Śiva's Brainchild

Śiva's Brainchild

From Hinduism to the Brain

Brian Capleton

Amarilli Books

Amarilli Books Onyx Edition

First Printing, 2023

CONTENTS

Presentation Notes 1

Introduction 2

1 The Horns of a Rabbit 18

2 The Hindu Picture 22

3 The Causal Ocean 44

4 Expansion of Being 48

5 Gunas, Purusa, and Prakrti 57

6 Śiva 79

7 Expansion and Involution 90

8 The Transpersonal 99

9 The Divine Couple 110

10 Viśnu and Brahma 130

11 The First Great Dispute 138

12 | Sex and Divine Love 151

13 | Svarūpa and the Infinite 180

14 | The Transcendental and the Mirror 188

15 | Brahma and the Universe 195

16 | Soma 202

17 | The Seven Oceans 214

18 | The Origins of the Saptadvīpa 241

19 | Mind and World 249

20 | The Sun 252

21 | The Bhu Mandala 262

22 | The Arising of Prakrti 272

23 | Kaleidoscope 283

24 | The Creation of the Senses 294

25 | The Churning of the Ocean 303

26 | Beyond the Poison 324

27 | The Core 336

28 | Yogamaya and Mahamaya 344

Presentation Notes

Some of the source translations consulted for this book contain transliterated words followed by plain brackets containing an explanation of some kind. These annotations are generally included in quoted material, in the same plain parentheses. The use of square brackets in a quotation or paraphrase denotes inserted explanatory content that is not directly from or derived from the original translation.

Italics are used both to make certain words more salient, deliberately linking their occurrences together, and for emphasis in general. Italics are also generally used where words are transliterations, especially if they include ś, ī, ū or ā pronunciations for which there may be no true English equivalent.

However, sometimes this principle is not followed in order not to over-italicise a length of text. Pronunciation indications are limited to the ś, ī, ū and ā characters, which Westerners often render approximately as "sh", "ee", "oo" and "ah" respectively. The use of the ā, ī, ū and ī characters is usually applied where these appear in the transliteration, or where transliterated words in the translation are being specifically referenced.

' *Śiva* ' is used rather than ' Shiva ', and ' *Viśnu* ' rather than ' Vishnu ', and both are italicised except in reproducing a book title as it stands, such as referencing a Purana translation.

' *Brahma* ' is generally used rather than ' *Brahmā* ', except in some cases where the name has been reproduced as it appears in the translation consulted and discussed. 'Krsna' is used rather than 'Krishna', and together with 'Radha' is most often written without italicisation.

' *Brahman* ' is always italicised whilst ' Brahma ' is always not, in order to make the distinction between these two similar words, always clear.

'Rig Veda' is used rather than ' *Rg Veda* '. However, the condensed form *rt*, rather than *rit*, (as in, for example *amrta*), is adhered to. In these cases the r is pronounced approximately *ri*.

Introduction

Some things are deep, and some things are shallow. And there is much in between. When a mind encounters something deep, from deeper than it has ever been before, then it can often seem difficult. If we are speaking of human experience, then the communication of such things is often in the form of parable, allegory, fable or fiction. Which is a perfectly valid medium of communication.

It's not necessarily so, that what's deeper than our ordinary, direct experience of everyday human affairs, is difficult in itself. It's just that talking about it requires a change of mindset, or even, in the case of what is deepest, the transcendence of ubiquitous, ordinary thought.

One idea that is deep when taken seriously, is that this, that we are living as our lives, is a living myth, a dream, a metaphor, played out in an illusion called time. It may well be that the easiest way to communicate such a thing, is through fable, or fiction. But then, what we are talking about is something in which the whole idea of the difference between fact and fiction, or fiction and actuality, begins to dissolve.

This recognition of *time* as the supporting structure of an illusion, and the awakening from the belief in the duality of fact and fiction, or fiction and actuality, is not an alien idea, in the sense that I am certainly not the first to speak of it. Many artists and writers and philosophers have sensed it or known it.

It is already inherent in Hinduism, which we are going to be talking about, but not in a way that puts it inside a box, and makes it exclusive. Hindus naturally believe that Hinduism contains the truth. The truth about our constitution and situation. I suggest that Truth isn't anything that can be contained in anything. Rather, if there is indeed Truth in Hinduism, which I contend there is, then we should understand that Hinduism doesn't so much contain it, as express it, in its own way, through its own cultural fabric.

So Hinduism isn't the only expression about time and being, in which what happens in time is portrayed as an illusion - a play of being. That is, to be more accurate, in Hinduism, it is portrayed as something called *Maya*, which *gives rise to* what the Hindu corpus calls "delusion" in those who are caught up in the play of it. The play of it is something that Hinduism calls a *lila*.

Many artists, writers, philosophers, and spiritual teachers, in their work, have been concerned with time and being, and the relation between time and being, in their own way. It's not something just confined to Hinduism. It's not even confined to the East, or for example to Buddhism, which arose out of Hinduism. The recognition of the connection between time and being is already here, even in our popular Western literature. So let's talk to begin with, in these terms.

For example, Joan Lindsay's unusual consciousness of time was expressed in her novels *Time Without Clocks*, and her best-selling story *Picnic at Hanging Rock*. In the Mythic Symbolism of *Picnic at Hanging Rock*, Joan quite explicitly (for those who can see it) draws on a deeper understanding of time as the fabric of our experience, and as something that is all around us, rather than in a "straight line" from past to future, in the way that the Western mind usually likes to see it.

In her video interviews she related how her own experience of things went beyond the idea of "what comes before" and "what comes after". A little research will reveal that apart from her remembering St Valentine's Day (on which she was married), dates, like clock time, had very little meaning for her, to the extent that at one point in her life she had to ask a friend to find out when she had been born. And when she was told, she remarked that she was apparently not present at her own birth. (See Terence O'Neill, *Joan Lindsay: a time for everything*, La Trobe Journal, 83, 2009, 41-52).

The timeless is played out in her books, and, indeed, in *Picnic at Hanging Rock* events that determine the spreading of a pattern of disruption through lives, happens early-on in the story, literally whilst the clocks are inexplicably stopped.

Set in Australia on Valentine's day, 1900, in *Picnic* what happens in this *timeless time* whilst the clocks are stopped, is the disappearance of three schoolgirls and a teacher, in their ascent up a "rock", whose own timescale is enormous compared to actual human lives (a point explicitly played out in the dialogue when the girls are still approaching the Hanging Rock).

Their disappearance cannot be translated back into "rational" actuality or fact, or "clock time". Not even by reading the missing Chapter Eighteen (now available) revealing what was at the top of the ascent. This chapter, the publisher left out of the book, turning Joan Lindsay's own brand of mysticism into a conventional but compelling mystery woven with elements of the supernatural.

In a note at the beginning of *Picnic* Lindsay states that the question of whether the story is fact or fiction readers themselves must decide. The reason she gives is that because the picnic took place in 1900, all the characters are long since dead, and so it seems unimportant.

Lindsay is leading the reader here. But few take the clue. In truth, every human being who has ever lived is consigned to this status, because all human beings die and soon become long since dead. The status of persons and happenings in all stories of persons, whether you want to think of it as fact or fiction, is, as Joan Lindsay knew, unimportant in time.

But not according to those who believe in the reality of clock time as something separate from our experience of being as human beings. Unlike Joan Lindsay, most people do believe clock time to be "reality". And so when it comes to Joan Lindsay's work countless people have endeavoured to find out and satisfy themselves as to the *facts* of "what really happened on the rock". They believe in an actuality, unfolding in clock time, without ever understanding that the actuality experienced by human beings, is a fiction, a myth, even as it is happening.

In clock time there is history. And even then, history is only a matter of interpretation. History, as they say, is written by the victors. Go beyond clock time, see-through it, and there you begin to discover a different reality and truth behind what is happening in human experience and human affairs. A different reality behind human perceptions and experiences. A realm in which the idea of a factual truth in something called actuality, turns out to be a delusion (in Hinduism a delusion based on what the Puranas call "false ego", the preserving the personal idea of "who I am" as a separate being).

The relation of time to spiritual ascent is subtly reflected in *Picnic*. In the story, the girl who leads the ascent up "the rock" is Miranda. Joan depicts Miranda as the most spiritual of all the characters, saying how Irma wonders how God makes some people so disagreeable whilst others beautiful like Miranda.

Just before Miranda leads the ascent up "the rock", she is explicitly recognised by the French teacher, who says "Mon Dieu! (My God!) Now I know...", realising the beautiful Miranda is a Botticelli angel that she had seen at the Uffizi.

In contrast, of those who ascend "the rock", the girl depicted the least spiritually is Edith, whom the character list describes as 'the college dunce', and whom in the prose is also called 'as plain as a frog'. She is actually the one to whom Irma is referring, in the passage above.

Edith finds the ascent too arduous, and fails to make it, finally running back down, screaming. Irma, a wealthy beauty, almost succeeds, but in clock time is found unconscious and alive on the "rock" a week later, as if she had been there only a few hours. Much is made of the fact that such a survival in the outback for that length of clock time would be expected to be impossible, but she is unharmed, except for a few scratches and bruises.

The ordinary, everyday, rational understanding of the world, is based on understanding things as they unfold in clock time. But it is only an understanding of "what happens" in something called "time", that is not itself really understood.

The higher understanding is to understand that what is really going on is something that is continuously *creating* time. And for that, you have to have an appreciation that time and being are inseparable. Is this such a strange and unfamiliar idea? Not if you are familiar with the Hindu corpus.

The great scheme of things in both Hinduism and Buddhism is one in which anything that seems to exist only does so in the context of what Hinduism calls the *lila* - a play of being - of which it is a part. In Buddhism this relativity is called *dependent arising* or *dependent origination*, or *pratītyasamutpāda*. In Hinduism time and being is subject to this principle, and ultimately, every moment of time-bound being arises from an immeasurable expansion and involution of the one Being that Hinduism calls the *Brahman*.

The result is that every moment of time in our little human experience of being is already created from eternally preserved, timeless stories of being in which we are participating, derived from the "ether" or "space" of Hindu cosmology, the eternally recreated and timeless *Ākāśa*.

And so also, does Joan Lindsay in *Picnic* say that there is no moment on Earth that is not by ordinary standards of time immeasurable. She considers each moment a "fragment of eternity" unrelated to clock time.

In *Picnic* as it was published, minus that last chapter (Chapter Eighteen), and with a few adjustments to make the omission work, during the ascent of the girls the prose speaks of shadows lengthening on the Hanging Rock. But in the missing Chapter Eighteen the description is more explicit, stating that the whole scene of the girls' ascent up the rock is essentially happening forever, and will go on happening until the end of time, acted out in what Joan Lindsay calls a "tepid twilight" of a present without a past. She speaks of their emotions being "forever new".

If you are familiar with the Hindu corpus it is easy to see that this is Joan Lindsay's own description of what also appears in the fabric of Hinduism, as the timeless "memory" of the *Ākāśa* at the root of what we experience as time.

We should therefore also not be surprised to find that in *Picnic*, after the disappearance of Miranda, Irma remembers Miranda saying that everything always begins and ends at exactly the right time and place. As Miranda walks away from the plain towards the Rock and the ascent, she turns and smiles to the French teacher, assuring her that the girls will only be gone a little while.

In Hinduism, the higher the spiritual ascent, the more time elapses on the "lower slopes", until eventually, at the threshold to the transcendental, there is the *Ākāśa* in which everything is happening now, and will "go on happening until the end of time". In the Hindu scheme this *Ākāśa* is "air", "atmosphere" or "ether", from which the "unmanifest one", the *Brahman*, the Being, descends through further "coverings" of the "egg" through which material existence is created.

In the missing final Chapter Eighteen, the girls who complete the ascent, remove their corsets (the constraint of their bodies), and cast them off the rock, but there, instead of falling, they too, remain, 'stuck fast in *time*'. They are 'becalmed on the windless air'. The girls have arrived at a place where there are 'no shadows', and 'the light too is unchanging'.

From the position "on the plain" below, the mind that believes in clock time also wants to believe in an objective actuality in human affairs, in which we can find what is the truth, and what is not the truth. But as both Hinduism and Buddhism recognise, what we experience as the world, is only what we experience as our own mind.

Another Western writer, Vita Sackville-West, recognises and plays on the illusion of objective actuality in *Seducers in Ecuador*, in which the protagonist's state of mind and perception is represented by the wearing of different coloured glasses. And in her novel *The Edwardians* (Penguin Vintage Classics, 2016, p. 54), the explorer Anquetil, previously believing in an objective actuality defined by 'objects, relationships, and situations', begins to realise under the candle-lit influence of the great old house Chevron, that actuality is a fiction dependent 'solely on the observer, his mood, and his prejudice'.

There is another language for all this, a scientific one. All this is a reflection of the modern scientific fact that anything we perceive, experience, or understand, is a construct of brain function. Including, actually, what we experience as the thing we call the material world.

This is perhaps a more demanding fact to come to terms with, even than what we have been talking about. From the point of view of materialist science there is nothing in our head except brain function.

And it is this actual electrochemical complex network activity, that is what we are experiencing as our self and the world.

But then, perhaps still more demanding, is the fact that it is only *through* this complex electrochemical activity, that this complex electrochemical activity comes to be known as such, in the thing we now call science. The world in as much as we can ever know it, is a construct of brain function, and brains are part of that construct.

There is indeed an *objective* aspect of this material world, that is not dependent on anyone's *individual* brain function. But aside from scientific facts, any idea we might hold that there is some objective actuality of meaning or truth in the world, separate from our own mind, is mistaken. It is, as we shall come to see, what the Hindu corpus regards as a *delusion*. A delusion caused by what Hinduism calls *Maya*, the very appearance itself, of the material world.

Let us turn one last time to *Picnic at Hanging Rock*, in which Irma, having ascended some way up "the rock" (the spiritual ascent), looks down upon the picnic ground, the plain, and wonders what all the people can be doing down there, like a lot of ants.

By now she is already looking down from a higher place, a place from where what she observes, is not unrelated to Hinduism, even though *Picnic* has apparently absolutely nothing to do with Hinduism. If anything, as some have argued, it reflects aspect of the Australian aboriginal *dreamtime*. But then, aboriginal dreamtime, and Hinduism, also share something in common: the *dream*.

As she looks down upon the plain, Irma goes on to see, from her vantage point higher in the ascent that many people are "without purpose", except that they are probably involved in some function unknown to themselves. What a strange observation. Or is it? Not strange at all, in the context of the Hindu corpus, and indeed, Hinduism even has its own word for this very state of affairs: *karma*.

In Hinduism, *time* and *being* are inseparable. In fact, according to the Purana stories, time is linked inextricably to *Being*. And time, as we all know, is measured in cycles. In Hinduism *being* and *time* "comes in cycles", as it were, cycles of being in the great scheme of things.

What we shall see in the course of this book, is how the Hindu corpus tells us our own experience of being and world, is a *play of being*, a *lila*, created in cycles through a thing called time, from an infinite expansion and involution of the one Being. The Being that Hinduism calls the *Brahman*.

* * *

So now let's talk about the Hindu corpus. The story content of the Indian Puranas is sometimes referred to by the West as a "mythology". But it is not "myth" in the modern, popular sense of the word, meaning something that is merely a mistaken belief. It is much more than that. Rather, if we are going to call it "myth" then we ought to distinguish it from the former meaning, through the use of an uppercase M. Very often, Myth, or Mythic symbolism, is not recognised for what it is. Whether it arises in a work such as *Picnic at Hanging Rock*, or in the Puranas.

We will be looking at *meaning*, and there isn't always only one meaning, because the language in the Hindu corpus is often polysemic. In fact, as we see at one point, the content of the corpus itself, explicitly declares itself to be that.

To glean anything of any value we have to look beyond the belief that core scriptural stories in religions in general, are merely myth in the sense of mistaken understanding, or fiction. At yet at the same time we cannot become trapped in the mistaken belief that these stories *must* be taken *literally* in just one way, in order to glean the deepest truth.

Myth is a particular kind of story-telling that appears in religions, that rather too easily allows, or arguably even encourages, modern rational materialism to call it nonsense or imaginative fiction. The truth is that many of these stories actually contain a depth of meaning that we respect in this book by using the upper case words Myth and Mythology. The Hindu Mythology that we refer to, is just one such example.

Some Hindus might well still object to the idea of calling the stories in the Puranas a Mythology, even if we *are* using an uppercase M. And actually, in a particular way, they have a point. They have a point, because using the word Myth *suggests* that the stories in the Puranas have some kind of different status to our lives now and the world in which we live. But as it turns out, it doesn't really suggest that, at all.

This is not to propose that you *must* believe a scripture *literally* and unquestioningly because you are not meant to understand it in any deeper way, and that if you don't just take it at face value, then you are being sacrilegious and you don't love God, Jesus, or understand the Buddha, and so forth. Indeed, by doing that you will mould your mind into nothing but cognitive bias.

Rather, this whole question of what Myth *is*, is also a question about the nature of our world. It becomes a question about whether our life, and the world in which we are living now, is actually anything other than a living Myth.

Indeed, the Hindu corpus in particular, together with the Buddhist corpus, amongst all the great religions, are prominent in questioning common presumptions about the very nature of the world in which we live.

So calling something Myth is not to denigrate it. There is even a modern scientific sense in which the whole world in which we live, is already, essentially a Myth. We can give the word the uppercase M here, because the world in which we live is not just fiction. Certainly, some of it is, and we would be a fool if we could not see that. But you cannot just dismiss love, or suffering, as fiction.

Nevertheless, as a whole, there is a very modern and scientific sense in which our whole world is already taken by some modern minds of a scientific disposition, to be essentially a Myth.

This is because it is a modern scientific fact that there is nothing we know or experience of our world, including our own bodies, and our mind, that is not materially just a construct of biological brain function. This is not some baseless, speculative theory. Rather, it is an evidence-supported modern scientific fact.

The common tendency is to want to believe that there really is a world "out there" that has nothing to do with brain function, other than that our brains happen to arise within it. And so perhaps the most popular interpretation of this relatively new fact of neuroscience is that the brain is creating a "predictive model" of a material world, a world that has is itself, nothing to do with brain function.

But actually, there are no pressing scientific reasons to believe that the so-called "predictive model" created by the human brain is a model of a world that in itself, is not a construct of brain function in general (rather than of one specific brain).

Rather, our situation is somewhat different. Because in material terms *everything* we know and experience, *including* the experience of understanding, measuring, thinking, and learning about science and how the brain works, is all *a construct of brain function*.

No brain organ came into existence by itself, and there is no reason to suppose that we can understand our "consciousness" of "the world" that we experience, solely on the basis of the functioning of an *individual brain organ*, considered in isolation. That is, in isolation from other brains, and in isolation from the whole of nature and the evolution that gives rise to it.

So even from the position of modern scientific materialism, *Myth* emerges. When we realise that our world is a construct of brain function, then in this very contemporary way, we can very well say that our whole world, which as human beings is our *world of being*, is a *living Myth*.

The bottom line here is not so very different from what the Hindu corpus is saying about the world. Which essentially, is that our human experience of self *includes* the world that we experience, and is essentially what can be described as a *dream*. It's not our *personal* dream. In Mythical terms, pertaining to Hinduism, it is, specifically, the dream of *Viśnu*. The Hindu corpus itself doesn't call it a Myth, though. That's a Western word. Hinduism has its own word for it: *Maya*.

It is a Myth, or dream, that we are experiencing the *being of*, and this picture of our situation even has that same scientific correlation. What our experience of being and world *is*, as far as science is concerned, is just a construct, specifically, a construct of *brain function*.

If we are going to be all very contemporary about it, like this, then we have to admit that it is a Myth, or dream, of a very special kind. Because unlike so many stories in the religions, and unlike the world of Hindu Mythology, what science calls "the universe", or our "material world", is not a world in which literally just anything can happen. Unlike the case in the stories in the Puranas.

On the contrary, ours is a world, or a Myth, in which - the experience of miracles aside - what can happen is really rather restricted. It is restricted by things that modern science calls *the laws of nature.*

As far as modern science is concerned, whilst what we *experience* is always a construct that is materially one of brain function, there is one *thing* in what we experience that does not depend on anyone's *individual* brain function. This is precisely the objective aspect of the material world that science studies and comes to understand.

What the Hindu corpus describes as "the universe" is not at all the same thing that modern science refers to as "the universe". It's not that they are two different approaches to the same thing. Rather, the Hindu corpus and modern science are each actually talking about something different, when they each talk about "the universe". And that is a fact that is frequently overlooked by so many people examining the Hindu corpus, even Hindus themselves.

What modern science talks about and describes as "the universe", is the objective material phenomena that can be scientifically measured. If what we are calling "the universe" is not that, then it's not part of what modern science calls "the universe". It may perhaps be part of what *you* or someone else *calls* "the universe", or what the Hindu corpus calls "the universe", but it's not part of "the universe" that modern science describes, understands, and talks about.

This does not mean that what the Hindu corpus calls "the universe" is a Mythology about something that is a completely separate and *alternative world*, other than the one in which we are living. No religion regards what it is talking about, as that. Christians don't in general regard the stories of Jesus as a Mythology, separate from the world in which we are living. And the same is true for many Buddhists, regarding their stories. Even when they involve enlightened individuals being born from a lotus flower in the middle of a lake.

The truth is that what you experience is what you experience. And the same is true for any *collective* of people. What that experiencing is, as far as modern science is concerned, is a construct of brain function. However, we can also say that *all our scientific knowledge* is also *a construct of brain function*. Even the experience of measuring, and deducing, in science, are all things that we only encounter in the first place as a construct of brain function.

The fundamental fact that our experience of being and mind and world is a construct of brain function, means that there is no true separation between belief, experience, and scientific knowledge. They all meet together, in brain function. However, scientific knowledge goes beyond belief and subjective experience, because it deals with what is beyond the construct created through anyone's individual brain function.

Since the scientific revolution of the 17th century there has grown and matured the underlying idea in scientific thinking that the material world in which we live, material nature itself, has nothing to do with us except that we happen to have arisen in it, and are now affecting our part of it.

This is, however, only a relatively modern idea, even in the West. It is an idea that grew with the arising of modern science, precisely because modern science is concerned with the objective nature of the world.

But it is an idea that is now undermined by what we now know about the brain. And, some would argue, it is also undermined by the facts of quantum physics.

It's not just Hinduism that disagrees with this idea that material nature has in itself, nothing to do with us, other than that we happen to be in it, perceiving it and experiencing it. All the great religions essentially disagree with that. And there is a now a steadily growing contemporary secular movement of opposition to it, too.

Hinduism itself disagrees with the idea, but its foundation corpus, is *pre-scientific*. Hinduism has come into the West now, and has already established a base that many Westerners have been attracted to in the search for spiritual truth or a deeper understanding of the nature of our existence. Hinduism exhibits *no knowledge about the human brain*, and says nothing about human brain function. The corpus nonetheless forms the *cultural basis* on which Eastern Masters have been expressing spiritual teaching to the West, for some time now.

On this planet we are taking the first small steps towards a major revolution in our understanding. A revolution of an unprecedented kind, actually, a completely new knowledge of our constitution and situation. This will eventually arise out of the scientific understanding of the brain.

* * *

Hinduism is generally conceived as dividing into four major branches. These are *Shaivism* (worshipping *Śiva* as supreme), *Vaishnavism* (worshipping *Viśnu* as supreme), *Shaktism* (worshipping *Devi* as supreme) and *Smartism* (worshipping *Śiva*, *Viśnu*, *Śakti*, *Surya*, and *Ganeśa*, equally). However, in Hinduism there are many, many more than just four "belief systems" or approaches to Truth, God, or the Divine.

All the different types of Hinduism have their origination in the Vedas, from which has evolved its great corpus, which includes, over time, many new branches condensing and distilling the teachings of the former. Buddhism itself arose out of this expansion.

The word *Vedas* does not necessarily refer to what is written down. It is based on the Sanskrit root *vid*, literally meaning "Divine knowledge", and it refers in general to the "revealed knowledge" of the original *rsis*, or seers. This knowledge is generally thought to have been passed on by oral transmission before being written down.

The term Rig Veda, however, does refer to *written* wisdom. Whilst the original scriptures in the Rig Veda are believed to have been arranged and compiled early in the Common Era, they are acknowledged to have been passed down orally, perhaps for thousands of years or longer.[1]

It is easy to see from the very nature of Hinduism that within the confines of a single book such as this, only a limited or selected part of the content of the corpus can be referenced. Furthermore, this is not a book of Indology or Sanskrit scholarship.

However, what is included here, is based primarily on scholarly translations by Indians, into English from the Sanskrit sources. So in the course of this book, we are at least, so to speak, in reasonably close contact with the sources themselves, rather than relying on informal secondary interpretations, or re-tellings of the stories.

In this book we are not even going to get into most of the stories that are popularly transmitted as part of Hindu culture. We are not even really interested in the stories just as entertaining stories of personalised beings. What we are interested in, is deeper meaning. There are different "layers" in Hindu Mythology and in the way it is told, and popular knowledge of the Mythology is not our destination here.

There is a very large tract of time over which what is now the Hindu corpus became established. So the Puranas contain many different styles of writing, from different periods, and include the transmission of accounts and stories by a process that we could regard as "informed repetition".

In consulting the translations by Indian scholars, it is clear that some Sanskrit sources themselves may contain instances of defective text, spelling errors, redundant repetition, and the "passing down" of material whose content and sometimes even meaning, the writer is at least *apparently* not confident about.

Some of the material is in the style of authoritative declaration. However, the presentation is often in the style of formalised hearsay, relying on terms (or equivalents) such as "It is remembered that...", or "The sages say", and so on. Although we may consider this to be authoritative too, this style is about *transmission*, and a deferring of authority to the past.

Another important feature that we can see in the translations is the interweaving of different *modes* of belief, thought, insight, and knowledge. The texts arise *out of* a particular culture, and they *speak to* a particular culture.

Sometimes the material contains a mode of thinking about the nature of the world, that is clearly a *prescientific forerunner* to the fully materialistic modern, scientific view. But it is nevertheless still *prescientific* and *not* scientific.

Take the use of numbers, and "measurements", for example. As far as modern science is concerned, in the Puranas these are pre-scientific because they have not been obtained through empirical *measurement*, in the modern scientific sense. Nor are they the results of calculations based on such measurements. But then, they do not even claim to have been. Rather, they constitute a form of "revealed knowledge". This knowledge is not of the scientific kind.

The meaning and purpose of the use of numbers in this context, is often misunderstood by modern readers as having *scientific* meaning, or as being scientific assertions, according to how modern science is understood. Some of the quantities spoken of in the sources do correlate to some modern scientific measurements. This unfortunately encourages some modern readers to perpetuate the confusion between spiritual truth and scientific fact.

There is a good deal of figurative material in the Puranas that superficially *seems* to the modern mind to be a way of understanding and explaining the nature of what the corpus calls "the universe", in terms of *structures*. However, these descriptions do not imply that the thinking in the Hindu corpus is even *remotely comparable* to the modern scientific way of thinking about the material world in the scientific, objective way. Rather, the true content has a much *deeper* meaning. It is not *materialist*. It is not *scientific*.

Even though the deeper *content* of the corpus is expressed through the fabric of a specific culture and its own evolution, this content shines out, as a true light, when the fabric is seen through. We don't have to be Hindu. It's not that the fabric is unnecessary, though. On the contrary, it is the very medium through which this light shines.

And why not? Human beings only learn and experience and express, through the brain. Every culture, every religion, is a particular formulation in the one principle of the human brain. And that is because the very nature of the brain is all about such formulations.

So the conceptual communication of spiritual truth has to come through the stuff of mind and brain and culture. However, the truth is that no mind or brain is genuinely isolated, or existent by itself. No brain ever came into existence by itself, or evolved in isolation. On the contrary, every mind and brain is an instance drawn from an aggregate. And the final aggregate is all of humanity.

Materially, using today's language of contemporary Western understanding, we would say that the existential aggregate is a thing that we now call a *network*. Just as every individual mind is part of a network of minds, so also every particular religion or culture, or belief system, is also always an aggregate.

None of our different aggregates are truly separate. All these aggregates are drawn from one larger aggregate that modern science doesn't yet truly know the nature of. That is, the still greater aggregate of humanity as a whole.

What that is, in the Hindu picture, is not a network of separate parts, but a play of being, a *lila*, in the play of *Maya*. It is the Myth that has been created through the *expansion* of the one Being, that Hinduism calls the *Brahman*.

1

The Horns of a Rabbit

In Hinduism, in the *Yoga Vasishta*, the idea that the materiality of the world in which we live is something separate from the nature of our own mind, is declared to be as false as the horns of a rabbit.[2]

This is one just tiny corner of the Hindu corpus in which we can immediately see there is something in it, that is taking us in a direction very different to the mainstream thrust of the busy, Westernised, global world.

What we are reading there, some people would say is beginning to sound like Buddhism. That is perhaps not surprising, because Buddhism arose out of Hinduism.

This book, even though it says relatively little about Buddhism or Christianity, is indirectly about those other religions, too. It is not proselytising for any religion, but not far under the surface it is about *all* religions.

This is not because it is going to say that they can all be "explained" by science or the brain. The point of a religion is the search for God. And you cannot "explain" the search for God, in terms of something that is not the search for God. If you think you can, then really, you have never really understood the search for God, or what it means.

But then also, you could say, this book not really about religion, as such, at all. Because it's also about the brain. And the brain isn't a religion, or something that any of the great religions, in their scriptures, say anything about.

You might perhaps think that talking about the brain is irrelevant to what the religions are concerned with, precisely because they are concerned with the Divine. But in the perspective of modern science, specifically neuroscience, the two are connected. Because as far as the materialist approach to modern neuroscience is concerned, there is nothing about us, including even the experience of the Divine, that does not have something to do with brain function.

The truth is that talking about God, or the Being, or the Self, all of which are ways that God is spoken of in the East, cannot simply be considered as irrelevant to what we now know about the brain, and us, as a matter of modern science. Because it is about our experience, and that is something that is delivered through brain function.

And this is where the horns of the rabbit come in.

You see, it's very easy for the busy, Westernised, modern mind, to believe it understands the world in which we are living, by labelling things as "isms". Just as it's also too easy for it to understand and label a certain, major part of what human beings are doing, as "religion". So that what is going on there, can be conveniently compartmentalised. Not least because compartmentalised understanding is already a major feature of the way contemporary, Western society, operates.

But then, its understanding remains shallow.

Hinduism is the oldest living "ism", as a cultural and religious fabric, in the world. And like Buddhism, and certain areas of modern science, Hinduism is upfront about challenging the modern mind's common idea of the basic nature of the very world in which we live. In that way, it has something in common with what certain areas of modern science are also doing.

Actually, very close indeed. We are not so much talking here about the exotic facts of quantum physics. Rather, the *essence* of the Hindu corpus stands hand-in-hand, harmoniously, with the *most fundamental* scientific fact of modern neuroscience.

That fact is that what we are experiencing as our world, indeed, what we are encountering in our "consciousness" and senses, as the objective, material world itself, is a *construct of brain function.*

The *prima facie* thing about *brain function* in human beings is that it gives rise to our experience of self. This is our *conditional experience of being,* as our experience of self, as mind, body, psyche, and our experience of the world. It all arises through one and the same means as the way the world arises for us - as a construct of brain function.

So not just in the *Yoga Vasishta,* but also as far as the fundamental fact modern neuroscience is concerned, the idea that the world we experience living in, is separate from the nature of our own mind, or our own brain function, could well be considered to be as false as the horns of a rabbit.

If this essence of the Hindu corpus stands hand-in-hand, harmoniously, with the most fundamental fact of modern brain science, then modern brain science, perhaps without realising it, also stands hand-in-hand with this essence of the Hindu corpus.

It's just that, to get to the essence of the Hindu corpus, might, for many people, require some effort. Because it is probably the most elaborate, exotic, and extensive corpus of any religion on the planet. Nevertheless, for that very reason, it is a very rich resource. This book, although reading it of course requires some attention, is like a shortcut into that very deep resource.

There is a big question at the centre of modern neuroscience. Specifically, the question of how it is that the electrochemical activity in this jelly-like complexus of connected biological cells in our head, equates to our own experience of being, as self, mind, thought, and the world around us that we experience.

In short, it is the question of how it is that the brain gives rise to our "consciousness". And that's something that is sometimes being called the "hard problem of consciousness". At least, it is by those who regard it as a problem. Which is something you try to solve, using this intelligence that arises through the brain.

Some people think this problem will remain forever insoluble. They would say that the secret of the brain is inscrutable. Others say it is only a question of *time*, before science understands it. Some others think they already understand it. But they have a hard time getting the whole scientific community to go along with them.

So what is this book saying? It is saying this: The secret of the brain is accessible to us. But you can't *deduce it*. And you can't understand it using the intelligence that arises through this material phenomena of the brain, in its default condition. Rather, it can only be *realised* through what Hinduism calls *the churning of the ocean*. And that's something that we will be coming to, in due course.

2

The Hindu Picture

The Hindu corpus is a very rich resource. Really, it is not the corpus of just *one* religion. Hinduism is more like many related but different religions. Often, its different branches and schools have contrasting views about certain things. But considered as one, then it is the oldest religion on Earth, and it has a vast corpus at many different levels of accessibility.

The entertaining stories in the Puranas are still passed on orally, from generation to generation. However, the written scriptures themselves clearly have more than one layer of meaning, from the superficially entertaining, to the esoteric. They often use polysemic language.

From the point of view of the modern scientific facts of the brain, if we are suggesting anything in Hinduism relates to *the principle of the brain*, then for fairly obvious reasons we would have to be going deeper into Hinduism than its surface. And what we discover would have to relate to *every* brain and *every* culture on Earth. Not just Hindus or those immersed in Hinduism.

So as far as the connection between Hinduism and the brain is concerned, the cultural fabric through which its content is expressed, cannot be the same thing as its core meaning.

However, because what the corpus is saying is expressed *through* that fabric, and in terms of that fabric, we have to speak in terms of that fabric, too. We have to use the same mode of expression. And at the same time, we have to refine out of it, the essence.

Causal Background

In Hinduism the "causal background" to the whole world, including our brain, is called the *causal ocean*.

So the *causal ocean*, variously called the *kāraṇa-samudra*, *kārana-jala*, *kārakavat samudra*, or *kāranatāsamudra*, and so on, represents in Hinduism the *cause* of both what the corpus calls "the universe", and the stuff of our human mind, psyche and experience of being. Which of course is part of the universe.

Let's unpack all that.

Let's begin with the widely known popular Hindu image of the *Trimurti* of three beings, called *Śiva*, *Viśnu*, and Brahma. Just as Christianity has the Trinity, so Hinduism has this *Trimurti*. They are not the same thing. But you'll notice they both consist of *three*.

In popular understanding, Brahma is known as the "creator", *Viśnu* as the "sustainer", and *Śiva* as the "destroyer". But this is all rather simplistic, and just under the surface, is something much more interesting.

Probably one of the best known pictorial representations in Hinduism is the image of the deity *Viśnu*, depicted lying on a "couch" that is the multi-headed serpent *Ananta Śeśa*, floating on the causal ocean. A lotus flower emerges from his navel, and from the flower, emerges Brahma. *Viśnu*'s consort *Lakśmī*, massages *Viśnu*'s feet.

Now things get a little more interesting. In the corpus as a whole, *including* the Krsna-Bhakti texts, there are actually *three* specific *Viśnus* contained, as it were, in the one *Viśnu*. These *Viśnus* are related to each other in a way that we shall be referring to as a "nested *expansion*". The expansion is an *expansion of being*.

That is, the great *Viśnu* who is depicted in the popular imagery, appears a little deeper in the Hindu corpus as *Maha-Viśnu* or

Kāranodakaśāyī Viśnu who lays, indeed, on the causal ocean - the *kāraṇa* ocean.

But this Being *expands* to create and become another being, *Garbhodakaśāyī Viśnu* who lays on the *Garbha* ocean (*Garbha* means "womb"). It is from *Garbhodakaśāyī Viśnu* that Brahma emerges, specifically, from a Lotus flower that comes out of *Viśnu*'s navel. And then *Garbhodakaśāyī Viśnu* expands into *Ksīrodakaśāyī Viśnu*, who lays on the Ocean of Milk.[3]

So occasionally one can find that *Viśnu* is referred to as laying on the Ocean of Milk. And sometimes people talk in terms of the "ocean of bliss". We will have much more to say about the Ocean of Milk, and all of this, later.

All three of these *Viśnus* are "wrapped up", as it were, in *Maha-Viśnu*, the great *Viśnu*, or *Kāranodakaśāyī Viśnu*.

So it is actually from the navel of *Garbhodakaśāyī Viśnu* that the lotus flower, and then Brahma, emerges.[4] As communicated in Śrīmad Bhāgavatam, Maha-Viśnu (*Kāranodakaśāyī Viśnu*), who is *transcendental*, enters *Garbhodakaśāyī Viśnu*, who is already his own expansion, to create the lotus. So here we see already, the important principle that Being *expands*, creating the illusion of another Being, and is then able to *enter* that expansion.

Essentially, we are told, Maha-Viśnu (*Kāranodakaśāyī Viśnu*) impregnates the lotus flower with all the "modes of material nature", thus creating Brahma, who then emerges from the lotus, ready to create the material world.[5]

Modern, Westernised, rational minds, would not be likely to accept that the material world we live in, has been created in such a way. At least, not without a great deal more explanation.

However, in a point that we will be coming back to emphasise again and again, what we must know and remember, is that what the Hindu corpus refers to as the "the universe" or the "material world", that gets created, is actually not the same thing as what modern science or engineering, and so on, measures and understands, as the universe or the material world. We will say more about this later.

So as we mentioned, the name *Garbhodakaśāyī Viśnu* is built on the word *Garbha* which refers to "womb".[6] We were also talking about *Kāranodakaśāyī Viśnu* entering *Garbhodakaśāyī Viśnu*, and the general principle of Being expanding as, and becoming the illusion of other Beings.

In the Hindu picture we human beings have been created through Brahma, who emerged from *Garbhodakaśāyī Viśnu. Ksīrodakaśāyī Viśnu*, as we said, is an *expansion* of *Garbhodakaśāyī Viśnu. Ksīrodakaśāyī* Viśnu who lies on the *Ksīra Sāgara*, the Ocean of Milk, 'lives in the heart of every living being.'[7] So *Ksīrodakaśāyī* Viśnu and the "Ocean of Milk" is within us.

What we are looking at here, is a creation that takes place through a great principle that we will have much more to say about later. It is the principle of *expansion of being*. This expansion is a "multidimensional" expansion, rather than something simple, linear, and straightforward.

Overall, as we shall be seeing, the *causal ocean* is so-called because it is a vast ocean of *expansion of being* that is *beneath* the transcendental. The transcendental is represented in the imagery we have so far been talking about, as *Maha Viśnu*. Hence, *Viśnu* is depicted as floating on this ocean, rather than immersed in it. Of course, as you might guess, this picture itself is part of a bigger picture, which we will also come to later.

In Hinduism the *causal ocean* is the deep cause of what we know as existence, or the material universe. And just as in modern science there is a "many universes" theory, so also in Hinduism there are many universes. Infinitely many. We are part of the *effect* of that oceanic *cause*. The effect is what we know as our selves and our world. And that *effect*, in the Hindu picture, is created through the Being called Brahma. Hence, Brahma is known as *the creator*.

The *effect*, here, has two meanings of the word *effect*. Firstly it is an effect following from the cause - the *causal ocean*. Secondly, it is an *effect*, in the same sense that we might talk about something giving the impression of being something that it isn't. Like an illusion. And in Hinduism, that is precisely how the universe is viewed. As an illusion. That illusion is called *Maya*.

Ultimately, the Hindu picture is based on the *infinite*, because it is based on Infinite Being. And in the Hindu picture, there are actually infinitely many Brahmas,[8] creating infinitely many universes.

There is much talk in the corpus, of the Supreme Being. And there is also much talk of various "different" Beings each declaring that they are the Supreme Being. This is because all Beings, and actually, *everything*, is an *expansion of being*, of the one Supreme Being.

However, there are two things to consider. There is what Hinduism calls the *Maya* of "the universe", which gives rise to our ordinary, every-day, conditional experience of being as human beings. The expansion that is going on here, is a mundane continuation of a higher kind of expansion, in transcendental Life and Being. Transcendental Life and Being is the Reality behind *Maya*.

So part of the corpus recognises that our human life, as *Maya*, is a continuing expansion of the Being, which Hinduism calls the *Brahman* (not to be confused with Brahma). However, the Bhakti texts recognise that the *Brahman* as it is first realised, in spiritual illumination, is only the effulgence of Transcendental Life and Being, which is a still higher Reality.

The Brahman

There is an awkward closeness in Hinduism between the name Brahma and the word *Brahman*, which is not to be confused with Brahma. The *Brahman* that we will be talking about, is absolute, unconditional, radiant Being, not dependent on anything. It is realised as the Self. Although the Self is the Source of Love and Joy, and beauty and bliss and compassion, its nature is impersonal. To not only realise That Being, but also to become grounded in it as the reality of your

Identity, is sometimes referred to as "liberation". This means that the experience of being as the Self, is beyond suffering.

Within the Hindu corpus there is a tendency in Bhakti writings to deride what is referred to as this realisation of the "impersonal *Brahman*", not least because of the contention between Hinduism and Buddhism which arose out of it.

Buddhism tends to relate to what the Bhakti tradition calls the "impersonal *Brahman*", because it refers to "liberation" associated with the disappearance of the personal "I" or sense of self based on that.

The Bhakti writings teach that impersonal "liberation" falls short of a full realisation of the Truth, the *Brahman,* as transcendental Life and Being. In Krsna-Bhakti, above the realisation of the "impersonal *Brahman*" is the realisation of transcendental Life and Being, which is the realisation of the original transcendental *Krsna,* and this realisation of Krsna is called "personal".

All this has the potential to lead to considerable confusion for the Western mind, and probably for Eastern minds, too. The Self, realised without a full blown realisation of Transcendental Life and Being, and its associated Gnostic knowledge, is *impersonal,* but absolutely not in the way that "impersonal" is understood by ordinary, personal mind, especially in Western culture.

That usual idea of "impersonal" is in comparison with personal self, and the personal "who I am" idea, or idea of "myself" or "me", and especially "my emotions", as a separate being. All of that, is the personal ego, self, and mind. The common understanding by personal self and mind, of "impersonal", is something that is devoid of compassion, or love, or experiential joy. But this in no way represents the spiritually "impersonal".

The *Brahman* is *radiant Being,* it is Self-effulgent absolute *Being* that transcends the human self, the natural ego, and in that sense, it is *impersonal* because it transcends personal self. But it is not "impersonal" in the sense that it has no relation to love, joy, compassion, and devotion to the Divine. It is the opposite. Sufficiently deeply realised, it is explosively full of Joy and Love, and the spontaneous love and joyous knowledge of the Absolute Being, or God.

It is only "impersonal" in the sense that it is not about self-conception, it is not of the personal *idea* of "who I am" as a *separate* being called a "person". It transcends all of that. In the *Brahman*, there *is no* separation, or genuinely separate beings. There is only the Being. And it is realised, and known as the Self. In that sense, is it "impersonal". But it is only impersonal in that it is above, and above the need of, individual, separate, being-identity, as ordinary personal self, and especially personal self-conception, with the personal *idea* of "who I am".

The Fabric

Let's talk about the fabric of the Hindu corpus. One has to bear in mind that even in the Hindu corpus itself are variations of clarity and quality of content. And it does not follow that everything, just because it is in the Hindu corpus, must consist of pure Divine wisdom. Much of it is *cultural fabric*. In other words, *Maya*. Furthermore, being from an ancient culture, some of it is ancient cultural fabric that some today might argue is a very long way indeed from being the representation of Divine love.

We will begin by looking at the Śiva Purana because it is a particularly rich resource for our purposes here. But it also contains parts that, especially to the modern, Western mind, might be regarded as socially ignorant and in particular even misogynistic. In contrast, there are other parts of the very same Purana, and many more parts of the Krsna-Bhakti texts, that communicate conscious spiritual love between male and female beings, rather than mere relations.

The basic elements of many of the stories in the Puranas are naturally part of the cultural fabric of Hinduism, but we have to look for content that, although it is expressed in terms of the cultural fabric, is not dependent on it.

The Universe

So now let's talk about what the Hindu corpus calls "the universe".

In Hindu Mythology, hierarchically speaking, "beneath" *Viśnu* and the *causal ocean* on which he floats, is what Hinduism calls *Brahmānda*. This is sometimes translated as "the material universe".[9]

As we will be repeatedly emphasising, the idea of "material", here, is not generally the same when used by commentators in the Bhakti tradition, or as it may appear in translations of Śrīmad Bhāgavatam and Caitanya-caritamrta, as when it is used by modern scientists. The importance of this point cannot be overstressed.

So whilst one often finds *Brahmānda* referred to as meaning "the material world", this is quite misleading if one is relating Hinduism to anything else outside Hinduism, and in particular, if it is related to the modern world of science and technology, or modern, Western culture.

Brahmānda is a word that literally means "Brahma's egg", sometimes called the "cosmic egg", and is often just called "the universe". We must remember that in writings about Hinduism, when *Brahmānda* or anything in it is called "the material world" or "material universe", this terminology comes into conflict with the modern scientific concept of what constitutes "material".

The Motilal Banarsidass translation of the Brahmānda Purana, 2002, states that the term *Brahmānda* 'connotes a mixture of ancient Indian concepts about cosmography, cosmology and cosmogony'.[10] It certainly does. But as far as modern science is concerned, what the "material universe" consists of is what is *scientifically measurable.*

Actually, even in the everyday sense, without science, in the West it is not usual to regard, for example, worlds of "life after death", as part of the "material universe" or "material world".

Conflating the term "the material universe", with the idea of "the universe" as it appears in the Hindu corpus, is a mistake. Conflating what the Hindu corpus calls "the universe" with what modern science calls "the universe" is a mistake.

It can lead to a great deal of misunderstanding when the meaning of the term "material universe" in modern science is not appreciated, and the two ideas, the Hindu and the modern scientific, are mistakenly presumed to be talking about the same thing.

Many Hindu texts contain what appear to be "measurements" of various parts of what it calls the "the universe". This still does not mean that the two ideas coincide. This remains the case *even if* some of the Hindu "measurements" *do* arguably coincide with actual scientific measurements of what science calls "the universe".

Another thing that should be mentioned is that a *scientific measurement* is not a mere *declaration* of a measurement, even if it is on Divine authority. Many such declarations appear in the Hindu corpus. Rather, a *scientific measurement* is a piece of *empirical data* that is acquired through the act of scientifically measuring.

The Hindu universe takes a form well known to Hindus as the *Bhū-mandala*. It is sometimes described as the "cosmic egg". Amongst other things it contains a set of seven concentric oceans, positioned around seven concentric islands or *dvīpas*, sometimes called "continents" (somewhat reminiscent, and not merely coincidentally, of Plato's Atlantis).[11] In Hinduism the islands are sometimes referred to as "planets". This system of seven concentric islands, and oceans is known as the *saptadvīpa*.

We are going to talk much more about the *saptadvīpa* later, but let's go ahead and just introduce it now.

Although the islands or *dvīpas* are sometimes referred to as "planets", there is also some cross-referencing in the literature in general between the Mythological descriptions and the geography of Earth - as understood by modern science - on which we live.

This is not dissimilar to how, for example, islands and places in the Greek Myths coincide with actual geographic places that exist now, such as, for example, Knossos, in Crete, where in the Greek Myths Theseus defeated the Minotaur, in the Labyrinth.

The island at the centre of the *saptadvīpa* is called Jambu, Jambu *dvīpa*, or *Jambudvīpa*, the word transliterated as *dvīpa* meaning "island".

At the centre of *Jambudvīpa* is Mount Meru, a golden mountain. Mount Meru is placed the centre of the scheme in most Indic cosmologies.[12]

In the *saptadvīpa*, going outwards from the most central ocean that surrounds the central island Jambudvīpa, the seven oceans are often described as concentric oceans of:

1. salt water,
2. sugarcane juice or molasses,
3. wine or liquor,
4. clarified butter,
5. milk, or curds and whey,[13]
6. milk,[14] yoghurt,[15] or churned yoghurt,[16]
7. fresh water,[17] clear water,[18] or sweet or very tasteful water.[19]

The meaning of the seven *dvīpas* (islands or continents) and their oceans, together with all their symbolic features, is woven into the Hindu Mythology. Essentially, they represent higher *worlds* from which souls who have not attained *liberation* from the endless process of reincarnation, must eventually be reborn to material existence on Earth, and hence again to suffering and what the Puranas often call "anxiety".

These islands and oceans, and the other "worlds" that are spoken of, are a basis of what Buddhism, which developed out of Hinduism, further evolves into all kinds of complicated systems of "heavens", depending on the particular school of Buddhism.[20]

In the context of this spiritual "landscape", beyond the "outermost" *dvīpa* and its ocean (furthest from Jambudvīpa which is at the centre), is a place called *Lokaloka*.

The name *Lokaloka* is a compound word that can be translated as "place and no place". Then, beyond Lokaloka's far side is the *causal ocean*,[21] which is described as infinite and unfathomed.[22]

We will come back to the seven islands and their oceans, called the *saptadvīpa*, shortly, and again in much more detail, later. Also later, we will look at the other "worlds" which are like spheres within this *Brahmānda* or "egg of Brahma", or "cosmic egg".

The Material and Spiritual Worlds

In the Hindu teachings the *causal ocean* around the "cosmic egg" can be considered Hinduism's "causal background" to everything in material existence. Because inside the "egg" is what Hinduism calls "the universe".

The *causal ocean* is also conceived as a "border" and sometimes called the Viraja river.[23] It is said to lie *between* the material and spiritual worlds, as a region that can only be crossed through spiritual awakening.[24]

Let's be absolutely clear about this. The *Viraja river* and the *causal ocean* in the Hindu corpus *are alternative names for the same thing*,[25] a "barrier" that can only be crossed through spiritual practice.[26]

On one side of it is where we find ourselves by default, as a human self, and on the other side, is the spiritual world or what Hinduism called the "spiritual sky",[27] or the transcendental world that the Hindu corpus calls *Vaikunthaloka*.[28] There are numerous references to it in the Hindu corpus.[29]

In Hinduism there is an infinity of universes *in* the waters of the causal ocean, or *on* the waters of the river Viraja.[30] In the popular imagery these "waters" are the waters of the ocean on which *Viśnu* floats (on the serpent *Ananta Śeśa*). This is depicted in the Puranas.[31]

The *causal ocean*, or Viraja river, is what we must cross, in order to realise what is beyond it, or "above" it. The concept of "crossing" this ocean or river is therefore synonymous with *transcending* the *Brahmānda*.

The *Viraja river* or *causal ocean* does not refer to an "object" in some world whose origins are separate from us. It actually refers to something we must discover *within ourselves*. That is where we "cross" it, and discover the Spiritual Reality beyond it.

So the "causal ocean" is not part of some "structure" of some world that is "outside" and separate from, any individual human being.

In the context of modern scientific facts, we might like to say it is not outside the *construct of brain function* that we are experiencing as our self, mind, emotions, and material world.

As the more advanced or perhaps esoteric parts of the Hindu corpus make unambiguously clear, the crossing of the *causal ocean* happens *in the individual*, in the "expansion" or awakening of spiritual consciousness, which is a matter of spiritual practice.[32]

What Hinduism calls "the universe" is the effect, or illusion, that we spoke of earlier, which is *Maya*.[33] In contemporary scientific terms, this is exactly what you would expect, once you understand that it is, just as we encounter it, *a construct of brain function*. Which in reductionist terms, consists of nothing but mathematical quantum correlations.

The point to note there, however, is that what mathematics itself, *is*, what numbers, themselves, *are*, is not something that is really being understood in science, in terms of the construct of brain function that our understanding of them consists of.

This is just a facet of the fact that nothing that is currently scientifically understood is really understood in its full context, until there is sufficient knowledge of the mind that is doing the understanding.

The Seven Oceans and Beyond

So in the part of the Mythological "landscape" or cosmology that we are talking about there are seven oceans, *not including* the causal ocean (the Viraja river). These oceans each surround one of seven concentric "lands" or *dvīpas* (not unlike Plato's description of Atlantis in *Timaeus* and *Critias*).

The account of the seven *dvīpas* and seven oceans are widely distributed across the Hindu corpus.[34] The seven oceans are arranged concentrically,[35] sometimes described as concentric circles, and in other sources described as like part of a lotus flower.

All together they are all surrounded by a golden region that "shines like the surface of a golden mirror",[36] containing the *Lokaloka* mountain. It is said that any thing that reaches this land is never found again, and so this land has been abandoned by all living entities.[37]

The speech here is figurative, in the sense that within the overall meaning, this golden mirror-land only appears to have been *abandoned*, as such, because no living entity can actually *reach* this land *and* ever be known again.

This isn't an *ominous* thing, although it may sound like it to begin with. On the contrary, it is the mythical representation of *spiritual liberation*.[38] Going beyond Lokaloka means transcending the cycle of reincarnation back into the gross body, and hence suffering.

In both Hinduism and Buddhism the message that *there is reincarnation* is not something to be joyous or relieved about. This is a point that is commonly misunderstood. Rather, it is the opposite. Because of reincarnation inevitably leads back into suffering.

In traditional Hinduism the caste system is inseparably linked to the idea of reincarnation. It is an expression of it. But in Hinduism the "aim" of spiritual practice is not merely to attain more favourable conditions of reincarnation in "the next life" in human existence. Rather, it is to attain liberation from the whole business of reincarnation, as it were.

The same is true in Buddhism. The four Noble Truths of Buddhism begin by recognising that human existence is synonymous with suffering. There are many, many human beings, particularly in the privileged West, who may not consider this to be the case. Rather, they may think it is more a case that human existence from time to time, *includes* suffering. And they may consider that it is a rather negative outlook to say that it consists of suffering.

However, they are not regarding human life in this way from a platform of spiritual awakening as what Hinduism calls the realisation of the *Brahman*. Rather, from the point of view of both Hinduism and Buddhism they are temporarily enjoying a temporary condition of being as a consequence of karma, of which they have no real realisation or understanding.

Belief in reincarnation is not at all the same thing as the spiritual realisation of immortality, and in both Hinduism and Buddhism immortality is not something that belongs to the one who is incarnated. However, personal mind and ego in general picks up on the idea of reincarnation as the suggestion of its own survival beyond physical death, and as a result invests personal belief in it.

But really, this kind of interpretation of reincarnation, as the transmigration of the soul, from one human life to the next, is just a convenient "interpretation" for the sake of giving hope to the personal ego and mind. In the West this was recognised by Schopenhauer, who, in *The World as Will and Representation* calls reincarnation *metempsychosis* rather than *transmigration*.

The third of the Four Noble Truths of Buddhism - the truth that *there is an end to suffering* - is expressed also in Hinduism in terms of this earlier (than Buddhism) Mythology as *going beyond Lokaloka*. Beyond Lokaloka is the realisation of the *Brahman*, and spiritual liberation.[39]

Hinduism has an entire Mythology to describe more than one path to the realisation of the *Brahman*, and it is a rich resource for the discussion of these matters. However, we shouldn't lose track of the fact that this is an expression through one particular, cultural fabric.

The Being we already really are, we could say, to put this into context, is not dependent on any particular cultural expression of its Realisation. On the contrary, the Being - that Hinduism calls the *Brahman* - is not dependent on existence, or anything in it.

But let's continue our exploration in terms of the Hindu fabric, which describes the "spiritual landscape" pretty much literally as a "landscape".

In Hinduism the "Lokaloka mountain" divides this final region beyond the seven *dvīpas* and their oceans, into two. These two parts of Lokaloka are the golden sunlit part closest to the seven oceans (*Loka*), and the perpetual darkness (of *Aloka*) on the other side of the mountain.[40]

This doesn't actually mean that beyond the sunlit side there is nothing but spiritual darkness, or ignorance. Rather, it is the opposite. It means that from the sunlit side, which is "the universe", in which we have our conditional experience of being, what is beyond the Lokaloka Mountain is unknowable to us, and its perpetual darkness actually represents *our* ignorance of what is there. Because what is there, is the transcendental.

Now let's see what the corpus itself says about this. We mentioned earlier that *Loka* means "world" and *Aloka* means "no world". How do we interpret this?

What is beyond "Loka" is "Aloka" or "no world", because any kind of world as a *world of being* that we find on the Loka side, is not to be found there. This is the meaning.

The *Caitanya-caritamrta* tells us that beyond Lokaloka is the region known as *Vaikuntha*, and *Vrndavana*, or *Krsnaloka*, the supreme transcendental home of Krsna.[41] The highest abode there, is Goluka, also known as Vraja, and the White Island (*Śvetadvīpa*).[42] We will be talking more about this later. In other words, beyond Lokaloka is transcendental Life and Being. But it is not knowable by life and being that occurs "beneath" it.

In terms of the Hindu "landscape" or cosmology, what is "beneath" the transcendental, and ignorant of it, is represented as what is *within* the "egg of Brahma" or Brahmanda, or Bhu mandala, which we will talk much more about later.

So in other words, the transcendental is "outside" the "egg" or Brahmanda, and it is what is *within* the "egg" or Brahmanda, or within Brahma, that is what creates our own conditional experience of being, and the material world we experience as our world of being.

Inside this "egg" are numerous "worlds", together with the *Saptadvīpa*, the system of seven islands and oceans, that we will also talk much more about, later.

The "cosmic egg" of creation in Hinduism is sometimes called *Hiranyagarbha*, which means "golden womb" or "golden egg". This is the "sunlit side" of Lokaloka that "shines like the surface of a golden mirror".[43] The *effulgence* or *Brahmajyoti* from which comes the Brahma-created world - *Brahmaloka* - is also like the effulgence around the Sun, obscuring what is inside the Sun.[44]

We can put this another way. Looking "up" towards the transcendental, from where we are in our ignorance of it, in human existence, is in the Hindu "landscape" or cosmology the same as looking "out" from within the "egg" of Brahma, towards the "surrounding" transcendental.

There, in this imagery, we see the "sunlit side" of Lokaloka. It "shines like the surface of a golden mirror". That means, what we see "in" it, is a reflection. It is not that what we see reflected in it, is the content of an "egg" that is called "the universe", where "the universe" is real, and independent, and the mirror just reflects it.

Rather, to see this "golden mirror" is the initial realisation of the *Brahman*, and to see that everything that we call "the universe" is just a *reflection in* the Reality of the *Brahman*. But what is it a reflection of, then?

It is a reflection of the one who realises the *Brahman*. Which means, as the Hindu corpus repeatedly states, throughout it, to realise "I am *Brahman*". So what is reflected in this "golden mirror" is none other than the one who is seeing the reflection. And also, what is reflected, is what we call "the universe".

The way in which the *Brahman* has *become* the being who realises "I am *Brahman*", the way in which That Being has become "the universe", in which arises this being, is none other than the *expansion of being*, that we have already talked about, and are going to be talking a great deal more about.

Another way in which this "golden mirror", which is the initial realisation of the *Brahman*, another way in which it is described, in the Bhakti literature, is as the *Brahman effulgence.*

Just a little earlier we mentioned that the *causal ocean* or Viraja river must be crossed through spiritual practice. The *Caitanya-caritamrta* makes it clear that this *going beyond* the Viraja river is synonymous with penetrating the walls of this universe - the *Brahmānda* in which we live - *into* the *Brahman effulgence.*

This too, can then be penetrated or gone beyond, into the "spiritual sky", and the Spiritual Reality that the Bhakti tradition calls *Goloka Vrndavana.*[45] And it is here that there is transcendental Life and Being. And we are not really talking about something different here, to what we are talking about when we are speaking of transcendental Life and Being realised in Christian mysticism. It is just that the cultural fabric of its expression is different according to the religious culture through which it is realised.

So the "perpetual darkness" of the *Aloka* side of *Lokaloka* is only "darkness" when seen from the "materially sunlit" side of the *dvīpas* and their oceans. It basically means that the spiritual Light beyond the *causal ocean* surrounding the "cosmic egg" (and also beyond specific "coverings" of the egg that we will talk about later), is inaccessible to beings who live in the *Brahmānda*. Until, that is, all the "coverings" of the "egg" are penetrated, which is to cross the *causal ocean.*

So what is beyond *Lokaloka* is not really darkness, even though in the corpus it is often described as such, from the point of view of *Brahmānda* or "the universe" inside the "cosmic egg". Rather, what is there, *beyond* the "egg", as the *Śrīmad Bhāgavatam* states, is the eternal transcendental *Light* of the spiritual realm.[46] This is transcendental Life and Being. The Hindu scriptures are explicit about this.

The basic allegory should now be relatively clear. What we are looking here at is an allegorical representation - a Mythical symbolisation - as a "spiritual landscape", rather than just facts about material things.

As we have already briefly mentioned, this "landscape" painted by the Hindu sources is part of an overall conceptual object known as the *Bhū mandala.*[47] Within the mandala are a number of "worlds" together with the seven *dvīpas* and their oceans surrounding the Meru mountain at the centre.

This "structure" is sometimes described as a "planetary system".48 Again, we must remember that this is not a "structure" in the ordinary, material sense. And we will be misled if for the term "planet" we tried to substitute the modern, scientific concept of a planet. Rather, if we want to understand the real meaning we should consider anything said in the Mythology to be a "planet", as a world, in the more general sense, even if it does have an associated celestial body.

Understanding the Perspective

We must always remember that what is called "the universe" in the Hindu corpus is not at all the same thing as what modern science calls "the universe". Modern science refers to what is scientifically, empirically, measurable. What the Hindu corpus refers to, is not that. But there is a "meeting ground" between the two, which is our sentient *experience* of the material world. *That*, however, requires the brain. And that is not something that the Hindu corpus mentions or talks about. Because the Hindu corpus is prescientific.

When the Hindu corpus speaks of "planets" it is talking about our sentient experience, and not about what is scientifically measurable, according to the definitions of modern science. Our sentient experience of "planets" that are observed in the sky, is an experience of mind.

This experience as we have it, first requires the human brain. It first requires the human mind. There is nothing "there", separate from us, that this experience exists us. Similarly, there is nothing "there", separate from the intelligence we are being, in anything we understand scientifically about it, that this understanding or knowledge exists as. It is all a construct of brain function, and all a product of the mind we are being.

What the Hindu corpus is essentially saying is that these objects, which we perceive as part of our experience of mind, are material representations in *our* world of being, of *other* worlds of being.

So precisely where is the difference between a material planet or any other celestial object as observed by science, and the "world of being", or indeed, in terms of the personalised accounts in the Puranas, the Being, that according to the Hindu picture the scientifically observed object represents?

The answer is actually remarkably simple. In scientific terms the scientifically observed celestial object is a material construct. In reductionist terms it is a material construct of super-complexity. As is the human brain itself. A planet or a star may look like a single "thing", but in fact, it is a super-complex construct. And ultimately, in terms of our current science, it is a super-complex construct, whose "base layer" so to speak, is structures of relations between quantum particles.

In terms of the Big Bang theory it has arisen out of the condensation into this structure, of what came out of the Big Bang. It is, to put it simply, a very big thing formed out of countless layers of complexity and complex relations between very small things.

In a process of infinite involution, or mathematically speaking, iteration or recurrence, such as we encounter in fractals, the same kinds of objects occur again and again at different levels of "magnification". In a fractal such as a Julia set, where do we find the smallest object? There isn't one. The involution is infinite. But the larger objects are nonetheless recurrent "representations" of the smaller ones.

In our own world of being, our material world, we see, for example, the principle of the orbit on the cosmic scale, but it also occurs at the scale of the atom. The reason is that there is a common abstract mathematical structure to both.

The abstract mathematical structures themselves are in the process of involution and recurrence. In our material world, which we have knowledge and experience of through the principle of the brain, the biggest material things, like planets and stars, or the cosmic web, are the biggest complex structures, although not necessarily the most complex. Because that's the nature of complexity. It also produces "simplexity". But counterintuitively perhaps, marrying together for a moment modern science with the Hindu picture, it is the smallest things known to science, that represent or symbolise the greatest aspects of our origins in Being, in terms of the Hindu picture.

When a large thing like a planet, comes to represent a god or a Being, the large observable material object is essentially a "fractal reiteration" of what it represents, crudely similar to the way that the geometric object we call the Mandelbrot set, is a "fractal reiteration" generated from the much simpler, "smaller", iterations that produce it.

Expansion and complexity produces structures, often relatively simple looking, from simpler structures of things that are much smaller. That's how it is in our material world. The Hindu picture views it all in terms of Being. In terms of Being, the smallest things in our material world, are representations of the greatest aspects of Being. But they are only material representations.

As far as the Hindu picture is concerned, the material world is an "external" representation of internal psychical experience. The way in which this internal psychical experience comes about, is part of the same "system" through which the material world comes about. In the Hindu corpus this "system" is the Bhu mandala.

How is it from the point of view of the modern scientific knowledge of the brain? The parallel should be clear enough. What we experience as the material world is a construct of brain function. And it is this construct of brain function through which arises our inner, psychical experience.

Whichever way you look at it, there is the "inner" and the "outer". The "outer" is the mundane or gross world of matter, which is constrained by laws of structure and behaviour that are independent of anyone's mind or brain. These, we call in science, the "laws of nature".

However, everyone's mind and brain arises through this same gross world. The "outer", in its entirety, is not what is separate from anyone's nervous system or body. Rather, the nervous system or body arises as part of it. What we encounter as this "outer", is nonetheless a structure of brain function.

The way in which each individual brain organ gives rise to the experience of this world, is something that mainstream scientific thinking currently regards as the "outer" giving rise to the "inner". The Hindu corpus sees things the other way around. In it, the "inner" gives rise to the "outer".

We shall look in detail at the way this is described, later. The "outer" still gives rise to "inner" experience, in that light enters the eye, for example, and in doing so creates the corresponding brain function. Or on a larger scale the loss of a loved one may give rise to grief.

However, the way in which this happens, is a matter of time. Experience always arises as experience, regardless of our understanding of it in terms of "what comes before" and "what comes after". The "what comes before" and "what comes after", is part of the fabric of the "outer". It is determined by the constraints we call the "laws of nature" that determine material cause and effect, which is basically what time is.

Experience itself, however, is psychical, and of the "inner". Our psychical experience is constantly unfolding in cycles and patterns, and as far as the Hindu picture is concerned this propagation of cycles and patterns across the ocean of itself, is the "prior" thing from which the "external" is manifested.

The real question is whether or not we are conscious of these cycles and patterns, which actually, we can only become fully conscious of, to the degree to which we are no longer identified with the experiences they produce.

In science, we already know that the constraints put on the "outer" by what we understand as the "laws of physics", whilst never disappearing as such, actually begin to dissolve into a structure of just statistical relations both at the fundamental smallest scale of quantum particles, and in respect of large-scale phenomena of our world that scientifically speaking, is phenomenal complexity and nonlinearity.

Examples of this are the weather, natural disasters, the question of who is going to win the next election, or whether or not you are going to fall in love, which no knowledge of the "laws of physics" is going to enable you to predict.

However, our knowledge of the "inner" psychical world of experience has a direct bearing on *how* we experience the "inner" in relation to the "outer". And, eventually, as this knowledge increases, the apparent separation of the "inner" from the "outer", dissolves.

In terms of the "inner" the "outer" becomes part of the experience of self that is the "inner". In terms of the "outer", the "inner" is understood to be a construct of brain function, which is part of the "outer".

But the idea that the "inner" or self is confined to "my body", and that the "outer" sense-perceived world has nothing to do with the self other than that the self happens to be in it, falls down. In Hinduism and Buddhism this is called Advaita.

The Hindu picture begins with the Being, the *Brahman*, and is *about* beings. All these beings are conditional experiences of being, created from the *Brahman*. Anything that the corpus talks about, is always in that context. Even when it is using numbers, and talking about distances and dimensions, and so forth.

Everything, in the Hindu picture, is an expansion of the Being, the *Brahman*. This is a completely different mode of speech and expression, to the one used by modern science. You cannot simply put both side-by-side, and transfer from one to the other, without understanding what the bridge, and connection is. And without understanding how that bridge and connection works.

The bridge and connection is, of course, the human brain.

3

The Causal Ocean

So let's now look at the Hindu representation of the "causal background" to everything. In contemporary terms, that means the causal background to the brain itself, and our experience of being in our world (our *world of being*) that arises through brain function.

In Hinduism the "causal background" to *everything* here, in our existence, is called the *causal ocean*.

The Tenth Canto of the *Śrīmad Bhāgavatam* relates the story of *Arjuna and the Brahmana's son*. In this story (we don't need to go into the full details of the story here) Arjuna is taken in Lord Krsna's transcendental chariot across the seven *dvīpas* and seven oceans, to the region of the vast darkness of *Aloka*.[49] Remember this is the "outer side" of Lokaloka.

Krsna lights the way by his *Sudarśana Chakra* ("wheel of auspicious vision") which is depicted in the myths as an invincible weapon.[50]

A weapon? What kind of weapon is it? The underlying truth of it is not about its mythical, physical characteristics. Any of those are just symbolic. Rather, it is a "weapon of truth" against ignorance. Krsna's *Sudarśana Chakra* is, like everything else in the Myths, a symbol, and furthermore, is *explicitly explained* in the texts themselves as being *religion*, *truth*, and the *original vision of the Lord*.[51]

It is also described as being like an inauspicious comet for demons, whose effulgence is as quick as the mind.[52] We can see that this idea is related to the "lions roar" in Buddhism, which is the ability of a Buddha to confront and overcome ignorance that has gathered itself in the form of conceptualising mind.

The notion of the "weapon" in the Vedas, in the later Hindu corpus in general, and in Buddhism, is certainly not merely about the common, modern meaning of the word "weapon". It is invariably a part of colourful and figurative language describing a metaphorical "weapon" of *truth* against *ignorance*.

In Vajrayana Buddhism the *vajra* is a "weapon" sometimes called the "thunderbolt". But it's not an actual weapon, used to attack other people with. It takes the form of a psychic object of meditation, used in the process of overcoming ignorance *in oneself*. Buddhist *vajras* do also exist as actual, physical things are *symbolic objects*. They are objects of art and ritual, usually coupled with the Buddhist bell, another object symbolising wisdom.

In a well-known story from the Puranas a *vajra* is made (we are now in the world of figurative and symbolic language again) from the bones of the sage *Dadhīci* who gives up his life in his material body so that Indra can defeat the demon *Vṛtāsura* on the "battlefield". The "bones" from which the *vajra* in the story is made, represent the spiritual power attained by *Dadhīci*.[53]

If you don't know any of this, or *want* to know any of this, then of course you can just go with the drama and the action of any Purana story. And you still have a nice, entertaining story. But as with the entire corpus of the Puranas, that surface appearance is not what it is really all about.

The essential idea in the story of *Arjuna and the Brahmana's son* is the *vajra* as a "weapon" of truth, consisting of *spiritual knowledge and realisation*, attained by *Dadhīci* during his life in the body.

It means that through spiritual practice during his life he obtained sufficient spiritual knowledge that could be considered as a "weapon" of truth against ignorance, in this figurative language. In the language of the story, the "weapon" can then be used against *ignorance* (personified in the stories as *Asuras* or demons).

In the story *Dadhīci* has to *give up his life in the body*, in order for his "bones" - his spiritual realisation - to become available for others, in the "battle for truth". The message is clear, but not everyone can see it. It is also possible just to be embroiled in the cartoon-like entertainment of the story.

The parallel here to the principle of the sacrifices made by the saints, and at the very pinnacle of this principle, of course, the parallel to Christ, really, is *obvious*. But you can't see it, unless you contemplate the meaning.

So in the story about Arjuna that we were talking about, Krsna lights the way across the region of the vast darkness of *Aloka* part of Lokaloka, that is beyond the *seven dvīpas and seven oceans*. He lights it by the light of his *Sudarśana Chakra* ("wheel of auspicious vision") which is depicted in the Myths as an invincible weapon.[54] An invincible weapon of spiritual truth against ignorance.[55]

With the help of Krsna and his *Sudarśana Chakra*, shining like a thousand suns,[56] and cutting through the darkness (ignorance) of *Aloka* with the *speed of mind*,[57] Krsna and Arjuna reach the all-pervasive, transcendental Light, so bright that in the story Arjuna has to shut his eyes. This Light is the spiritual Light of the Being, often referred to in the Bhakti parts of the Hindu corpus as the *Brahman effulgence*.

They then *enter into* the *Brahman effulgence*. Here they then enter water (in the mythical imagery), blown by wind into huge waves, with wondrous ornaments, effulgent with brilliantly shining gems, and with thousands of beautiful columns (signifying structures or worlds).[58]

And here, we are told in the narrative, is the huge and effulgent *Ananta Śesa*, the serpent that in the widely known popular Mythology, Mahā-Viśnu (popularly just called Viśnu) floats on, on the *causal ocean*.[59]

What is this *meant* to be all about? It is meant to be about spiritual truth. Despite the mode of presentation, it is not about some fantastical place that can be truly understood as an object. It is not about the antics of various "persons" in that place. And yet so often it is presented or understood in that way.

It is then no wonder that many materialist Western minds reject it as imaginative nonsense, or myth as falsehood rather than true Myth as allegory, and then fail to connect with its truth and value.

The Hindu sources contain much text and thought whose *fabric* is a matter of time, place, and *culture of the time and place*, which is often completely out of kilter with modern, materialist, Western understanding. They use language and ideas about societal structures that are obsolete. The texts sometimes contain, for example, material that would be regarded by many in contemporary Western culture as socially unacceptable and misogynistic.[60]

But this aspect of the text should never be alighted on by any modern mind, East or West, in order to dismiss the whole text as irrelevant to modern understanding. It is just that in some sources, or at least in part of them, there is just more weight of the cultural past than there is the light of Truth.

In the story we just related, the "water" entered by Krsna and Arjuna, with its "huge waves" and "wondrous ornaments, effulgent with brilliantly shining gems, and with thousands of beautiful columns" (signifying structures or worlds),[61] is none other than what elsewhere in the corpus is called the *causal ocean*, or the Viraja river.

It is one and the same as the *Brahman effulgence*. Sometimes it is called the *Virāt*, or *Viraj*. We spoke of this before, and we shall speak of it again.

4

Expansion of Being

The Godhead is called *Brahman* because it is immense and it expands.[62]

- Śiva Purana

When, in the popular Mythology, *Viśnu* is pictured as "laying on the ocean", floating on a "couch" that is the serpent called *Ananta Śeśa*, this does not describe the whole picture.

Anyone with some familiarity with the Hindu corpus would probably be amused by that statement. Because it is an understatement, to say the least.

We have talked about how parts of the Hindu corpus describe *Viśnu* (as His expansion of Being) as having different *expansions*, as *Kāranodakaśāyī Viśnu*, who lays on the causal ocean, *Garbhodakaśāyī Viśnu*, who lays on the *Garbhodaka* ocean of living entities (*jivas*), and *Ksīrodakaśāyī Viśnu*, who lays on "the Ocean of Milk".[63]

What is going on here is one small example of the principle of the *expansion of being*, that we will come to talk much more about in due course.

The principle of the *expansion of being* even takes place in its own way, in human reproduction. Of course it's not quite the same thing there, that we are talking about in the case of *Viśnu*, because human reproduction is a material, genetic expansion.

Nevertheless, the way in which nature expands the numbers of human beings is still an expansion in the principle of *experience of being*. Because human beings, even as material, biological beings, still constitute *experience of being*.

You can even see particular aspects of *expansion*, in terms of personal characteristics, in the way that children inherit features and characteristics genetically, from their parents. And, indeed, the way we all do, from our ancestors in general.[64]

As we have already seen, in the case of *Viśnu*, essentially, *Garbhodakaśāyī Viśnu* is an *expansion of being* of *Kāranodakaśāyī Viśnu*, and *Ksīrodakaśāyī Viśnu* is an *expansion of being* of *Garbhodakaśāyī Viśnu*.

So *Ksīrodakaśāyī Viśnu* is also an expansion of the Being of *Kāranodakaśāyī Viśnu*, but one that only takes place *through* the intermediate Being called *Garbhodakaśāyī Viśnu*.

So in the three *Viśnu*s we are getting our first glimpse of the principle of *expansion of being*. It's not really where expansion of being begins, but it is where we first start to talk about it.

Bear in mind that whilst this has the appearance of a *hierarchy*, from *Kāranodakaśāyī* to *Garbhodakaśāyī* to *Ksīrodakaśāyī*, not all expansion of being in the Hindu picture is hierarchical in appearance, in this way.

Describing it conceptually, in this way, if you were to represent hierarchies as vertical, then you would also have to show "lateral" expansions too. And that's only the beginning of the ways in which the *Being* can expand. Ultimately, it is all an expansion of the *Brahman*, or in an alternative terminology, the One (as referred to by the early Greeks).

As we have already mentioned, in the Hindu corpus, more than one Being declares themselves alone to be the Supreme Being, even though the Supreme Being is one Being. This is because *all beings*, ultimately, are expansions of the one Being. If reading the corpus, this is a really important thing to remember.

The oneness of all beings in that they are all really the one Being, or all an *expansion* of what Hinduism sometimes calls the Supreme Being, is not a plural, collective oneness, of "us". Rather, it is the realisation that "who I am" is *Brahman*, the Being.

Appreciating this is crucial to seeing what is really going on in the Purana stories. The underlying framework of *all* that goes on, that isn't always explicitly declared, is all about this *expansion of being*, from the one Being, the *Brahman*.

But at the same time, the only way in which anything is *happening*, or going on, in these stories in the first place, is through "forgetfulness" of the Being that is everyone's (in the stories) true Identity. Even Brahma, "the creator" of all other beings after the Trimurti, forgets his true Identity. But he does realise, through penance, that He is the *Brahman*, the Being.

In the Hindu corpus *creation itself* - the thing called "the universe" - comes from the *expansion of being*, originating from the Supreme Being. This expansion, after *Śiva*, is *Śakti*, and *Maya*, as the Śiva Purana states, as we shall come to see. But, as we have emphasised before, we must remember this:

In this 21st-century global civilisation in which we are living, what, *in the world of science and technology* - is called "the material world", or "the universe", is *not the same thing* that the Hindu corpus calls "the universe" or "the material world". We will repeatedly talk about this throughout this book. The conflating of one with the other tends to come about from not really understanding the *modus operandi* of modern science. We will talk more about this in due course.

The great *expansion of being* as represented in the Hindu corpus is actually a kind of descent, and involution, and convolution, of *being*, or *experience of being*, from the Supreme Being.

With the exception of the *Brahman*, every part and aspect of this great *expansion of being*, from the Being, is represented in the corpus by personified beings. As we shall come to see, places are beings, principles are beings, even *time*, is a being.

And it is perhaps a little too easy to forget that all this is what Hinduism calls *Maya*. That is, it is illusory, in the sense that it is the cause of what the corpus refers to as "delusion".

Hinduism, in one particular way, could be said to be ahead of science in that it already recognises that the material world is primarily a world that we *experience*, rather than a world that has nothing to do with us, other than that we happen to be experiencing it.

This is completely in line with the scientific fact that what we encounter as the material world we encounter as a construct of brain function. And yet in the mainstream, we continue to regard our world in science, as though it has nothing to do with us other than that we happen to be in it.

So long before the rise of modern science, the Hindu corpus *already innately recognised* in its own pre-scientific way, something that in modern terms we can put in another way: the world we live in is something we only ever encounter as a construct of brain function. Therefore, we only encounter it in conjunction with our experience of self. No matter how *objective* we are being. And therefore it has everything to do with us, in other words, it is not separate from us.

We only know it, and experience it, and understand anything about it, through the brain. All that knowing, experiencing, and understanding, is *a construct of brain function*. Our experiencing of the world, our scientific thinking about it, our comprehension of it, our understanding of it, is all brain function.

In science all this thinking and understanding circulates around what is *objective* about the world. It is about what can be objectively observed or measured. And it works because the world indeed does have an objective aspect to it. However, this simply means that this aspect is not at all dependent on anyone's individual mind or brain, or on any network of minds or brains.

It doesn't mean that our experience and understanding of it is not a construct of brain function. It doesn't mean that *the world* is not a construct of brain function. And the *prima facie* characteristic of our brain function, actually, is to create our experience of self.

Everything we study and understand, changes the brain. In many cases, when human beings study something, it changes the brain, creating belief, and cognitive bias. This is especially true of religious texts. But it is also true of scientific texts. That's partly why there have always been such things as scientific paradigms, that are *believed in*.

Studying the Hindu corpus doesn't increase our knowledge of what is objective about the world. But at the same time, studying it from outside the culture, doesn't *necessarily* only create a belief system and cognitive bias.

Rather, the Hindu corpus takes the reader towards the realisation of its central message, which is the realisation of something that doesn't even ultimately depend on that particular Mythology or cultural fabric.

In terms of Saivism, the entire thing is a *much ado about nothing* in the light of its own central message about *Brahman*, which burns everything else up as in a sacrificial fire, and out of the ashes rises *Śiva* - not as a personalised being, but as what *Śiva* means.

Scientific knowledge doesn't make the central message of Hinduism, fall down. Because the knowledge of how an illusion arises cannot be deduced by studying the illusion. Rather, one has to realise how the magician is creating the illusion.

The Hindu Puranas are about *Maya*, and *Maya* is, as it were, the trick of the magician. The message in the Puranas is not so much about the inner mechanics that manifest through the trick, as how the illusion is created in the first place.

It's just that, the way the trick is done, results in an aspect of its appearance, that enables the subsequent creation, within the trick, of a thing called science, as we understand it in the modern way.

* * *

So let's get back to what we were talking about, in the Hindu picture the various *Viśnus* we were mentioning above. The *Viśnu*s are *expansions of being* from the Supreme Being, the *Brahman*.

Ksīrodakaśāyī Viśnu is said to lie on "the Ocean of Milk". *Ksīro* here just means milk. We will talk much more about the Ocean of Milk, and what it means, later.

To "lie on" or "lie in" an ocean, as talked about in the Hindu corpus, is a description of *expansion of being*. In other words, the *Ocean of Milk* is the *expansion of being* of *Ksīrodakaśāyī Viśnu*. But, as we shall be seeing later, what is meant by the *Ocean of Milk* is more far reaching than this limited glimpse of it.

Ksīrodakaśāyī Viśnu is an *expansion of being* of *Garbhodakaśāyī Viśnu*. And *Garbhodakaśāyī Viśnu* is an expansion of being of *Kāranodakaśāyī Viśnu*. And all, are expansions of being of the Supreme Being. So in other words, the Ocean of Milk is an *expansion of being* of the Supreme Being.

Out of this expansion comes Brahma. And out of Brahma comes the world of the rest of the Mythology, with all its beings.

Expansion of being is not a simple, one-dimensional thread, so to speak. It is multifarious with all kinds of different expansions, some of them complete, some of them partial. In the Hindu pantheon, if a being expands to become an apparently "other" being then this "other" being may be declared in the text to be "non-different" (*abhinnā* or *abheda*) to its progenitor. In other words, it is an apparently separate being, but actually, it is the same being.

They may appear to be two beings in the play of *Maya*, illusion, but both may be two different instances of the same being. Each experiences their identity as that original being, or becomes one with the original being, when they *realise* their true identity.

For example, at the very pinnacle of this principle, in the Bhakti texts, the lovers Rādhā and Krsna appear in the play of *Maya* as two separate beings, female and male, but really, they are both one and the same being.[65] The whole point of their appearing as two "separate" beings, is so that the nature of the love of the Being can be realised, and enjoyed.[66]

In Hinduism, the Being who realises his identity as this conjugal love of Rādhā and Krsna, as the combined *Rādhā-Krsna*, is Lord Caitanya.[67] Lord Caitanya is the realised Being of that aspect of God, or Krsna, which is the union and exchange of love of Rādhā and Krsna.[68]

Rādhā (*Rādhārāni*) is not separate from Krsna, except, as His Divine Grace A.C. Bhaktivedanta Prabhupāda puts it, in order to 'understand Himself through the agency of Rādhā', so He unites with Rādhārāni, and 'that unification is called Lord Caitanya'.[69]

This, in Hinduism, in Bhakti, is the pinnacle of conscious realisation of the nature of the Being, through the combination of different aspects of the Being.

In Hinduism beings also multiply by *Śrsti* (Sarshti) or *Prajanana*. We see multiplication by *Prajanana* where two beings personified as male and female create offspring, just as we also see it in sexual reproduction.

We also see multiplication by *expansion of being* from just one being. We see it in the expansion of being from *Śiva* to *Viśnu*, and from *Viśnu* to Brahma. We see it where *Śiva* creates *Śivā* (*Śakti*) also often called *Satī*. We see it where Brahma creates numerous "mind born" or psychic sons, and his consort and his daughter.

Where there is a fullness of *expansion of being* from the Supreme Being, then the play of expansion of beings is such that many beings are appearing also as expansions of themselves, and the interaction of beings is therefore correspondingly complex.

When described in terms of personalised beings, as it is in the Hindu corpus, the "world" into which the overall *expansion of being* takes place, is a world that to the modern, educated, Western mind, is clearly "mythological".

Going Beyond the Cultural Fabric

In general the Hindu corpus is fully imbued with the characteristics of times, places and culture of the world in which the Puranas arose - namely the culture of India and ancient India in particular. So there is much in the sources pertaining to rituals and fire sacrifices, and so on. There is also ample suggestion of "worship", that appears to be no more than obsequiousness and ritual idol worship.

So the corpus material is of course specifically linked to *India* and *Indian culture*. Being Indian in origin, in the Puranas, we would expect to see a cultural bias of time and place, in the account of creation. This, we do indeed see. But then, all cultures and their associated religions, in their accounts of creation, see the world and its origins with the same kind of bias.

The ancient name of *Bhārata* refers to India, and it occurs, as we shall later see, according to some parts of the corpus itself, as the only place from which salvation can be attained. Nevertheless, we should be wise enough to at least recognise that God, the Divine, or Spiritual Reality, cannot be bound by any specific culture, religion, human belief, or human behaviour.

The Hindu corpus is vast and detailed. But a great deal of the detail is specific to the Indian mind and culture. And in that, we can expect the corpus to contain not just wisdom, but also some ignorance of the kind that can be found in *all* cultures. Because *all* cultures contain ignorance.

However, regardless of the fabric, if you look at it, you can see that the principle of *the expansion of being* is a principle in its own right. It is not just something that *has to be* expressed in the form of its *Indian cultural expression*, with its particular *personifications* and names of beings. God doesn't *only* create the *Indian* mind and brain.

It is just that the Indian mind and brain must *realise* what there is to be realised, through the Indian mind and brain. Just as the Chinese, or the Japanese, or the American or the European, must do so through the Chinese or Japanese or American or European mind and brain, respectively. Unless it happens otherwise. And the more globally interconnected we become, as we have been becoming for a very, very long time, long before modern global connectivity, the more likely this is to happen.

Ultimately though, we must be prepared for something that transcends completely, all culture, and cultural expressions. We must be prepared for something beyond the brain. And in that, it doesn't make any difference whether you call it the *Brahman*, the Being, the Self, God, or *Satori*.

5

Gunas, Purusa, and Prakrti

In addition to the Puranic stories of personalised beings, and interwoven with these stories, the Indian sources contain a parallel account of creation that can appear to be somewhat more impersonal, and technical sounding.

This is the account in terms of *Purusa*, *Prakrti* and the *Gunas*.

Purusa literally means "man". It is an aspect of the Being first referred to in the Vedas. In terms of the great *expansion of being*, Purusa can be regarded as the nature of the *Being* as it "enters" the part of its own expansion that is behind the creation of what we have come to know as material existence. Across the Puranas, Purusa is spoken of as "entering *Prakrti*".

In contemporary interpretations of Hinduism *Prakrti* is therefore often associated with the *matter* of the material world. But actually, as we shall see, *Prakrti* is about human experience. And furthermore, *Prakrti*, in the corpus, is *female* and explicitly identified with *Śakti* and *Maya*, and in modern language is also related to what in human beings is love and sex.

Whilst even today we may still sometimes refer to "nature" as female, there is nothing in the *matter* of the material world that makes modern physics regard matter as fundamentally female. The mainstream position of modern science is to regard love and sex as something that arises *secondarily* to the material universe. In the mainstream view of modern science the material universe in itself has nothing to do with matters such as love, sex, or gender. Rather, the idea is that it was here before, and will be here after.

In contrast, in Hinduism, what in human beings is gender, love and sex, is an expression of principles that are inseparable from the universe, and go right to the origin of material existence itself.

So Hinduism speaks of *Prakrti* as consisting of the three *Gunas*. The three Gunas are *Sattva*, *Rajas* and *Tamas*, but sometimes appear with variations on those words. There are many different ways in which the three *Gunas* are described and talked about by modern writers. *Sattva* is often described as calm, stillness, mindfulness, and so on. *Raja* is activity and excitement, the need to do, emotionality and restlessness, and so on. *Tamas* is often described as dullness, lethargy, slowness, and emotional darkness. A general term is *ignorance*.

But actually, in interpreting the corpus, the three *Gunas*, as *Sattva*, *Rajas* and *Tamas*, can be sufficiently understood as *goodness*, *passion*, and *ignorance*, respectively. This is basically how the words are translated by Swami Prabhupāda.[70]

However, it is important to realise that "goodness" here, isn't a "virtue" that can be judged or objectified, according to ordinary, personal ideas about what is "good" or "bad", or "right" or "wrong". This "goodness" has to be appreciated in the context of the *Gunas* as a whole. It is not alien to what Plato talks about as "the Good".

The *Gunas* begin with ignorance. This, *fundamentally*, before it morphs into all kinds of other things, and personal attributes, is the ignorance of the Being, an ignorance that is inherent in the condition we are in. We have to understand that "ignorance" in this context doesn't just refer to lack of intellectual understanding or mental command of facts. Rather, the core of human ignorance is a matter of being, and contains what is psychical, visceral and experiential.

In this context what we might call "my personal emotions" based on our personalised and ego-based idea of "who I am", are actually this ignorance. In the bigger picture the experiential part of our true being is not about these emotions. This is in stark contrast to the fact that they are held so highly by current Western society, and its cultural conditioning, in the erroneous idea that they constitute our spirituality, and the highest part of our being.

Rather, the highest part of our experiential sensibility as a human being, is transcendental *rasa*. And what appears as self and ego-based emotionality is essentially a subsequent creation, that arises through the fall of the consciousness of who we really are, into ignorance of our true Identity.

Rasa has a spectrum that extends from aesthetic sensitivities and awareness of the energies of human situations, all the way up to *peak experience* in which the Being is experienced so directly and powerfully that it spontaneously dissolves emotional self and ego in what may even look like ordinary emotionality.

Our conditional experience of being as individual, "separate" self, that we ordinarily have, arises through the body and the brain. And the visceral, experiential substance of it is personal, *emotional self*. It exists in us whether or not we happen at the time to be experiencing it consciously, or not.

But the Joy of *rasa* is where we begin, as experience of being, before we become immersed in this ignorance. We tend to think of our experience of self as being in the present. But in the great expansion of being, where we are, when immersed in this ignorance of personal emotionality, is in the past, and we awaken out of that by coming into the presence of the Being. Where there is the joy of *rasa*.

So ignorance gives rise to the emotions, but ignorance isn't the only thing that is in us. There is also Divine love. Because love, the love of the Being, it is at the root of the entire *expansion of being*. This isn't the personal love belonging to the personal idea of "who I am" based on emotional self, and ego, but rather, is the love of the Being. That's already here, along with the ignorance. This love is at the root of *Sattva*.

It even gets into the emotions and stirs them up. This love, together with the basic ignorance, or *Tamas*, actually *creates* the emotions.

Rajas, or passion, is the basis of the whole *play* of our existence. It is the means by which ignorance plays itself out, in a play of the overcoming of the *Tamas* by *Sattva*. So now we are talking about ignorance and passion. And passion can be loved-based, and/or ignorance-based. And in general is both.

Human beings in general carry around a personal *idea* of "who I am" that isn't actually the same thing as the *visceral feeling* of "who I am" in any moment. The *visceral feeling* of "who I am" is the experience of self. And in general, we cannot come to truly know this self, to see it for what it is, and to penetrate into it, because that process of self-knowledge is blocked by the personal "who I am" *idea*.

The actual visceral experience of self is, in modern scientific terms, the sum of all experience being delivered through brain function. And fundamentally, like biological brain function itself, it happens impersonally. But because we are by default, completely identified with it, we make it personal.

But we don't have to be identified with it in this way. The beginning of our awakening into the consciousness we already really are, is usually by becoming consciously aware of the emotional content of our experience, from a platform of pure awareness of it. Even though the very nature of emotional self is to draw us into identification with it.

It is because we are subconsciously and unconsciously attached to the *personal idea* of "who I am", *through* this emotionality, that we become trapped in personal misidentification with the emotionality. It is like a vicious circle between the idea of "who I am", and the experience of emotional self. The one leads into the other. But this emotional self that we are experiencing being, is not who we really are, at all. In fact, it is a blockage.

When we are blocked in this way, we end up holding other people and the world responsible for the nature of what is in this "who am" experience of self. And that is pretty much the zeitgeist of contemporary Western society at the moment. It is a zeitgeist in which the practice of holding others responsible for our emotional self, is actually eulogised.

In love-based passion the love isn't originally personal at all. We just *make* it personal through the imposition of the personal *idea* of "who I am". The truth is that we don't *need* the personal *idea* of "who I am", in order have the "I am" experience. When the true nature of the "I am" experience is realised, then the nature of the "who" is different.

And if you don't relate to the *experience* of "who I am" through the personal *idea* of "who I am", then the experience of "who I am" becomes freed from that blockage. It becomes freed from that constraint. And in that freedom there is then the possibility of transmutation and transcendence, and the discovery of the Self, the *Brahman*.

There is the possibility of the experience of "who I am" as it stands, identified with the ignorance of self, being transcended, and *trans-personal consciousness and being*, as "who I am", being discovered.

Love-based passion, of course, isn't the only kind of passion. When you start getting into ignorance-based passion, then you start going down into every aspect of what has long been called "the passions", and that contains all the emotional negativity in human nature. And of course this isn't the way to go. Not if we want to find the truth of our own true Identity. Which is the Being.

Throughout the Hindu corpus the *Brahman*, the Being, is said to be above and beyond the *Gunas*. So the consciousness of our own true Identity, as the Being, is completely beyond the *Gunas*. *Sattva*, or "goodness", is only what the love of the Being becomes when it enters the realm of the *Gunas*.

Actually, to be more specific, *Sattva*, or goodness, is what the love of the Being becomes when it enters the realm of ignorance and passion.

So it can quell the negative passions, like anger and resentment, and even quell the apparently "positive" passions that are still based on ignorance, such as jumping up and down with personal excitement. Because it pulls everything towards the love of the Being. And so *Sattva* is associated with stillness and peace. And finally, in Hindu terms, with what is called *transcendental mellow*.

So *Sattva* is a symptom of the consciousness of the Being. But the consciousness of the Being, the love of the Being, is above and beyond all the *Gunas*.

The Gunas are also sometimes referred to in the Hindu corpus, as *attributes* or *qualities*. So when we find, in the corpus, references to being with or without *attributes* or *qualities*, for example, this is in general reference to the *Gunas*.

Prakrti and Purusa

So *Prakrti* consists of the three *Gunas*. That is, *sattva*, *rajas*, and *tamas*. Which we can translate when they appear in the Puranas, as *goodness*, *passion*, and *ignorance*, respectively.[71] However, it is important to remember that this "goodness" has nothing to do with personal ideas of "good" versus "bad", or "right" versus "wrong".

In short, *Prakrti* is not some mysterious primordial "material" that has nothing to do with human experience. On the contrary, *Prakrti* is all about the human condition and experience of being. It is very much about the experience of "who I am".

Purusa and *Prakrti* together form the whole crux of the matter. *Purusa* is as it were, the consciousness in the *Prakrti*. But all along, the *Prakrti* itself, like everything else, is the *Brahman*, or more specifically, an *expansion* of the *Brahman*. *Prakrti* is created by the Being, through the *expansion of being*, and as such, consists of consciousness, into which consciousness, as Purusa, then enters.

The tendency, in modern intellectual materialism, is to try to want to understand this as separate things, or as a system of parts. But it is not that. Later, we will come to see that the corpus itself tells us this. Rather, the talk of Purusa entering *Prakrti* is a way of communicating a principle in the expansion of being. It is, after all, all the *Brahman*, and all the expansion of the *Brahman*.

One way of looking at this, is that the expansion enters itself, in what is otherwise called *involution*. The Being, the Brahman, always remains throughout the expansion. At any point in the expansion, so to speak, the Being is still arising, as *Purusa*, but also, the *expansion* of the Being, as *Prakrti* is what the *Purusa* arises *in*. Whereupon the Purusa has *entered* the *Prakrti*.

But the origin of the Purusa is transcendental, and has no dependence on *Prakrti*. This transcendental origin of the Purusa is the *Brahman*. And the first transcendental creation from the *Brahman*, the Śiva Purana states, is *Śiva*, who immediately manifests transcendentally as the Divine Couple *Śiva* and *Śivā* in "the blissful forest".

We will see in due course that in the "descent" into the expansion and involution, the first Purusa is the direct expansion of *Viśnu*, called *Garbhodakaśāyī Viśnu*, that we have already talked about.

This *Purusa* and *Prakrti* is the central expression of the fact that in Hinduism, the material universe is not taken to be something *separate* from *what we are being*, or something that we just happen to arise in.

Our conditional experience of being as material beings, comes down to *goodness*, *passion*, and *ignorance*, which are not material, scientific measurables, but rather, they are features of our own experience of being, self and mind. *Purusa* and *Prakrti* are part of a picture in which the material universe is *us*.

That's because the Hindu picture views the universe as *inseparable from our experience of being*, and the universe's existence as inseparable from our arising in it.

And that brings it close to the fundamental fact of modern neuroscience. That is, if we accept the scientific evidence that our thought, and our learning, and everything we know about, and experience of the universe, is in fact, a construct of brain function. Through which also arises, as the *prima facie* thing about the brain, our conditional experience of being, as body, self and mind.

The Trimurti and the Gunas

The Trimurti, that is, the three Beings *Śiva*, *Viśnu* and Brahma, are popularly understood to each represent one of the three *Gunas.*

Specifically, *Śiva* is said to be *Tamas*, *Viśnu* is said to be *Sattva*, and Brahma is said to be *Rajas*. However, taking the whole corpus into account, this is merely a simplification that serves the purpose of superficial understanding.

In this simplified view, the role of *Śiva* is not really understood, and rather, is just represented as *Tamas*, or ignorance.

The Śiva Purana tells us the whole story. In the Śiva Purana, Śiva (who in the Purana later becomes Rudra) says he is the author of creation, protection and dissolution through the "attributes" which are the *Gunas*, and yet he is different from the *Gunas* and directly beyond both *Prakrti* and Purusa.

He says he is the supreme Brahman, eternal, endless, perfect and unsullied. He then goes on to say that *Viśnu* has *Tamas* within but *Sattva* outside, Hara [*Śiva*] who causes dissolution of three worlds has *Sattva* within but *Tamas* outside, and Brahma who creates the three worlds has *Rajas* both within and without.[72]

As a corollary, Brahma in a different Chapter says that *Viśnu*, Rudra [*Śiva*] and himself represent the three *Gunas*, but *Śiva* is free from *Gunas*. He calls *Śiva* the supreme *Brahman*, and says that although Brahma is *Rajas*, and Rudra [*Śiva*] is *Tamas*, this is only in terms of activities in the world. In fact it is otherwise. Brahma also says *Viśnu* is *Tamasika* within and *Sattvika* without, Rudra [*Śiva*] is *Sattvika* within but *Tamasic* on the outside, and that he himself is *Rajasic* throughout.[73]

Let's just summarise the essence of this.

Śiva is *Sattva* within, but *Tamas* outside. *Viśnu* is *Tamas* within, but *Sattva* outside. Brahma is *Rajas* both within and outside.

Just to be clear, Rudra is an epithet for *Śiva*. However, there is a little more to say about this. In the great *expansion of being*, *Śiva becomes* Rudra, by expansion, which is something we will talk about in detail, later.

There are no *Gunas* in the transcendental, and *Śiva* is transcendental, which is why it is said here that *Śiva* is free from *Gunas*. But the first Rudra to appear in the *Prakrti* is none other than *Śiva*, but as appearing in the *Prakrti*. So this first Rudra is taken across the corpus to be an alternative name for *Śiva*.

In the corpus at large, the realisation of transcendental Reality is when a being realises their true identity as the Self, the *Brahman*, and says "I am *Brahman*", or "I alone am the Supreme Being", or makes a similar declaration. However, this can be confusing if we are not careful, because more than one being makes this declaration. And that leads to the idea of different "schools" of belief as to who is the Supreme Being.

Actually, the Supreme Being, of which all other beings are an *expansion*, is the *Brahman*, which is realised as the Self. There is only one *Brahman*, there is only one Self, but this Being expands into all other beings. This is why, in the corpus, different beings arising in the *Prakrti* realise themselves to be the *Brahman*.

Even the Krsna-Bhakti tradition that declares Krsna, rather than one of the members of Trimurti, to be the Supreme Being, also identifies Krsna and *Brahman* as one and the same. We look at this, and the specific sources that say so, in more detail later. It is just that in Krsna-Bhakti the realisation of Krsna as God is declared to be a higher realisation of the same *Brahman*. Essentially, the *Brahman* in its *impersonal* realisation as the Self, is regarded in Bhakti as less than a full realisation of God.

So *Śiva*, as we see here, is "with and without" *Gunas* (or "qualities" as they are frequently called),[74] and is beyond *Prakrti*.[75] *Śiva* extends, as it were, from the transcendental, into the *Prakrti*, from which then arises the material world. And the *Prakrti* which is not in itself transcendental, comes from and *is* the great *transcendental* expansion of the transcendental Being.

Essentially, the *Brahman*, the Being, the Self, expands into what eventually becomes *Prakrti*, even though the *Brahman* itself does not depend on *Prakrti*. The *Brahman* is realised as "who I am", the Self, the Being, by beings - specifically we humans - who arise in the *Prakrti*, which is the *expansion of being* of the *Brahman*. And what is realised in this way as the *Brahman*, the Self, by beings who arise in the *Prakrti* (us), is the effulgence of the *transcendental* expansion of Being, beyond and above the *Prakrti*.

The Brain

In contemporary terms, if we wanted to weave this into scientific fact, *Prakrti* is inseparable from the *principle of the brain*, whose functioning is the construct we experience as the world.

The "bridge" between material brain function and human "consciousness", is what is sometimes now being posited in neuroscience as the "hard problem of consciousness". In other words, it is the "problem" of how is it that mere biological brain function is also our "conscious experience of being and world", as self, mind, body and psyche.

In Hinduism this is not a "problem". The "bridge" is in the fact that material brain function, being material, is something that is arising through the infinite expansion and involution of the Being.

The Being cannot be scientifically *deduced* from the stuff of its expansion, or scientifically *measured*, in terms of it. Rather, it has to be *realised*. The "outermost" stuff of its expansion, for us, is what we encounter as the material world. Which, precisely as we encounter it, is none other than a construct of brain function.

The idea of the "hard problem of consciousness" merely arises out of the way our scientific ignorance of the brain is being characterised, and couched as a "problem". It is being incorrectly presumed that the world has nothing to do with us except that we happen to be in it. And that it is separate from us, separate from what we experience as self, and in short, is other than our self.

So *Prakrti* is not simply synonymous with the matter of the material world as science studies it. And nor is it the case that the matter of the material world has nothing in itself to do with our experience of being, as self. Rather, the matter of the material world - which is a construct of brain function - is part of the way nature, through the principle of the brain, creates our conditional experience of being as self. It is just that through the "who I am" idea, we psychologically separate the world from our idea of our self.

That mechanism involves the creation of the *objective facet* of the world, the facet on which the success of science rests. The objective facet of the world rests on the feature of the way our brain function gives rise to our experience of being that is independent of the functioning of any particular brain organ. Just as the principle of DNA, for example, doesn't depend on any particular DNA molecule.

The Hindu picture is a picture of our situation as human beings, prior to the modern scientific discovery that our whole experience of self and world is a construct of brain function. And in the great scheme of things, that is why, in the corpus, what is conceived as "the universe", which is everything it describes of being inside what it calls the "cosmic egg", is not at all the same thing as what modern science conceives as "the universe". Because nothing inside the "cosmic egg" of Hinduism is a scientifically measurable thing.

It's not that Hinduism is mistaken about what modern science calls "the universe". It's not that Hinduism offers a fanciful, Mythological substitute for that. And it's not that science now has the "correct" view of what Hinduism calls "the universe". Rather, they are just two completely different, although related, things.

What relates them, is the brain.

The Hindu corpus stops short of talking about the truly *objective* facet of the world that science studies, and its significance. That's because, whilst the corpus may be an expression of spiritual truth, it was expressed at a time *before the conscious discovery* of the truly objective facet of the world, and the establishing of modern scientific method that is based on it.

The truly objective facet of the world in which we live is an undeniable facet of it. And it remains so whether or not you see the world as *Maya* or illusion, or a dream, or any other way in which you wish to see it.

So what Hinduism *calls* "the universe" or "the material world", as we shall soon come to see in some considerable detail, is not that. Whilst what modern science calls "the universe" or "the material world" is precisely that. What links the two, is none other than the brain.

In Hinduism the Being or Self is called the *Brahman*. In other spiritual disciplines, and sometimes in Hinduism too, it is just called the Self. The *realisation* of the Being is not irrelevant to the scientific investigation of the brain. But this not because there is some way in which scientific theory and understanding can start to deal with anything other than the truly objective facet of nature. Rather, it is because it changes the nature of the way our intelligence is working, because it brings us into *transpersonal consciousness and being*.

There are limits to our scientific powers of comprehension that arise from the fact that objective thinking and understanding is not the same thing as being *transpersonal*. For too long, there has been the assumption around, that our understanding is either *subjective* or *objective*. In our personal lives we are subjective. Science clearly relies on being objective. But our powers of comprehension aren't limited to the subjective and objective.

There is a whole other layer of comprehension that arises from *transpersonal consciousness and being*. And because that changes the way we see things and comprehend things, that will have an effect in science, too. Especially when it comes to our understanding of the brain, through which arises our experience of consciousness and being, through which we are *doing* our scientific understanding about the brain.

Purusa

We were saying that in Hinduism the way our experience of being and world arises, begins with the entry of Purusa into the *Prakrti*. But this is the entry of the Being into its own expansion. And that is something that happens infinitely, and recursively.

So there are many Purusas referred to in the Hindu corpus.[76] But in general we may regard an otherwise unqualified reference to "Purusa" as in most cases referring, depending on the text, to *Śiva* or *Viśnu*. If it is *Viśnu* then more specifically, it is *Kāranodakaśāyī Viśnu* otherwise called *Maha-Viśnu* who is identified in the Caitanya-caritamrta as the first Purusa, or Maha-Purusa.[77] So in other words *Kāranodakaśāyī Viśnu* represents the *first* Purusa in the part of the expansion where *Prakrti* arises.

Purusa is essentially the consciousness of the Being, but is usually referenced from a particular "stage" onwards in the expansion of the Being. This is where what the corpus calls "the universe" or "the material world" *begins* to arise out of the expansion. In the "technical" descriptions this is the beginnings of the formation of the "cosmic egg" that gives rise to what the corpus calls "the universe".

This is where *Kāranodakaśāyī Viśnu* arises. And of course, as we have seen, *Kāranodakaśāyī Viśnu* expands as *Garbhodakaśāyī Viśnu*, and then Brahma expands from *Garbhodakaśāyī Viśnu*. This is where in the Mythology Brahma emerges from the lotus flower that emerges from the navel of *Garbhodakaśāyī Viśnu*.

And then from Brahma (who is here given the epithet and appellation *Viśvakarman*, the "architect of the gods") expands the initial "stages" of creation, and then the "mind born sons" of Brahma, and so on. Around about this point, the expansion has already "exploded" into an infinity of Brahmas, who are creating an infinity of "universes".[78]

This is the "gradual arising" through the expansion, of what the corpus calls "the universe" (or infinitely many universes). However, this understanding of the expansion in *stages*, or as a "process", or as "gradual", is only a convenient way of representing of what we are talking about.

Most importantly, the Brahmanda Purana states that it all happens "unpremeditated" and instantaneously, like lightning.[79] Firstly, by "unpremeditated" the Purana means that it is *spontaneous*. The fact that it all happens instantaneously, "like lightning", is because it doesn't happen "in time". Rather, *time* is something that emerges *within it*, and *from it*.

The corpus spends a lot of time (excuse the pun) explaining things in terms of time, such as how many "Divine years" a being performs penance for, before achieving their spiritual aim. There is a whole Hindu "time scheme" in which beings in different parts of the expansion are living in different "time scales", with different lifetime lengths, and different lengths of "day", relative to each other, so to speak. We will talk in a little more detail about this later.

The further out into the expansion we go, the "faster time passes", compared to further back in the expansion. In the Mythology the expansion contains different "worlds of being", realms, or *dhāmas*, or *lokas*, of the various beings. Time is part of the expansion, rather than the expansion taking place in time.

The idea that time *emerges from* a world, rather than the world taking place in time separate from it, is not alien to modern physics.

In physics we now understand a way in which *time* in the universe *emerges from* the universe, from structures of quantum correlations that are static.[80] So in other words, understood in terms of quantum correlations, the universe we live in is a structure in which nothing is happening. Rather, in a manner of speaking, it has all already happened, and it happened instantaneously, "like lightning".

In the "technical-sounding" accounts the Hindu corpus also describes the point at which Purusa arises, in terms of the formation of the "cosmic egg" inside which arises "the universe". We will look at this "egg" in more detail, later, but basically, the "egg" is conceived as being formed from the outside in, in "layers" called "coverings", which are *coverings of the universe* in more than one sense.

Importantly, one of the meanings of the idea of "coverings" is that these "coverings" obscure the truth behind the universe. These "coverings" then become later understood in Buddhism as pertaining to our own individual psychical constitution and experience of being. Which, indeed, can then be transcended through meditation and spiritual practice.

What Purusa *signifies*, is consciousness, from the unsullied transcendental radiance of unconditional Being, or the *Brahman*, to where it arises in *Prakrti*. And *Prakrti* is what the great expansion of the Being has become.

The whole expansion consists of both a "straightforward expansion" of the Being *and* the re-entering of consciousness of the Being into its own expansion. What is generally called *incarnation* or the creation of an *avatara*, or the creation of an *amśa* from an *amśi*, is an example.

We can think of this in the following way: In transcendental Life and Being, all life and being is the Being, and everything is the Joyous consciousness of the Being in a way that cannot be mundanely understood. It can be realised in spiritual realisation but it simply cannot be understood in a mundane way. It is a completely different kind of consciousness to that which arises through *Prakrti*, which includes the consciousness of human beings. In other words, in modern terms, the consciousness that arises through brain function.

"Prior" to the creation of the material world, *Prakrti* is the "outer limit" of brilliant consciousness expanded from the Being, but now without form or variety. She is the pure radiance of the Being. She is the result of the infinite variety of expansion and involution of the Being in the transcendental. She is like an undifferentiated and indistinct echo or image of the Source, now radiating from That Source at the "outer extremity" of the transcendental, reached by the expansion.

Prakrti is essentially the result of all transcendental Life and Being that has explored its own expansion to the point where it is now "sleeping" in the transcendental equivalent of "dreamless sleep". It is just infinite, radiant, unconditional Being that remains as the result of the expansion.

In alternative Western imagery, just as the sleeping beauty needs to be awakened by the handsome prince, so the Purusa must enter the

Prakrti in order for both to fulfil their destiny through the continuing exploration of life and being in the material.

So the *Prakrti* arises at the "outer limit" of the transcendental expansion. But the principle of the *expansion of being* doesn't cease. It never halts, it is eternal. The expansion goes on to create *us*. And the *Brahman*, the Being, can be *realised* by us. When it is realised, the self we are being as a human being, is transcended in that realisation.

When we realise this radiant, unconditional Being through the *Prakrti* we are being, then the original, unmodified *Prakrti* where it first arises in the expansion, is inherent in what we realise.

We realise it as our true Self - the *Brahman,* and awaken into the Reality of That Being. But the Being, the Self, the *Brahman*, is not merely *Prakrti*, and is completely free from any dependence on *Prakrti*. Just as the Sun is not dependent on its radiance that we see and feel, on the Earth.

In the realisation of the Self, we realise liberation from dependence, dependence on existence or anything in it, as our own true Identity, as this radiant Being. So the realisation is spontaneously filled with indescribable Joy and Gratitude, for the truth of This Being, that we are.

In realising the Self *everything* is the Self, the *Brahman*, the Being, but the *Brahman* realised where the *Prakrti* begins in the great expansion, is just the *effulgence* of the transcendental Life and Being from which it comes.

The explosion of Joy and Gratitude that attends the temporary release from self is a Bhakti realisation. In India, in the corpus of Krsna-Bhakti, the *Brahman* is equated with Krsna, *as that* transcendental Life and Being whose effulgence is realised as the Self.[81] It is just that the way we have described it here is nonpartisan (except to Hinduism in general).

Compared to transcendental Life and Being, *Prakrti* is "featureless", pure Being, in the transcendental equivalent of deep sleep. So in the Caitanya-caritamrta *Prakrti* is interpreted as "dull and inert".[82]

Here, because this is a Bhakti text, the entire great expansion emanates from Krsna. Krsna "infusing his energy into the dull, inert material nature", is what is described elsewhere in the corpus as the entry of Purusa into the *Prakrti*. Compared with Transcendental Life and Being, *Prakrti* is dull and inert.

But there is nothing "dull" about *Prakrti* as far as human beings are concerned. The Śiva Purana describes *Prakrti* as having a brilliant that can hardly be conceived.[83]

Here, the union is with *Śiva* rather than Krsna, because this is the Śiva Purana speaking, rather than a Bhakti text.

Note here that *Prakrti* is *Māyā*, the dancing illusion. *Prakrti* is only an echo, so to speak, of the transcendental Reality of Life and Being. Being an *expansion* of the Being, created from infinite involution of the Being, *Prakrti* contains ignorance of her Source, the Being, even though she *is* the expansion of the Being in the "form" of the limit of the Being's own transcendental expansion.

So in *Prakrti* the full conscious knowledge of transcendental Life and Being has been lost in the expansion and involution. And yet, at the same time, the *whole of the transcendental expansion* is somehow still enfolded within the *Prakrti*.

Note also in the quote, that it is from her union with *Śiva* that *Prakrti* becomes *manifest Prakrti* "in various forms". *Prakrti* before this union is sometimes called *Pradhana* or *Mulaprakrti*.

It is only at the point in the great expansion where the expansion is becoming the *Prakrti*, that the immediate Purusa who enters *Prakrti*, arises. The Purusa here is usually regarded as *Viśnu*, or specifically *Kāranodakaśāyī Viśnu*. And yet this far out in the expansion, *Viśnu* arises in ignorance of the Source, His own Identity.

This is represented in the Mythology as *Viśnu* falling asleep. And then from his navel emerges the lotus, the expansion of consciousness from "above" the sleeping Viśnu, as it were, further into the expansion, where it manifests as Brahma. And by now, in terms of the other "impersonal" kinds of description in the corpus, the Purusa has entered into the *Prakrti*, becoming Brahma.

Brahma is widely referred to in the corpus as "the self-born one". This is not dissimilar to the way in which the self you are, in a dream, when you are asleep in bed dreaming, *as that experience of self*, is a self-born one. In much the same sense, *Viśnu* is not Brahma, Brahma is self-born, but only because of *Viśnu*.

To *realise* you are "self-born" as a human being, is to transcend the personal idea of "who I am" based on identification with the body and the way in which it arises in material terms, from parents and biology, and so on. This is the state of consciousness of the *risi*, or seer.[84]

When *Viśnu* enters his own surrounding *Prakrti*, which is his *Śakti*, when he enters this as Purusa, *Viśnu*'s transcendental nature, free from *Gunas*, becomes *Sattva* in the world of *Prakrti*, which is none other than the *Gunas*. It becomes the goodness in *Prakrti*. This is why, as we saw above, the Śiva Purana tells us in no uncertain terms that *Viśnu* is *Sattva* "on the outside" - where *Viśnu* is *continuing into* the great expansion.

But also we are told He is *Tamas*, or ignorance, *within*. This is because He knows "I am Brahman", but he doesn't have the full knowledge of Transcendental Life and Being, that we have been talking about. This is why the entry into the *Prakrti* is taking place in the first instance. *Viśnu* at the point of entering the *Prakrti* is not only the Being, but also already an *expansion* of the Being, in which the full knowledge of transcendental Life and Being has been lost. Hence, as the Śiva Purana says, Viśnu is "ignorant within". In the other terminology, this knowledge has become "covered".

All the descriptions of *Śiva* (or *Viśnu*) as having *Gunas* or "qualities" ("qualities" is often used as a synonym for *Gunas*) are referring to the "position" in the great expansion where *Prakrti* is arising.

The Gunas and the Brain

According to the more "technical-sounding" parts of the Hindu corpus that we have been talking about, the creation of the universe is achieved by *agitating* the *Gunas* into a condition of *disequilibrium*. For example, the Kurma Purana says that it is only when the three *Gunas* are not in equilibrium that creation happens. It clearly states that when they are in equilibrium creation is dissolved.[85] We are told:

> When there is complete equilibrium of the *Gunas*, and the Purusa abides in his own blissful state, one should know that it is the original state of *Prakrti*, or the dissolution pertaining to *Prakrti* till the creation of the Universe.[86]

Behind the surface of this text is something that we will be mentioning again, and again, throughout this book. Throughout the corpus there is this equation between the *Gunas* in their "agitated" condition, or in disequilibrium, and what the corpus calls "creation" or "the universe". And similarly, when the Gunas are "in equilibrium" what is called "the universe" dissolves.

Today, in the times in which we are living, the true meaning of this is *easier* to see, for those who have the potential to see it. What the Hindu corpus refers to as "the universe" or "creation", that is, the "creation" made by Brahma, is not what so many readers of the Hindu corpus mistake it to be.

The fact is that it is synonymous with what, in the corpus, is called the Bhu mandala, or the "cosmic egg". Or the "egg of Brahma". And so on. Sometimes it is called *Brahmanda*. All of this is the Bhu mandala. And the clue is in the name.

It is arguably true to say that as far as Hinduism is concerned, what modern science is studying, and calls "the universe", is, unbeknown to modern science, the Bhu mandala. But it is not true to say that the Bhu mandala is what modern science calls "the universe" and is becoming knowledgeable of.

As we said, the clue is in the name. The Bhu mandala is a *mandala*, and modern science doesn't study mandalas. There is nothing in any of the descriptions of the content of the "cosmic egg" or the Bhu mandala, that we are given in the Hindu corpus, that is a part of what modern science measures, and comes to knowledge of. On the contrary, it is a completely different thing.

So when the corpus talks about the dissolution of "the universe" it is actually talking about the dissolution of the Bhu mandala. Or the "cosmic egg". That is, the creation of Brahma.

The Bhu mandala is not the "universe" that modern science gathers data about, and understand the laws of, which basically exist very usefully in the form of mathematical structures. This knowledge is then what then enables us to create various technologies. Rather, the Bhu mandala is Hinduism's own description of what *underlies the appearance of* what science calls "the universe", that we are learning about scientifically. It is the description of how that comes in the first place, to be in our mind and experience of being.

So when the Hindu corpus refers to the *dissolution* of what *it* calls "the universe", it is referring to the dissolution of the Bhu mandala. And therefore, it is referring to the dissolution of *the means by which* "the universe" that is measured and understood by modern science - which is most definitely not the same thing as the Bhu mandala - comes in the first place, to be in our mind and experience of being. In terms of modern science, this *means by which this happens*, is none other than *brain function*.

In short, if you want to talk about "the universe" as something separate from you, then it is no good talking about what the Hindu corpus calls "the universe", because you are making a mistake. That's not what the Hindu corpus is talking about.

But if you want to talk about "the universe" as something that is not separate from you, then you can either talk about the Bhu mandala, or the construct of brain function that you experience as self, and the world.

You can go either way, they are two different approaches. But ultimately, they come together. When it comes to putting the Hindu corpus side by side with modern science, then apart from the distraction of the cultural fabric, there isn't really any conflict.

There is nothing in modern science that is equivalent to the Bhu mandala, and there is nothing in the Hindu corpus that is equivalent to modern science. But neither are the two *essentially* in conflict.

This, really, underlines what we have been saying about *Prakrti*. The original state of *Prakrti* - its "equilibrium" - is synonymous with the realisation of the *Brahman* - the Purusa in its own blissful state.

Prakrti is not *separate from* Purusa. The *Prakrti* is none other than the expansion of the Purusa. The next "step" so to speak, in the great expansion and involution, is another expansion and involution where the Purusa *enters* this expansion. But now, this is where the transcendental ends. Now, there is the creation of the *Gunas* as separate or "agitated" *Sattva*, *Rajas* and *Tamas*.

Misunderstanding about what is meant by "the dissolution of the universe" arises when the difference between what Hinduism refers to as "the universe" and what modern science refers to as "the universe", is not recognised.

The words *Mulaprakrti* or *Pradhana* are often used to mean the *Prakrti* when it is "in equilibrium". The *Prakrti* "agitated" or in "disequilibrium", as it is often referred to in the corpus, is the three apparently separate *Gunas*, as *Sattva*, *Rajas* and *Tamas*.

This is not something that can be described by modern science in its current condition. *Sattva*, *Rajas* and *Tamas* can be called, as we have said, goodness, passion, and ignorance, respectively. These three things do not pertain to any fundamental description of the universe used by modern science. Rather, they pertain to the condition in *us*.

When they are in equilibrium then we are conscious of the good, we still contain passion, and we are still the embodiment of ignorance. And yet we are not being what we would be if they were in disequilibrium. Which is the normal, default condition of the mind and the self.

Rather, they are in equilibrium when *Sattva* dominates and we are not *identified* with this whole conditional experience of being that arises through the "agitated" Gunas. We are then at least *transpersonal.* And possibly in consciousness of the Being.

Sattva, *Rajas* and *Tamas*, or goodness, passion, and ignorance, as far as modern science is concerned, are things that pertain *to the brain* and *brain function*. Without which there would be no goodness, passion, or ignorance.

When we understand that what we encounter as "the universe" - as conceived by science - is in fact *a construct of brain function*, then the idea of understanding it in terms of human attributes, is not so strange.

6

Śiva

The Śiva Purana tells us:

> *Śiva* alone is glorified as *Nikala* (nameless and formless) since He is identical with supreme *Brahman*. He is also *Sakala* as He has an embodied form. He is both *Sakala* and *Nikala*.[87]

Śiva is transcendental consciousness. But here, the Purana is telling us that *Śiva* is at once both transcendental (*Nikala*) and, we are told, *Sakala*, with "embodied form".

Sakala means "consisting of parts, divisible, material, complete, entire, whole, all, and everybody".[88] It also means "affected by the elements of the material world".[89] It is also a word used when talking about a soul "which has not advanced beyond the lowest stage of progress".[90]

So what this passage is really saying is that *Śiva* is all at once both transcendental Being *and* the entirety of mundane material existence with all its beings, *and in all its ignorance*.

Yes, *Śiva* is transcendental Being. But also, yes, *Śiva* is precisely the whole of this material existence in which we are living. In all its ignorance.

In other words, our existence, the world in which we live, and we ourselves, in all ignorance of the Being, literally *are Śiva*. This is why the Śiva Purana, as we have already seen, tells us that *Śiva* is ignorance "on the outside". We are the living *Tamas* of *Śiva*. And so what is *within Śiva*, which as we know, is *Sattva*, is also *within us*.

We shall see shortly that transcendental *Viśnu* in the Mythology is created at the behest of transcendental *Śiva*, precisely so that *Śiva* and his *Śakti*, his consort, *Śivā*, the manifestation of his love, can remain eternally united in "the blissful forest", without getting involved in the ignorance of creation.

So more fully, we, and our world of being, which we call the material world, is an actually an "outward" manifestation in the stuff of ignorance, *Tamas*, of the Divine Couple, *Śiva-Śivā* in "the blissful forest". In other words, this is the transcendental meaning behind the nature of our existence.

Simply, the message is this: The underlying true nature of our world, our material existence, is not the aspect of its nature that science studies, assuming it to be separate from us. That aspect certainly is what it is, as science studies it, but *why* it all is the way it is, is not understood. The reason is tied up in *the principle of the brain*, which is not yet understood by the network mind that is doing the science.

"The universe" that science talks about and studies is not the same thing that the Hindu corpus calls "the universe". So the scientific understanding of "the universe", which is currently devoid of understanding the principle of the brain, is not about the underlying nature of our world. The underlying nature of our world is in the principle of the brain.

We only *encounter* our material world in the first instance through *the same brain function* that as a whole creates our experience of being as a human self. So what we are saying is that ultimately the structure and nature of the world is about the human self. That's why the brain exists.

The Hindu corpus doesn't say anything explicitly about the brain, or about any other aspect of modern science, understandably. But it does understand that the structure and nature of our world is about the human self.

The world has *everything to do with* the nature of our self. And the underlying dynamic and meaning in it is not about physics, but about our own experience of being. Just as the greatest frontier in science is not in physics, but in understanding the principle of the brain.

Hinduism says the Source, the Being, *Brahman*, is who we really are. That is the whole, central message, of the Hindu corpus. We are living in the form of ignorance of That Being. That's what we are being, as our human *self*, and our attendant *world of being*. Which we just call the material world. And that world, *at every level*, whoever we appear to be, is an expansion of our own true Identity.

Śiva represents a way back in. The way back into the realisation of our own true Identity. As we have seen, or as we have been told, *Śiva* is ignorance "on the outside", but goodness within. We, as material beings in material existence, *are Śiva* "on the outside". We are our own true Identity, but being expressed in the stuff of ignorance. Which is what *Śiva* is, "on the outside".

Furthermore, as we shall come to talk more about, in the account of "the beginning" in the Śiva Purana, the first thing *Śiva* does (as an *expansion of being*) is to create *Śivā*, his lover. And simultaneously *Śiva* and *Śivā*, as the Divine lovers, are in "the blissful forest". But then, through the great *expansion of being*, and then through the entry of Purusa into the *Prakrti* that arises from it, there arises a material existence.

In other words this material existence in which we live is a reflection, in the stuff of ignorance or on the "outside" of *Śiva*, it is a reflection of the eternal lovers *Śiva* and *Śivā*, in "the blissful forest".

In the Krsna-Bhakti tradition, this has its own expression, in what is called Radha-Krsna. There, the Divine couple, the Divine lovers, are Krsna and Radha, in the blissful forests of *Vrndavana*. They are not really separable, because Radha is an expansion of Krsna. The love that is Radha-Krsna is known and "manifest" in the transcendental Reality of Life and Being, through this expansion. But then Radha-Krsna and the glorious *Vrndavana*, too, must also expand into the great expansion, where "reflections" of it arise. We will have more to say about this, later, too.

The Śiva Purana tells us in poetic language that the Being creates *Śiva* as an auspicious form with all power and knowledge, that basically becomes everything and satisfies that everything should be created.[91]

The Purana also says:

> He has five faces. He is always joyful. He has ten arms. He holds the Trident. He is as pure and white as camphor. His body is entirely dusted with ash.[92]

These two quite *different* types of narrative pervade the Puranas. But not everyone can see that they are different. Being able to see the difference is key to unlocking the true power of the Puranas. The first takes the individual reader directly into the esoteric energy and content of the Puranas. The second is about symbolism, culture, and appearances.

Both provide routes into talking about the Puranas, but here we are going to take a closer look at Śiva mainly through the first kind of narrative.

Vanishing

We have been saying that everything is an expansion of *the Brahman*. And that the *Brahman* is eternal, radiant Being. But we are also saying that whilst this *Brahman* is indeed radiant, unconditional Being, Absolute Being, and Self Real, this is not the end of the story. Because we are saying that even when this is discovered, or realised, by spiritual awakening as That Being, this is not the end of the story.

The beginning of the story, so to speak, appears in the Śiva Purana. The story of creation in the Śiva Purana states that as soon as *Śiva* is created, *Brahman* vanishes.[93] *Why* would *Brahman* vanish?

Sometimes this has been interpreted by saying that *Brahman* is *sacrificed* in order to bring about *Śiva*. But really, this is a materialistic interpretation.

The "sacrifice" idea would fit in nicely with the background cultural fabric of the Vedas, and early Indian corpus. The ancient Indian *culture* here is clearly one of *sacrifice to the gods*, and ritual associated with that sacrifice. Later it is about what many Westerners would see as idol worship. The corpus is imbued with this cultural aspect, and some parts of the corpus are about little else.

But really, the only true meaning of sacrifice in spiritual pursuit is the sacrifice of one's self or aspects of one's self. Even *within the Indian culture itself* it has been recognised (by the Indian saint *Ānandamayī Mā*) that the true meaning of sacrifice is the sacrificing of one's lower (animal) nature, in the aspiration to realise our inherent Divine nature.[94]

The idea of sacrificing *Brahman* goes back to a certain Western way of interpreting of the Vedas, especially the Purusa Suktam, but we shouldn't deviate into that here.

Khanda IX of the Subala Upanishad extensively teaches that whatever disappears into something else, or whatever being disappears into "another" being, *becomes* that thing or being. It is a principle that goes both "up" towards the Being as well as "down" from the Being into human existence.[95]

So when, in the Purana story we are looking at, the *Brahman* Being (the Self) *vanishes* on the arising of *Śiva*, it simply means that in *Śiva*, the *Brahman* has *become Śiva*. But this doesn't mean that there is no more *Brahman*. It just means that the story has shifted to *Śiva*. Here, *Śiva* is an *expansion* of *Brahman*.

As it happens, also, throughout the Puranic stories, deities sometimes suddenly appear just as they suddenly vanish from the scene of action, like actors entering and exiting the stage. The meaning of the vanishing of a deity is generally just that the vanished deity is no longer the focus of attention in the story, or immediately in the consciousness of the being or beings still in the scene of action.

So when we are told that *Śiva* manifests, and the Supreme *Brahman* vanishes,[96] this *doesn't mean* that *Brahman* ceases to Be. The *Brahman* never ceases to Be. In fact, the Purana states about *Brahman*, the original Being, that it never decays and illuminates everything.[97]

Simultaneously, *Śiva* realises his Identity as the supreme *Brahman*, saying that *sat-chit-ananda* (being-consciousness-bliss) constitutes his characteristics.[98]

Śivā and Prakrti

The Śiva Purana goes on to tell us that this *form* of the formless Being, the *form* called *Sadaśiva* (the original form of *Śiva*):

> ...though alone, then created the physical form *Śakti* from his body. This *Śakti* did not affect his body in any way. This *Śakti* is called by various names. *Pradhāna*, *Prakrti*, *Māyā*...[99]

Now we are talking again of the *expansion of being*. *Śiva* manifests his own *Śakti* from his "body", his being. At least, from the point of view of *Śiva*, so to speak, this is what happens. From the point of view of *Śakti*, she manifested herself from the body (*i.e.* the being) of *Śiva*.[100] Both points of view are correct.

But from the point of view of *Śiva*, so to speak, *Śiva*'s *Śakti* is himself, as well as his own radiant expansion. This is why he creates *Śakti* "though alone", and why *Śakti* is said to be created as a "physical form" *from his body*. She is himself. And the text here does not mean "physical" or "body" in a modern scientific or biological way.

Creating *Śakti* "though alone", which means *Śiva* is able to do it even though he is alone, means it is "multiplication" of beings just from the one being, as distinct from requiring two "beings" to produce "offspring".

We are then told that *Śakti* is also known as *Pradhāna*, *Prakrti*, *Māyā*, *Gunavatī*, *Parā*. She is the mother of *Buddha Tattva* (cosmic intelligence), and she is the goddess of all, *Vikrtivajitā* which means without *Gunas* [*i.e* "modification"], and is the mother of the Trimurti.[101]

We are also told:

> She is the generating cause of all. She sprang up singly as *Māyā*. In her union she manifested in various forms.[102]

So the first expansion of *Śiva* is *everything* that "subsequently" will expand from the expansion. *Maya* here, as we shall soon be talking more of, means "magic" or "illusion". *Śakti* is the power or potency of the Being, in its expansion, through which it creates the *Maya*.

So we know that *Śivā* is associated with the female gender, and that she is *Prakrti* and *Māyā*. We also know that she is the "prime cause and the mother of the three deities" who are *Śiva*, *Viśnu* and Brahma.

So to hear what is being said here, we must give up any idea of beings creating other beings one after the other or in the biological way. Phrases like "the mother of the three deities" is not speaking in that way.

Śiva's Śakti here, as created by *Śiva*, is a potency or power of *Śiva*. As the Śiva Purana says in the narrative, this *Śakti* is *Prakrti.* She is created from *Śiva*'s "body", so she is already inherent in *Śiva*'s radiance. And as we are told, she is also *Śiva*'s *Māyā*. *Śiva*'s radiance, and all the possibilities for the expansion of his being, are all *Māyā*.

However, the Nirālamba Upanishad tells us:

> What is *Prakrti*? It is nothing else but the *Śakti* of *Brahman*...[103]

So the *Prakrti* created by, and emanating from, *Śiva*, in the form of his *Śakti*, has come from *Brahman*. It is part of *Brahman*'s *Śakti*.

We looking here at the "process" of *expansion of being* from *Brahman*. The original Being here, *Brahman*, is transcendental to *Prakrti*, but has unmanifest *Prakrti* as part of its radiance, its Self effulgence. This, we have already spoken of.

The Being (*Brahman*) creates a *form* of itself called *Śiva*, through whom *Prakrti* is then manifested as *Śiva*'s *Śakti*. *Śiva* has also emerged in the first place from the effulgent original Being.

This is a "process" of *expansion of being* of the one, original Being, the Self, that is the radiant *Brahman*. And the realisation of that Being, through *Prakrti*, is not the end of the story. That Being, when realised through *Prakrti*, is the emanating radiance of the transcendental expansion of Life and Being, above the first realisation of the *Brahman* as Absolute Being.

The Blissful Forest

What happens now that there is *Śiva* and his *Śakti*?

The Purana tells us that *Brahman* [now manifested in form as *Śiva*] has the form of time, (*Kāla*), and together with *Śakti* created the holy place called *Śivaloka*, otherwise called *Kāśikā*. It shines over everything and is the seat of salvation. Its nature is extreme bliss and these primordial lovers, supremely beautiful, have this beautiful place as their perpetual abode.[104]

Most importantly, we are told that even at the time of the Great Dissolution [the end of "the universe"] this place is never free from *Śiva and Śivā* (*Śakti*). Hence it is called *Avimukta*. *Śiva* calls this place "the blissful forest" and later "*Avimukta*".[105]

Śivā, by the way, if you come to read the Puranas, is also often called *Satī* (not to be confused with *Śakti*).

The couple then go on to stay happily in the blissful forest, free from worries (of creation), roaming as they please, and sporting in the forest.[106]

And that would be the end of the story, if it were not for the creation of another being, *Viśnu*, and then another, Brahma. But we will return to that, later.

So to summarise in part, "the seat of salvation shining over and above everything" has been created by *Brahman* in the form of *time*.

This is a very deep statement. It clearly says that the abode of *Śiva*, called *Śivaloka* (*loka* means "place" or "abode"), has been created from *time* and *Śakti*. But this "holy centre" is also "shining over and above everything." And that sounds like a description of the transcendental. It *is* a description of the transcendental.

Śivaloka, or "the blissful forest", or *Kaśi* (as talked about here, rather than as a geographical place in India), whichever we want to call it, *is* transcendental, and "the seat of salvation shining over and above everything", and yet it is also created through *time* and *Śakti*. This is what the Purana says.

When we are talking about the great *expansion of being*, then time, as cycles, begins in the transcendental. But there, it is "transcendental time", for want of a better description, rather than the "material time" that we actually experience in our conditional experience of being as human beings.

What we ordinarily think of a time, is only our "take on it", our conception of it, based on the way time manifests *objectively*, in the material world in which we live. Such that we can measure it. Invariably by measuring things that *cycle*.

"Material time" is material because it arises in material phenomena. In general, in modern scientific thought, in the background of our thinking, we make the mistake of presuming that material phenomena has, as a whole, nothing to do with brain function. This arises because of the pre-existing psychological bias in which we believe the world as a whole has nothing to do with our self, other than that we happen to be in it. But the material facts of brain science itself, evidence the opposite. In this sense, we are ignoring the evidence.

So "material time" arises as the objective time that we encounter in the material phenomena of our world. But this material phenomena as we encounter it, is itself a construct of brain function. It is a construct of the functioning of the brain, which itself is part of that construct.

The materialist assumption in mainstream modern science is that human "consciousness" arises through the brain. And then there are alternative theories that consciousness is independent of the brain, and so on.

At the core of the Hindu corpus is the recognition that the material world is a "product of consciousness" so to speak, and although the corpus doesn't speak explicitly about the brain, it effectively says that the brain is a "product of consciousness".

The position of the Hindu corpus is not that there is something called "consciousness" that is *separate* from the brain. Rather, it is that consciousness is *beyond the brain*, but not separate from it, because nothing is truly separate from, or other than, the *Brahman*, which is at the root of our human "consciousness".

In the same way, in Hinduism the *Brahman* is beyond *Prakrti*. As we are told, *Prakrti*, which is none other than the *Śakti* of *Brahman*, is created together with time (*Kāla*). Time is actually part of the *Śakti* of *Brahman*. Time is manifest for us, in the form of material phenomena. And all that is *manifested* in this way is the *Śakti* of *Brahman*. And, indeed, is *Maya*. It is an illusory construct erected from *Brahman*.

As we have said, material time consists of cycles of material phenomena. As measured by science. The transcendental equivalent that begins with the *Brahman* taking the form of *Kāla*, is what we could call "transcendental time". But in the transcendental, it is not the cycling of anything other than conditional Being and world of Being. And as we shall come to see later, the parts of the Hindu corpus that talk about it are quite explicit in stating that in transcendental time there is no past or future.

There are various ways, across the Hindu corpus, in which cycles in the expansion of the Being are conceived in various teachings. These include "vibrations" and *prana*, or breath. But, as the Śiva Purana says, the first thing created, with this nature, is *Kāla*, which is *time*. And here, it is talking about "transcendental time".

In our material existence as we encounter it, time indeed consists of cycles. But apart from our subjective experience of time, these cycles that make what is commonly called "time" are cycles of things that are *objective*. Like, for example, the vibration of a caesium atom, or the rotation of the Earth around it axis, or its orbit around the Sun.

The *objectivity* of these things doesn't mean they are not part of the construct of brain function. It just means they do not depend on any specific, individual brain function. Material time is an essential part of the way in which our ordinary experience of being as a human being arises.

This, our *conditional experience of being*, is a *construct of brain function*. Time is a basic part of the way that construct works. But neither time, nor the construct, can be ultimately understood as part of a world that has nothing to do with us, other than that we happen to be in it.

In other words, objective, material time, is not something *separate from* brain function, such that, in itself it has nothing to do with brain function. The absence of this realisation is a major part of the obscurations under which science is currently working.

7

Expansion and Involution

We have seen that the Śiva Purana states that from the Being, the *Brahman*, arises "another" being, that Hinduism calls *Śiva*.

This "other" being, as we have seen, is stated to be identical with the Being, the *Brahman*.[107] In other words, *Śiva* is an aspect of *Brahman*, an *expansion* of *Brahman*.

So in this account all beings that arise through *Śiva*, only do so because *Śiva* arises in the first place from the Being, the *Brahman*.

In this way, all beings can be said to come *through* the initially created *form* of the *Brahman*, which is *Śiva*. In other words, the *Brahman* Being creates a form of being *through which* further beings can arise.

We are going to look at how this constitutes an *involution* of *Brahman*. And we are going to look at how in material terms the continuing and *expanding involution* of the *Brahman* leads to what modern science would recognise as complexity. And furthermore, not just complexity in general, but complexity of a special kind.

We ought to mention straightaway that in the Krsna-Bhakti tradition the *Brahman* as the Self effulgence of Being is recognised as the result of higher expansion from the what Krsna-Bhakti calls the *Supreme Personality of Godhead*, Krsna.

This can be slightly confusing for some people, because Krsna also appears in the corpus as an incarnation of *Viśnu*. We must remember that when Krsna-Bhakti talks about the *Supreme Personality of Godhead* it is talking about *transcendental* Krsna. And there tends to be emphasis on Krsna being a *person*, or a *personality*, because in general the Krsna-Bhakti movement takes exception to the part of Hinduism in which the *Brahman* is portrayed as *impersonal*.

But as we talk about in the course of this book, in this context, "impersonal" and "personal" tend to be weasel words. If you want to get into that, then you first have to be clear about what you mean by "person" and "personal". And in a spiritual context, "impersonal" does not necessarily mean merely mental, or devoid of love, beauty, compassion, or even adoration and devotion. It merely means transcendental to the human self-based personal ego.

These words tend to be weasel words woven around the very deep issue of the fact that Self realisation, the realisation of the *Brahman*, or the realisation of God, is not something that has only one level, so to speak, or only one "dimension". These are matters of aspects of pre-transcendental and transcendental realisation, that cannot be translated into ordinary, conceptual language. There *are* ways in which "models" are presented, but the *meaning* in terms of being and experience of being, gets lost in translation, as it were.

The way in which spiritual realisation happens, is not confined to one way. In the *Bhakti* tradition the path is one of *devotion* to God. In this sense, it shares some ground with Christianity. In much of the Yoga tradition it is one largely of *technique*. The path of *jnana* is one of aspiring to spiritual awakenings through meditation, scriptural study and spiritual practice of other kinds, and the attainment of higher transcendental knowledge. And so on.

In Buddhism, the path is about "extinguishing the flame", which essentially means the same thing. Buddhism speaks of *emptiness*, as a way of describing what the world actually is. But what it is really talking about is emptiness in the knower of the world. Hinduism speaks of *Maya*. They are just two different approaches. The antagonism between them arises, essentially, between intellectual interpretations, rather than from their different orbits around the same truth.

* * *

Here we are not looking at specific, different approaches. Rather, right now, we are only looking at the principle of the *expansion of being* that is found in the Puranas and other texts.

Overall, in Hinduism, it is not *Śiva*, or even *Viśnu* through whom the actual "activity" of creation is said to take place. Rather, it is Brahma. Brahma is the one who actually *creates*. Except, of course, that Brahma is actually an *expansion* of *Nārāyana* (*Viśnu*).

The Hindu *principle of expansion of being* is that all beings are *expansions of being*, in one way or another, from the Supreme Source. It is not that every single part of Hinduism understands the principle of *the expansion of being*. But it is that part of the Hindu corpus that interests us here. And the corpus as a whole clearly exhibits an expression of this principle.

Expansions can be partial or whole, and the corpus speaks of this resulting in *non-different* beings. This means beings who have the same identity. They are the same being, but that being is appearing in two different ways.

Non-different beings have the same identity in the way just explained, but they don't necessarily have the same *form*. Expansion also takes place such that a being may be an expansion of more than one other being.

The Laghu Bhagavatamrta speaks of different kinds of expansion. There is expansion as *prakāśa* beings,[108] and then there is expansion as *tad-ekātma-rupa* beings.[109] Let's have a quick look at what this means.

The original form, nature and beauty (*rūpa*)[110] of a being, is called *svayaṁ-rūpa*.[111] The presence of one *form* of *svayaṁ-rūpa* as apparently many, simultaneously, is what *prakāśa* means. The Laghu Bhagavatamrta tells us that one form manifesting in many places, whilst in all respects still the same original form, it is called *prakāśa*'.[112]

The Laghu Bhagavatamrta states that the *tad-ekātma-rūpa* type of expansion of being has two forms, *vilāsa* and *svāṁśa*, which respectively, each are less in "quality and power" than the *svayaṁ-rūpa*.[113] The implication here is that if *tad-ekātma-rūpa* beings themselves expand, then the principle of *vilāsa* and *svāṁśa* also expands further, resulting in less and less of "quality and power", in the resultant beings. And if the expansion is infinite, then this continues *ad infinitum*.

Recurrent *vilāsa* and *svāṁśa* expansions tend therefore towards the stage in the overall great *expansion of being* that results in forms of being that are drastically reduced in "quality and power", and yet, at the same time, are none other than an expansion of the Original Source, and whose true Identity is still That. Essentially, the transcendental *expansion of being* results in this way, in what across the corpus as a whole, is called *Prakrti*.

In one account, as clearly reported in the Śiva Purana, *Prakrti* is the first "offspring" from *Śiva*, and she is *Śivā*, *Śiva*'s consort, who is also *Maya*.[114] In another way, *Prakrti* arises at the limit of transcendental expansion, and goes on to create what Hinduism calls "the material world", by being *entered* by Purusa, who is *Viśnu* or *Śiva* (depending on which Purana you are reading).

Essentially this means that *Śiva's* expansion as *Prakrti* is not talking about expansion in the transcendental. There *is* expansion in the transcendental, but it is only extensively spoken of in the Bhakti sources. And there, it is the expansion of transcendental Krsna. In this context, *Śiva* must be identified with Krsna. But *Śiva* represents the part of the great expansion where transcendental Being is about to enter the limit of its own expansion, which is *Prakrti*.

As the Śiva Purana also tells us, this actual entry into *Prakrti* (*i.e.* the responsibility for creation, so that *Śiva* and *Śivā* can remain in "the blissful forest"), is left to *Viśnu*, who is an expansion of *Śiva*. And *Viśnu*, of course, then gives rise to Brahma, "the creator", who in the Mythology comes out of a Lotus flower that comes out of *Viśnu's* navel.

Śiva then "later" (in the great expansion) *enters* the *Prakrti* as Rudra. We will shortly talk about this in more detail. So in the corpus *Śiva* basically represents transcendental Life and Being which is referred to as "the blissful forest". But as a member of the Trimurti He becomes a kind of "tacit template" based on transcendental Life and Being, from which springs the creation in the *Prakrti*.

In the *Prakrti* is ignorance of transcendental Life and Being. In eternal cycles it forever endeavours to give rise, in the *Prakrti*, the transcendental Life and Being from which the *Prakrti* has originally come.

But it can never do it, because the fundamental from which it is built, is ignorance. The *Sattva* in it is the tendency of the three *Gunas* to re-combine back into the *Prakrti* in its pure form, before the entry of the Purusa into it.

The *dynamic* or passion in it is *Rajas*, the energy of which, arises in the first place, and is provided by, the entry of the Being, as Purusa, into the *Prakrti*. The parallel description here is the entry of God into the material. And there is of course also a literal parallel with what is called the passion of Christ.

This is why *Rajas* or passion, combined with *Sattva*, or goodness, is not to be eschewed, and leads anyway, to the great *Sattva*, the *transcendental mellow* that is the hallmark of transcendental realisation.

Expansions and Portions

The Bhakti scriptures talk about *portions*, and *partial expansions*, and *plenary portions* of beings. This is because if a being *expands wholly* to become "another" being, there are now "two beings", but both these beings are still the original being in their true Identity.

The duality is an illusory *lila* or *Maya*. It is not unlike a single actor taking two parts in a play, except that in that analogy, the actor can only take one part at a time.

Because both beings are the original being, there is a *plenary* consisting of both beings. And the second created being, because it has the same true identity as the first being, is dependent on the first being, and in order to be the second, on *both beings*.

Imagine that a being expands into *many* beings. If the expansion is such that all these beings have the same identity as the first, then each of these beings, if it knows it's true identity, will also know itself to be the *plenary* of *all* the beings. But because the beings made by the expansion are *dependent* on the original being, each is a *plenary portion* of the original being. And not *vice versa*. There are also beings who are *portions* of *plenary portions*.

Abodes or places are also expansions of the Being. Everything is created through the vast complexity of infinite *expansion of being*. And so it is that the Laghu Bhagavatamrta tells us that the entire creation, maintenance, and destruction of the universe are due to a mere fraction of an expansion of an expansion of Krsna.[115]

What we have been doing here, is to partially explain the great principle of *expansion of being* in an impersonal way. Without much reference to *personalised* beings.

The Hindu Bhakti corpus doesn't always do this, because it necessarily arises in the *cultural fabric* of itself, as a religion. And this kind of talk is not part of Bhakti. Bhakti is concerned with personal devotion to the Supreme *Personality* of Godhead. Not with abstracted, impersonal descriptions.

Nevertheless, principles are principles. In Bhakti the description of expansions are part of the development of understanding being pursued in service of devotion to God, as Krsna. But any human mind and brain through which this is happening, is itself essentially also an *expansion* of the cultural and religious mind of which it is a part. And that cultural and religious mind is only a part of the aggregate of all human minds.

"Identical"

So the Hindu corpus often refers to different, personalised beings, as being "identical".

To the rational mind, it is perfectly possible to have two things that are distinct, and yet identical. Like two billiard balls, or electrons, for example. When a Purana says that two beings are *identical*, it is *not* speaking in this way. Because although beings are presented *personalised*, as if they are separate "persons", these narratives are not really ultimately about separate *persons*. They are about the play of the *Being*. As *lila* or as *Maya*.

In this context, "identical" means not identical in appearance or properties or qualities, but literally having the same *identity* as "I". For example, *Śiva* is said to be both "with and without" *qualities*, or *Gunas*. But the *Brahman*, that *Śiva* is said to be *identical to*, is completely without *Gunas*. The *identity* is about the "who I am" of the being in question. Ultimately, when realised, the "who I am" of any being, is *Brahman*.

Involution in Science

In science and the material world *involution* essentially means a recursive re-entering, involving, or *enfolding*, by the process of things *re-entering into* or *passing through*, things that already are being created in this same recursive way. It is also possible to have limitless *different* infinite involutions interacting with each other, and, as it were, entering and "cross fertilising" through each other. So as you might imagine, *involution* is often associated with the production of *complexities*.

Also, *involution* is associated with the principle of *recursion* or *iteration*. In other words, something that repeats itself, cyclically. In a process of *recursion* or *iteration*, something "goes back into itself", so to speak, and by doing so, creates something apparently new, which can then, again, "go back into itself". This can happen *ad infinitum*. And it is then called *infinite recursion*.

Every experience we have arises because all the components of that experience must already exist as something we can "go into". In terms of the brain, and brain function, there is an equivalent explanation. Brain function takes place according to what brain function has already taken place. Even a new "neural pathway" has to be made from elements of former "neural pathways".

A version, as it were, of the principle of *expansion by recursion*, or recursion by expansion, which ever way you want to look at it, can actually be modelled in a *completely abstract way*, without the conceptualisation of personalised beings. We don't even have to be talking about *being*. It exists in our own material existence, in the intelligence that arises through our brain, as part of our knowledge of mathematics and metamathematics.

In fact, the objects that today we know as *fractal geometries* are things that consist of patterns within patterns within patterns, *ad infinitum*, generated using mathematical *recursion and involution*. They consist of expanding recursions, as a "fractal landscape", that emerges from the infinite mathematical recursions behind the creation of that geometric "landscape".

What that results in, is of course the multiplying of objects, rather than the multiplying of beings. But the *relations between* these objects, and the kind of "world" in which they appear, bears resemblance to the *relations between* the beings of the Hindu pantheon, and the cyclic and eternal nature of the world in which they appear.

The First Rudra

The *Rudra Sambita* of the Śiva Purana reveals the essence of the *involution of being*, or "incarnation", in Chapter Nine.

Here *Śiva* explains to *Viśnu* and *Brahma* how *Rudra* will *manifest himself*,[116] even though he will actually come into the world (this expanding *world of being*) through Brahma's body (meaning, through Brahma's being).[117]

Śiva explains how in *his own incarnation as* Rudra, He and Rudra are identical ("He is I. I am he").[118] He explains how all three beings, *Śiva*, *Brahma* and *Rudra*, will be of the same form, with no difference.[119] A form that is the Truth, the Knowledge, the Endless.[120]

Here we see how one being, in this case *Śiva*, *expands* through *involution*. He, as it were, *descends through* Brahma, to manifest as *Rudra*. But then also, Brahma has already been created by involution through *Viśnu*. And then, *Viśnu* also expands into the "material" world, by involution through Brahma.

In general, an expansion of being ín transcendental Life and Being is referred to in Bhakti sources as *amśi* and *amsa*, but if the expansion arises in the "material" world, in other words in *Prakrti*, then it is an *avatara* (an avatar) that arises in the *Prakrti*.

In the Śiva Purana, *Śiva* goes on to say that *Viśnu* and *Brahma* are born of *Prakrti*, but, like himself, this is not true of *Rudra*.[121] He then re-emphasises his own nature, which is that although he is said to be *with Tamas*, which are of course *Prakrti*, he is actually different from the *Gunas*, and directly beyond *Prakrti* and *Purusa*.[122]

Similarly, he says, as *Hara* he will appear to have variable *Gunas*, and *ego*, and is associated with *Tamas* or ignorance, but that will be "only in name and not in reality".[123]

He also speaks of *another Śakti* arising out of the *Prakrti*,[124] who will become *Viśnu*'s *Śakti*, and another *Śakti Kālī* whom he says "will surely share my part".[125]

All of this describes how the Being is entering its own expansion. The expansion of the Being, at the edge of the transcendental, is the *Prakrti*, where the transcendental ends, and what Hinduism calls "the universe" or "the material world", arises.

It is saying that it is possible for the Being or consciousness of the Being to arise in the *Prakrti* in such a way that the direct consciousness of the Being is not lost.

8

The Transpersonal

In the Hindu corpus everything and all beings in "material existence" - the content of the "cosmic egg" of Brahma - are the expansion of the Being, the *Brahman*. The *Brahman* is a word for God, or an aspect of God.

The corpus says the universe is the *Brahman* manifesting in form, as *Maya*, the cause of delusion, through *Brahman*'s inherent power of *Śakti*.

Compared to the commonplace *personal idea* of "who I am" as a separate being, a separate self, the *Brahman* is undivided, impersonal *Being*, appearing as everything.

The Krsna-Bhakti teachings such as the Caitanya-caritamrta are somewhat disparaging about the realisation of the *impersonal Brahman*, on the grounds that the realisation of it is inferior to the realisation of Krsna, that comes through the path of devotion.

As we have previously said, however, the words "personal" and "impersonal" tend to be weasel words unless we are very clear about what we mean by them, especially when Eastern teachings are being interpreted by Western minds.

Let's just reiterate a little of this. In *Maya*, the mind and the emotions appear to be at the centre of who we are. As a personal mind and self they seem to be our very core, and "who I am". But actually, in both the context of Hinduism and the context of brain function, the mind and the emotions *create* the "who I am" idea. And this "who I am" idea is not our true Identity.

The "who I am" idea is in effect, the mind's way of interpreting all the experience of mind and self that is delivered through brain function. And this interpretation is itself, an aspect of brain function.

So in a way, in *Maya*, we could say, the mind and the emotions orbit the "who I am" idea. That's how it seems. So that, at the centre, supposedly as yourself, is the "who I am" idea. That's the "delusion" referred to in the corpus, arising from *Maya*.

That's the ordinary, commonplace, *personal* mind. When being deluded by *Maya* is transcended, then *Brahman* is at the centre. And being at the centre, it is *Brahman*, that is *who we are*. Rather than the personal idea of "who I am". Throughout the corpus, is the statement made by beings who cease to deluded by *Maya*: "I am *Brahman*". Brahma often explains his misdemeanours by saying he was deluded by *Maya*.

To be clear then, our personal mind and emotions, interpreted through the personal "who I am" idea, is an expansion of *Brahman*, that is this very delusion. It is essentially the *Brahman* playing in, or dancing as, the illusion of personal existence as a separate being. This is all part of *Maya*.

So the personal "who I am" idea is a play, a dance of being, that is actually delusion, and ignorance of *Brahman*. It is ignorance of our true Identity, the *Brahman*, and that ignorance is what the Hindu corpus, in the texts, repeatedly calls *delusion*. In other words, because *Brahman* actually means God, it is delusion due to ignorance of God.

And so it is that traditionally, *Śiva* is depicted as the Lord of the Dance. He is depicted as dancing on ignorance, or delusion.[126]

As the corpus describes it, the way in which this play of being as *Maya*, comes about, is through what the corpus calls the "cosmic egg", or "egg of Brahma", or *Brahmanda*. This play of being, created through the "cosmic egg", becomes our conditional experience of being as a human being, or self, in a "material world" that appears to be separate from "who I am".

Speaking now in contemporary terms then, this play of being, the personal *idea* of "who I am", is only at the centre of our conditional experience of being, because it is maintained there, by the personal mind and emotions, the stuff of separate self, that seems to orbit around it. Really, though, unbeknown to the ego, the personal *idea* of "who I am", the ego, orbits around the mostly hidden substance of emotional self.

When the hidden stuff of emotional self is fully transcended, the personal "who I am" idea has nothing to orbit. Then it no longer seems to be who we are, and *Brahman* can be realised to be the center, as what is and has always been our true Identity. And hence, throughout the corpus, is the statement made by beings who realise this, that "I am *Brahman*".

So to reiterate, the creation of the "cosmic egg", which gives rise to our human experience of being and world, is all *Maya*. This gives rise to delusion, the delusion of being a separate being that is other than "who I am", rather than the direct knowledge "I am *Brahman*".

The experience of consciousness being that is not just completely immersed in misidentification with personal self, emotions, and mind, and its attendant *personal idea* of "who I am" as a separate being, is what *transpersonal* consciousness and being, is.

Now we have to bring this into the context of modern science.

Essentially, even within the context of Hinduism, modern science brings a new dimension of understanding about the nature of this *Maya*. *Maya* is essentially our experience of being, and our experience of the world.

There is an aspect of this world in which we find ourselves, an aspect of the way it is, and behaves, that is completely independent of anyone's personal experience of it. For that matter, it is completely independent of anyone's individual brain function. This aspect is the *objective* aspect of the material world, the aspect of it that science studies.

This is what science has discovered. And by learning about this aspect of our world, science is then able to lead on to technologies, and achievements, that wouldn't otherwise have been possible.

So the "universe" that the Hindu corpus refers to, the "cosmic egg", is not the "objective" phenomena that modern science calls "the universe" or "the material world", and is studying. What the Hindu corpus calls "the universe" is not just this "objective" aspect of our world, but rather, is the whole "cosmic egg".

We will look at the "cosmic egg" in more detail, later. In Hinduism there are infinitely many universes. There are an infinity of "cosmic eggs" that form through the expansion of the Being, from the transcendental into the *Prakrti*.

The human brain, as studied by modern science, is part of what modern science calls "the material world" and "the universe". It, itself, as part of the "objective". What neuroscience refers to as "brain function" refers to that, too.

The creation of the "cosmic egg" of our "universe" that Hinduism refers to, consists of a number of "layers" called "coverings". In the depiction of the "egg" they *begin* as the "shell", as it were, of the "egg". But as we shall see, even in that depiction, they penetrate right down into the interior of the "egg". Actually, they are "coverings" in the sense that they *obscure the truth*, the truth behind what we, as sentient beings, experience as the material universe.

As we shall see later, although a finite number of "coverings" are described, it is recognised in the corpus that their qualities are infinite and interpenetrating.

Inside the "cosmic egg" is not what science studies as "the material world", but rather, a Mythical object called the *Bhu mandala*. And only one small part of the central "island" at the centre of this mandala, a place called *Bharata*, which is an ancient name for India, experiences the four great ages of time in Hinduism, called the Yugas.

Throughout the corpus there is reference to "spheres" called "the worlds" that are contained within this "universe", which vary in number according to the text and the age of the text. These "worlds" are described as spheres inside the "cosmic egg". They are *worlds of being*.

The Nirālamba Upanishad says:

> *Brahman* itself, having through his *Śakti* called *Prakrti* created the *worlds* and *being* latent in them...[127]

We are reminded again here that *Prakrti* is *Brahman*'s *Śakti*. Through *Śakti* these *worlds of being* are created. The Nirālamba Upanishad then goes on to say:

> What is *Prakrti*? It is nothing else but the *Śakti* of *Brahman* which is the nature of *Buddhi* that is able to produce the many motley worlds by virtue of the mere presence of *Brahman*... That *Brahman* is Brahma, Viśnu, Rudra and Indra, Yama, Sun and Moon, *Devas*, *Asuras*, *Piśachas*, men, women, beasts, etc., the fixed ones, Brahmans [a caste of Indians] and others. Here there is no manyness in the least degree: all this is verily *Brahman*.[128]

So we can see here that all the beings and their worlds are expansions of the otherwise unconditional, infinite Being, the *Brahman*. *Everything* is an expansion of the *Brahman*. But we can also see, more specifically, that all the worlds (of being) are created by virtue of the mere presence of *Brahman*, created *through Brahman*'s *Śakti* which, as we have seen, in the Śiva Purana, is also the *Prakrti*.

The phrase "the mere presence *Brahman*" is indicative that *Brahman* isn't really directly involved in the further expansion in *Prakrti*. That happens through *Viśnu* and Brahma.

It *does* mean that the *Brahman* is *present* in what is created. And yet, at the same time, the *Brahman* is not encapsulated in what is created, *in terms of* what is created. Many beings are created, of which we are one kind. But the *Brahman*, as the origin of those beings, isn't necessarily realised by those beings, as their own origin and actually, true Identity.

The realisation of the *Brahman* has a kind of material equivalent. In science there is a growing understanding of the content and vastness of the material universe studied by astronomy. There *is* most definitely in science the realisation of something of mind blowing magnitude, and beauty, and of amazing order that we are still endeavouring to scientifically understand. In a way, those who study this, and appreciate it for what it is, are already sensing with both the intellectual and aesthetic parts of the mind, something of the Being. But it is not generally thought about in that way.

The awe-inspiring aspect of what science calls the universe is in its mind-boggling grandeur and magnitude, and magnificent creative order. Within it is the whole of our solar system, and then our individual selves, appearing to be vanishingly insignificant and small.

This "material reality" is no less "real" than it materially is. However, our appreciation and experience of its magnitude and beauty, as well as of the staggering mathematical beauty of it, arises *in us*. That aspect of it is part of *us*. It is not part of the material cosmos as studied by science, as something *separate* from us.

In the absence of Self realisation the very *objectivity* of science causes the mind to continue to separate this material magnificence from us, and from "the observer". Which actually, is us. And that presumption of separation, that presumption of its independence from who we are, is a consequence not of science's objectivity, but of the fact that this objective mind and thinking in which we are engaged in science, for all its objectivity, is not yet *transpersonal*.

Good scientific thinking is already completely transpersonal when it comes to its study and understanding of what it calls "the material world". But its idea of what this "material world" *is*, and what its relation is to the one who is studying it, is completely *not* yet transpersonal.

Simply, because the mind itself, that is doing the studying, is not yet transpersonal. The ability to be scientifically objective, and being transpersonal, are two quite different things.

However, someone who spends all their time immersed in impersonal, objective contemplation of the world, or of any part of it, which many scientists do, will have, in many cases, already developed a kind of preparatory condition from which it is possible to step up into the transpersonal. Some scientists are already transpersonal. But the mainstream collective isn't.

Stepping up into the transpersonal requires the same dispassionate and detached view that works behind good science, but applied to the self and the self's experience of phenomena.

However, merely "understanding" the self as consisting of material brain function that has evolved in a material world that has nothing to do with us other than that we happen to have evolved within it, is certainly not the same thing.

The dispassionate and detached view has to be applied not to the scientific *concept* of the self, but to the actual *experience of being it.* It is not merely the ability to "explain" what you experience according to what you understand scientifically.

That's not the same thing at all. Rather, that's like taking a book that you haven't really read, and saying you understand the content of the book because you understand that it is all the content of a book, as printed ink on pages, following rules of language and grammar.

The process of self knowledge requires actually coming to know the self. And that's not the same thing as coming to know how science "explains" it. This is *completely irrespectively* of whether or not science's scientific "explanation" is "correct".

There is no point in getting into arguments about whether it is correct or not, because it is irrelevant. *Explanations* are not *self knowledge.* Explanations support being objective, and being objective supports explanations. But neither is the same thing as being transpersonal.

So many scientists and people who are used to objective understanding, are in many ways more transpersonal to a certain degree than many people who are only ever immersed in personal self and life. And in constant personal thinking and personal emoting.

People of the latter kind are always more concerned with their idea of "who I am", and relating to, and understanding the world, in terms of that, than in any way of relating to, and understanding the world, that leaves this personal idea of "who I am" out of the picture.

This latter way of *understanding* the world is something scientists are engaged in. But in the way they *relate* to the world the personal idea of "who I am" isn't necessarily out of the picture. It's just that unlike the first kind of person, they may not talk about it so much. They may not be quite so self obsessed with it. Because for them, it is not as interesting as what they are understanding about the world, through science and objectivity.

Nonetheless, this self must come to be known, if we are to become transpersonal. And it cannot come to be known just through the application of the kind of knowledge that science consists of. Only the scientific *concept* of it can come to be known in that way.

To awaken into the reality of the Self, which is beyond all concepts and all conceptual understanding, demands that the illusory play of individual separate self and mind, be known for what it is, and as it is. Not by conceptual learning about it, but by *consciously passing through* the stuff of it. And literally awakening from it, as the Consciousness of the Self, or *Brahman*.

There are multiple ways in which this is happening. It is always happening to many human beings all over the Earth. But you won't hear about it in the daily News.

The *universal way* is something that Hinduism calls the *churning of the ocean*. That's something we will come to talk about in detail later. It is also possible for it to happen in a sudden, Zen like way, or literally, through the way of Zen. But even if it does happen "in a flash" of Satori, in a Zen like way, *the churning of the ocean* still happens, albeit in a different kind of way.

In the Hindu corpus, there are different "branches" or "schools" that speak of this in various different ways, and using different language. The ancient tantric master Abhinavagupta speaks of it (in *Tantrāloka* and other works) in terms of the intellect, *prana* (the breath and all manifestations of bodily experience and cycles), and the body, in which the reflection of the Ultimate arises.[129]

Let's put it into modern language. The realisation of the Ultimate by a human being, which is the realisation of the Self, may arise through the practice of *yoga*, but it may also arise by other means, in other ways. And even if it arises suddenly, in a Zen like way, this doesn't necessarily obviate its continuation into a necessary process of yoga that really, is *the churning of the ocean* of the ignorance that remains in the individual. In order for what has been realised to be assimilated into the individual, human, conditional experience of being.

In other words, the realisation of the Being, as the Consciousness of the Self, the realisation of the *Brahman*, that transcends bodily identification, is all very well, but it still has to be "brought down" into and established in the stuff of the body and mind that it transcends.

In one way or another, there is going to be a *churning of the ocean*.

* * *

The second passage from the Nirālamba Upanishad says that the *Śakti* of *Brahman*, which is *Prakrti*, is the nature of *Buddhi*. *Buddhi*, in the descriptions of the formation of the "cosmic egg", right across the corpus, is often referred to as the "cosmic intellect".

The corpus is telling us that the "cosmic intellect" or *Buddhi*, is the one intellect behind the multiple instantiations of intellect in human beings.

This, too, relates to the transpersonal. A person can be very *intellectual* without being transpersonal. Another person can be not very "intellectual" at all, and yet be transpersonal. But always, someone who is transpersonal has at least a part of their consciousness that is operating in detachment from identification with their person.

Unfortunately, the words "personal" and "impersonal", because they appear not only in the Hindu corpus and its surrounding literature, but also in the everyday Western world, become weasel words. For this reason, the word *transpersonal* is perhaps a better word than "impersonal".

The *transpersonal* leads into the *impersonal*, but impersonal love, compassion, consciousness, and being, is not anything that can be understood from the point of view of the personal *idea* of "who I am" as a being who is separate from other beings, and something other than the universe as a whole.

In essence, in the Hindu picture, as we saw in the Śiva Purana, at the very beginning of how "the universe" arises, is the *Being*, the *Brahman*. Out of the *Brahman* comes *Śiva*, as the *representative* of transcendental Life and Being, of the *Brahman*.

Śiva is represented in the corpus, as the Divine couple, *Śiva* and *Śivā*, in "the blissful forest". The Bhakti part of the corpus then recognises this as Krsna and Radha. But of course there is also *Viśnu* and *Brahma*, who are alternative aspects of the realisation of the *Brahman*.

Viśnu gives rise to Brahma, who in the Mythology emerges from the lotus that emerges from *Viśnu*'s navel. In other parts of the Mythology *Viśnu* emerges from Brahma's mouth, which represents "the word" of Truth, or *Viśnu*, that is forever transmitted across everything that Brahma subsequently creates.

The *Viśnu* realisation of *Brahman*, is the realisation of the Being, the Self. But the Being, the Self, is also engaged in transcendental Life and Being, which is generally only really explicitly recognised in the Bhakti part of the corpus.

However, the *Śiva* Purana recognises transcendental Life and Being in the transcendental form of *Śiva*, as the Divine couple that it calls *Śiva* and *Śivā*, in "the blissful forest". In the Bhakti part of the corpus, such as the Srimad Bhagavatam and the Caitanya-caritamrta, transcendental Life and Being is recognised as the transcendental Divine couple Krsna and Radha, in Vrndavana.

The corpus is saying that the *Brahman* is the light at the root of the human experience of being, and mind, and world. Our world, "the universe" that science studies, is just our human world of being.

The *Brahman* is actually the light at the root of the human experience of self. And the *Brahman* is the light of the Self. This light is the same light that Plato speaks of, in the *allegory of the cave*, in which we are sitting with our backs to the fire, watching our own shadows on the wall of the cave.

The play of shadows, is in Hinduism, the play of *Prakrti*, or *Maya*. We are a conditional experience of being and world, that arises through *Prakrti*, which is essentially just ignorance of the great expansion of transcendental Life and the Being. And the Source of that Light is the Divine couple in "the blissful forest", or *Vrndavana*.

9

The Divine Couple

We have been talking about *expansion of being*. The *multiplication of beings* that underlies the whole fabric of the Hindu pantheon cannot be truly understood in the same way as understanding "family trees" or "personal relations" or "lines of descent" as in human relations. Because it is not that. Rather, it is an *expansion of being*.

Behind the surface appearances, one of the fundamental messages of the corpus is that the reality of the being we are is not a matter of personal identity, personal family, and imagined, personal roots, of "who I am". All of which is based on the mistake of identification with the body, the mistake of misidentification. Rather than the realisation of *Brahman* as one's true Identity.

We have seen that in the Śiva Purana *the story of creation* begins with the *Brahman* Being, which is the Self. It is the effulgent Joy of absolute, liberated, unconditional Being, eternally free from all dependence on existence. This Being, as we saw, creates what the Śiva Purana calls the *manifest form* of itself as *Śiva*.

In reading such things it is a mistake to presume that we are reading about something that is separate from our self. The real secret of the Puranas is not in difficult to understand polysemic layers about something else, other than our self, the reader. The real secret is that they speak directly to the reader, direct to the individual.

The Purana, in talking about the manifest form of the Being, as *Śiva*, is talking about the manifest form of our own true Identity. We *are* the what the Puranas call "the unmanifest one", manifesting as what is manifest. Even as an individual, we are the manifest *Śiva*, we exist as the play of *Śiva*, as this part of it, created through the principle of infinite expansion, and who we really are, is the Being, the same Being from which, as the Purana states, *Śiva* comes.

Śiva is essentially the personalised name Hinduism gives to the manifest form of the *Brahman* Being. The "manifest form" in terms of our own experience of being, as human beings, is what we call "the world".

Of course, in the Puranas *Śiva* is often depicted in a personalised away. But *Śiva* isn't really personal. Any *personalised* form is just the manifest illusion, the *Maya* of *Brahman*. However, in Hinduism, this is sometimes treated as a contentious point.

Some Bhakti Hindus, based not least on the content of the Srimad Bhagavatam and the Caitanya-caritamrta, tend to denigrate what they call "impersonal liberation" - the realisation of the *Brahman* as impersonal Being - in comparison with the realisation of the *Brahman* as Krsna, which they say is personal.

But "personal" and "impersonal" are weasel words. At least, they can be. Especially to Western ears and minds, looking for spiritual Truth through Eastern culture.

The truth is that the spiritually impersonal is not impersonal in the way that modern *persons* in the West commonly think of "impersonal". That is, as something devoid of feeling, love, compassion, and so on. Such as something that is merely a mental, intellectual understanding. Like, shall we say, the rules of chemistry, or the wording of the law, or mathematics, for example.

Rather, what is spiritually impersonal, still refers to love, and compassion, and joy. The spiritual impersonal, when realised, is full of impersonal love, impersonal compassion, feeling experience, and adoration of the Divine. But it's not personal. Because it's not based on the personal *idea* of "who I am" as a person, in the way that always was, and has now become in a new way a central obsession in contemporary Western society.

The spiritual impersonal is impersonal because it is not based on the personal, ego-based *idea* of "me". It's not based on the human stuff of separate self. It's not based on the personal ego.

The reality of the being in a human being, as an experience of being arising through the impersonal biology of the body and brain, is *transpersonal*. Transpersonal basically means to go beyond of the person and the personal. Not into something "impersonal" like the laws of chemistry, but into the spiritually impersonal. In which personal self, and personal ego, and the personal *idea* of "who I am", is not the most important thing.

What the Puranas call "the unmanifest" begins *beyond* the personal *idea* of "who I am" which is all just part of the personal ego. And brain function itself, of course, through which our conditional experience of being arises, is of course *impersonal* biology. In material terms, it is the way our play of experience, the play of being, is delivered. In Puranic terms it is the actuality of the manifest *Śiva*.

The Divine Couple *Śiva* and *Śivā* that we have been talking about represent a level of realisation of transcendental Life and Being that the Bhakti tradition knows as the Divine Couple Krsna and Radha, whose combined consciousness is *Radha-Krsna*.

It is this that the *Bhakti* tradition revering Krsna as the highest manifestation of the Supreme Being, puts into some context. It does so by declaring the *Brahman* realised impersonally to be the effulgence - the *Brahman effulgence* - of still higher Being - the *Supreme Personality of Godhead* - which is *Krsna*.

Śivā and Śivā

Śiva has *form*, the form of *the auspicious one* (the word *Śiva* means "the auspicious one")[130] in "the blissful forest".

Śiva is portrayed as Being, who, being one with the *Brahman*, has the *Brahman* as his true Identity. Remember that in the texts *Śiva* is frequently explicitly stated to be identical with *Brahman*.[131]

Really, despite being called *Brahman*, the *Brahman* Being has no dependence on any particular name for its Identity. That Being is both nameless and formless. It is radiant, infinite Being, incomprehensible, and yet *it can be realised* by beings who have been given *form*.

So *Śiva* is both nameless and formless since He is identical with That Being, the supreme *Brahman*. The Śiva Purana tells us that he is both without embodied form.[132]

An "embodied form", here, doesn't necessarily mean a material form. As far as the texts are concerned all material form is a manifestation of *Śiva*, but "embodiment" in the context of the Hindu corpus doesn't refer to matter, as science understands it. Rather, it refers to *svarūpa*, which is essentially *experience of being*.

So as a *manifest form* of the *Brahman*, *Śiva* has this "embodied form". A form in which he is both *Śiva* and *Śivā*, and also "the blissful forest", which is the *world of being* in which *Śiva* and *Śivā* enjoy "dalliances" and "sports".[133]

They enjoy *form of being*, in a *world of being*, all of which has been provided as the Divine Idea of the Divine Couple in their Divine world - "the blissful forest".

Śiva, with his consort *Śivā*, in "the blissful forest" in which they enjoy their love, is a creation of the Divine, the *Brahman*. But remember *Śiva* is identical with *Brahman*.[134] So this *world of being* enjoyed by *Śiva* and *Śivā* is still potent with the possibility of further creation.

So the Purana goes on to say that *Śiva* and *Śivā* whilst sporting in the "blissful forest" wished for another Being to be created.[135]

Śiva says:

> "Another being shall be created by me [a being that will be *Viśnu*]. Let him create everything, protect it and in the end let him dissolve it with my blessing. Having entrusted everything to him we two,

> remaining in *Kāśī* shall roam as we please keeping only the prerogative of conferring salvation. We can stay happily in this blissful forest being free from worries".[136]

In other words, "the blissful forest", of *Śiva* and *Śivā* is also called *Kāśī*. The Divine Couple live here eternally, irrespective of the material creation and its destruction.

The Purana tells us then that "the divine forest" is called *Avinmukta* and *Kāśī*. And in the texts, more widely, it is also called *Vārānasī*, which is the name of the holy city in India, in Uttar Pradesh, also known as *Kāśī*.

Vārānasī

So *Kāśī* or *Avinmukta* is also called *Vārānasī*. And *Vārānasī* is also the name of the holy city in India, in Uttar Pradesh, (also sometimes called *Kāśī*). But the real meaning here is not about geographical locations.

The names of geographical places in India are woven into its Mythology, just as the Mythology is woven into the places. (We see essentially the same thing in the case of the Greek Myths, and other cultures). So in Indian culture the city of Vārānasī in Uttar Pradesh is believed to have been founded by *Śiva*.

Hindus also believe that dying in Vārānasī and being cremated there by the river Ganges, ensures salvation. As part of the Indian culture such beliefs have their roots articulated in the Scriptures. However, we get a much deeper reading out of these texts if we see the transcendental context.

The first thing to be clear about is what is meant by *salvation*. We are of course talking Hinduism here, so we are talking about *reincarnation*.

Many people in the West may regard the idea of reincarnation as a kind of "comfort" to counteract the fact that as a human being you are going to die. But of course in Hinduism, as in Buddhism, this is not how reincarnation is viewed, at all.

On the contrary, reincarnation is the thing to be avoided, and salvation is liberation or *moksha* or *freedom from the whole cycle* of reincarnation and death, and rebirth into suffering.

In the Kurma Purana God (*Iśvara*) speaks of Vārānasī saying that it is his sacred place *Avinmukta*. He says that shrines in heaven, on Earth, and in cremation grounds are all found here.[137] He says Vārānasī is His secret-most holy centre that enables living beings to cross the ocean of worldly existence.[138]

Most importantly He says his abode (*Avinmukta*) he's not even in contact with the Earth, but rather, is in the firmament. Only the liberated perceive it through the mind.[139]

For now, let's just focus on why we can say this clearly contains a deeper meaning under the surface, without for the time being worrying about what that meaning is.

Obviously, the *material*, holy city of Vārānasī is *not in itself*, for anyone seeing it ordinarily, *in the firmament* [heaven]. And the *material*, sacred city of Vārānasī is certainly not *in itself*, a place that is *secret*. It is one place in India that probably everyone knows about, being India's most holy city.

The text as a whole in this chapter of the Kurma Purana mixes statements that explicitly refer to the actual material city of Vārānasī, with statements about *the transcendental* that cannot be understood mundanely.

So the meaning in this particular passage isn't mundane. The Puranas in general contain much material with multiple levels of meaning. In particular, this part of the Kurma Purana and corresponding parts of the Skanda Purana present cultural material suitable as directions for ritual belief, but the texts *also* have esoteric meaning suitable for more spiritually advanced understanding.

Staying in Kāśī and Dying in Kāśī

There are two salient things pertaining to *Kāśī*, Vārānasī or *Avinmukta*, that the Scriptures talk about. Firstly, there is "entering", or "staying in". Secondly, there is "dying in". Both these aspects are frequently referred to in both the Kurma Purana and the Skanda Purana (and elsewhere of course).

The Kurma Purana tells us that all accumulated from thousands of births are destroyed as soon as one enters the holy centre of *Avinmukta* [*Kāśī*].[140]

However, this clearly does not in itself constitute liberation from the cycle of death and reincarnation, and hence worldly existence and suffering, because the Purana also states that liberation from worldly existence comes only to him *who dies there*.[141]

So liberation is not attained until you *die in Kāśī* (Vārānasī or *Avinmukta*). But in the meantime, one must *stay* in *Kāśī* (Vārānasī or *Avinmukta*).

Now the Skanda Purana says that anyone who goes to the city "stays behind" or does not return.[142]

But the Purana also says that the unwise go elsewhere after attaining *Kāśī*, or liberation. We are told that even salvation is lost by those who abandon *Kāśī*.[143]

Hence, the Skanda Purana emphasises that the wise do not return from *Kāśī*.[144]

So what kind of place is it, then, that offers salvation, that is an accumulation of "liberation"? What kind of place is it where *whoever* goes to that city *stays behind*, but is at the same time a place that can be abandoned by the unwise?

What kind of place is it, that is the abode of *Śiva* and *Śivā*, and is the eternal "blissful forest", where all sins accumulated previously in the course of thousands of births are annihilated, the moment you enter. And yet at the same time, is a place you can "fall" from?

"Staying in Vārānasī" and "Dying in Vārānasī" clearly doesn't really refer just to physically staying and dying in the sacred city of Vārānasī in Uttar Pradesh in India. No matter how much that may be culturally believed.

On the contrary, what "Staying in Vārānasī" refers to is a "process" of accumulating innate spiritual merit or wisdom, through countless rebirths, until one can "die in *Kāśī*".

And that's a process in which what is accumulated is never really lost, which is why whoever goes there stays behind [*i.e.* does not return].[145]

"Going to that city" means to be consciously on that spiritual path, following the pursuit of liberation, a path that is the process of accumulation of merit.

Once on the path, what is accumulated as merit is never lost. Nevertheless, one can still fall from the effects of the "merit" one has gained, if one becomes re-immersed in worldly attachments and pursuits, abandoning the spiritual path.[146]

The salvation which has been achieved here, the "mass of salvation" is the merit accumulated over many lifetimes.

The effect of merit or "staying in *Kāśī*" appears in actual worldly circumstances. This is understood as a matter of *Karma*. In India, as elsewhere in the Eastern religions, pursuing the spiritual path leads to better rebirth. *Karma* is gradually improved, over many lifetimes. As one works at the spiritual path, rebirth leads into circumstances that draws one onto the spiritual path. You "pick up" where you "left off".

But the progress gained can "slip out of the hands". It is possible, in a given lifetime, to temporarily "fall from grace". However, the merit itself, is never really lost.

The climbing and the falling, is inevitably part of the picture. To come "off the path", to "leave Vārānasī", is to start to create troublesome karma. It is to "fall down" from the climb. The "merit" gets "covered over" and loses its effect.

The ancient Indian "board" game of *Moksha Patam* (meaning *moksha path* - the path of liberation) models this very idea and is the forerunner to the modern game known in the West as *Snakes and Ladders*.

By persisting, over many lifetimes, eventually, the opportunity to "*die* in *Kāśī*" arises. But first, one must tenaciously stay on the path, one must "stay in *Kāśī*" no matter what happens in one's worldly existence. And so it is that the Kurma Purana, when talking about *Kāśī*, says that a person must stay in *Kāśī* even when beset with calamities.[147]

The reason is that the goal is to *die in Kāśī*. Death in *Kāśī* is not to be feared, it says. It is a death that cannot be understood in the material way, although physical death may be the entrance to it.

To *stay in Kāśī* and to *die in Kāśī* each have a double esoteric meaning.

Firstly, to "stay in *Kāśī*" means simply to stay on the spiritual path, as we have seen. But secondly, it refers also to *ego death*. Ego death is the *transcending* of misidentification with everything that constitutes the individual and personal ego - the separate self - by awakening into our true Identity as the Self.

We can even say what this means in terms of brain function. It is to awaken Identity beyond everything that brain function constructs as the experience of self, and "I am", based on the totality of experience delivered through brain function.

You might want to say "Well, surely *anything* we experience, including the Self, must be delivered through brain function"? That's a reasonable conjecture to be made in the absence of Self realisation, but it is not so. Because what brain function constructs is our *conditional experience of being*. That is, the experience of being the body, the experience of the mind, the emotions, and the world at large. All this is a construct of brain function. But it is only possible in the first place, we are saying, because of the Reality of the Being. Which is realised as the Self, or *Brahman*.

The Reality of the Being is not something that can be understood from the position of the *conditional* experience of being and mind, arising in *Prakrti*. The Reality of the Being is beyond thought, beyond the mind, beyond the conditional experience of being, beyond the need of *anything*.

Beyond existence, or any need of existence, or anything in it. There is simply no *understanding* it, through thought structures, or conceptual understanding, or any mind still identified with the self as it arises through brain function.

The Being is only *realised* and knowable by *awakening as* That Being. It is becoming a little more widely known now, that this is synonymous with what is called *ego death*. We could also call it transcendence of the ego, but there is a very good reason why it is referred to as ego *death*.

Because it is (usually as a temporary occurrence to begin with) psychological and/or emotional death. This is not something that can be imagined or speculated about, or understood conceptually. It is what "happens" when the consciousness we already really are, *completely drops* the construct of *self* and *mind* that gives rise to the ordinary human experience of identity, as self identified with the body.

As a result, consciousness continues but is awakened into the direct experience of itself as the Being, in which there is spontaneous adoration as ecstatic transcendental Love and Joy, and Gratitude to the Being, for the Truth of the Being. Which is that it has no dependence on anything outside its Self, no *need* of existence, or of anything in it. So what dies, in the realisation is not the Being, but the ego, the separate, little idea and conditional experience of "who I am", that arises through the principle of the brain.

We ordinarily recognise three "states of consciousness" which are the "waking state", the "dreaming state", and complete unconsciousness, or deep, dreamless sleep. Actually, the state of unconsciousness is more than one "level", as any anaesthetist will tell you, but we can regard it as one.

It has long been recognised in the East that there is a "fourth state", the *Turiya*, in which there is "consciousness in the unconscious". This is not, it must be said immediately, the same thing as consciousness under anaesthesia, called "waking anaesthesia", which can also happen.

What separates the ordinary first three states from *Turiya*, is ego death, or "the band of death".[148] In *Turiya* it is directly realised and known that *death* as it is commonly understood is an illusion. Certainly, bodies die, persons die, but it is only by falsely identifying with the body in the first instance, that death *seems to be* something that applies to the Being we already really are. Ego death can be encountered as temporary, in terms of the time in which the temporal, conditional experience of being, of a human being, occurs.

The first esoteric meaning of "staying in *Kāśī*" is to stay on the spiritual path, but there is a second esoteric meaning which is to be able to remain in the state of spiritual equilibrium, even, as the Kurma Purana says, "if buffeted by hundreds of calamities". This is only truly possible where there is permanent ego death. Otherwise, it is a question of remaining spiritually conscious and not identifying with, as much as possible, what arises as emotional disturbance.

To "die in *Kāśī*" also then has its own double esoteric meaning. Firstly, it means to physically die having realised ego death. Secondly, it means permanent ego death, in terms of the human experience of time.

The Skanda Purana says that *Kāśī* is the *personified form of Viśnu*'s *Maya*, which enchants and deludes the whole universe.[149]

What does this mean? In Hinduism the entire universe is the *Maya* of *Viśnu*, it is, in effect, the dream of *Viśnu* when *Viśnu* falls asleep on the causal ocean.

So this passage is saying that *Kāśī* - the Divine Couple in "the blissful forest" - is the *personified form* of the *Maya* of the whole universe.

In other words, *everything*, the *whole universe*, all of this *Maya*, is the illusory or veiled manifestation, through *expansion*, of *Kāśī*, the Divine Couple in "the blissful forest". Everything is this, all material phenomena is this. This is what the passage is saying.

If, alternatively, we were to speak in terms of Krsna-bhakti, then we would be saying that everything is Krsna and the transcendental pastimes of Krsna, but corrupted by material manifestation.

It is all being represented or "reproduced" in a way that is translated into Time (*Kala*) and *Prakrti*. And through infinite expansions and involution, the "Divine pastimes" of transcendental Life and Being, now translated into the phenomena of *Prakrti*, become all but "lost in translation".

In terms of the Śiva Purana, the whole universe is the illusory, material representation of *Kāśī*, in matter and time (and space) and ego (*ahamkara*) born of *Prakrti*. *Kāśī* of course being "the blissful forest" in which *Śiva* and *Śivā* enjoy their sporting and dalliances.

Śiva and *Śiva* in "the blissful forest", in the Śiva Purana, are none other than the representation of the Spiritual Reality (above the *Brahman*) of transcendental Life and Being, that the Krsna-Bhakti texts communicate as Radha-Krsna, and the Divine transcendental world of Goloka.

If we wanted to express this in nonpartisan terms, outside Hinduism, we might call it the Divine Idea of Man, Woman, and the Earth.

The Enchanting Herb

In the Skanda Purana *Śiva* says:

> Oh *Kāśī* ! I know you well that you have a great power of bewitching others [*Śiva* himself here, in *Kāśi,* is not bewitched by *Kāśī*]. Those who are conversant with affairs of long-ago praise you as the destroyer of great delusion. But they do not know this aspect of *Kāśī* that it is a place possessing a great power of creating delusion. I shall be sending all others and you will enchant them. Thus I know, *Kāśī*, you, the enchanting herb.[150]

So *Kāśī* or *Avinmukta*, "the blissful forest", is actually referred to by *Śiva*, knowingly, as "the enchanting herb." And it is a place to which *Śiva* will be "sending all others and you will enchant them."

Of course, herbs are referred to in the Puranas, often apparently literally, just meaning herbs, that is, plants. But the Puranas have multiple layers of meaning, so there is also a deeper meaning.

Like everything in the Puranas, herbs are created as *beings*. The transliteration of the word is usually *oṣadhi*. This indeed means "herb" or "plant", but it also means "containing light".[151]

The Brahmānda Purana speaks of the "souls of medicinal herbs",[152] and includes extensive passages on the spiritual origin of "herbs".[153]

We have to bear in mind that these texts are also the product of a religious culture deriving from the time of the Vedas, a culture of fire sacrifices and the ingestion of a psychoactive plant or herb called *Soma* - which also means the Moon - in order to attain union with that Being.

So finding that the texts talk about herbs in a way that dissolves the distinction between material plant and realms of Being, is not really surprising. Herbs in the Puranas symbolise aspects of the overall spiritual and cosmic picture, as well as supporting more mundane meanings.

But there is no doubt that the meaning of "herb" (*oṣadhi*) in the Indian sources is not limited to the mundane. For example, the Brahmānda Purana speaks of the Earth milking the mountains and the yield being embodied forms of medicinal herbs, together with various gems and jewels.[154]

The Harivamsha similarly states:

> 'I have heard that the mountains again milked her [the Earth] for the herbs in forms of various jewels'.[155]

It later tells how

> 'Luminous bodies and herbs, shorn of lustre, flew about in the sky'.[156]

In the account of *The Churning of the Ocean* (which we will talk about later) in the Harivamsha, the Hindu scholar and translator Manmatha Nath Dutt states that the herbs (*oṣadhis*), which are also said to be fragrant flowers - herbs that the *Dānavas* will grind in the water - represent bodily attachment, which is to be drowned in true knowledge.[157]

The bodily attachments are "fragrant flowers" because they are based on the addictive experiences of the senses that come through bodily being.

The casting of bodily attachments into the water of true knowledge has much the same meaning as the attainment of spiritual knowledge, given that the latter is synonymous with the transcending of identification with the body.

(The Harivamsha account of *The Churning of the Ocean* is a somewhat different account to that usually found in the Puranas. The ocean referred to in Harivamsha is the ocean of salt water, whilst more generally in the Puranas the account is of the Ocean of Milk, and is often called in full, *The Churning of the Ocean of Milk*. Both oceans are part of a set of seven oceans called the *saptadvīpa* that we will talk more about, later. In the Harivamsha account the ambrosia or *Amrta*, the "nectar of immortality" that arises from the churning of the ocean of salt water, is in the form of milk).[158]

When *Śivā* speaks of *Kāśī*, and calls it "the enchanting herb", there is a difference between the status of *Śiva* and *Śivā* who are eternally *in Kāśī*, and the status of those generally, who "stay in *Kāśī*".

Śiva and *Śivā* as we saw above, are to remain in *Kāśī* conferring salvation but remaining happily in the "beautiful forest" free from concern with creation.[159]

But for "others", the truth is that one has to "die in *Kāśī*", to attain liberation.

In the Skanda Purana, *Skanda* says that even great spiritual seekers do not compare with those who die in *Kāśī*. The language is highly figurative saying that "in the state of a corpse" a creature does not become unclean in *Kāśī*.[160] *Skanda* says he himself will touch its ear [an Indian cultural action of respect, reverence, or repentance].[161]

There is a great deal of symbolic language in this. But it clearly indicates that to *die in Kāśī* is to transcend even *Brahma* and *Viśnu*.

Śiva and his lover *Śivā* are remaining forever in *Kāśi*, "the blissful forest". If it is transcendental Life and Being that is represented by *Śiva* and his lover *Śivā*, sporting in "the transcendental forest", or *Kaśi*, then why does *Śiva* say, in the quote from the Skanda Purana, that *Kaśi* is the "enchanting herb" that both destroys delusion, and creates it. And that he will be sending all others to this place?

What does this mean?

Here is the difference between the Krsna-Bhakti scriptures, and the corpus in general. In the *Śiva* Purana, as we have seen, *Śiva* is created (by expansion) as the first *form* of the *Being*. *Śiva is* the Being, and because this is an *expansion of being*, so He is both with and without form.

Throughout the corpus, *Brahman* is without form, and above and free from the *Gunas*. And because *Śiva* is created from the *Brahman*, and not just arising in the *Prakrti*, or *Gunas*, he is both with and without *Gunas*, which are the *Śakti* of *Brahman*. But He is, nonetheless, created from the *Brahman*, which here, has a particular meaning, and refers to a particular aspect of the *Brahman*. An aspect that, in general, only the Bhakti texts speak of.

Although *Śiva* represents transcendental Life and Being as the Divine couple in "the blissful forest", He springs from the *Brahman* "with and without Gunas". This means that *Śiva*'s place as a member of the Trimurti is as one who has sprung from the "outer limit" of the expansion of transcendental Life and Being, at the point where the *Prakrti* arises.

The *Prakrti* somehow contains the "impression" of that transcendental Life and Being, because it is the expansion of it. But how? *Śiva*, as the Purusa, coming from transcendental Life and Being, from which He springs, then enters the *Prakrti*. And henceforth, the *Prakrti* contains the "impression" of transcendental Life and Being. The *Prakrti*, which comes from it anyway, is then "impregnated" with that "impression".

And it is not that this is an idea based on human life and sexuality, but rather, that human life and sexuality is a continuing expansion of the Being, a continuing expansion and involution, that carries this involution of the Purusa and *Prakrti*, within it.

Here, again, we are talking about "stages". Again, just as a way of "explaining". As happens in the Puranas. But really, there are no "stages". As we said a little earlier, as the Brahmanda Purana states, it all "happens" instantaneously, "like lightning".

It is happening where we are, as human beings. But for us, the expansion and involution has become what we call "time", as something that is happening objectively, in a world that we mistakenly consider to be separate from us. Which is, in fact, a feature of the construct of brain function. Without which, we would have no such conditional experience of being.

We each have our subjective experience of time. But there is also this objective facet of time, which is independent of anyone of us, individually. The aspect measured by clocks. Everything that is "happening" objectively, in our world of being, is "happening" according to objective time. And that world of objective time is what science calls "the universe" and "the material world". Which is not what the Puranas call "the universe" and "the material world".

The bridge between the two, the Puranas, and modern science, is the brain. The principle of the brain is the place in which objective time arises. But modern science doesn't yet know what the principle of the brain is. That is, the principle by which the brain and its functioning equates to our whole conditional experience of being, of self, mind, psyche, body, thought, memory, imagination, emotions, and world.

And of the past that knowledge is currently blocked by attachment to the misinterpretation of the world itself. The misinterpretation of it as something other than a construct of brain function.

The Puranas didn't know or explicate anything about the brain. And modern science, as a whole, doesn't know anything about the true content of the Puranas. Beyond its religious and cultural fabric.

Śiva and *Śivā*, the Divine couple, in "the blissful forest", as we have just described, are implicit in the expansion of the *Brahman*, from the point of the arising of *Prakrti* onwards. Which means, *Śiva* and *Śivā*, where *Śiva* is a member of the Trimurti, and their "blissful forest" called *Kaśi*, arise at the "outer extremity" of the expansion of *transcendental* Life and Being.

The expansion of transcendental Life and Being is only really something that the Bhakti texts, such as the Brahma Samhitā, the Padma Purana, the Srimad Bhagavatam, the Caitanya-caritamrta, the Brihad Bhagavatamrta, and so on, talk about. The rest of the corpus is only really concerned with the *Brahman* realised as what the Bhakti texts call the *Brahman* effulgence, which is the *effulgence* of transcendental Life and Being at the outer extremity of the expansion.

Śiva and *Śivā*, the Divine couple, in "the blissful forest", as spoken of in the Śiva Purana, are the *representation* of transcendental Life and Being, in the great expansion, at the point where the *Prakrti* arises. That same transcendental Life and Being, from its Origin to well before the arising of *Prakrti*, the Bhakti texts speak of, in their own religious and cultural fabric, as the Divine pastimes of the Divine couple Radha and Krsna, in *Vrndavana*.

The Śiva Purana says Śiva sends "all others" to *Kaśi*, where delusion is destroyed. That's what the Purana says. But it *also* says that *Kaśi creates* delusion. Because *Kaśi* - "the blissful forest" is only the way transcendental Life and Being is *represented* by the Beings called *Śiva* and *Śivā*, in *Kaśi*.

In short, "the blissful forest" of *Śiva* and *Śivā* is the eternal "impression" at the extremity of the transcendental expansion of Life and Being, where the *Prakrti* arises. It is the archetypal form inherent in the continuing expansion, whose origin is the transcendental expansion of Life and Being, the Krsna-Bhakti characterises as Radha-Krsna in *Vrndavana*.

The "impression" of this that remains in the expansion of *Prakrti* remains "covered", but is still there, in everything that arises out of *Prakrti*, which means *us*, our conditional experience of being, and our world.

To awaken from *Maya* or the delusion of it, we have to *realise Kaśi*. That means, to realise that what this is really all about, this human life, is *Kaśi*. Which is "the blissful forest" in which we experience our own love for the Being we are. Which, through the *Śakti* of creation, appears as the *Maya* of each other, and the world.

And not everything else that human beings tend to think their existence is about. If we realise *Kaśi*, and stay with it, then we are "staying in *Kaśi*". But in the great scheme of things, as understood in both Hinduism and Buddhism, and, indeed, in other religions, we have to *die* in *Kaśi* if we are not to fall back into delusion in rebirth.

Our existence as a human beings is actually *already in Kaśi*, but mostly, we do not realise it. When we realise it, then we make *Kaśi* consciously realised in our own experience. And we have to stay there, if we are not to be drawn back into the delusion of what the human mind mistakenly thinks human existence is all about. Which is something other than the love of the Being we all, already really are.

The Brain

Our conditional experience of being, as human beings, is one that arises through the principle of the brain. The brain *does not* arise in the universe as a way for "the universe" that *science* speaks of, to come to "know itself".

Not if we are talking about "the universe" that science refers to. Because, in the mainstream, what science conceives of as "the universe" is something has nothing to do with us, other than that we happen to be in it. This idea that the brain arises in "the universe" such that "the universe" - the one that science studies and refers to - comes to know itself, is now quite a popular idea. But for these reasons it is duplicitous and shallow.

It is a misunderstanding about the nature of the universe, and the nature of consciousness. Because it is not true that there is a universe "coming to know itself", that is other than the self we already are. The brain doesn't exist in order for the universe that science studies and talks about, to come to know itself. In terms of Hinduism that idea is part of *Maya*, part of the delusion.

Extending the basis of Hinduism, it would be more true to say that the brain exists so that we can come to know our self. Which in any case, is inseparable from the universe as a whole. The universe as a whole is the macrocosm, and our self is the microcosm. When we transcend the microcosm the universe is experientially known to be the Being, which is also our true Identity.

Mainstream scientific thought is oblivious of this. There are many scientists who will try to tell us that that science already has the answers to why there is something rather than nothing, to why the universe exists, to human "consciousness", and pretty much everything else. But it is simply not true.

Firstly, because it is simply not true that all these things have been settled and established by science, even in scientific terms. But more importantly, because "the universe" they are talking about is being thought of as something that is other than a construct of brain function. Something that fundamentally has nothing to do with us.

There may be a few scientists who realise, in scientific terms, that what science is studying as "the universe" or "the material world" is the same thing as a construct of brain function. Some may even deduce that the world must be the self. But *deduction* isn't the same thing as *realisation.*

The realisation is experiential. And it is the experiential condition that is the foundation of a concomitant intellectual understanding. Just as the intellectual understanding still unconsciously based on the principle of preserving the *idea* of "who I am" associated with the body but not the entire universe, has its own concomitant intellectual understanding.

The *realisation* of it is part of what the true content of the Hindu corpus is all about. The main part being the realisation of the *Brahman* - the Being.

As part of the realisation, as it occurs in human beings in these times, the human brain is seem to be arising as part of the great scheme of things. Which is undeniable, because it is here. And our experience of being as a human being arises through it.

We could say it arises as a way for "the universe" to come to know itself, but if we want to say that then we have to appreciate that the "universe" this applies to is not the one that science talks about.

Rather, it is the human self that we are talking about. That's what "the universe" in Hinduism is. And that's none other than the thing that in modern science, we recognise as *the principle of the brain*, even if we cannot scientifically say what it is.

It's the thing that Hinduism, in its own way, through its own religious and cultural fabric, talks about. And that's the thing that each one of us, in our own way, has to come to know. Whether or not we know anything about Hinduism. Because it's only in that way that we can discover who we really are, and what the brain is really all about.

That Being - or in terms of Hinduism the *Brahman* - isn't an object, or an objective system or principle, or anything that science can understand or model. As both our true Identity and our unfathomable infinite Source, it expresses itself the world over, in all its various ways. The ignorance of it in human beings is also expressed, the world over, in the form of belief. In which, in general, it is just called God.

10

Viśnu and Brahma

So *Viśnu* is an expansion of the *Brahman*. And in the Śiva Purana, more specifically, *Viśnu* is an expansion of *Śiva* who is an expansion of the *Brahman*.

In the Puranas it is perfectly in order for *Viśnu* to declare "I am *Brahman*". Provided, of course, that this indeed the state of *Viśnu*'s consciousness and realisation of his true Identity. And in the Puranas, it is.

It is important to know that there is a difference between the *condition* of a being's identity, or *svarūpa*, and that being's Source Identity - the *Brahman*.

Ultimately, as described in Hinduism, the true identity of *all beings* is the *Brahman* (or *Krsna*, if you are in the Bhakti tradition). The Being then expands through the principle of *the expansion of being*, to become all the other beings, who themselves may also expand in various ways.

So this expansion creates a vast ocean of complexity, because the principle of *the expansion of being* carries on through, in the eternal *great expansion*. And so it is that even human beings, way down at the "bottom" of this great expansion, still have this power of *expansion of being*, albeit in a constrained way.

Human beings literally "expand" their numbers, but only by interacting and mixing, as material bodies, sexually and biologically.

As a result of this, it is possible for a child to be very *like* one or both of their parents, but it is not possible for the consciousness or mind or *experience of being* of a child to *awaken as* the actual consciousness or mind or experience of being of their parent or parents.

As a human self our experience of being and identity is under the ordinance of the *principle of the brain*. Only in the very rare cases of conjoined twins who share brain matter, can there be an overlap in identity. But in the principle of the *expansion of being* that permeates the Hindu corpus, the "sharing" of identity is not a rare thing, at all.

The objective, material world, with its objective laws of nature, is a construct that creates our human experience of sentient being. And where we are now, in science, we already understand our experience of this to be *a construct of brain function*. But in the mainstream, there is difficulty in accepting that our world is also this.

So as a living human being, our human self is our *conditional being identity*. And that remains the case, even if we realise the *Brahman* or Self. However, it is not uncommon for humans who initially realise the Self, to make the subsequent mistake, after the ego reconstitutes itself, of confusing that realisation of true Identity, with their *conditional being identity*, as a human being.

And so it is that sometimes, the incoming or developing realisation of the Self can lead to delusions of grandeur. There are some aspects of Self realisation that the wider world at large is unable to distinguish from more commonplace mental illness or psychosis.

Viśnu is the Being, *Brahman*, but is associated with the expansion of *Brahman* that, through Brahma, becomes the material world. The *Brahman*, realised by beings in that world (us), is realised as as the Self, as pure, unconditional Being, without any form, or need of this creation.

This is where, in the Bhakti texts we looked at earlier, *Viśnu*, as Maha-*Viśnu* also called *Kāranodakaśāyī Viśnu*, is said to expand into to *Garbhodakaśāyī Viśnu*, and then into *Ksīrodakaśāyī Viśnu* who is in the heart of every living being.[162]

Viśnu is Purusa, the consciousness of Being, and in the Padma Purana *Viśnu* speaks of being awake, full of reflection and having "self consciousness".[163]

This means "self-consciousness" in a very literal sense, rather than the "self consciousness" of human beings, such as may be experienced, for example, in embarrassment.

Viśnu also says he is involved in the movements of the world and has sense organs and form, and is called *Taijasa* (*i.e.* bright).[164]

This essentially means that *Viśnu* is also conditional sentient life (including us) in the material world. This is because the material world has been created as an expansion of *Viśnu*.

Viśnu then says that when he he is without understanding or action he is in a state of sleep.[165]

The statement is self-explanatory when merely applied to the living beings in the material world. However, it also refers to *Viśnu* as the Purusa.

In the Mythology, when the material world is created, *Kāran-odakaśāyī Viśnu* sleeps on the *Kārana Samudra*, the causal ocean. So essentially, the conditional beings in the material world are created without understanding. Essentially, in this way, they are dream beings, of the dream of *Viśnu*, unaware that they are the product of dreaming.

As *Ksīrodakaśāyī Viśnu*, *Viśnu* is the Purusa, the consciousness of being, within us. Then he says he is in a state of deep sleep.[166]

This, again, is self-explanatory, when applied to biological beings. But he goes on to say:

> As *Turiya* (*i.e.* in the fourth state) I am without any modification and void of properties. With my form reflected everywhere I am unattached and (am just) like a witness. I am the individual soul still sticking to the worldly defilements.[167]

Turiya, the "fourth state", is "fourth" in addition to the human waking state, dream-sleep, and state of deep, dreamless sleep. *Turiya* is, essentially, the state of consciousness that shares characteristics of both deep, dreamless sleep, and the waking state.

The phrase "without any modification" here refers to the *Gunas*. Whenever the Puranas talk about "modification" or "agitation", they are invariably talking about the *Gunas*. "Without modification" means that the *Prakrti* is still in the state of Pradhana or Mulaprakrti, not "modified" or "agitated" into the three *Gunas*, by the entry of Purusa into it, but rather, is in its original, pristine state. This is the "brilliant" state of *Prakrti* that we talked about earlier.

In the *Turiya* state of consciousness the Purusa in the *Prakrti* has awakened into the consciousness of the Being. It is the access to the realisation "I am Brahman", the beginning of the realisation of *Bhagavan*, as spoken of in Bhakti.

It is still in the *Prakrti*, but the *Prakrti* is now no longer "agitated" or in "disequilibrium". This state of consciousness can be brought about about as a result of meditation, and spiritual practice, together with what we will later talk about as *the churning of the ocean*.

The Purusa, or consciousness of being, is still arising *in* the *Prakrti*. And so it is that *Viśnu* says here "I am the individual soul still sticking to the worldly defilements".

We could put this in another way. We could say that at this level the Purusa realises the reality of Being as the individual, evolving identity or soul, still stuck in material being, or "still sticking to the worldly defilements".

Above this level of realisation are higher levels of realisation of the *Brahman* where what is realised is consciousness and joy, as the eternal, immutable *Brahman*.[168]

The *Brahman*, is also acknowledged in the Padma Purana to be the effulgence of higher transcendental Life and Being,[169] which requires still higher levels of realisation, in order to be directly known, as *Bhagavan*.

Beyond Personalisation

In the Mythology *Śiva*, *Viśnu* and Brahma each appear as "separate" *personalised* beings. But this is just a mode of expression.

In the Hindu picture the universe is infinitely periodically created and destroyed and recreated, in periods called *Kalpas*. During the destruction the three members of the Trimurti become merged in *Prakrti.*[170]

The Śiva Purana tells us that in a former *Kalpa* (the period of creation and dissolution of the universe), *Brahma* and *Viśnu* were created by *Rudra* (*Śiva*), but in another *Kalpa* Brahma created *Rudra* and *Viśnu*. And then, in another, *Viśnu* was similarly the creator of the other two Deities. Therefore, in different *Kalpas*, *Brahma*, *Viśnu* and *Rudra* are cyclically born from one another.[171]

Here we can see the principle that Buddhism calls *dependent arising* or *dependent origination* (*Pratītyasamutpāda*). That is to say, the principle that something can only be, because it is part of a whole of things that must all arise together in order for any one of those things to be.

We can also see the principle of *cycles*, and the fact that in the greater scheme of things, none of the personalised members of the Trimurti are absolute.

The Emergence of Brahma

In the Mythology *Brahma* is said to emerge from an infinite lotus flower that itself emerges from *Viśnu*'s navel. The Lotus is the "standard" symbol in the Hindu picture, for things of great wonder and beauty, and actually, for the "structure" of consciousness as it expands into the exploration of its own possibilities.

This lotus that emerges from *Viśnu*'s body is not a *plant*, anymore than *Viśnu* is a human being. Any "lotus" referred to in this way in these mythological accounts is clearly a *symbol*. It's a symbol of something *transcendental* that cannot be understand just by conceiving it in a material way.

If there is any doubt about the meaning in these texts, of the *lotus*, and *lotus petals*, and seeds, and so on, any doubt about what lotuses and lotus petals and seed vessels are trying to portray, then one should consult the Padma Purana V.69.6-55; 60-78, or the Brahma Samhita 3-4; 26.

Lotuses and lotus petals, and the lotus pericarp or seed vessel, represent infinite *worlds of being*, of transcendental joys. They represent transcendental "places" or *dhāmas*. And furthermore, they represent transcendental "stories" of *being*.

On a sufficiently careful reading of the Padma Purana it is not difficult to see the portrayal of infinite "worlds within worlds", and "seeds" that when *entered into* are themselves infinite worlds of being (reference to "a thousand" in texts of this kind may be a synonym of "infinite").

In other Eastern texts they may be referred to as "jewels", and Indian texts such as the *Brihad Bhagavatamrita* refers to these features of transcendental *world of Being*, as "*cintāmani* jewels", the *cintāmani* then also occurring as the merely material "wish fulfilling stone" that exists in Indian culture.

Just as in mundane human existence we may imagine, or may enter into imagination as an alternative world of being, through something such as a "story" that we may hear, so in the transcendental context, at a far higher level of Reality, the *cintāmani* provides entry of consciousness into another world of being.

Although what we are talking about is literally inconceivable, in much more contemporary terminology, with its science and technology and mathematics, a conceptually comparable principle is encapsulated in objective form in infinite *fractal phenomena*. What mathematicians call "fractal geometry" in complex dimensions, is essentially a mathematical "landscape" that has these kinds of infinite characteristics.

Of course in these Puranic descriptions of the transcendental, we are not talking about *objective phenomena*, of that kind, rather, we are talking about transcendental *worlds* or *world of being*, and of *stories of being*, or *worlds of stories of being*.

We also see here, in the Padma Purana (V.69.70-78) that *Vrndavana*, the abode of Krsna, is the seed-vessel of an infinite-petalled lotus, and that it is 'non-different from Govinda's [Krsna's] "body". It is the abode of joy of (reaching) the complete *Brahman*'. In other words, the highest realisation of *Brahman*. Krsna "body" of course, means the Being of Krsna.

Note that the Purana says that Krsna's body, or the beautiful, transcendental, wider abode of Krsna called *Vrndavana*, is explicitly stated to be the joy of reaching *Brahman*'.[172]

In other words, even the *Brahman*, realised as Absolute, unconditional Being, liberated from all dependence on anything, shining with the infinite Radiance of its own Reality, is nonetheless not the realisation of the "complete *Brahman*". This is central to the Bhakti view.

Were we to consider the realisation of the *Brahman* Being as the spiritual equivalent of seeing and realising the Sun, then this text is saying that the full realisation of the Being, *as Krsna*, is by the same analogy equivalent to realising what is *within* the Sun.

The Purana is saying that the *world of Being* called *Goloka*, as the Being of Krsna Himself, spontaneously creates other *worlds of Being* and *stories of Being*, other places and *forests* and *groves*, and *pastimes*, within the infinite petals of this "lotus".

In *Harivamsha* we see that that this "lotus" that is the origin of Brahma, emerging from "Viśnu's navel", is eternal and *identical with the universe*.[173] It has infinite petals, is golden, and effulgent like the Sun.[174]

In the Padma Purana it is of infinite colours, bright like the sun, made of gold, bright like the blazing flames of fire, prominent and like the clear autumnal sun.[175]

Again these are visionary descriptions expressed in terms of, actually, phenomena that is already familiar to human beings. And it is very difficult for some human beings to realise precisely that they are *only visionary descriptions*.

So from what we have said it should begin to be clear that what emerges "from Viśnu's navel" is not just a personified person called

Brahma, just because in their mode of communication the Puranas *personalise* what they are talking about. The Padma Purana is perfectly explicit here.

This "lotus" of Brahma is *identical with the universe.*[176] But it is 'of infinite colours, bright like the sun, made of gold, bright like the blazing flames of fire, prominent and like the clear autumnal sun.' In other words, it *is* the universe, but still here essentially it is the universe in the image the totality of *Being* and *worlds of Being* from which it has come.

The Śiva Purana then also tells us that this "lotus" emerging "from Viśnu's navel" is *infinite*. But it does this, in the form of the story, by describing how Brahma attempts to explore the "lotus".

When Brahma narrates on his own origin, he says, referring to *Viśnu*, that he was deluded by His *Maya*, and did not know where he had come from, other than the lotus.[177]

For "body", remember, we are talking about "self", *being*, or *consciousness*. So Brahma asks himself "who am I"? He asks where he has come from, what is his duty, and to whom was he born a son? He wants to know by whom he has been created.[178]

Rather than remain confused Brahma decides that it will be easy enough to find the answer, by exploring the lotus. So he decides to go down the stalk to find the source of the lotus. But after descending for a hundred years, he cannot find it.

So then he decides to try to find the top of the Lotus. After another hundred years he cannot find the top, either. After a further hundred years of "wandering on the lotus" he finally receives Divine inspiration to perform penance, which he does for twelve years.[179]

And then at last as a result of the penance he has a vision of *Viśnu*, but does not recognise Him. Speaking as the narrator of the story, Brahma says he now realises that at the time he was deluded by *Śiva*'s *Maya*.

And now it is, that things start to get rather interesting. There are different accounts of the story, in different Puranas, highlighting different aspects. We, here, are going to draw on both the Śiva Purana and the Kurma Purana, to give a fuller account.

11

The First Great Dispute

In more than one culture, the Swan has been a symbol of purity, a symbol of the spiritual, of the Divine. Perhaps because its neck reaches up, like the spiritual path. And conversely, the boar symbolises the tenacious exploration in search of something, by rooting down. This represents self inquiry, and self-knowledge.

In our own existence, what there *is*, to go down into, is *ignorance*. It is ignorance of our self. It is the ignorance of human nature, but also the ignorance of the Being, our own true Identity. A journey down into ignorance, is often born of the search for the truth.

There is a spiritual principle that it is sometimes necessary to go down into something, something that is ignorance, in order to become enlightened with the knowledge of the truth of it, and to become free of it. One of the tacit messages in the Puranas is that material existence *as a whole*, is like this.

We don't all necessarily always have to be swans, as it were, in order to be on the spiritual path. Part of the spiritual path itself, involves being the boar, rooting down. And it is a "truth of *Śiva*", that one who we may see rooting down into ignorance like a boar, is often, like Śiva, only ignorance "on the outside".

In other words, in appearance only. Like *Śiva*, whom as we have already seen, is ignorance "on the outside", whilst goodness within. The cultural form of *Śiva* as a naked person covered in ash with matted hair, or in the Purana stories as a person who apparently behaves badly, is in part a symbol of this principle.

Of course, in the stories we have been looking at, as you will remember, the original *Śiva* remains forever in "the blissful forest", together with his lover, *Śivā*.

Except that he doesn't.

Because he also appears in numerous other stories, where he has "descended" into existence in these other stories, sometimes referred to as *Śiva*, and sometimes referred to as *Rudra*. And sometimes taking other forms. Because all this is possible, within *the expansion of being*.

So one of the ways in which this happens, is that *Śiva* becomes, through *the expansion of being*, *Viśnu*. Even though the *condition of being*, of *Viśnu*, is not *Śiva*. There is a difference between our *condition of being*, and the Being we are. The conditional experience of being is known in Hinduism as *svarūpa*. And when that conditional experience of being is created by *Śakti*, then it is a *svarūpa-śakti*. In the whole *expansion*, really, all *svarūpa* is *svarūpa-śakti*.

Viśnu of course, as we saw described in the Śiva Purana, is ignorance *within*, but goodness "on the outside". At the same time, as we have seen, *Viśnu* is a "nested expansion" of being, as the three *Viśnu*s.

The highest part of *Viśnu*'s Being is above the *Gunas*. It is above goodness, passion, and ignorance. It is Being, in realisation of the *Brahman*. And in the Bhakti texts, it is Being, in realisation of the transcendental Being and abode of Being, of Krsna.

The expansion of *Viśnu* isn't something that "floats" above the rest of the great *expansion of being*, separate from ordinary human existence. The expansion of *Viśnu* pervades the entire expansion of being, and becomes *Ksīrodakaśāyī Viśnu* (laying on "the Ocean of Milk"), who is "in the heart of" every living being (in material existence).[180]

As far as the aspect of *Viśnu* that has *Gunas* is concerned, the part that goes into the expansion, he would be ignorance *within*, of course, because he is a direct *expansion of being*, of *Śiva*. So in this sense, he is "outside" *Śiva*. And *Śiva*, as we know, is ignorance "on the outside".

Viśnu knows himself to be the *Brahman*, and this he declares in many places in the Puranas.[181] There, in his true Identity, he is free of condition, or qualities, or *Gunas*. But in the developing world of *Prakrti* and the ignorance of *Tamas*, where *Viśnu*'s *condition of being* appears, he is *Tamas within* and *Sattva* "on the outside". As the Purusa who enters the *Prakrti* of the expansion, he is without *Gunas*, but in his entering of the *Prakrti*, he is with *Gunas*.

Being *Tamas* or ignorance *within*, *Viśnu*, as a being considered "separate from" or "other than" the *Brahman*, simply *does not know himself*. As *Tamas* he is ignorant of what is "within" him. Nevertheless, his true Identity is the *Brahman*, which is all consciousness, knowledge, and bliss, and devoid of the *Gunas*.[182]

In that realisation, in knowing he is *Brahman*, in his realisation that he is *Brahman*, *Viśnu* transcends his *Prakrti*-bound *svarūpa*, he transcends this *condition of being* in which he has *Gunas*. Just as human beings, too, can also transcend human self, and realise "I am *Brahman*".

Viśnu, personified in Hinduism as the source of Brahma and "above" creation, has to explore this ignorance, he has to "dig down" into it, in order to enlighten it. This, by delegating the task to Brahma, he does eternally, in cycles. So just as *Śiva* maintains his position in "the blissful forest", and yet also descends by expansion into the world created through *the expansion of being*, so *Viśnu* does the same thing.

He maintains his position "out of existence", whilst *from him*, through *the expansion of being*, is created Brahma, who will literally "do the work" of this exploration, *down into existence* or *creation*. It is spoken of as *creation*, but it is a *rooting down* into the *ignorance*.

Brahma represents the beginning of that ignorance, in the descent. And so Brahma will have to "go up" in pursuit of the truth of his origins.

The Divine *dream within a dream*, continues on, and down, or out into this expansion and creation of existence, through the principle of *the expansion of being*, and *involution*. Which ends up in the thing that we do not yet understand, in the modern scientific world, called *the principle of the brain*.

In the Hindu picture, Brahma has neither goodness nor ignorance. As we have already seen, he is *Rajas* - passion or agitation - within and without. His *condition of being* is all *Rajas*.

Of course this condition of being is still something that is all part of the "ignorance" that we spoke of earlier, that is inherent in the *Prakrti*. And so it is that even *Viśnu* who frequently declares himself in the Puranas to be the supreme *Brahman*, because he *realises Brahman* is still ignorant when in his *condition of being* that is permeating the *Prakrti*. This ignorance is ignorance of the transcendental Life and Being that *Śiva* and *Śivā*, in "the blissful forest", represents.

And the only way out of this ignorance, the only way to transcend it, is by descending into the created existence that follows from this ignorance. That is, by descending into the world of the *Gunas*, the world created from *Prakrti*. Goodness alone, is not sufficient to do it. So by Grace (in the story, specifically by the Grace of *Śiva*), Brahma is created, in whose passion this exploration can be done.

Having been created by the descent, as it were, away from the transcendental, the need of Brahma and everything that Brahma creates is to go "up" in search of the truth, the Source. We will shortly see this depicted in the story. It is to reach up, in search of the Divine Source of our own experience of being.

But as passion, we cannot just go up and expect to find the Truth. We would never find the Source, that way. It has to be done *also* through the exploration of existence in the form of *Prakrti*, which is all the *Gunas*. All three *Gunas*, goodness, ignorance, and passion.

It has to be done through the exploration of our existence. Because, in terms of the *expansion of being*, in the Hindu picture we are made from both Brahma who reaches up to the Divine, and *Viśnu* who descends through Brahma, into the exploration of existence.

In the Hindu picture everything in this existence is in the domain of Brahma, through whom it has been created. We know Brahma's passion directly as our own passion. Whatever it may be passion *for*. Our "passion for life" is Brahma's *condition of being*. But passion is not Brahma's true Identity, nor is it our true Identity. That, in the first instance, is the *Brahman*. The supreme *Brahman* that is described in the corpus as being above all *Gunas*.[183]

So is the creation of *Brahman* we have to go "up". We will have to, as it were, assume the form of the Swan. As we will see, in due course.

The purpose of "being born", and having to explore existence, is to have the passion to *consciously pass through* the experience of it, and awaken from the illusion of it. The passion to do that, is the passion of Brahma's *condition of being*.

And the passion of existence (*Śakti* or the Earth, the Divine feminine) is to allow and create this exploration, for the sake of Divine Love.

Our existence is existential *Śiva*. It is the rendering of "the blissful forest" into the world of matter, time and space, sentience, and material being. It can only be known through the *Prakrti* of goodness, passion, and ignorance.

Existence and its exploration must be done where there is ignorance. It's something that only applies, as it were, on the "outside" of *Brahman*, or in terms of ascending towards the Divine, from *beneath* the *Brahman*. Whichever way you look at it, the exploration of existence is the exploration of ignorance of the Truth of the *Brahman*, the Being, the Being has no dependence on this existence.

What there is, "outside" the *Brahman*, or beneath it - depending on which way you want to look at it - is nothing but ignorance. Firstly, this is ignorance of the *Brahman*. But also, secondly, it is ignorance that is inherent in the expansion of the *Brahman* itself, where the *Prakrti* - the expansion and involution of the Being - arises. The *Brahman* isn't separate from us. It is *who we are*, as our true Self, when it is realised. But as the stuff of existence it is ignorance of its own Source. And even our first realisation of That Being, the *Brahman*, that is our true Identity, is nonetheless still ignorant.

When the realisation happens, the truth of the Self is realised, and the human *ignorance* of the Self, the *Brahman* Being that is our true Identity - is overcome and transcended. We are then free from that particular ignorance. However, that is not the end of the story because there is still ignorance.

There is something beyond the realisation of the Being as the Self, or as unconditional, Absolute Being, realised by *awakening as* That Being, beyond dependence on anything in existence.

Beyond it, it is realised that even this realisation of the Being, is only *an effect of ignorance*. The ignorance of the full creative power of That Being. The full creative power, that is *transcendental*, and not the "creation" that is the material world and our being in it. The full creative power that in its higher expansion is transcendental Life and Being.

Where there is still this ignorance, as there *is* in human existence, this ignorance *must* be explored. Which is why even though the Self is realised by a human being, the human being lives on.

All along, ignorance isn't something that *exists*, independently, separately, from the Reality of the Being. On the contrary, it is something that *doesn't exist*, and *has no reality*, except as illusion, *Maya*, happening in itself. Not independently of the Being, but *as* the *Maya* of the Being.

For as long as it takes, the journey into ignorance, the exploration of existence, recurs, until it disappears in the full awakening of the Being. The awakening into the conscious knowledge of the Reality of the Being, in its full creative power.

And so we shall see shortly the story in which *Viśnu* must become like a boar, in order to "root down", in search of the Source of this ignorance, whilst Brahma must become like a swan, in order to fly up in search of the Divine Source.

But both *Viśnu* and Brahma, each being *a condition of being*, are doing this eternally. As a condition of being, they never find the Source of themselves, by going down in goodness (which is what *Viśnu* does), or by going upwards in passion (which is what Brahma does).

Because existence, our material existence as human beings, the whole ocean of it, is like a mirror. A mirror in which the Truth, the truth of *Śiva* and *Śivā*, in "the blissful forest", is reflected. And our experience of it is this eternal going down and rising up, as in the Myth of *Viśnu* and *Brahma*. The living real Myth in which *Viśnu* is forever exploring downwards, and *Brahma* is forever striving upwards.

The Dispute

So getting back to the story, *Viśnu* then appears to Brahma, who has been searching for his Source, his progenitor. And finding that beautiful Being, he is struck with wonder.[184] But he does not recognise him. "Who are you", he asks.

There is no answer at first because that Eternal Being is asleep.[185] This is the main Mythological image of *Viśnu* asleep on the causal ocean. It is none other than Brahma who tries to awaken him. It is only *because* of Brahma, that *Viśnu* awakens. This is very important to realise. Brahma is an expansion of *Viśnu*. But it is only through Brahma, that *Viśnu* awakens. Brahma is necessary.

So because Brahma tries to awaken Him, which in the story require some effort, eventually, *Viśnu* awakens.

"Welcome, welcome to you, dear child", he says.[186]

Being all passion, Brahma is insulted. "How is it that you speak of me trivially as "Dear child", he retorts. "I am the creator of world, the direct activiser of *Prakrti*, unborn, the eternal, all-pervasive *Brahmā*. I am born of *Viśnu*. I am the soul of the universe, the originator, creator, and the lotus-eyed, and the excellent supreme Being. You must explain quickly why you speak like this".[187]

Viśnu then proceeds to put Brahma right on the matter, at length, and in no uncertain terms.

In the Śiva Purana account this angers Brahma and leads to a straightforward battle between Brahma and *Viśnu*. But the Kurma Purana account is deeper:

Firstly, *Viśnu* [*Nārāyana*] is sleeping on the couch of *Śeśa* [*Ananta Śeśa*, the infinite serpent].[188] He floats on the ocean (the causal ocean, or the milky ocean).

Viśnu assumes the form of 'one with thousand heads, thousand eyes, thousand feet, and thousand arms'.[189] This is a reference to *Purusa*, referring back to the Vedas in which there is the description of *Purusa* in these terms (in the Purusa Saktam).[190]

It is possible to regard this in the following way. When we fall asleep and start dreaming, we re-create a sense of self, and "I" in the dreamworld. This, by analogy, is the "*Purusa*" we have created, in the dreamworld.

While *Viśnu* is sleeping, a 'divine wonderful lotus that was the quintessence of the three worlds, shone in his umbilical region, for the sake of his diversion'.[191] (The three worlds are often interpreted as heaven, atmosphere and earth, or the physical, subtle and causal, and so on. They are "worlds" of Being within the "cosmic egg" of creation, and the Bhu mandala, which later in the corpus become many more "worlds". We will have more to say about "the worlds", later).

This is the "lotus" emerging from Viśnu's navel that we have already discussed. There then follows the confrontation between Brahma and *Viśnu* that we just described above. However, in the Kurma Purana account instead of developing into a battle, what happens next is that Brahma, knowing himself to be the creator of the universe, and knowing himself to contain the whole universe, he invites *Viśnu* to enter his "body" in order to see that this is the truth.

This, *Viśnu* does, after which he comes out of Brahma's mouth. Thus, in this sense, Brahma creates Viśnu. It has another meaning in that *Viśnu* becomes "the word of Brahma" (in the Vedas), but we are not going to go into that here.

Viśnu then invites Brahma to do the same, and to enter *his* "body". This Brahma does, by going back down the lotus. Whilst inside *Viśnu*, Brahma finds the self-same worlds (the universe), but inside *Viśnu*. While he is in there, *Viśnu* closes all the exits from his "body". However,

Brahma finds an opening in the navel, and emerges from the *Viśnu*'s navel. Essentially, we have "gone round in a circle". The whole play of the story represents expansion and involution.

So here we see how the *expansion of being* plays out in the inseparable relation of *Viśnu* and Brahma. The *expansion of being*, from the *Brahman*, creates, through *Śiva*, both *Viśnu* and then from further expansion, Brahma. Brahma is created by the continuing *expansion of being* "passing through" as it were, *Viśnu*, who is the first *expansion of being* from *Śiva*.

Although this has to be described as a "process" in the Puranas, the entire creation, maintenance and destruction, of "the universe" is not something that takes place "in time" as separate framework or theatre of action, from the *Maya* that it all is. Rather, everything is *already done*, and eternal, as *Śiva*. As stated in the passages in the Kurma Purana that we have been looking at, *Śiva* becomes time (*Kāla*) in order to create, protect, and destroy the universe.[192]

Time itself, in other words, is just an illusory form of *Śiva*. It is *Maya*. *Śiva* is eternal, and eternally in "the blissful forest". And everything that then appears to "happen in time" is just the "working out" (*karma*) of *ignorance*, ignorance of the full Truth of the Being, that is only transcended by *dying in Kāśī*. Which we have talked about earlier.

So there isn't really a situation in which there is *Viśnu* and then afterwards, another being called Brahma. Rather, Brahma is always already implied in *Viśnu*, just as *Viśnu* is already implied in Brahma. And the same thing applies to everything else that is created. Ultimately, the *Brahman* is implied in *us*. Actually, it all arises together, according to the principle that Buddhism then comes to recognise and understand as *dependent arising*, or *Pratītyasamutpāda*.

The Being (*Brahman*) expands somewhat like like waves on the shore, expanding from the greater ocean. Some waves break in one place, before going very far into shore, but they are "passed through" by other incoming waves, that then break further into shore.

This very principle persists even in the physics of material phenomena. We find it in the nature of waves in general. Not just waves in material water, but any waves, because it is in the *principle* of waves. Waves can "pass through", as it were, other waves. But also waves can *superpose* on each other, to create something new. And yet "hidden" in the new, so to speak, is still the original waves. The essential principle manifests even in pure mathematics in what is known as the Fourier series, and the Fourier transformation.

So getting back to the story, in which Brahma has just seen that both he and *Viśnu* each contain the same, whole universe, Brahma then says:

> "What is this that has been done by you, desirous of your own victory? I am the only powerful one and no one else. Who will dare attack me"?[193]

In the Purana, *Viśnu* appeases Brahma and asks him to be his son. Brahma, eventually realises that they are both the eternal *Brahman*, and agrees to this.[194]

However, he is still deluded and declares:

> "There is no superior ruler of the worlds other than we two. We, *Nārāyana*[195] [*Viśnu*] and *Brahmā* (the grandsire of the universe) are about one single body divided into two".[196]

Now this is not the truth. It is not the truth of the *Brahman*. The *Brahman*, the Being or Self, that has just been realised by Brahma, firstly, does not "divide" into two or into any other number. Rather, the *Brahman* undergoes what is described in the corpus as *expansion of being*, which we have already said so much about, and which is not the same thing as division.

Secondly, Brahma is confusing his realised own true Identity as *Brahman*, with his *conditional experience of being* (*svarūpa*) as Brahma. This is not unlike the situation in which a human being realises the Self,

(*Brahman*) and then mistakenly presumes their individual identity or personal self to be omniscient.

So in the story *Viśnu* attempts to correct Brahma. But Brahma insists:

> "Certainly I know myself as that Supreme imperishable Brahman, the sole *Ātman* [soul] of all the worlds, the highest region. There exists no other Supreme Ruler of the world other than we both".[197]

Viśnu then attempts to convince Brahma that he is still making a mistake, because he is deluded by the *Maya* of the Supreme Ruler.[198] He then remains silent.

But now *Śiva himself* who is not unaware of the dispute, manifests himself to confer Grace on Brahma.[199] Brahma does not recognise *Śiva*, but *Viśnu* helps him to realise who *Śiva* is. As he talks about *Śiva* to Brahma, he sees *Śiva* shining brilliantly in the translucent water, which is the "water" of creation (the causal ocean).[200]

In other words, really, the whole of our existence (creation) as we encounter it, is just the *reflection* of *Śiva*, in the waters. Material existence is literally a reflection of the Truth. The Truth of *Śiva*, who is the Divine couple (*Śiva* is His *Śakti*) in "the blissful forest".

The waters are the waters of creation, the causal ocean, and the ocean of milk. They are what we will later see, is *the churning of the ocean*. They are everything that as we will come to see, is "inside" the "cosmic egg" of what Hinduism calls "the universe". And where everything there, comes from, originally, is the *transcendental*.

The Linga

There is another account of how the dispute is settled, in the Śiva Purana. Here, *Śiva* sees that as a result of the fierce battle between *Brahmā* and *Viśnu* the world is about to meet untimely dissolution. So to assuage the weapons he assumes the form of a huge column of fire in the midst of *Brahmā* and *Viśnu*.[201]

The Śiva Purana tells us that the weapons were enough to destroy the entire world, and yet they fill in to the column of fire. This made *Brahmā* and *Viśnu* wonder what this amazing column of fire was. They realised it was "beyond the range of the senses", and they determined to find its top and bottom.[202]

What has appeared, a form of *Śiva*, is known as the *Linga*.

Brahma recognises the *Linga* as the great *Ātman* (*Brahman*).[203] In order for this pair of deities to find the root of it at the bottom, and the top of it, *Viśnu* assumes the form of a boar and goes in search of the root, whilst Brahma in the form of a swan goes up in search of the top.[204]

Neither succeeded in their quest. The Vāyu Purana says *Viśnu* went downwards for a thousand years and still could not find the root.[205] The descriptions indicate that the effulgent *Linga* is infinite.

Brahma, however, on his way up, meets a *Ketakī* flower 'of mysterious nature' falling from above.[206]

Unknown to Brahma, the *Ketakī* flower has fallen from *Śiva*, who is shaking his head laughing at *Viśnu* and Brahma's dispute. Although the flower has been falling for many years, 'neither its fragrance nor its lustre has been diminished even a bit'. It was intended to bless *Viśnu* and Brahma.[207] We can take the *Ketakī* flower as a representative of "the blissful forest".

Brahma then asks the *Ketakī* flower "Who has been wearing you, and why are you falling"? The flower replies:

> "I am falling down from the middle of this primordial column that is inscrutable. It has taken me a long time. Hence I do not see how you can see the top".[208]

Brahma then persuades the *Ketakī* flower to be a false witness for him back at the battleground, where he intends to say untruthfully that he has found the top of the infinite column.[209]

This trick is of course visible to *Śiva*, as a result of which, Brahma gets the fifth of his five heads chopped off,[210] leaving him with the famous four heads of his cultural image.

Notice that the *Ketakī* flower is found falling from the "middle of the column". It represents the truth, the truth of "the blissful forest" where *Śiva* and *Śivā* are, the truth of the transcendental. But it cannot truly bear witness to that, because it has fallen. And if we ever find the *Ketakī* flower in our ascent, and claim it as evidence of our reaching the top, whilst we are still in the domain of Brahma, then it is not the truth.

12

Sex and Divine Love

Now let's unpack some of this.

This *Śiva Linga* in the story is something whose manifestation is variously described in different Puranas. But essentially, as in the Purana stories we have already related, it is an *infinite*, effulgent column, often described as a column of "fire". It goes infinitely "up" and it goes infinitely "down".

It is *Śiva*, who is the *Brahman*, manifesting in a particular form. This is perfectly explicitly stated in the Śiva Purana. The fact that it is a column of "fire" is not merely incidental. "Fire" in Hindu cosmology is part of the "coverings" of the "egg" of Brahma, one of the so-called "elements". We will come to talk about these in detail, later.

Essentially, though, "fire" is the last "stage", in the Hindu description, in the "descent" from the "unmanifest one" or *Avyakta*, to "Earth", before the matter of the "Earth" is created. Descending, as it were, from *Avyakta* to Earth, there are various "stages", which we will come to talk about later, ending in what are usually called "the elements". As we will discuss in detail later, these are not "elements" in the scientific sense of being "simpler components".

As we shall see later, each "stage" leads to the next, but actually, all "stages" are infinite, interpenetrating, and really, there are infinitely many "stages" or "coverings" of the "egg". All this we will come to look at in more detail later. So "fire" is the last "stage" before "Earth", or matter.

What "fire" actually consists of, what goes on *inside* "fire", so to speak, in order to create the matter of the "Earth", is not something that the descriptions of this "descent" in the Puranas really talk about.

However, one way that it appears, in this part of the Puranas, is as the Linga. Firstly, it is a symbolic manifestation of *the infinite*, that is, the *infinite Being* of *Śiva* (*Brahman*). That it represents infinity, is clear from the story. One way of considering this, is to say that because the Linga is a manifestation of *Śiva*, who is infinite, then the Linga is infinite. But its infinity is of a different kind, because it is this "fire", through which is created "Earth" or matter.

The Puranas often tend to segregate different aspects of the great picture or scheme of things that they are representing. When we pull them together, we start to see the bigger picture.

The most salient feature here, not mentioned in this particular story about the dispute between *Viśnu* and Brahma, is that the Linga, the "fire", is also about sex. But the reference to this is only elsewhere in the Puranas. We will come back to this shortly.

Because the *Linga* is a manifestation of *Śiva*, it is of course connected with what *Śiva* in the Purana story means and represents. This, principally, is that *Śiva* is the *manifest form* of the *Brahman* Being, as explicitly stated in the Śiva Purana. But it is also that *Śiva* remains eternally in "the blissful forest" together with his Divine lover *Śivā*, as the Divine couple. Which as we have seen, is also explicitly stated.

It is through the manifest form of the *Brahman* being, as the Linga, and the so-called "element" called "fire", that the "Earth" is manifested, which is our own existence in matter. In this way, "the blissful forest" is translated into matter, it descends through Brahma, the "egg", to Earth. Where for the most part, in human experience, it has become lost in translation.

The Linga

In the story we have been looking at, both *Viśnu* and Brahma fail to find the top or the bottom of the great *Linga* that appears before them. Of course, this is because it is infinite.

Infinity is also represented in *Ananta Śesa*, the serpent who forms the "couch" on whom *Viśnu* floats, on the ocean. *Ananta* means "infinite" and *Śesa* means "remainder". *Ananta Śesa* extends from the ocean, on which he literally supports *Viśnu*, to a position above *Viśnu*'s head.

This arrangement is reflected in kundalini yoga in which the "serpent" of the kundalini energy (Kundalini being implicitly female, by the way) is drawn up from the lower regions to the top of the head, and above the top of the head.[211]

In Christianity the serpent in the garden of Eden has been considered to be representative of sex, and in kundalini yoga, and in various forms of Vajrayana Buddhism and meditation, it is also sex energy that is "raised", in the various meditation techniques. Parts of the Hindu corpus explicitly mention yogis "drawing semen up to the head", but parts of Vajrayana Buddhism meditation involve the "white drop" that "falls" from its psychic position. However, the point of this is the transmutation into higher consciousness, and so that also constitutes a "raising".

Ananta Śesa ("infinite remainder") essentially refers to infinite cycles of conditional experience of being created from "what remains as ignorance". This ignorance is everything created through the causal ocean on which *Viśnu* floats. Not only does *Ananta Śesa* keep *Viśnu* afloat, preventing him from sinking into the ocean, but also, *Ananta Śesa* reaches from the ocean to above *Viśnu*'s head. The knowledge that *Ananta Śesa* represents literally "goes above *Viśnu*'s head".

The "process" of infinite cycles of conditional *being-time* (the cycles of birth and death) is only escaped from, by *awakening* from the whole process, into the "unmanifest" that is "outside" the "cosmic egg" or "egg of Brahma" (*Brahmanda*). Brahma is the Mahat,[212] the Great Principle, and the "outer shell" of the "egg" is the causal ocean, beyond which, is the *Brahman*.

In terms of the Mythological imagery, this awakening is clearly the awakening of *Viśnu*, who in the well-known Mythology, falls asleep on the causal ocean, floating on *Ananta Śesa*, and is periodically awoken by Brahma, who himself has emerged from *Viśnu*'s navel. In human terms, the awakening is our own awakening into the realisation of the Being.

However, as the Śiva Purana reveals, beyond the Truth of *Viśnu* is the Truth of *Śiva*. This is the Truth that *Ananta Śesa* reaches up towards.

The Truth of *Viśnu* is the impersonal *Brahman* behind the appearance of the whole mandala (called the Bhu mandala) of matter and our own material existence. Beyond that Truth of *Viśnu* is the still higher Truth of *Śiva*. In terms of Krsna-Bhakti the higher truth of *Viśnu* is Balarama (often referred to as Krsna's brother) and finally, of course, Krsna.

Viśnu could be called the Truth of the unconditional Being, as we may realise That Being in our existence. *Śiva* could be called the hidden order in existence as we experience it. Or more specifically, as we experience "moving" through it, through our experience of being born, and then the continual process of change and ageing as we "grow up", with all its crazy "ups" and "downs", as we "move" through all our life experiences, continually ageing, and eventually dying. In Western terms, *Śiva* is *Gnostic.*

We mentioned how the Śiva Purana talks about *Kaśi* as another name for "the blissful forest". To say *Śiva* and *Śivā* are in "the blissful forest" is the same as saying *Śiva* and *Śivā* are in *Kaśi.*

Mostly, for most of the human population, we don't "die in *Kaśi*", as the Śiva Purana talks about, in the deeper, metaphysical sense (nor in the mundane sense - *Kaśi* is also a name of an actual place in India).

Dying in *Kaśi* as far as the material existence is concerned essentially refers to ego death. But *transcendentally*, it refers to the expansion of the Being into its own "reflection", as it were, in the form of the Divine couple. Through the conjugal "mixing" of the Divine couple, the full Love of the Being, comes to be known by the Being.

In other words, the Being appears as Radha and Krsna, or Laksmī and Nārāyana, and so on, in whose conjugal union as Laksmī-Nārāyana or Radha-Krsna, and so on, is the awakening of the Being into the Knowledge of its own Love.[213]

The truth of *Śiva*, as the Śiva Purana makes clear, is none other than *Śiva* and *Śivā* "in *Kaśi*", as the *transcendental lovers*, in "the blissful forest". We may still get a glimpse of *Kaśi* in the deeper sense, a glimpse of *Śiva*, distilled out of human experience, even in the human condition. Translated into our existence as human beings, "the blissful forest" of the conjugal love of *Śiva* and *Śivā* becomes the ideal of the Earth that the material Earth and nature represents, and the play or enjoyment of the Being as *Śiva* and *Śivā* becomes in translation the relation between human lovers, and conjugal love in material bodies.

There is hidden order in the dream (of *Viśnu*) in which we are engaged. This order comes from *Śiva*. This Truth of *Śiva* is not just the Truth of the *Brahman* from which arises our own existence, and which is Viśnu's Truth, but it also contains the knowledge of the hidden sexual order in the whole mandala of our existence.

We can take this order in the mandala (the Bhu mandala) to be what we unwittingly experience in our ordinary everyday life as a human being, as the meaningful nonsense that we are invariably fooled by, according to the narratives that we attach ourselves to. Especially regarding love and sex. Behind those narratives is this one Supreme Truth behind the nature of the whole mandala, which is encapsulated in the Śiva Purana, as the Divine Couple, *Śiva* and *Śivā*, in "the blissful forest". Alternatively, in the Bhakti texts, this underlying order is encapsulated in Radha-Krsna, and especially in the *Rasa Dance*.

So the *hidden order* in this mandala of our experience as human beings, is, in terms of the Śiva Purana, this Truth of *Śiva*. Whilst the unconditional nature of the Being that we really are, is represented in *Viśnu*.

Śiva appears not "in" but *as* this mandala. But He also appears "in" this mandala because every part of this mandala is already *Śiva*. And then again, *Śiva* only appears as this mandala in the first instance, literally through his love, *Śivā*, who is already a transcendental *expansion* of *Śiva*, as His *Maya*, and His *Śakti*. So the whole of this mandala, all of material existence, is *Śakti*. Who is *Śiva*'s *Śakti*.

As a human being we experience the mandala as this world of being that we inhabit as human beings. Our *world of being* is not just the material world separate from our body. It includes *everything* about our *experience of being*. That is, self, mind, psyche, thoughts, imagination, emotion, and so on. *All of it*, the inner and the outer, the material and the immaterial, is the mandala - the mandala of our own conditional experience of being as a human being - as we experience it.

In the Purana story of the Linga, *Viśnu*, through whom Brahma emerges in order to bring about the creation of the mandala, roots *down* the *Linga* to try to find the bottom. Because he is going down, he takes the form of a boar who roots down deep, looking for the prize. The descent is infinite, just as the *expansion of being* is infinite. Just as the mandala is infinite.

At the same time as *Viśnu* goes down, Brahma tries to fly to the top. Because he is going up, he takes the form of a swan. The clue that "the blissful forest" of *Śiva* and *Śivā* is up there, is in his encountering a Ketakī flower that is falling down. Because it has come from the Truth, it has, as the story in the Śiva Purana relates, lost none of its fragrance or beauty.

But even the Ketakī flower, now that it is falling, has no knowledge of where it has come from. The meaning is that is not possible to find "the blissful forest" as an upper limit of the *Linga*. The *Linga* is not the nature of the transcendental Life and Being that it represents. Rather, the *Linga* is another representation of the entire Bhu mandala, everything that is created through the "egg of Brahma".

There is something else in all this, that we should be conscious of. We can put it like this: In order for *Viśnu* to take the form of a boar, there first has to be the idea of a boar. In order for Brahma to take the form of a swan, there first has to be the idea of a swan.

In terms of the great *expansion of being*, this is *Viśnu* and Brahma entering into something that is already part of the great *expansion of being*. The boar and the swan are already *Prakrti*. So here, *Viśnu* and Brahma are each a Purusa, entering into the *Prakrti*.

When any part of Being in any part of the expansion enters into a part of the expansion, that Being is essentially the aggregate of what has been entered into. So, for example, *Garbhodakaśāyī Viśnu* is the Supersoul of the aggregate of living entities,[214] and his expanded form is *Ksīrodakaśāyī Viśnu* who is "in the heart of" every living being (in material existence).[215]

Garbhodakaśāyī Viśnu is, we could say, more "energetic" than *Ksīrodakaśāyī Viśnu*. But *Garbhodakaśāyī Viśnu* is an expansion of *Kāranodakaśāyī Viśnu*, and so we could say *Kāranodakaśāyī Viśnu* is in turn more "energetic" than *Garbhodakaśāyī Viśnu*. And so on, all the way up to the Supreme Being of inconceivable energy.

If *Viśnu* takes the form of a boar and Brahma takes the form of a swan, indeed, when any being takes the form of "another" being, in a world in which there are conceptual forms, such as the boar and the swan, what does this represent? This does not just happen in Hindu Mythology. Beings taking the form of "other" beings, or who are even represented as "taking over" other beings who have already taken form, is also part of other Mythologies, not least the Greek Myths.

In terms of the Hindu picture it would represent part of ongoing involution and expansion, in which the *Prakrti* is entered by Purusa. Or perhaps more accurately, at later stages in the great expansion, is once again *re-entered*. Because these are infinite cycles of entry of the Purusas into the *Prakrti*. That, after all, is the nature of infinite involution.

Now suppose there is a point in this involution where expansion and involution reaches a kind of limit, so that the expansion or *Prakrti* undergoes an eversion, from involution to evolution. It begins to create a world *lila* that has the *potential to be* - although it isn't yet that - what we now know as physical matter, time, and space. This of course is the stuff of our sentient *body-mind* experience of being in a world in which our immediate somatic field of experience of being a bodily self is part of what takes place in a surrounding world of this material phenomena.

Such a world, unrealised, still *as potential only*, in the now evolving expansion of being, is still essentially *Prakrti*. But at a given point in what is now its expansion as *evolution*, *Prakrti* would be ripe for the entry of the descended Purusa (of Viśnu or Krsna) into this *Prakrti*. Whereupon Purusa experiences this *evolutionary energy* of itself as the reflection, in this exciting *evolutionary* medium, of the Purusa's own energy.

Here, the already conditional experience of being is able to enter into its own expansion, to experience the being of that expansion, as a new kind of evolutionary *svarūpa*. A new kind of self, that is the representation of all that is happening in this tremendously condensed evolutionary expansion, as bodily being in this new theatre of being.

Without the entry of the Purusa, the *Prakrti* is nothing materially, nothing but a possibility, inherent as a structure of interrelations between the consequences of the expansion of the Purusa as it is. We cannot say whether this Purusa is *devolving from* the Being, the *Brahman*, into this primordial light or soup of *Prakrti*, or evolving towards the *Brahman*, the Being free from the need of *Prakrti*. It is both. We can even see this Purusa as having *evolved from* this primordial soup of *Prakrti*.

In any case, this ripe new theatre for conditional experience of being, would offer a completely new kind of experience of being, and world of being, as much to be *awoken into*, from within the primordial soup, as *entered into*, from "above", by Purusa.

But it would be highly charged with both the energy of separation (the illusion of separate beings) and the whole energy of the eversion through which this new dream of conditional experience of being comes about. It would be an entry, that across the aggregate of all the ignorance in the *Prakrti*, would be of Bacchanalian proportions.

Essentially, and in Mythical terms, what we are talking about here, is where, through the sleep and dreaming of *Viśnu*, through the churning of his mind as the Śiva Purana calls it,[216] the causal ocean, the expansion of *Viśnu*, finally comes to the shore, as the primordial "egg". The shore of the land that is the beginning of this new possibility of material experience of being, before, in a manner of speaking, the *saptadvīpa* even begins to form.

Again, does the *saptadvīpa* that we all know about from reading the Puranas, evolve out of experience of being in the middle of Brahmanda, the "egg", or does the *saptadvīpa* devolve from the Being, the *Brahman*, descending into the "egg"? Again, we cannot say, it is both.

The colours of the rainbow do not form from violet to red, or from red to violet. They are just inherently there, in the nature of sunlight and rain or atmosphere, even if we see a rainbow forming one colour at a time. And really, there are no such colours except by virtue of how we see them. From the point of view of physics, they are just zones in a spectrum of electromagnetic wavelengths. This is essentially how we should understand the whole nature of our mind, and, indeed, the description of it as a arising through the expansion of being. For a description of the nature of the mind we are being, is indeed what the Hindu picture of *Brahmanda*, is.

Consider then, this point of eversion in the expansion of being, where involution becomes evolution. The Purusas then enter this world, taking the form of "other" beings, contributing to the great eversion, by their awakening "other" beings into this new conditional experience of being. It happens in an orgy of formation, and its attendant unconscious creation of further consequences, which are the evolutionary, lower past, the evolution coming up, as it were, to meet the involution.

How would we describe this, in terms of the involution of the highest Being, *Brahman*, Krsna or the *Viśnu*, into the *Śakti* of its own expansion? This turning from involution into evolution, this eversion, of *Prakrti* into the material, is where - in the exploration in the great expansion of being and creation of time, the Divine Being, setting out from the eternal "blissful forest" - transcendental Love or *Prema*, or the conjugal Love and Life of the Divine couple, finally "falls asleep" in the *Prakrti* it has been creating, still intoxicated with that higher past. Only to become intoxicated with the liquor of the entry into this lower evolutionary expansion.

It is here that we would meet the first metamorphoses for the sake of sexual intoxication. It is here that the Divine yoga or union of the Divine couple, stumbles on the path of expansion towards the evolving creation of material sex.

We might alternatively talk about this in terms of the Divine couple, Krsna and Radha, exhausted after their transcendental sporting, resorting to rest in the root of a transcendental tree. Hinduism's Ashvattha tree is an *inverted tree*, with its roots in the Truth, and in the proliferation of its branches everything that has been expanded from that Truth, as the evolving world.

In their transcendental sporting the Divine couple were enjoying the expansion of being in the transcendental groves of *Vrndavana*, where their proper pastimes above time had not even entered the vernal "air" or "wind" on all sides, which would then become the "water", the ocean, and then the "fire", and then the material Earth.

A complete description appears in the Padma Purana, of how Krsna and Radha, after their sporting, "endowed with vernal breezes on all sides", fall to the root of a tree and "drink liquor". They fall asleep holding each other's hands, under the influence of Cupid, and "stumbling on the path" sport like a female elephant with the male of the herd. The passage tells us that Krsna assumes multiple bodies in order to satisfy all the female elephants, and afterwards take them with his beloved to the lake for more sporting.[217]

What is this but the creation of sex out of the primordial light? In the Srimad Bhagavatam also, Krsna is said to be like an intoxicated elephant with his she-elephants.[218]

Just as *Siva* and *Śivā* remain always in "the blissful forest" despite the expansion of being, so also we are told that the gopīs [cowherd women who were Krsna's lovers] always had their desires fulfilled by Krsna, but that these "transcendental affairs" do not constitute mundane sex desire as known by human beings.[219]

We are talking about the cusp between the transcendental and the material. The eversion can only be described in the stuff of Myth. Which in turn serves as the Mythical explanation of the origin of what in our experience, is the lower human energy and experience of sex.

As far as the Hindu picture is concerned it is all, all of it, still *Maya*. Such a thing would indeed be a Myth. But then, so is the human experience of self and world, as it stands.

Conjugal Love of God

Naturally, this *Śiva Linga* as it appears in the Purana story, because it *is Śiva*, represents *Śiva* and *Śivā* as the Divine Couple in "the blissful forest". Their eternal conjugal love in union becomes of course, further out in the great *expansion of being*, the Divine union of Purusa and *Prakrti.*

That union of Purusa and *Prakrti* first occurs in the "first Purusa", most often said to be *Viśnu* (*Maha-Viśnu*) and his *Maya*, his *Śakti*. The Bhakti tradition may refer to the "first Purusa" as Balarama.

The well-known *personified representation* of Viśnu's *Śakti* as his consort or wife, is *Lakśmī*. But of course, *Viśnu* is already an expansion of *Śiva and Śivā,* in "the blissful forest", eternally above the whole cyclic creation process.

The conjugal love of the Divine Couple, is *transcendental to* the Bhu mandala itself. In Hinduism this conjugal love is what reveals the realisation of God Himself, or in transliterated Sanskrit, *Svayam Bhagavān* or *Bhagavān Svayam*.[220]

The '*Svayam Bhagavān*' term for God or the what Bhakti calls the *Supreme Personality of Godhead*, appears in the Śrīmad Bhāgavatam, and extensively in the Caitanya-caritamrta, in all three *lilas*, and elsewhere, such as the Brahma Samhitā.

In the Puranas and Upanishads, the declaration "I am *Brahman*", declared by any being who realises *Brahman*, or as recited as a mantra by an aspirant seeking that realisation, is a salient feature of these scriptures. But in these sources, no being, even when realising the *Brahman* Being as their own true Identity, no being able to declare "I am *Brahman*", necessarily also realises what Bhakti calls *Bhagavān Svayam.*

This is because the realisation "I am *Brahman*" is the realisation of the Self, but is not yet the full transcendental realisation of the glory of *Bhagavān Svayam*, the glory of God, and transcendental Life and Being, which Krsna-Bhakti calls *Krsna*, as *Radha-Krsna* in Vrndavana.

The impersonal realisation of the *Brahman* is itself something that has different aspects and "levels". At a deep level it is still God realisation, but it's not necessarily complete in the awakening of knowledge and realisation of *Bhagavān Svayam.*

Svayam means "Self" or "One's Self".[221] It is sometimes translated as "personally". *Bhagavān* is given the meaning 'God', or 'the Supreme Lord', or 'the Supreme Personality of Godhead', in various contexts, depending on the source. In the Krsna-Bhakti Hindu texts such as the Caitanya-caritamrta, the Śrīmad Bhāgavatam, and the Brihad Bhagavatamrita, only the transcendental original Being, Krsna, is *Svayam Bhagavān.*

It is only in these texts that the knowledge of transcendental Reality begins to be revealed. So the realisation of the *Brahman* is the realisation of the unconditional Being, and the Being is indeed the Being of God. But this realisation is not necessarily the realisation of the *Brahman* as *Bhagavān Svayam.*

In this Bhakti representation, Radha is the transcendental expansion of Krsna, so that Krsna is able to enjoy conscious knowledge of conjugal love of the Being, the highest *rasa* in Bhakti. This conjugal love is literally the love of the Being.

In these terms, in our human existence we generally only encounter conjugal love *through* ignorance inherent in the *Prakrti* in which we arise. We experience it "translated down", as it were, in our love of another human being. Another human being who as a being, appears to be separate from us. But this separation is only an appearance brought about by the part of the great expansion of being, that is the Bhu mandala. This is *Maya*.

Really, we *are* the Being. We are the Being engaged in a play, or *lila*, of separateness. In the Hindu depiction this illusion of separateness is created through *Prakrti*. And *Prakrti* is the three *Gunas*. And the three *Gunas* can be understood as goodness, ignorance, and passion. The truth, the Being, and transcendental Life and Being, is beyond even goodness in this existence.

To bring the three *Gunas* into "equilibrium", means that there is not turbulence. Rather, there is stillness. There is still ignorance, there is still passion, but they are experienced in the stillness of the transpersonal consciousness that we already really are.

And through that, what Hinduism calls "the unmanifest one" - which is who we in any case really are - is realised. The highest potential in human experience itself, is the awakening of this conjugal love of the Being.

Śiva and *Śivā* in "the blissful forest", as depicted in the *Śiva* Purana, is the Śiva Purana's alternative representation of what in Bhakti texts is Krsna and Radha in Goloka. It doesn't really matter whether you want to interpret *Śiva* and *Śivā* in "the blissful forest" as being a different kind of account of Krsna and Radha in Goloka but with a less full exposition, or as an account of a further *expansion* of Krsna and Radha in Goloka.

However, some might want to take the descriptions of *the Dalliances of Satī and Śiva* given in the Śiva Purana[222] as an expansion of the pastimes of Krsna and Radha in Goloka, because the Dalliance of *Satī* and *Śiva* are said to take place on the Himalayas. The Himalayas are part of the material realm, that is, they are part of creation "inside the egg", whilst Goloka has a clearly transcendental meaning in the Bhakti texts.

In the Hindu picture, the transcendental Divine union becomes the union between male and female, as *Purusa entering Prakrti*, and finally we find it as the sexual union of material human beings.

But in Hinduism, this union, where it begins, before reaching that degree of expansion, is in the transcendental realm. This appears in its fullest description in the part of the corpus that deals with as the *transcendental pastimes* of Radha and Krsna. This is something that most people can relate to very easily, just at the superficial, literal level. But its true meaning is much deeper.

The account of *Śiva* and *Śivā* in "the blissful forest" given in the Śiva Purana, is not really in contradiction to the accounts of Radha-Krsna in the Krsna-Bhakti parts of the corpus. The Krsna-Bhakti texts about the Divine *pastimes of Krsna* deal with the relations of Krsna and his lover Radha, and with the *gopis* (cowherd girls). It is true, this does have a much less developed counterpart in the Śiva Purana's account the Dalliance of *Satī* and *Śiva*. But nevertheless, essentially, in one way or another, *Śiva* is as an alternative representation of transcendental Krsna.

The salient connection between the two is transcendental Life and Being.

The Linga Again

Let's return now to talking about the *Śiva Linga*.

As stated in the Śiva Purana and other Puranas, the *Śiva Linga*, that manifests during the dispute between Viśnu and Brahma, is *Śiva*. It is the same *Śiva* who as the Śiva Purana tells us, is eternally in "the blissful forest" with his consort *Śivā*, who is his *Śakti*. They are the Divine couple. But this manifest Linga is as seen from within the Bhu mandala.

The Śiva Purana describes the *Linga* as 'a terrific form of a huge column of fire'.[223] The Linga Purana describes 'a brilliant Linga' with 'thousands of clusters of flames'. It goes on to say that it is comparable to hundreds of fires, and does not diminish or increase. It also tells us that it has no beginning, middle, or end, and basically, is the incomprehensible source of the universe. We are told that both Lord *Viśnu* and Brahma were deluded by it. They both then seek to "test this fiery Being".[224]

The Kurma Purana compares it to the end of the world, and also states that it has no increase or decrease, beginning, middle, or end.[225]

The Kurma Purana also explicitly states that the *Linga* is 'the Supreme form of the *Brahman*'.[226] Why the supreme form? Specifically, because it is the Truth of *Śiva* and *Śiva* in "the blissful forest", it is their combination, their union. This supreme form of the Brahman is one and the same as *Krsna*, who expands as the Divine couple Krsna and Radha, in the Krsna-Bhakti part of Hinduism.

The Linga, as is often not understood, is the *combination* of the "male" and the "female". It's not just symbolic of the male part.

Śiva, as we have already said, is the *manifest form* of the *Brahman*. *Śiva* takes many forms in the Puranas, in some of the stories appearing essentially as wisdom in the disguise of ignorance. But here we are seeing that the *Supreme form* he takes is the *Linga*, which is symbolised in the story as an infinite column of fire, but is also symbolised as a phallic object. So the *Linga* is known to the Western mind as phallic, and is consequently sometimes misinterpreted as a sex-cult object. This is a very crude misunderstanding.

The *Linga* as it appears in the story of the dispute between *Viśnu* and Brahma, is indeed the source of the *phallic emblem* worshipped as *Śiva* in Hinduism.[227] But the meaning of this has possibly not been widely understood in the West. And as the Śiva Purana itself explains, the origins of worship of phallic emblems in general, has its roots in the transcendental *Śiva Linga* that we encounter in the dispute between Brahma and Viśnu.[228]

The *Linga* doesn't represent just the male organ. The Śiva Purana is quite explicit about this. It represents the *unification and fusion* of *Śiva* and *Śakti*, as *Śivā-Śiva*.[229] The *Śivā-Śiva* relation and energy is of course the equivalent in terms of *Śiva* and *Śakti*, of the Radha-Krsna relation and energy, in Krsna-Bhakti.

It is through the combining of the two *principles*, of *Śiva* and *Śakti*, or indeed Radha and Krsna, even well out into the great *expansion of being*, that the Divine Source of *Śiva* and *Śakti*, the *Bhagavān Svayam*, can be realised.

In the world of *Prakrti*, in materiality, the merging of the principles can bring about the realisation of the Purusa. And so the Śiva Purana tells us that the unification and fusion of the symbols of *Śiva* and *Śakti* is called *Linga*.[230]

In the Hindu culture the human-made idol object called the *Śiva Lingam* is indeed a phallic emblem, as it is clearly called in the Śiva Purana.[231] But the context is not easily seen by mainstream Western mind. In the full Hindu picture, the *Linga* is the *combination* of God with the *expansion* of God, in the *Prakrti* that creates the universe.

To say it again, what Hinduism calls the Linga is not, as we have already said, just the male part. On the contrary, it is already the fusion of both the "male" and the "female", where the "female", *Śakti*, is the radiant expansion of the Divine.

The Whole Universe Is the Linga

So in the Hindu picture there is nothing, really, in material existence, that is not the "phallus". Not when it is understood that by "phallus" we are talking about the *combination* of the male and female principles. The *Linga* and the *Yoni* (the female part) are not *separable*. Their very appearance as *separated* things, is *Maya*. And so it is that the Śiva Purana tells us there is no limit to the number of phallic images. In fact, it states, the entire universe is in the form of a phallus.[232]

It is necessary to understand this before attempting to interpret the meaning of the *Linga*. Also, one must understand how sex is viewed in the Hindu corpus in general, and therefore where the *Linga* is in relation to that view.

As far as Hinduism is concerned, the whole of the created universe, *and its destruction*, is all the *Linga*. The Reality of the Linga is the *infinite unmanifest* into which the universe merges and dissolves, but it is also the material cause of the universe. It is the "body" or *svarūpa* of *Śiva* and *Śivā*, combined, and is *Siva*'s state of Being as *Linga*.[233] It is also, in terms of Bhakti, the *svarūpa* of Krsna and Radha, in their conjugal union. Bhakti calls this consciousness *Chaitanya*.

In this way, the material world is *Śiva* in existential form. Or, if you prefer, if you are in the Bhakti tradition, it is Krsna. However, as the Śiva Purana states about *Śiva* and *Śivā*, their having the *Linga* as their body (their *svarūpa*) is not the ultimate Reality.[234]

The Śiva Purana states that the *Linga* is only the "body" of *Śiva* and *Śivā* 'in a secondary sense'.[235] This "body" (or *svarūpa*) of *Śiva* and *Śivā* combined, in other words the *Linga*, is in fact, we are clearly told, the great *Śakti* of *Śiva*, and none other than the great Ātman (the Being). Its glory cannot be described even in a hundred years, and both Viśnu and Brahma were deluded by it at the outset.[236]

And yet it is not the ultimate Reality.[237] The Ultimate Reality is still the Being. The *Linga* is the manifestation of the Being of *Śiva*, it is the creation of material existence. Material existence itself is ignorant of the Being. But it is necessary for ignorance to transcend itself, and come to know the Being, because it *is* the Being, and only in this way can this aspect of the Being come to know its Self.

"Let us test this fiery Being",[238] said *Viśnu* when the transcendental *Linga* manifested to *Viśnu* and Brahma. And as we have seen above, the entire Earth, the entire universe, is a manifestation of the Being, and is in the form of what Hinduism calls the phallus. So the exploration of the Linga, upwards and downwards, by Brahma and *Viśnu*, respectively, is what *we* are engaged in, in our exploration of our conditional experience of being as human beings.

Of course, part of that conditional experience of being, *the very thing that brings us into existence*, is what we call sex. In these terms, the whole of material existence is *Śakti*, which is the expansion of the Being. But it is a part of the great expansion that comes through something that then we experience, in our conditional experience of being, as sex.

Sex, not the sex act, but sex itself, doesn't have a beginning, and it doesn't have an end. Even if you transcend it, it carries on, where it has not been transcended. Material existence comes through it, because there is no material or mineral existence that is not a construct of brain function.

So the Linga, the phallus, the material world or universe that we live in, doesn't have a bottom, and it doesn't have a top. You cannot discover its origin, its root, by going down to try to find it by reductionism or measurement. If you do that, you end up with infinity and zero. And no matter how high you spiritually rise, within it, you can only ever pretend that you have found the top, perhaps by using a falling Ketakī flower that you will encounter on your way up, to try to corroborate your claim.

The Reality of the Being cannot be truly understood or imagined from within the mandala. Within the mandala, which is the mandala of our own individual existence - our conditional experience of being as an individual human being - we are already immersed in something that is the very means of realising the *Brahman*.

This is why, for example, in the Radha Tantra, in the tantric tradition, it is repeatedly stated that without the 'clan behaviour' (sexual union) *Brahman* 'is like a dead corpse'. The Tripura says to Vāsudeva (Krsna) that without "clan behaviour" perfection cannot be attained.[239]

This is given as a constructive criticism against austerities. 'Laksmī is born from a portion of Me; why have you given her up to engage in austerities?',[240] asks the Tripura.

Vāsudeva is given the instruction to engage sexually with *Śakti* because without enjoyment spiritual knowledge cannot be perfected.[241]

In Buddhism, our conditional experience of being, as human beings, is sometimes referred to as the *body-mind*. In terms of Hinduism, and I am now somewhat mixing the languages, the message is that body-mind is created through the great expansion of being, *as a result of which*, it comes into existence through what becomes in us, sex.

Nevertheless, even though sex is very means of our existence, it is, itself, actually only a small part of all that goes into creating our conditional experience of being as the body-mind. As a conditional experience of being, we are not actually separated from the transcendental. In the Hindu picture, it is all part of the great expansion.

Our *body-mind* experience of being and world contains a rich, multidimensional mix of components of mind and experience, as any intelligent human being will know. Much of it has nothing directly to do with human sexuality, even though our coming to participate in human life and experience is dependent, in the first place, through what appears in our experience, as sex.

Siva Teaches the Brahmins about Sex

There is a story in the Śiva Purana itself (*The reason for Śiva assuming the phallic form*)[242] that provides some real perspective:

The story says that once, *Śiva* appeared in a hideous form in order to test the devotion of the brahmins.[243] He appeared stark naked, covered in ashes, holding his male organ and began engaging in "perverse activities".

The wives of the sages (the holy men aspiring to the Divine) were frightened at this sight, but the other women (not engaged in the pursuit of the Divine) became excited and approached and embraced him, holding his hands, and struggling with one another.

The sages approached and insisted that he stopped, and gave up his sexual excitement. This, *Śiva* did, but then his male organ began to burn the whole universe, causing problems and disasters.

On praying to Brahma, the sages are told by him that the mistake was theirs; they should have treated *Śiva* as a guest, and *Pārvati* (*Śivā*) should be propitiated to assume the form of a vaginal passage, so that 'that penis will become steady'.[244]

Then *Śiva* himself speaks. He says "If my penis is supported in a vaginal passage there will be happiness".[245] And he is referring to the fact that the whole world is currently being burned by this unaddressed ignorance of sex.

Actually, according to the story, this disaster for the world only happened in the first place because the sages had interfered with and stopped *Śiva*'s ignorant expression of sex, rather than treating him, and his manifestation of ignorant sexuality, as a guest.

The symbolism is that as a result of simply ignoring or stopping sexuality and trying to overcome it, through convention, and social construct, that same sexual ignorance will go everywhere and "burn" everything. This is indeed what happens in our world.

Collectively, our own world gets burned in all kinds of trouble simply because of not understanding the nature of the "guest" of our own ignorant sexuality. And the mistake of either trying to reject it, or just indulge in it, or treat it as a recreation, or just as a means of procreation, or as a means of cementing *personal* relationship based on the egoic idea of "who I am". Rather than treat it rightly.

The solution, the way of embracing it rightly, is not just to allow free sexual expression and indulgence, and illicit sex, and so on, with no context other than the "who I am" idea and sex itself. In ignorance of what it is, and of one's own true nature.

Śiva says:

> Except *Pārvatī* [the common name for the wife of *Śiva*], no other woman can hold my penis. Held by her my penis will immediately become quiet.[246]

To "immediately become quiet" means that the sex energy as ignorance and passion, or *Tamas* and *Rajas*, becomes *Sattva*.

When *Śiva* says "my penis" he is essentially also saying *your* penis to any man whom he is addressing. After all, the true Identity of a man is no less than *Śiva* himself.

And when he says *Pārvatī* he is also talking to every human woman, after all, the true Identity of a woman is no less than *Śivā*. Similarly, to "propitiate *Pārvatī*" so that she 'assumes the form of a vaginal passage' refers to the woman partner in a human couple. In other words, her state must be spiritual, in pursuit of realising her own true Identity as *Pārvatī* or *Śakti*, 'for the sake of virtue'.[247]

So this story is *the opposite of* the promotion of illicit sex, and free sexuality for the sake of sex itself. Rather, is about the pursuit of the Divine. The first (and actually lowest) meaning, might be interpreted simply as marital fidelity. But there is really this higher, or deeper meaning, because marital fidelity in itself, isn't necessarily the same thing as treating sexuality as a guest, and knowing how to embrace it rightly.

Carefully interjected into the narrative in the Purana is a passage where Brahma instructs the Brahmins on how to make and worship a *Śiva Linga* idol. This is a phallic idol still widely used in Hinduism.

However, it is very important to realise that despite the cultural and religious worshipping of *Linga* idols called *Śiva Lingams* (or "Śivlings" as they have sometimes become colloquially known in the West), this *idol worship* was only promoted in the scriptures in the first place, for a particular purpose.

That is, for the sake of those who are not sufficiently spiritually advanced to understand how to consciously treat sexuality as a guest, and to embrace it rightly. This fact is explicated in the following. So for the less spiritually advanced, instructions for idol worship are given.

But for those ready to understand it, Brahma reveals the truth about the *Linga* in the Śiva Purana, telling us the *linga* is of two types: the exterior and the interior, the gross (material) and the subtle (psychical). It states that worshipping the gross *linga* [the phallic idol] is only for those who are unable to meditate on the subtle. Masters of true knowledge, it tells us, perceive the subtle, whilst those who are not yogins regard only the material one.[248]

The "exterior" type of *linga* referred to here is of course is the constructed physical idol. This *Śiva-linga* object is the *gross linga* that the passage is talking about. The "subtle linga" referred to is about *inner experience and knowledge*. It is about making our sexuality *conscious*, rather than it being just an expression of the *Rajas* and *Tamas*, that by default, it begins as.

It is important to remember here that in the Hindu picture, as we have already said above, the "phallus" does not mean merely the male organ, but the *union* of the male and the female.

The Purana says at the end of the story, that when *Śiva*'s advice was followed, 'the excellent penis became static',[249] and *Śiva* and *Pārvatī* became delighted, and 'the phallus was held by her in that form then'.[250]

The essential meaning is this: It is in effect saying that spiritually orientated love making gets rid of the trouble. It is saying that all the trouble in the world is originally caused by sexual ignorance, in other words, the unconscious expression of sex as just *Rajas* and *Tamas*. Rather than treating sex as a guest in our spiritual pursuit, which means to come to conscious knowledge of it, and through it, to realise the Divine union and conjugal love of the Being, that it represents.

The transcendental meaning is that in the origin of the universe, the transcendental origin of the phallus (which as we have said is the entire universe, and all of *Maya*) is the union of *Śiva* and his expansion as *Śivā*. Or, indeed, in Krsna-Bhakti, the eternal energy of conjugal love of the Divine, as Radha-Krsna.

The passage is saying that when sex is engaged in, in ignorance, then the ignorance inherent in it is "ignited" and causes all the trouble in the world. Collectively, the whole world will be set on fire by it.

So it should come as no surprise really, that in the 1960s when the influence of Eastern spiritual teachers was entering a peak in the West, the West translated the essence of the teaching as "Make love, not war". Sure, that was in the political context too, of objection to the Vietnam war, but the origin of the idea that we should make love, not war, came from the influence of Eastern Masters.

And so it is that the Purana states that when the "phallus was stabilised", 'there was welfare throughout the worlds'.[251]

The phallus that the Purana speaks of, the Purana also tells us is then known as *Hāteśa*,[252] which means *without desire*. By worshipping it, it tells us, people become happy, and eventually it gives a final liberation.[253]

"Worshipping" here does not refer to ritual idol worship. It actually refers to the realisation of the truth behind sex energy and what it represents. Without "treating it as a guest" in the pursuit of the spiritual, it is a blockage to that pursuit. But when "treated as a guest", it becomes the *key* to realisation.

The message here, in the story as a whole, is not just some ancient piece of Mythology, that is now irrelevant. On the contrary, it is completely relevant now.

It is about how to approach sex, treating it as a "guest", rather than just indulging in it, or pointing the finger at it as a sin. Treating it as a guest doesn't mean *using* it, for personal purposes, whether for recreation, procreation, or even for cementing personal relationships. When a guest comes to your house, you do not, if you treat them as a guest, dictate to them what *they* are all about, or what they should *be* about.

To some people, there may well seem to be some degree of "twilight language" here. And it is no accident that in the development of many of the *tantras* (spiritual texts which are much more specific in their sexual focus), the deliberate use of quite sophisticated "twilight language" evolved.

The fact is that pretty much all deeper spiritual literature includes polysemic language, simply because it is impossible to render the spiritually transcendental into what we call *language*, except poetically, or without something getting eventually "lost in translation".

So there is nothing intentionally "twilight" about any of this. It is just that we human beings undeniably only exist in the first place, through sex. So we shouldn't be surprised to find that it is only through the self-knowledge of sex, only through making love, that we can reach the highest knowledge of the Truth behind our own existence.

The Expansion

The message in these Hindu texts is that sex in human beings is something that has been created out of the vast *expansion of being* of the Divine, and that in human beings it is but a shadow of something transcendental.

That is not, however, to ignore the fact that as the core cause of our existence in the first place, sex is also a "hub" in what is going on to create our experience of being, as a human being. And therefore, closely connected into it, is all the trouble. So as such, in Christianity, for example, it is recognised as *the fall.*

But this does not mean that it does not have its transcendental counterpart. It is just that, in Hindu terms, to be able to find it, there is going to have to be a *churning of the ocean* through sexuality itself. But also, out of that, comes the *Amrta* - the nectar of immortality.

That transcendental counterpart of sexual love in human being is is none other than what Krsna-Bhakti portrays in its own polysemic language, as the transcendental Divine pastimes of Krsna, Radha and the Gopis.

Even that, is a partial picture. Because Krsna's expansion as Radha and the Gopis, and the other beings, and the Joy and play of those pastimes, itself expands, and goes on expanding. In an unimaginably vast expansion and involution of both being and opulences of being, worlds of being, enjoyments of being, the Light of being, and eventually, in the time created out of it, the shadows of Being.

Somewhere, on the "way down" or on the "way out" into the expansion from the transcendental, in the great *expansion of being*, something happens, that introduces the basic problem into human nature. Which whether we realise it or not, circulates around sex, the very thing through which we come into existence. This is essentially why Christianity regards sex as *the fall.*

Let it suffice here to say that in the materialistic, Westernised mind, what is spoken of in the Hindu corpus as the *Linga* and the *Yoni*, are often *incorrectly* taken to be symbols of the penis and the vagina of *human beings*.

The truth, the truth that is essentially explicated in the Hindu corpus, is the other way around. It is that these parts of the human experience of being - because that is what they are - these parts of our *experience* that also arise in the *appearance* of the human body, are the *symbol* of the *Linga* and the *Yoni*. Rather than the other way around.

The human bodily parts are a symbol, a projection in the form of the mind and experience of being that we are being. Our whole existence is a projection. And it is full of symbolism. Not merely physical symbols but *experiential* symbols.

The human body, its visual appearance, is in all its aspects a symbol of how it comes to be. And the experience of *being* a human body, is an *experiential* symbol of that.

We are being a conditional experience of being, that in the first instance, is the way in which we are entangled in material existence, as the theatre for our conditional experience of being. It is none other than a *dhāma* realm. Our body constitutes a somatic field of experience, but it is most certainly not the case that every aspect of our experience of being, originates in this somatic field of experience.

Rather, it is just that all aspects of our experience of being that we have here, are *enabled through* this somatic field of experience - the body. It is not that experience of being *per se*, requires this somatic field of experience. But in order to know that, in order to discover that, we have to go beyond identification with this somatic field of experience. And that means going beyond identification with the body, and that means going beyond attachment to material sex.

However, we cannot in general go beyond identification with this somatic field of experience without coming to know it, first. Even if we do suddenly transcend it, we must still then come to know it, if we are to communicate anything about what we have discovered. Because human experience arises through the somatic field of experience.

Nonetheless, in general, the human somatic field of experience is not very well consciously known. Rather, in most human beings in the modern world, attention is directed out into the world, without first truly knowing the somatic field of experience. Our somatic field of experience isn't merely physical, bodily sensation. That's only its surface. The field goes right down into the "psyche" through which the experience of being the body is produced. And it's the ignorance of that, that is the lack of knowledge of the somatic field of experience.

In general, yoga practices are aimed at addressing this imbalance. But the default condition in "society" is reliance on the mind, whose formulations of thought for understanding the surrounding world are based on ignorance of the somatic field of experience.

The network of all this outward focused thought then forms a *network mind*, which in turn then contribute to configuring the minds that make up the network mind. It all arises through brain function - which by default gives rise to mind in which there is self-conception as a separate being. It is the *union* that as we have seen, the word *Linga* really refers to, that is the key to the missing knowledge of our somatic field of experience.

Union is *yoga*. That's actually what the word *yoga* means. The appearance of *separation*, the appearance of distinct experiences of being, as different beings, is the human condition. It arises through the principle of the brain. The appearance of separation happens in a field of experience of being that consists of what we know as matter, time, and space. Things are separate in matter, time in space. Human beings are separate in matter, time in space. But they are not separate in the principle of the brain. And in Hindu terminology, they are certainly not separate in being, because we are all the *Brahman*.

But actually, in the first instance, by default, it's not in those terms that we encounter our apparent separation. Rather, separation is encountered through the "who I am" idea of self-conception. Which by default is always an idea of a separate "who I am". This is the personal ego. It's the personal ego that creates the primary separation. And it is that, that perpetuates the ignorance of sex.

In the great scheme of the creation of the "cosmic egg" that Hinduism depicts, very close to the beginning of the appearance of "the universe" is the creation of the *Ahamkara* - the transliterated Sanskrit word for ego. And the word "ego", as we know, also has a Western root that just means "I", before it comes to mean all the other things that it comes to mean in everyday parlance.

Our apparent separateness, as human beings, is literally embodied in our bodies, which are separate bodies, in terms of matter, time, and space. Matter, time and space, is the theatre of separation. However, it is in this very theatre that the reality of our being, beyond identification with our somatic field of experience, is reflected.

It is just that if we put our attention into the world external to our body, and try to understand it without first knowing our somatic field of experience, then we start to understand it only with the ego mind, and in terms of separation. Because the ego mind always wants to preserve its "who I am" idea. We can never get beyond the brain, that way.

Everything in the world including the nature of our own bodily experience is essentially a symbol. The symbolism of the world is both experiential and about comprehension. We are not really comprehending the world until we understand what an experiential symbol is, and what it means.

Every part of our experience of self is centred on our somatic field of experience, through which it comes. But not everyone is conscious of this. All our sexual feelings come through it, all our emotional attachments come through it, all our thinking about "I", the ego, comes through it.

Just as scientifically speaking, everything we experience is a construct of our own brain function, so the surrounding world that we experience is actually part of this "I" experience, of natural ego. Materially, it is actually a construct of brain function.

It's true, it's not created just through our own, individual brain, because our own individual brain is just an *instantiation* of the principle of the brain. Nonetheless, the surrounding world is actually part of this "I" experience, of natural ego, and is only ever experienced as a construct of brain function. This is the trick of nature, in creating our conditional experience of being, as a human being. This is what nature is really all about, and what nature is really up to.

The entire world of apparently separate things, and separate beings, as we know it and experience it, is in Hindu terms the *Ahamkara*. The entire material universe. Just as anything we can ever know of it, or experience of it, is a construct of brain function.

It is actually our somatic field of experience that provides our conditional experience of being in the first place, and creates this appearance of separateness. Just as everything we experience as the world, and everything we experience as our being of the body, the whole of our somatic field of experience, is all a construct of our brain function. Which itself, is part of this construct.

It is this *whole world* of apparent separateness, in which we live, that is, as we have seen from the Śiva Purana, the Linga. Not just some part of it. Not just the Western idea of the phallus. And the *Śiva*-Lingam, the material idol object worshipped in Hindu culture, is the not just the phallus, but the combination of both the Linga and the Yoni, both *Śiva* and *Śivā*. The combination spoken of in the story in the Śiva Purana that we have been looking at.

Our somatic field of experience begins with our body. But actually, it facilitates our experience of the entire world. We can have no experience of the world, nor any understanding of the world, that is not a construct of brain function. It all comes through the brain, and through the nervous system of the body, which is an extension of the brain.

Translating the Hindu picture again into this language, any individual brain function, any individual nervous system, although confined to a body that is separate in matter and time and space, is not really separate from the whole. That is, the whole of that which creates this appearance of separation. Which is only an appearance, a symbol, in the intelligence we are being, of the *Ahamkara*.

Proper knowledge of our somatic field of experience, coincides with a proper *psychical* knowledge of sex. And that coincides with the realisation that sex, once purified of the ignorance attached to it, it is the experiential arising in this *lila* of our existence, of the Divine love of the Being.

13

Svarūpa and the Infinite

Svarūpa means one's 'own form or shape, condition, peculiarity, character, or nature'.[254] To put it another way, it is the name given to what a being experiences itself, or himself or herself, to be, in some conditional experience of being.

Sva means "oneself". *Rūpa* means "outward appearance, dreamy or phantom shapes, likeness, image or reflection, a play or drama", and even "an integer".[255]

All of these meanings of *rūpa* are appropriate for *svarūpa*, when it arises as a *lila* (a "dance" or "play" of being) or part of *Maya*. We humans have a common prosaic word for it, applied to ourselves. The word is *self*.

The *Brahman* can be realised through a *svarūpa*, as his or her or its own true, unconditional Identity, the unconditional, radiant Being from which this *svarūpa* has somehow been created.

This realisation of the Being, the *Brahman*, is made when identity with the *svarūpa* or self is transcended. This is sometimes called ego death. Which may be temporary. Not just as the transcendence of the personal psychology behind the personal idea of "who I am", which is the commonplace and mutable personal ego, but also as the transcendence of the natural (and actually impersonal) self experience as it arises through brain function.

In the Purana stories when beings are referred to as having a "body", it is really the *svarūpa* that is being referred to as the "body" of this or that being. Our *svarūpa* by default is based on the experience of being our body, and then also on all the rest of the experience delivered through brain function.

So, when *Śiva* has *Śivā* as his *Śakti* created from his "body", as it says in the Śiva Purana, what that really means is that she is created from his *svarūpa*. This is not so unlike the way in which, in the Mythology of Christianity, in the Book of Genesis, Eve is said to have been created from a rib from Adam's body.

The eternal, unconditional, Self Radiant Being, that Hinduism calls the *Brahman*, has an associated *svarūpa* too. This is the *svarūpa* of the *Bhagavān* who realises the *Brahman* by *awakening as* That Being.

The realisation of the Being, is to realise *svarūpa* as being completely free from dependence on anything, free from any condition, and as the effulgent Reality and Joy of liberated Being. It is the realisation of our true Identity as the Self. The *svarūpa* of the *Brahman* - unconditional, infinite Being - is *our own svarūpa*, beyond our *conditional svarūpa*, of our experience of being as a separate self.

As a matter of scientific fact our *conditional* experience of being, or *conditional svarūpa*, is provided through *the principle of the brain*. But *the principle of the brain itself*, is not something that is dependent on, or just arises through, any individual brain organ.

So human "out of the body experiences", or *experiences of being* during what is medically called "brain death", and so on, are not *experiences of being* beyond *the principle of the brain*.

Only the realisation of the Being, as the *Brahman*, is beyond the principle of the brain. Sure, the principle of the brain is still *in the picture* in order for this realisation to arise in a human being. But the picture relies on the *Brahman*, and not the other way around.

The underlying message in what Hinduism says about the *Brahman*, is that there is Conscious Being that is not dependent on *any* condition. Such as, for example, the condition of *brain function*.

This unconditionality, and inherent liberation from anything other than what the Being Is, the inherent liberation from all doubt, the inherent, intrinsic Knowledge of the Self, the awakening of consciousness into the unlimited Joy of that Knowledge and That Being, simply cannot be *understood*, or *related to*, by mind that has not been illuminated with the *realisation* of That Being.

And this can appear to be the difficulty in the communication of it, to the general field of mind that has no illumination. However, where there *is* a *communication of it*, - even though any attempt at describing the Reality of That Being gets "lost in translation" when put into words - then there is arguably inherent in the mind that *hears* what is being said, already some implicit *realisation* of it, even if it is, as it were, "underneath the surface".

What we realise as the *Brahman*, as our own true Identity, as the Self, is only the beginning of awakening of Knowledge of That Being. The *realisation* of the *Brahman* through a being's *svarūpa*, as a man, woman, child, or any other form, is for that being to *awaken as* the *Brahman*, realising the *Brahman* as one's own true Identity. But it is only a beginning.

To begin with, the *Brahman* is the radiance or *Self effulgence* of That Being. Its "quality" is the Radiant Reality of the Self, as unconditional Consciousness. It is not an effulgence of Being that is observed by a "person" who is separate from it, observing it. In the realisation of the *Brahman* the self, together with all self-conception as a separate being, drops away, or dies. So it is the *Brahman* that realises the *Brahman*. The Self cannot be observed by something or some being, separate from it.

On the contrary, it is an *awakening* of, and as, That Being. And yet it happens through a human body and brain. Arising through the principle of the brain. It is the human body and brain that is, just as Hinduism puts it, an *expansion* of That Being. And similarly, That Being is actually an expansion of a higher realm, that in the Indian Bhakti tradition is known as *Goloka*.

But then the attempts to communicate that are translated down into forms suitable for the comprehension of minds that can only identify with the personal self and "who I am" idea based on identification with the body and the mind.

And so just as there is the *svarūpa* above the self, of the one who realises the *Brahman*, there is *svarūpa* above that too. All *svarūpa* below it, such as the experience of being a human self, is created through the *expansion* of the *Brahman*. This means, in effect, that it happens in the Radiance of That Being, the Self, where in general the *svarūpa* does not realise its Source - the *Brahman*, the Self that we already really are.

The *Brahman* is already a Radiance of Being, realised as the pure, infinite, unconditional, *Being I Am*, full of Consciousness and Joy, and Gratitude, for this intrinsically liberated Reality of Being. But it is nonetheless the Radiance of still higher Spiritual Reality, waiting to be Realised.

So the human experience of *self*, our ordinary everyday *svarūpa*, is an expansion of That Being that the Hindus call the *Brahman*. And the Hindu corpus seeks to explain how this creation of the human being comes about, through the expansion of the *Brahman*, in the ways that we see in the Mythology of the Puranas. Which are in general not ways using the kind of language that we have just used here. But nonetheless, we are talking about the same thing.

The mainstream Western view sees human beings arising in terms of time. Hinduism sees time itself in terms of Being. And the appearance of our arising in time, as an illusory play in the expansion of That Being.

The Infinite Lotus

The Being, conceived in the Bhakti tradition as Krsna, has infinite expansions that initially manifest in ways invariably described in the Indian literature in terms of the imagery of *the lotus*, lotus stalks, the pericarp and lotus petals. A description of the transcendental in these terms is intensely and beautifully described in an extensive text of the Padma Purana.[256]

The use of the lotus motif also appears in the Garga Samhita, in which the thousand-petalled [infinite-petalled] lotus is referred to as a great circle of light.[257]

Remember that in these texts references to "a thousand" or "thousands", or "hundreds of thousands", or "innumerable", and so on, are generally just synonyms for *infinity* or *infinities*.

Circles of light, as mentioned here, are not uncommonly encountered in these kinds of descriptions.

In the part of the great *expansion of being* where the transcendental turns into the material, we encounter the "demigods". Here is where in the popular imagery, *Viśnu* "floats on the ocean", reclining on a Being called Lord *Śesa* (*Ananta Śesa* - the infinite-headed serpent, also called *Śeśa Naga*).

In the Bhakti understanding *Ananta Śesa* (*Anantadeva*) is a partial expansion of *Balarama* (*Baladeva*), the Being who is a direct expansion of Krsna.[258]

Just as *Viśnu* is inseparable from the "place" called *Viśnuloka*, otherwise known as *Vaikuntha*, so also Lord *Śesa* is a "place". To reiterate, realms, or "places", and beings are all *Being*.

And so it is that the Garga Samhita describes how Brahma sees *Śeśa Naga*:

> In that circle of light he saw the form of a peaceful transcendental realm. When the demigods saw in that realm the very wonderful white lotus stem of thousand-faced [infinite-headed] Lord *Śesa* they bowed down to offer respect to Him.[259]

So here we see the imagery of *Śesa* who is otherwise depicted as a serpent, now depicted as both a lotus, and as a *transcendental realm*. We are already well beyond the superficial interpretation of the Mythology.

In Hindu imagery the serpent *Śesa* has an infinity of heads around Viśnu's head, like a halo. The Garga Samhita goes on to say that the transcendental realm of *Goloka* is on *Śesa*'s head, and here illusion, ego, and the materiality of the *mahat-tattva* cannot enter.[260]

Here, the mahat-tattva is the cosmic principle (whereby the material world and the experience of being therein, is created).261 It is sometimes referred to as the total material energy. The phrase "time, the Conqueror of the proud" refers to karma and death. The material mind, heart, intelligence, and ego - all part of our conditional experience of being of human beings - have to be shed and transcended in order to enter Goloka. And given that all these are a construct of brain function, we can be sure that Goloka is beyond the principle of the brain.

Into the Material

There is some considerable symbolism in the widely depicted imagery of *Viśnu* floating on the ocean, reclining on *Śesa*, whose infinite heads surround *Viśnu*'s head like a halo.

Firstly, as we have said, there are actually the three *Viśnus* who are nested expansions. There is the *Kāranodakaśāyī Viśnu* who lays on the causal ocean, *Garbhodakaśāyī Viśnu* who lays on the *Garbha* ocean, and *Ksīrodakaśāyī Viśnu* who lays on the Ocean of Milk.

So *Viśnu* may be variously found depicted as laying on any of these three oceans. The oceans themselves are nested expansions, expanding from the causal ocean, to the collective *Garbha* ocean, the "womb" of existence, to the Ocean of Milk that is still to be found in the individual human consciousness of self and world. Sometimes the ocean *Viśnu* lays on is just generally referred to as "the ocean of bliss".

Ananta Śesa - the infinite-headed serpent - is an infinite expansion from *Viśnu* (as well as a partial expansion of *Baladeva*), but is also *Rudra* in the form of *Sankarsarna*.[262] At the direction of *Śiva* this "serpent" *Ananta Śesa* or *Anantadeva* supports the fourteen worlds, extending above and below the Earth.[263] In other words, *Śesa* supports the whole universe.[264]

We also find in the Kurma Purana that *Nārāyana* (Maha-*Viśnu*) is the immanent soul of all living beings.[265] (In the Krsna-Bhakti texts this is in the form of the expansion of *Nārāyana* as *Ksīrodakaśāyī Viśnu*). Here, *Nārāyana* is also identified as *Vāsudeva* (Krsna), who is the 'first form of the Lord, the 'blemishless embodiment of knowledge'.[266] This first form of *Nārāyana* we are told is beyond all *Gunas*, *Niskala* (meaning formless and without parts), indivisible and unsullied. So in other words, the first form of *Maha-Viśnu* is the transcendental Krsna.

The text then goes on to say that the second form of *Nārāyana* is *Kāla*, the destroyer, characterised by *Tamas* and designated as *Śiva*, *Śesa* or *Sankarsana*.[267] This, it says is the highest form of *Viśnu*, the destroyer of everything in the end.[268] In other words, *Śesa* who is a form of *Sankarsana*, who in turn is a form of *Rudra*, is the highest form of *Viśnu* - which is also none other than *Śiva* the destroyer.

We are told by the text that the 'permanent nature of' *Viśnu* is then the third form of *Nārāyana*, which is the one usually spoken of as *Viśnu*, the sustainer, with *Sattva Guna*.[269] Finally, the fourth form of *Nārāyana* is Brahma.[270]

So in all this we can see the *expansion of being* of *Nārāyana* begins as an expansion from *Vāsudeva* (Krsna) without *Gunas*, into what rapidly becomes a complex web of identities, that also expands "outwards" in three forms. That is, as *Śiva*, *Viśnu*, and Brahma.

In the expansion, *Śiva* gives rise to the well-known *Śiva* the destroyer, or *Kāla*. This is not the original "unexpanded" *Śiva* we first spoke of, who remains in "the blissful forest" together with his consort and *Śakti*, called *Śivā*. As we saw earlier, the Śiva Purana explicitly explains this Divine Couple does not get involved in creation or destruction, but rather, they remain in *Kaśi* and 'confer salvation'.[271]

Even just concerning the beings we have mentioned, which is a tiny part of the whole picture, what we are looking at here is a complex web of beings who are all *expansions* of the *transcendental Vāsudeva* (Krsna).

Within the overall infinite expansion, the *Gunas* and hence *Prakrti* begin to be introduced at that point in the expansion that we have already talked about, that the corpus refers to as the *causal ocean*.

14

The Transcendental and the Mirror

In the Kurma Purana when *Viśnu* emerges from the mouth of Brahma, it is said that *Viśnu* has *Śesa* as his *abode.*[272] So here again we are seeing *being*, and "*place*", *realm*, or *abode*, as one. Essentially, *svarūpa* and *dhāma* can be one.

In the Hindu picture, as a human being, ordinarily, the meaning of *svarūpa* is our *self.* Our *dhāma realm* is what we would ordinarily just call "our world". That is, our *dhāma* is the total environment of our conditional experience of being, including our relationships, our activities, our creativity, our troubles, and the spiritual teaching and practice we may be involved in.

Not only can *svarūpa* and *dhāma* be one, but the apparent separation between *dhāma* and *svarūpa*, to begin with, is only part of *Maya*. Beyond the delusion cast by *Maya*, *dhāma* and *svarūpa* are one. In our situation as human beings, beyond the appearance cast by *Maya*, the self and the world in which as self we find ourselves, are inseparable.

The contemporary correlation of this is that in terms of the brain, both the self and the world we experience from the point of view of this self, are one construct of the brain function of the one, individual brain.

If you shut out the experience of the world through sleep or sensory deprivation, the brain either reconstructs another apparent world, of dream or hallucination, or there is complete unconsciousness without experience of self. The Self is still there, but not the apparently separate self, as the mind and the emotions, and the personal idea of "who I am". We cannot have consciousness of this self, without some world, even if that is very limited, such as in a liminal experience of body.

The material world is not dependent on the consciousness of any individual, and has its own rules of existence and behaviour that are completely independent of any individual brain function. We call this aspect "the laws of nature", and it is this aspect that makes the scientific study of physics possible. But none of this means that the material world is anything other than a construct of brain function. Which itself, is part of the material world.

It is just that every individual brain organ has functioning that results in our individual experience of self and world, through a *principle of nature* that does not depend on any individual brain.

The idea that the world is separate from us, and other than self, is purely psychological. There is nothing in it that is a matter of scientific fact. And so it is that looking for how a brain organ "creates consciousness" as an isolated thing, is misguided.

Transcending the natural illusion of separateness is ordinarily blocked by the personal ego, which is our misidentification with the sum of all experience being delivered through brain function. And this is upheld by the subsequent personal idea of "who I am" and "me" and its attendant "I" thought.

The only problem for we human beings in coming to comprehend this, is not that there is something difficult to learn, but rather, that it only becomes revealed, and easy to see, in the actual realisation of it, which is through our actually encountering the Being in our own experience.

* * *

The highest realm of the transcendental in the Hindu picture, is called, amongst other names, *Goloka*. This is of course, also part of

Hindu cultural fabric, and it literally means "the place of the cows". This comprehension of it is inseparable from Hindu culture. Its whole expression is part of the Hindu cultural fabric.

Above *Śesa*, the Garga Samhita tells us, is the transcendental realm of *Goloka*.[273] This, in the Krsna-Bhakti texts, is the transcendental realm of Krsna. It is "above" the *causal ocean*. In the corpus there are numerous poetical descriptions of *Krsnaloka*, *Goloka*, or *Vrndavana*, in terms of the imagery of Indian culture.

These descriptions are by no means ineffectual, and are psycholinguistically potent even in their English translations. But they should never be taken to be literal descriptions of the transcendental and transcendental Being. The Garga Samhita speaks of Krsna as the unborn Supreme, indescribable, and beyond the material world. It says that Krsna cannot be described by even the greatest philosophers.[274]

So we have to understand that in the numerous texts ancient and modern, the original purpose of the descriptions of the transcendental, of Goloka, and so on, is not to convey literal imagery or "information" about the transcendental.

Rather, it is to provide a literary form of experience through which readers without direct realisation of the transcendental can engage in certain psychological transformations that work towards that aim. If there is attachment to belief in this descriptive material as being factual, literal descriptions and information about the transcendental, then there is a blockage.

In Hinduism there are infinitely many Brahmas.[275] These all arise from the *Brahman*. The Brahma Samhita tells us that the *Brahmajyoti* (the *Brahman effulgence* or radiance) contains infinite universes and worlds.[276]

Really, we can see the whole of the *expansion of being* as a play of *svarūpa*. The Source, the Being, or Krsna, if you are in that tradition, or in any tradition, God, is infinitely beyond any *svarūpa* in the play of *svarūpa*. And yet it is due to the great expansion that there *is* that *svarūpa*. And in this, is the immanence and the transcendence of God.

In human beings natural ego arises as experience of self, through the body and the brain as the sum of all experience delivered by the brain. But really, this *natural* ego, without the personal idea of "who I am", is *impersonal*. If we can come to *see it* impersonally, and as impersonal, then our relation with it changes.

Ordinarily, it goes on to expand further, through the mechanisms of the brain, into the personal *idea* of "who I am", which is not really the natural self, or the natural ego, but just an *idea* of "who I am". It is the personal "I thought" *subsequent* to the *natural ego* arising through brain function, as the experience of self.

This becomes a deep part of our psychology that colors the way our mind is working. It results in constant subconscious and unconscious reflection on this idea. And surrounding this idea is a field of emotional experience, emotional past, that causes us to continue to be attached to an idea of "who I am" based on past identity and experience of being. We can reinvent the idea of "who I am" if we wish, but this doesn't liberate us from this deep psychological attachment.

Ultimately these deep psychological attachments are a reservoir of energy of being experience, the experience of self or *svarūpa* that still remains as a component in our current *svarūpa*. The way in which we are actually freed from attachment to this reservoir, which Buddhism calls *vasanas*, is something that in Hinduism is called *the churning of the ocean*. Later, we will talk about this in more detail.

The Mirror

The experience of *self* that we have, our natural ego, arising through the body and the brain, *requires the world* - which is our *world of being* - in order to come about. As we have already mentioned, we cannot separate our experience of self from our experience of "world".

Underlying this basic fact is the deeper truth found both in the Indian Vedanta and in the work of some Western philosophers such as Schopenhauer, who familiarised themselves with the Indian corpus. This is that the world and self are inseparable.

In terms of the brain, what we experience as the world is inseparable from brain function. It is a construct of brain function. And what we experience as self, is inseparable from brain function. It is a construct of brain function. In fact, both arise together through the same thing - brain function.

In Hinduism everything is the *Brahman*. But it is the *Brahman* in the play of *Maya*. It is *Maya*, it is illusion, it happens in the *Śakti* of *Brahman*, but is nonetheless, still the *Brahman*. And so it is that not only is the world the Self, the Being, but it is also the ignorance of the Being, called the human self, experienced as this self.

Schopenhauer expressed this in the very opening statement of his book on the subject, as "*The world is my representation*".[277] Another way of putting this is that the world is a *projection* of the self, into the appearance of matter, space, and time.

This is not essentially any different to recognising that what we know and experience as *the world*, is always a construct of brain function. Our knowing of it and experiencing of it, requires this brain function, the same brain function that constructs our experience of self.

However, there is much more to our situation than this. Hinduism recognises that this experience of self and world, whether or not we realise that it is all the same thing, is in any case not the truth of our Being. It is only *Maya*.

The true Self we are (the *Brahman*) doesn't require the world in order to Be. It is completely free, liberated, from that need. Rather, what we experience as human self and world is, as it were, *ignorance* of our own true Identity. It is, quite literally, this ignorance *in motion*. As matter in time and space.

In the Hindu picture we humans, each one of us, as a human self, is a partial expansion of the Trimurti member Brahma (sometimes called by the name *Hiraṇyagarbha* which means "golden womb"). Altogether, we constitute the "manifested body" of Brahma. But the Brahma *behind* all this expansion, the Brahma depicted as a personified being in the Hindu corpus, the Brahma from which everything in our existence is an *expansion*, remains *unmanifested*.

And so it is that the Paingala Upanishad, for example, states:

> He (*Hiraṇyagarbha*) [Brahma] has a body, both manifested and unmanifested. From *Vikshepa Śakṭi* [projection] of *Hiraṇyagarbha* arose, through the preponderance of *Ṭamas* [ignorance], the gross *Śakṭi* called *ahaṅkāra* [ego]. That which is reflected in it is *Virat-Chaitanya*.[278]

In other words, the expansion of Brahma (mostly as complex, partial expansions) is what leads to our individual experience of being as *self* and the world. This principle of expansion or "projection", called *Vikshepa Śakṭi*, is overall, mostly a projection of *ignorance* (*Tamas*). This ignorance is fundamentally ignorance of the *Brahman*.

It results in our conditional experience of being as *ego*, or individual *ahaṅkāra*, our experience of self, and world, as two separate things, and all the consequential mental and emotional nonsense surrounding the personal *idea* of "who I am", and "me", that arises from it.

The last line of that paragraph from the Paingala Upanishad, however, adds an entirely new dimension. It is saying that this *ahaṅkāra*, this ego, or experience of self and world (which really is all one thing), essentially, *is like a mirror*.

Because it says:

> That which is reflected in it is *Virat-Chaitanya*.

Virat-Chaitanya basically means "consciousness". But it implies a great deal more. It doesn't just mean the "consciousness" of a human being, a human mind, in which there is this idea of "who I am" as a separate self.

What *Virat-Chaitanya* refers to is the effulgent, shining consciousness, or *Virat* that is *Chaitanya*. *Chaitanya* means consciousness,[279] the Universal Soul or Spirit,[280] or "living force".[281]

In the Bhakti part of Hinduism, the 15th century Hindu mystic saint Chaitanya Mahāprabhu is said to have become frequently absorbed in ecstatic spiritual rapture, in direct knowledge of the Divine. He is recognised in Bhakti to have been an incarnation or *avatara* of the Divine Love and union of Radha-Krsna, the *Chaitanya* consciousness of the Divine Couple.[282]

The Paingala Upanishad is saying, therefore, that our experience of self and world, as a human being, is essentially a mirror. A mirror in which is reflected what in Hinduism is called the Divine pastimes of Krsna and Radha, in which there is our own true Identity.

Alternatively, in the terms of the Śiva Purana, as we have already seen, the world is a projection in which there is the reflection of the Divine lovers *Śiva* and *Śivā* in "the blissful forest".

When we look out into the world, especially as Westernised mind, we tend to see only the material fact of the world. But the material world itself is an externalised expression or projection, in the stuff of matter, time and space, of something that is eternal.

When immersed in Western mind, our "understanding" of it, and hence our way of relating to it, rationally, is attached to a mode of mind in which we are, as the Bhakti tradition calls it, *bewildered*.

We are still to this day just as bewildered as we were as a newborn. But we have covered that over with the rational understanding. When we stop being *bewildered* then the mirror that is the world, begins to reflect something profoundly beautiful, extraordinary, and consciousness-changing. Which is none other than our own true Identity. It is the Consciousness of the Being we already really are, entering the *Śakti* that we are merely playing at being.

15

Brahma and the Universe

In the Hindu corpus *Viśnu* expands into Brahma. But Brahma's *svarūpa* is different to *Viśnu*'s. Then Brahma's *svarūpa* expands beyond that, further into the great expansion that becomes the universe we know, and this expansion doesn't make Brahma into *Viśnu*. Only by Brahma meditating or performing penance, in the Purana stories, in other words, only by him *transcending* his *svarūpa*, can he realise his identity as *Viśnu*, or as the *Brahman,* which is in any case *Viśnu*'s true Identity.

The Indian corpus goes to great pains to introduce the concept of "non-different". That is to say one particular being is "non-different" to another particular being. It uses the concept frequently. And at other times it uses the concept "identical to".

In the scenario portrayed in the Hindu corpus, when a being or consciousness expands into "another" being or consciousness, there are apparently two "separate" beings. The corpus may say that the second being is an *amśa* of the first, which is the *amśi*. Or, it may say that the "second" being, if appearing in the stuff of materiality (specifically, *Prakrti* or the *Gunas*), is an *avatara* of the first.

Brahma is an expansion of *Viśnu*, and in the mythical or symbolic imagery he emerges from the lotus that emerges from *Viśnu*'s navel. The *Viśnu* spoken of in these particular stories, is actually *Garbhodakaśāyī*

Viśnu,[283] (who lays on the *Garbha* ocean), as stated in the Caitanya-caritamrta, the Brahma Samhita and other sources.

Remember that there are *three Viśnus* "wrapped up", as it were, in the one *Maha-Viśnu*. They are all part of the continuing great expansion. By "wrapped up" here, what we mean is that the three *Viśnus* are "enfolded" in *Maha-Viśnu* by the very fact that *Maha-Viśnu* expands as these three. But these three are themselves beings in which are enfolding countless "other" beings.

The way this is approached in the written sources of the Bhakti tradition is, as you might expect from the Bhakti tradition, to speak of the beings as *personified beings*, and in terms of *rasa* or "mood", and their various subordinations. We are taking a different path, of course. But not because that approach is in any way being rejected. Rather, we are going "steep and fast" into the relation between the Being and the brain. The brain, in terms of some of the fundamental scientific facts about it, that we now know.

As we have previously mentioned, *Maha-Viśnu* otherwise called *Karanadakaśāyī Viśnu* expands into *Garbhodakaśāyī Viśnu* who also expands into *Ksīrodakaśāyī Viśnu* (on "the Ocean of Milk"). So *Ksīrodakaśāyī Viśnu* therefore arises within the part of the great expansion that involves Brahma.

The Caitanya-caritamrta states that *Garbhodakaśāyī Viśnu* is known within the universe as *Hiranyagarbha.*[284] *Hiranyagarbha* sometimes refers to Brahma,[285] and is a compound of *Hiranya*, and *Garbha*. *Hiranya* means *gold* or *golden*, or even *semen*, or "*imperishable matter*".[286]

Garbha means *womb, foetus or embryo*, or "*offspring of the sky*" (as vapour drawn upwards by the rays of the Sun), or an *interior or sanctuary.*[287]

So *Hiranyagarbha* is most often taken to mean "golden womb", but as is often the case with Sanskrit, these various meanings "fit together" to maintain the overall meaning. For example, *Hiranyagarbha* contains the "seed" of existence and all living beings within it. Their Source in the *Hiranyagarbha* means that they are immortal (hence "imperishable matter"), although not yet eternal. They are indeed "offspring of the sky", but like the vapour drawn upwards by the rays of the Sun, they never *become* re-absorbed forever into the Sun, but rather, must return to the material Earth.

The Śrīmad Bhāgavatam tells us that a lotus flower sprouts from *Garbhodakaśāyī Viśnu*, that blazes like a thousand suns. This Lotus flower is the "reservoir of all conditions souls", which manifests as the first Being to emerge from *Garbhodakaśāyī Viśnu*, who is Brahma.[288]

The lotus flower, as we shall be talking more about a little later, is the motif here for part of the great expansion of the Being that is still *effulgent Being* and infinite *worlds of Being* or dhāmas, effulgent "like a thousand blazing suns".

So the lotus emerging from the navel of *Garbhodakaśāyī Viśnu* is part of the *infinite expansion* of Being that expands "outwards" from the effulgence of the *Brahman*, to become all living entities. The Caitanya-caritamrta describes *Garbhodakaśāyī Viśnu* as the "supersoul" of the aggregate of all living entities.[289]

As we have said, *Garbhodakaśāyī Viśnu* then expands into the next part of the great expansion, which is *Ksīrodakaśāyī Viśnu* (laying on "the Ocean of Milk"), who is "in the heart of" every living being (in material existence).[290]

The Hindu portrayal of the creation and destruction of "the universe", is not about some place separate from our own conditional experience of being. Rather, it is a portrayal of how the whole play of time is an illusion in the first place.

What Brahma creates is not something separate from us, called "the universe", but rather, is the very structure of the human mind and conditional experience of being, itself.

The Nature of the Aggregates

So the aggregate being of all living entities, or in Hinduism, the *Garbha* ocean, is presided over by what Hinduism calls *Garbhodakaśāyī Viśnu*.

Garbhodakaśāyī Viśnu is the one collective being or consciousness of all living entities (in material existence), which is then in cycles of time endlessly *instantiated* through the "Ocean of Milk" as the particular, unique form of each living entity.

The "Ocean of Milk" appears in the Hindu corpus, in the Mythology, superficially spoken of as if it is something separate from us, from which things emerge. But really, it is within us. And it is the role of *Ksīrodakaśāyī Viśnu* "in the heart", to command spiritual seeing of this "Ocean of Milk", which is our psyche, our self, our mind, our emotions.

Ksīrodakaśāyī Viśnu is, after all, just an expansion from the *Brahman*, and is therefore the way back to the realisation of the *Brahman*.

The aggregate of all living entities, the *Garbha ocean*, represents *all* life on Earth. But the aggregate of *all human beings*, is only part of that aggregate.

Anyone who exists as a member of a particular race, and so on, is already part of an aggregate that is only part of the aggregate of *all* human beings. Even a family is an aggregate. The total aggregate corresponding to *Garbhodakaśāyī Viśnu* consists of aggregates of aggregates of aggregates, and so on.

Every human mind and experience of being is an aggregate. Just as, in terms of brain function, the mind and experience of being of a human being is a construct created as the integration and aggregate of everything that brain function is doing.

Just as our experience of *self*, as a human being, is the integration of all components of the conditional experience of being that the brain is delivering, through its various functions, so each instance of this *self* experience, as a human being, is an *expansion* from an aggregate. But it's not an aggregate of separate parts.

Rather, our individual brain is an *instantiation* of the one principle of the brain. The one principle of the brain provides the objective nature of the world in which we live. Our particular, unique instantiation of that principle, provides our individual experience of it.

Even as beings with separate bodies, and separate brain organs, we are existentially connected as a network. This is something that in the "history" of humanity we have only recently come to realise.

But beyond that, our separation in space and time, and distinctions between bodies, is only an appearance. It is only true in certain terms. It is because each one of our individual brains is an institution of the one principle, that what we experience as our individual conditional experience of being, as a human being, is always part of the one overall *construct of brain function*.

Who Contains the Universe?

In the Purana story of the dispute between Brahma and *Viśnu*, when each invites the other to enter his "body", it doesn't matter who goes into whom, who enters the "body" or *svarūpa* of whom, the content is the same. And the content, for both *Viśnu* and Brahma, is *the entire universe*.

The "universe" spoken of is not what the Westernised mind tend to think of as "the universe". That is, in the Hindu story, it is not a world in its own right, made of "matter" or material energy, that has nothing to do with us other than that we happen to be it.

Rather, it is 'this entire set of the three worlds, including Devas [gods] Asuras [demons] and human beings',[291] that *Viśnu* and Brahma each see.

Of course, at this stage in the story, the human beings that are mentioned as being part of the universe, haven't even been created! But then, this is just a story, telling things *as though* they happen step-by-step, in time.

What is within *Viśnu* is the same as what is within Brahma. And that, is *everything*. There is only really one Being - the *Brahman*, from which Brahma and *Viśnu* both come to be, as *expansions*.

The "three worlds" spoken of in this text are conceived as *Bhu*, *Bhuvar* and *Svar*.[292] These are "spheres" inside the "cosmic egg" and part of the *Bhu mandala* that represents the way in which our existence arises.

Actually, elsewhere, the *later* Puranas speak of 14 worlds, or *lokas*, seven "higher" and seven "lower". And in this scheme our world is *Bhu*, the lowest of the seven "higher" worlds. *Bhuvar* and *Svar* are the next two in ascending order.

Viśnu is the "preserver" because what is being manifested through Brahma, *depends, in the first instance*, on *Viśnu*. It is only preserved as long as *Viśnu* is asleep on the causal ocean. Brahma is only an *expansion of being* from *Viśnu*, to begin with. Hence Brahma is known as the "creator" whilst *Viśnu* is known as the "preserver".

Expansion and Aggregates

The Adi-lila of the Caitanya-caritamrta, which is a Krsna-Bhakti scripture, states that just as the Sun might be reflected in countless jewels, so Govinda [Krsna] manifests Himself in the hearts of all living beings.[293] Essentially, then, here, *Ksīrodakaśāyī Viśnu* is considered to be an expansion of Krsna.

The subtleties and intricacies of all the expansions as the great expansion of being "passes through" the Trimurti, so to speak, are deep. We can see this, for example, in the Brahma Samhita, elucidated by Jiva Gosvami's commentary on it.[294]

Ultimately, in the Krsna-Bhakti view, Brahma is a particular "stage" in the great expansion of being. Brahma is an expansion of being of other expansions of being, of the Supreme Being.

And just as *Garbhodakaśāyī Viśnu* is the aggregate being of all the beings created through Brahma, so *Garbhodakaśāyī Viśnu* is also the "reservoir" of all the aggregates that this aggregate consist of, or even expands into. All this is Brahma.

One of the aggregates is the aggregate that is the overall *cultural mind* of Hinduism. And in terms of Hinduism itself, Brahma has created existence far and wide beyond Hinduism. And Hinduism itself states that there are infinitely many Brahmas,[295] creating infinitely many universes. Even in *this* universe, even on *this* planet, in which we live, the aggregate of all human beings is far greater than that which is found in Hinduism.

Names, words, sounds, mantras, understanding, and religion, are all aspects of an aggregate. Scientifically speaking, it all manifests through the principle of the brain. And *the principle of the brain* - the principle whereby brain function is also our experience of mind, being, self, and world - is not something that arises through any brain organ in isolation.

No brain organ exists in isolation, nor has any brain organ, in modern scientific understanding, ever evolved on the Earth in isolation. The very *principle of the brain* manifests from, and still is, pertaining to an *aggregate*.

To understand the *principle of the brain*, we need to understand not just the individual brain organ. We need to go beyond the mindset in which we are looking to understand *the principle of the brain*, in terms of an individual brain organ.

We need to understand that everything about our existence belongs to an aggregate. Everything here manifests out of aggregates. And there is an aggregate that in its entirety is in every individual brain as an *instantiation* of the one principle of the brain.

16

Soma

Verily, that One became threefold [the Trimurti]. He developed forth eightfold, elevenfold, twelvefold, into an infinite number of parts. Because of having developed forth, He is a created being (*bhūta*); has entered into and moves among created beings.

- Maitri Upanishad.[296]

Entheogens are "psychoactive substances" that when ingested have the potential to induce some kind of Divine or spiritual experience. In terms of the brain they release in some way the "mode of restraint" in the way the brain is normally working.

Perhaps, we might speculate, this is by allowing multiple, new paths of connections between neural networks, that are otherwise relatively isolated. And perhaps also by repressing certain neural circuits that would otherwise normally be active.

Essentially, it is not possible to *disentangle* this scientific question from the question of how it is that biological brain function equates to our experience of self and world, in the first place.

The question of the effect of entheogens on the brain is closely related to the content of the Hindu corpus. The reason is that the Vedas which are the oldest part of the corpus, and later parts of the corpus too, are based on "revealed knowledge" of *rsis* (seers) in the context of a religious culture of fire sacrifices, in which, it seems, there was the use of an entheogenic plant substance called *Soma*.

The Vedas are the earliest part of the corpus of the Indian scriptures. The Vedas alone exceed the extent of the Bible more than six times over.[297] *Soma* is mentioned frequently in the Vedas, as well as in the Puranas and Upanishads.

The Rig Veda is arranged in ten mandalas, consisting of "hymns" in which there is frequent mention of *Soma* and of drinking *Soma*. The entire ninth Mandala is dedicated to *Soma* and consists of 144 hymns to *Soma*.

Plants or "herbs" in Hinduism are more than just culinary things or food. The Skanda Purana, for example, refers to "medicinal herbs" regarded as "full of nectar and conducive to excellence of intellect",[298] and *Soma* was regarded as the 'Lord of all medicinal herbs'.[299]

As an ingested substance, *Soma* appears to have been prepared by mixing juice crushed from an actual plant, with milk.[300] The contextual background is a culture of fire sacrifices carried out under the influence of *Soma*, often called *Soma* sacrifices.

However, *Soma* clearly also refers to the moon. The moon, in the Hindu corpus, is a Being, and like all beings, is an expansion of the *Brahman*. *Soma* also infers attaining higher states of consciousness through the ingestion of the plant substance.

There is a contemporary analogy here. In the modern world of material understanding, and scientific materialism, we, as a species, landed on the moon in 1969. But the result was more than merely materialistic knowledge of the moon. One could argue it created an unprecedented shift in perspective, in the human mind, certainly in the Western world. Perhaps the icon of this is the famous "Earthrise" picture.

To this day, we now talk about "the planet" in everyday parlance, in a new way, that before, we never did. For the first time, we saw us, and our planetary home, in a new, more "cosmic" way.

The ingestion of *Soma*, which does seem to be what the sources are referring to, constitutes a psychical equivalent of this going to the moon, and then even beyond it, by going beyond the limitations of the material-bound *mind*. In Eastern spirituality generally, the moon is also associated with the mind.

If the *Soma* spoken of in the Vedas relates to an entheogenic plant substance, which certainly seems to be the case, then we can surmise that it was the plant that assisted the entering of the consciousness of the *risi* into the states from which came the chanting or verses that were eventually written down in the Rig Veda.

We need to remember that Hinduism primarily recognises that *all* beings ultimately come from the one Being - *Brahman*. In essence, it is through *becoming* the illuminated consciousness of *Soma*, that the reality of *being-consciousness-bliss* or *sat-chit-ananda* associated with the *Brahman* can be realised as *the Soma no one ever tastes*.[301]

In modern usage the effects of the psychoactives and entheogens that are currently known to science are not explicitly controllable. However, today, in the modern world of Western science, there is now a new thrust to scientifically investigate the brain and the experiences that arise through it whilst under the influence of psychedelic or entheogenic substances.

Perhaps one of the most promising areas in this respect is the scientific investigation of the effects of DMT on the brain, in terms of the *experience of being* and *world of being*, of a subject under its influence.

DMT - N,N-dimethyl tryptamine - is basically what we might consider a modern substitute for *Soma* (although it is not currently certain what *Soma* actually was). DMT would appear to be in this respect more promising even than the previously quite well-known "magic mushroom" substance, psilocybin.

DMT is a naturally produced substance that is also naturally found in the human brain.[302] *Ayahuasca*, the hallucinogenic drink that has long been traditionally used by some Amazonian tribes, is rich in DMT.[303]

One of the salient things that is emerging from the studies of the effects of DMT, is subjects reporting experiencing:

"... an autonomous alternate world rather than a dream or hallucination".[304]

One outstanding thing about reported experiences is that what is experienced seems "more real than real".[305] A large study of 2,561 individuals under the influence of DMT, published in 2020, reported that "entity encounters" experienced under the influence were said to be "more real than normal reality" in 81% of cases during the experience, and 65% after the experience.[306]

Also, the results showed that 'more than half of those who identified as atheist before the experience no longer identified as atheist afterwards', and that in 80% of cases 'the experience altered the respondent's fundamental conception of reality'.

The "more real than real" aspect of the experience is of course indicative that comparatively, the ordinary, everyday experience of the material world, so often referred to as "reality", is an experience of a world that is less "real", or more "dreamlike" than what is sometimes referred to as a "DMT breakthrough".

Considered as a construct of brain function our mind and conditional experience of being is a dynamic structure. Just as brain function is a dynamic structure. And anything that we know as thought or experience, is part of that structure. That structure hasn't come into existence in isolation, in just a single brain.

What we often don't *get*, at the current time, in considering how the brain "creates consciousness", is that no brain ever came into existence in isolation. There are not billions of different principles of the brain, with a different principle operating in each human brain.

Rather, there is one principle of the brain. And each individual human brain is a uniquely configured *instantiation* of that one principle in nature. Similarly, just as, in modern scientific terms, the mind arises as a construct of brain function, so also there is essentially only one human mind in nature, of which each individual human mind, is a uniquely configured instantiation. When put like this, this principle should be easier to see.

So there is only one human mind, but it's not anyone's individual, personal mind. Nor is anyone's individual mind, *separate* from this one human mind. Rather, everyone's individual mind and experience of being as a human being, is a uniquely configured *instantiation* of the one human mind. Just as the principle of the brain operating in everyone's individual brain is a uniquely configured instantiation of the *one* principle of the brain.

"Subsequently" to this, there arises in each human being the individual, *personal* mind, out of this natural mind. The personal mind is the natural, individually instantiated mind's creation. It is the aspect of the naturally arising mind that *interprets* this experience of natural mind and calls it "I". This is the personal ego.

What we experience as the world, is a construct of brain function. It is essentially mind. Similarly, from the point of view of our experience of it, what we experience as the world, is the one natural mind. So everything in the world is part of this natural mind.

It's not anyone's individual, *personal* mind, because that's just the personal ego, as we have just explained. So to walk around declaring that "everything is my mind" or "everything is your mind" from the point of view of the personal ego, would be delusion.

It is a delusion that actually sometimes happens, though, and it can be found in the now quite popular idea of "manifestation", which is the idea that as a person, you can "manifest" (through psychical or mental means) what you want.

Rather, everything in the world that is available to perceive or experience, or know about, or participate in, is part of the one natural mind (*i.e.* world), of which each individual natural human (impersonal) experience of self, is a uniquely configured instance.

But then, things become more complicated because an *involution* takes place. *Involution* is where one thing "folds itself" inside itself. So what happens is that the personal ego, that is, the principle of it, is *part of* the one principle of the mind, that every natural human mind is a uniquely configured instance of.

And so the arising of the personal ego becomes a kind of self-fulfilling prophecy, in the very existence of the world or natural mind. Nevertheless, everything in the world as a whole is the one natural mind created by nature, and each individual human being experiences a unique instance of it, as their experience of self. And entangled in that, is then the aspect of this natural mind, that is the personal ego. That gets there, through this *involution*.

So the blockage to being able to realise that what nature creates as the world, is one and the same as our experience of self, is the personal mind or ego, itself. Hence, when we start to become spiritually mature, and begin to awaken to this truth, concomitantly with that, we begin to become *transpersonal*.

The natural mind, in itself, in us, as it were, isn't personally problematic. Our personal problems as human beings, arise through the personal mind, the personal ego. Because it is a false interpretation of our situation and constitution. Out of it, arises a major part of what is called "the human condition".

In our experience of being this one natural mind, there are different "levels" of what we experience what we might call "real". For example, we might imagine something, and visualise it in our imagination, but then we might say that what we saw, wasn't "real" because it was only imagination. But actually, it was still "real", *as an artefact of mind*, and its associated experience. There is a certain level of "reality" in the experience of it, otherwise it wouldn't be experienced.

If we actually see something through our senses, rather than just in our imagination, then that's a different level of "reality of experience", because its a different aspect of brain function. Both experiences may actually involve some of the same parts of the brain, as we know from brain scanning, but what is actually going on in the brain, in each case, is different. What the DMT study shows is unusual "levels" of "reality of experience". But this "reality of experience" is still being delivered through brain function.

What is going on in the brain, is in any case only a uniquely configured instantiation of the one principle of the brain. So across humanity as a whole, imagination and sense perception are just as mixed up, as they are in an individual. But everyone "looks out" into this world and imagines that it is separate from the self, when actually, the world itself has known by human beings is the one human mind, of which our individual, natural mind, is an instantiation.

Modern scientific evidence itself, which reveals that everything we know and experience is a construct of brain function, actually points to this. But in general, we cannot understand the scientific evidence, or don't even know what to do with it, because there is an inherent blockage in our comprehension, that comes not from lack of scientific data, or lack of ability to think objectively, but rather, because we are not *transpersonal*.

So in the so-called "DMT breakthrough", it is often reported that what is experienced is "more real than real". That's because DMT changes the way the brain is working, and takes experience to a different "level" of "reality of experience", so to speak, in which what is experienced, is above, as it were, mere imagination, but also above ordinary sensory experience.

Anything that can be experienced or known through the one principle of the brain, is anything that that structure is capable of creating, as experience or knowledge. Different cultures, and religions, and even different DMT experiences, explore different aspects of this structure and its possibilities. But always, it is what is created through the principle of the brain.

It's perfectly possible to experience something that doesn't *seem to be* dependent upon the biological brain, such as an "out of the body experience", or experiences of "astral being" and so on, when actually that dependency is still there. This is all wrapped up in the fact that the biological brain organ, as we encounter it, is itself only encountered through the principle of the brain. The *principle* of the brain through which our experience of being and mind actually arises, transcends the merely material representation of that principle, which is what we encounter as the material, biological brain organ.

So where is "reality" in all this? This is not a modern question. It's just that before the times in which we are living now, it hasn't been addressed in these terms. The Hindu corpus *already answers it*, with the answer: the *Brahman*. It's just that the *Brahman* is not an object or a "thing". It's not a *principle*, like the mind is, and the brain is, and therefore, ultimately, something that can be mentally *understood*. It's not that.

As the Hindu corpus overall communicates, the *Brahman* is not something separate from us, that we discover. On the contrary, the *Brahman* is the reality of the Being that even in our limited, conditional experience of being, as a human being, we *already really are*.

This Reality of Being called the *Brahman*, is realised by *awakening as* that Reality of unconditional Being, in which there is Joy (or alternatively what the Hindu corpus in general calls *bliss*), Knowledge and Consciousness. This Consciousness is not merely the mind. It's not merely the one natural mind that everyone's individual, natural mind is an instantiation of. It's not merely the principle of the brain.

There is only one *Brahman*, just as there is only one principle of the brain. But also, just as everyone's individual experience of the principle of the brain, as individual self and mind, is different, so there is also more than one kind of *realisation* of the *Brahman*.

In general, when a human being realises the *Brahman*, the underlying realisation is the same, in all cases, which is realisation of the Self, as unconditional Being, not dependent on any condition of being, or on existence. An aspect of it is what the Hindu corpus calls *sat chit ananda* (or alternative spellings), which means "being consciousness bliss". But the actual realisation of it has different "levels" and "aspects". For example, the realisation may or may not include gnostic illumination.

The communication of it by an individual will be in some way unique, not just because communication is delivered through a unique individual, natural mind, but also because the realisation is itself unique. However, all realisations are of the One, the Being, Splendour, *Brahman* or Self, which means variant communications of it are recognisable for what they are, by any human being who has had the realisation.

Importantly, as we have been seeing, the Indian *Bhakti* tradition recognises that an initial realisation of the *Brahman* as the impersonal bliss of liberated, unconditional Being, is actually the effulgence or radiance of what Bhakti knows as *Krsna*. In other words, the Reality of transcendental Life and Being (*Vrndavana*) above the "impersonal" realisation of the *Brahman*.

So the initial realisation of the *Brahman* is transpersonal, and is of *impersonal, unconditional* Being. But above the "impersonal" realisation of the *Brahman*, is the realisation of transpersonal Life and Being, in which "personal" takes on an entirely new, transcendental meaning.

Everything, including the *Brahman* and the material world, is understood to be created through the *expansion of being*, of That Being. And Bhakti holds that the highest realisation of That Being is the realisation of the Spiritual Reality of the Divine Couple Radha-Krsna in *Vrndavana* - realised as Chaitanya.[307]

The *Brahman* is likened to seeing the Sun, whilst still higher, *inside* the Sun, is the true Spiritual Reality, the Source of this effulgence, that is the glorious, inconceivable Reality of the eternal Joy and love of the Being Krsna,[308] realised in *Chaitanya Consciousness* as Radha-Krsna in Vrndavana.[309]

This goes well beyond anything that the scientific investigation of the effects of DMT, can access or understand. The "more real than real" aspect of the DMT experience is just a preliminary indicator in the field of scientific investigation of the brain. It does highlight the questionability of clinging to *naive materialism* and *scientific materialism*, in which it is believed that the material world is a "reality" in its own right, separate from us and independent of brain function.

It is an indicator that *everything* we can ever know, actually falls in the first instance into the domain of the *experience of being*, and *world of being*. Because always, this is already in place to begin with, before we "know" or experience anything. Our *experience of being* is already in place first, *before* we measure anything in science, or understand anything at all about our world.

First, before we have any of this human experience, there is the brain. And the *prima facie* thing about the brain is that it creates our experience of being and world. If we are looking straight through this fact or beyond it, without noticing it, then we have failed to notice what "nature" is really all about.

DMT interferes with the working of the brain. As such, it interferes with the working of the mind. We must remember that in Hinduism and Buddhism, even though Hinduism is regarded as "theistic" and Buddhism is often regarded as "atheistic", the aim of spiritual practice is to discover God, *beyond the mind*. The *Brahman*, the Being, is not just beyond the mind, but as the great Hindu corpus communicates, it is the Source from which the mind is created.

The ingestion of DMT deconstructs the mind in some way. The effects of DMT in studies include a large variety of experience-types that depend on the individual. For example, the experiences include parallels to other experiences not under the influence of externally provided DMT, such as near death experiences, the experience of bodiless being, alien abduction, specific religious experiences, and so on. The beings encountered include "machine elves", hyper-intelligent beings, circus characters such as clowns, jesters, jokers, and so on.

Amongst the experiences are explosive translocation into other worlds, other "realities", flying through "other dimensions", and encountering DMT itself as a personified being (in parallel to how *Soma* appears in the Vedas).

There are encounters with many beings with specific roles, such as "the teacher" and "the trickster", which clearly correlate with Jung's archetypes. There are even encounters with "sentient geometry" and

Hyper-dimensional structures. Then there are also encounters with "messages" about the nature of the cosmos, love, and being.[310] There are also "encounters with God" and mystical experiences.[311]

These are just a few examples of what is experienced. They are all aspects of *the mind* itself, and of what can be reconstructed out of that structure. It is not the same thing as the realisation of the *Brahman*.

When we are talking about such things as "machine elves" and "alien abduction", and "black holes", then clearly we are talking about something that pertains to the times and culture in which the participants in such experiments are living.

We have to remember that the use of *Soma* in ancient Indian culture was taking place in ancient Indian culture, and was not "experimental" in this same way. It wasn't being "investigated" from an objective, materialist point of view, and wasn't being taken in the context of that setting. The thrust of the content of the Hindu corpus is not about "experiences you may have when taking *Soma*".

On the contrary, *Soma* in the Hindu corpus is just a part of a much bigger picture. And we need to recognise that so too, are the effects of any entheogens or psychedelics that are currently examined by science. This whole field is part of a much bigger picture.

That bigger picture, from the point of view the Hindu corpus, is about *Brahman*, or God. That is, knowledge or ignorance of *Brahman*, or God. From the point of view of the materialist Western mind, the bigger picture is also about our knowledge or ignorance of this bigger picture.

The question is, how do we get to see the bigger picture? Naive materialism is the blockage. In modern science-related terms, naive materialism is the naive presumption that the material world exists independently as something separate from us. It is the presumption that it must be other than a construct of brain function, erected on belief in the psychological and emotional conviction that it is other than our self.

That psychological and emotional conviction rests on the personal idea of "who I am", rather than on actual knowledge of this self, as an experience of being. It is in the way of things that increasing knowledge of this self dissolves the blockage, and there, behind what dissolves, is our already intrinsic natural knowledge of the true nature of the world in which we live.

No amount of data or scientific interpretation of data can provide this knowledge. Because it is necessarily experiential. But what science can do, is tip us towards awakening into this knowledge.

It is already trying to. Because in science, we already know that there is nothing we know, think, or experience, that is not a construct of electrochemical brain function. And that includes the material world that we experience, too.

The material world, within which, as part of it, arises the brain organ itself. The material world, that includes naturally occurring substances such as DMT and *Soma*, which help to break down this blockage of naive materialism, by taking the carpet out from under the feet of this personal idea of "who I am".

But there is another way in which this happens. It is what the Hindu corpus as a whole is all about, beyond the earliest parts of it in which *Soma* features. There is another way. Which is simply the realisation of the *Brahman*, as the Truth of our own Identity through spiritual pursuit and the Grace of God. And in the corpus of the Puranas as a whole, the central process through which this realisation happens, is called the churning of the ocean. Which is something we will come to talk about.

17

The Seven Oceans

As we mentioned earlier, the *Ocean of Milk*, amongst other things, is one of seven Mythological oceans in Hindu cosmology. These oceans are situated between seven concentric islands or *dvīpas*, the whole arrangement forming part of the *Bhu mandala.*

The *dvīpas* are described in the Puranas as lands free from suffering and anxiety, with fantastical features. Essentially, they correspond to what Western understanding would ordinarily call a description of spiritual "heavens".

The seven oceans, starting with the innermost one, and working outwards, are described in the Puranas as oceans of:

1. salt water,
2. sugarcane juice or molasses,
3. wine or liquor,
4. clarified butter,
5. milk, or curds and whey,[312]
6. curds,[313] or yoghurt,[314] or churned yoghurt,[315] or *dadhi-manda*,[316] or milk.[317]
7. fresh water,[318] clear water,[319] or 'sweet' water or 'very tasteful' water,[320] or drinking water.[321]

Here, in most accounts, the salt water ocean is the innermost ocean, surrounding the central island or continent of *Jambudvīpa*. The seven concentric islands or *dvīpas* are separated by respective concentric oceans. The arrangement is not unlike the way Plato's Atlantis is described in *Timaeus* and *Critias*.

The collected seven islands are known as the *Saptadvīpa*. The word *dvīpa* is often combined with the name of the island to make just one word. So for example, *Jambudvīpa* is Jambu *dvīpa*. The concentric islands are commonly said to double in size with each island as we travel out from the centre. Each island's surrounding ocean is commonly said to be the same size as the island it surrounds.

Whilst many attempts have been made to rationalise the *Saptadvīpa* and the seven oceans, the fact remains that this Mythology is a particular *cultural Mythology*, appropriately symbolising something in the form of its particular presentation in Hinduism. Furthermore, as we shall see, the descriptions vary across the Puranas.

As can be seen from the list above some of these islands have oceans that are of milk or milk products, and of course the "Ocean of Milk" features prominently in the Mythology. These accounts emerge out of an early culture in which cow-herding is the backbone of the culture, the cow is sacred, and milk products are central to the society. So the fact that milk and milk products feature in the Mythology is hardly surprising. That's just part of the cultural and religious *fabric* through which the Mythology is expressed.

However, there is *much* more to it than this. This is not *merely* cultural, or merely just a matter of prosaic things like the production of milk from cows, to sustain society. Far from it.

When texts - especially the Bhakti texts - speak of such things as "oceans of transcendental milk", and "transcendental cows", this has a much, much deeper meaning.[322] It's not just a matter of prosaic, cultural features.

The mode of expression and scenery of the Mythology arises out of the culture. But the point the corpus is making is that the very culture itself, with its cows and its milk, when seen through the eyes of spiritual illumination, is not just a prosaic form. It is, like everything, as this part of the corpus describes, a material manifestation from the transcendental. And so it is already a *material symbol*, so to speak, of the nature of things in the transcendental.

The symbolism used in the Mythology clearly arises out of the culture. Cows and milk are part of the mode of expression, especially in the Bhakti texts. But also, in the spiritual vision that the corpus itself communicates, the nature of the culture and its Mythology, arises, *like everything else*, out of the transcendental. It arises through the great *expansion of being*, from the transcendental Spiritual Reality, and then through the *causal ocean*.

So something called "the Ocean of Milk" is not part of some mystical objectified *structure*, in which there are different material liquids of the kind that we know in material existence.

On the contrary, in material existence itself, just as it is, milk is a symbol. Cows are a symbol. The production of milk and the giving of milk, is a symbol. And the churning of milk is a symbol. They are not symbols for other material things, but symbolise aspects of the transcendental.

Similarly, all these things *as they appear in the texts*, are *symbols* because they are *already symbols* in the actuality of material existence.

There is of course an interrelationship between the way spiritual knowledge or realisation is experienced, and the culture within which it happens. So when transcendental spiritual Reality is described in Hinduism in a way seemingly inseparable from the nature of Hindu culture, there is indeed a way in which this is true. However, basically the same principle in other religions and cultures, and is true there, too, with different characteristic modes of expression.

The truth, of course, is that what is transcendental is transcendental. It is transcendental to all culture, and all belief. That which is not, is something intermediate between a still limited, conditional experience of being, associated with the human condition, and the transcendental.

The Saptadvīpa

So in the Hindu corpus, we were saying, the set of seven concentric islands and their surrounding oceans is called the *saptadvīpa*. We were saying that most commonly, the order of the oceans going outwards from the central island of Jambu, around which is the Ocean of Salt Water, is often stated to be:

1. salt water,
2. sugarcane juice or molasses,
3. wine or liquor,
4. clarified butter,
5. milk, or curds and whey,[323]
6. curds,[324] or yoghurt,[325] or churned yoghurt,[326] or *dadhi-manda*,[327] or milk.[328]
7. fresh water,[329] clear water,[330] or 'sweet' water or 'very tasteful' water,[331] or drinking water.[332]

The commonly encountered list of names (outwards from the centre) of the concentric islands themselves (the *dvīpas*) is:[333]

1. Jambu,
2. Plaksa,
3. Śālmali,
4. Kuśa,
5. Kraunca,
6. Śaka,

7. Puskara.

The Śiva Purana says Puskara is divided into two, and says that it is always night there.[334] We are told that Brahma resides there, and that it is surrounded by an ocean of sweet water.[335]

Then we are told that beyond Puskara there are no living beings, and that the land is golden and has no living creatures.[336] Beyond it is the mountain Lokaloka.[337]

We met Lokaloka and this part of the "spiritual landscape" before. Beyond it, we saw, is the *causal ocean* or Viraja river.

According to the Śrīmad Bhāgavatam and other sources, the Ocean of Milk surrounds the island called *Krauna dvīpa*. And on the "outside" of the Ocean of Milk is *Śaka dvīpa*.

But we should not be complacent about this, thinking we have discovered here an objective structure, just because we have read one text.

The Srimad Devi Bhagavatam agrees with this order, for both islands and oceans. However, it also states:

> The Jambu *dvīpa* is surrounded by *Ksira Samudra* [the Ocean of Milk].[338]

It actually speaks of the Ocean of Milk as surrounding more than one *dvīpa*. And of course the easiest thing in the world is just to "take sides" with one "school" of Hinduism, or another. But that's not the way to get not just into it, but under it, into where it all comes from.

In the Hindu corpus, the Ocean of Milk turns up in all kinds of places, just as places turn up in the Ocean of Milk.

The "white island" called *Śvetadvīpa* is the case in point. We saw earlier that *Gokula*, *Vraja*, *Goloka*, *Śvetadvīpa* and *Vrndāvana* are all names of the *transcendental realm* of Krsna, beyond Lokaloka (a combined form of *loka-aloka*, meaning "place and no place").

The Caitanya-caritamrta says that Gokula is the highest of all, also called *Vraja*, *Goloka* [the "place of the cows"], and *Śvetadvīpa* [the white island] and *Vrndāvana*.[339]

We saw that in the tenth Canto of the *Śrīmad Bhāgavatam* Lord Krsna's transcendental chariot travels *across* the seven *dvīpas* and seven oceans, to the region of the vast darkness of *Aloka* [the "outermost" part of Lokaloka].[340] We saw that the *transcendental region* is well beyond this, beyond the *causal ocean*.[341]

And yet *Śvetadvīpa*, the abode of Lord *Viśnu*, is also declared in the Caitanya-caritamrta to lay *in* part of the Ocean of Milk.[342]

Śvetadvīpa here, is explicitly the abode of Lord *Viśnu*. But this is a Bhakti text, which upholds *Viśnu* to be *an expansion of* Krsna. So we can see clearly here that *Śvetadvīpa*, the abode of transcendental Krsna, is involved in the expansion of *Viśnu* from Krsna. It could even be said that it is an expansion of *Śvetadvīpa*, that occurs in the Ocean of Milk. The Mahabharata then states that the island of *Śvetadvīpa* is on the northern shores of the Ocean of Milk.[343]

The Laghu Bhagavatamrta says (about the Brahmānda Purana)[344] that *Śvetadvīpa* is surrounded by the milk ocean,[345] and also says that *Śvetadvīpa* is South East of Meru (the mountain at the centre of Jambu *dvīpa*).[346]

The Kurma Purana rather ambiguously states:

> Encircling the Śaka *dvīpa* is the ocean of milk, and in its middle is *Śvetadvīpa*.[347]

So although *Śvetadvīpa* (the white island) is, in the Bhakti texts, explicitly in the transcendental realm, and is the highest transcendental abode of Krsna, here, it turns up *in*, or *on the shores of*, the Ocean of Milk, in various different locations.

So what we actually have here, is an Ocean of Milk that isn't part of something that can be understood as a fixed, objective structure, in just one part of the Hindu cosmology.

A little later we shall see that the whole of the *saptadvīpa*, the seven islands and oceans, are "inside" what Hinduism calls the "cosmic egg" or "egg of Brahma". And that only "outside" this "egg" is the transcendental realm. So we have been looking at sources that state clearly *Śvetadvīpa* is *in* the transcendental realm, *and* sources that state clearly it is not.

This is not however, out of keeping with the corpus in general, in which not just "places" (which are also *Being*), but personified beings also, such as *Viśnu* and Krsna, are both *in the transcendental*, and arise within the creation, "inside" the "egg", through the principle of *the expansion of being*.

What is "inside" the "egg" is said to be "the material world". When the *expansion of being* reaches down, as it were, from the transcendental to "inside" the "egg", then this expansion of being is called an *avatara*, or avatar.

None of this should surprise us, because the Hindu corpus is not after all, really about objective structures. It is, it must be emphasised, about the realisation of God. We are not talking about a "geography" of spatially arranged distinct parts, or indeed about anything that can be represented in that way, with any fidelity.

However, having said that, the corpus does contain what is essentially often presented as a "cosmology" of parts in relation to each other. We will eventually come back to this. It is important to remember that this is not an objective structure, as science or engineering might recognise, or even the discipline of geography might understand, but rather, it is a *symbol*.

It is a symbol, in the same way that many particular drawings or objects in Buddhism are called *mandalas* (A Sanskrit word that more generally just means circles, paths or spheres). This cosmological symbol that we are beginning to look at here, presented in the Hindu corpus in a somewhat fragmented way, is indeed known as the *Bhu mandala*.

The Padma Purana says there is a four-fold manifestation of God by the great sages, consisting of *Vaikuntha* which it says is the highest heaven, *Viśnuloka*, *Śvetadvīpa* and the Milky Ocean.[348]

This makes it clear that we are here *not looking at a structure of distinct "things"*. We are talking about *Being*, and in particular about the *expansion of being*.

Let us go on with the accounts. The Padma Purana says that the Ocean of Milk surrounds *Śaka dvīpa*.[349] But we are also told that *Sakadvīpa* is twice the size of *Jambudvīpa*.

The general rule found across the corpus, is that each *dvīpa* is twice the size of the one next to it further in towards the centre, the central *dvīpa* being *Jambudvīpa*.

By other accounts, however, the island that is twice the size of *Jambudvīpa* is the next island out which is not *Sakadvīpa*, as mentioned here, but *Plaksadvīpa*. So here, the order of the islands themselves, has changed.

However, the idea that the Ocean of Milk surrounds *Saka dvīpa* is also found in the Brahma Purana, which says:

> The ocean of milk is *encircled by* Puskaradvīpa. Puskaradvīpa is twice as much as the Sakadvīpa in size.[350]

So here we see the Brahma Purana agrees with the Padma Purana that the Ocean of Milk surrounds *Śaka*, and is placed between *Śaka* and *Puskara*. This also agrees with the placement of it in the Siva Purana.[351]

Is this respect then, the Padma Purana, the Brahma Purana and the Siva Purana, all agree. They all say the Ocean of Milk surrounds *Plaksa dvīpa*. But the order of the islands is changed, in the Padma Purana.

The Motilal Barnarsidass scholarly edition of the Kurma Purana, (Delhi, 1998) lists the islands (*dvīpas*) in the same order as most other sources, the most usual order being:

1. Jambu,
2. Plaksa,
3. Śālmali,

4. Kuśa,
5. Kraunca,
6. Śaka,
7. Puskara.

The beginning of Chapter 45 of Part 1, then lists the seven oceans in order, but without specifically mentioning all the islands. Starting with the ocean surrounding Jambu, they are:[352]

1. salt water,
2. sugar-cane juice,
3. wine,
4. ghee (clarified butter),
5. curds,
6. milk,
7. sweet water.

However, later, *the same Purana* states the order to be:

1. milk,[353]
2. (unstated),
3. first states sugar can juice,[354] then later states wine,[355]
4. clarified butter,[356]
5. curds,[357]
6. milk,[358]
7. (unstated).

The "standard answer" to discrepancies like this, in the corpus, is to say that the situation is different in different *kalpas* or *Manvantaras*. So let's now take a short detour to talk about *cosmic time* in Hinduism.

Hindu Cosmic Time

In Hinduism Brahma, "the creator", is not eternally static, but rather, is himself created and dissolved in infinite cycles. *Viśnu* is eternal, but in an infinite cycle of sleeping and waking. Brahma emerges from the lotus that emerges from the navel of Viśnu.

Within each life-cycle of Brahma, are many "days and nights" or *kalpas* (Divine days) of Brahma. The whole cycle of creation, maintenance, and destruction of what Hinduism calls "the universe", takes place within just one "day and night" or *kalpa* of Brahma.

One life-cycle of *Brahma* consists of 42,200 *kalpas*.[359] So 42,200 Hindu universes are created and destroyed during the life-cycle of one *Brahma*. There are simultaneously infinitely many Brahmas,[360] and infinitely many universes in their cycles of creation, maintenance, and destruction.

So what Hinduism calls "the universe" is only ever one of infinitely many *cycles* of creation, maintenance, and dissolution, of "the universe". In fact, it is also only one of *infinitely many instances* of such infinite cycles of "universes", because there are simultaneously infinitely many *Brahmas* engaged in these cyclic creations of "universes".

So let's just reiterate that: what Hinduism called "the universe", is created, maintained, and destroyed within one Divine cycle or "day and night" of *Brahma*, - one *kalpa*. However, there are also the infinitely many *Brahmas*, each engaged in such cycles of creation of infinitely many "universes".

Ultimately, as well as the realisation of the *Brahman*, Hinduism is all about infinities, and infinite cycles and cycles within cycles.

There is a Being called *Manu*. A *Manvantara* is the life-cycle of the *Manu* Being, which is the Being "ruling over" that *Manu*'s *Manvantara*.

Fourteen *Manus* arise within each *kalpa*, so in each *kalpa*, or Divine "day of Brahma", that is, within each and every cycle of creation, maintenance, and destruction of the entire "universe", there are *fourteen Manvantaras*. So at any time in "the universe", it is "configured" or "ruled over" by one of fourteen different *Manus*.

A *Yuga* in the Hindu time-scheme is one of four *Yugas* or ages that take place in 71 cycles of all four, during one *kalpa*. The four Yugas in order are *Krita* (*Satya*) *Yuga*, *Treta Yuga*, *Dvapara Yuga*, and *Kali Yuga*, which represent four stages of time, progressively degenerating, in which people become more and more ignorant.[361]
Each Yuga is a fraction of the "length of time" of the previous one. In the same order, their time lengths are in the ratios 4:3:2:1.[362] There are special transition periods between one Yuga and the next.[363]

Only in the *Kali Yuga* are things terribly degenerate. The age we are living in, is usually said to be a *Kali Yuga*. After the degeneration is complete, at the end of the *Kali Yuga*, there is a dissolution, in which people become "scrupulously religious",[364] and the cycle of four *Yugas* starts all over again. The progression of Yugas is not a *wave form*, rather, we are specifically told, the beginning of Manvantaras is preceded by the ends of Manvantara.[365]

The duration of the Kali Yuga is stated in the Brahmanda Purana to be 360,000 human years,[366] and the duration of the four Yugas including the junctions or transition periods between Yugas, is stated to be 4,320,000 human years.[367]

A very important point about the Yugas is that although there is progressive spiritual degeneration from the *Krita* (*Satya*) *Yuga* through to the *Kali Yuga*, spiritual realisation (as the result of true *Dharma* or spiritual practice), becomes *quicker* (easier) in each age.[368]

One cycle of four *Yugas* is called a *Caturyuga*. So at the end of 71 *Caturyugas* which is 284 (71 X 4) *Yugas*, a *Manu* completes his life-span.[369]

So a Yuga is therefore approximately 0.00025 of a *kalpa*, or "day of Brahma".[370]

There is a kind of "standard answer" to discrepancies in the corpus, in that one can say conflicting accounts are talking about different *Manvantaras*.

Whilst talking about *Plaksa dvīpa*, the Brahma Purana states that time there is not subject to the changes of the Yugas but rather, is perpetually like the Treta Yuga.[371]

Also, when talking about *Plaksadvīpa* the Siva Purana states:

> ... the time there is on a par with Treta Yuga forever.[372]

The Kurma Purana, also talking about *Plaksadvīpa*, and "continents" within it, states that it has no cycles of the Yugas.[373]

There is here only one division in the whole of the *saptadvīpa* in which the four Yugas are taking place, and cycling. This is a small section of Jambudvīpa called *Bhārata* (an ancient name for India).

This part is known as the *karmabhūmi*, the "place of work", as distinct from the other parts of the *saptadvīpa* that are "places of pleasure".

The *Karmabhūmi* part of the "cosmic system" is spoken of in many other parts of the Hindu corpus. In some systems such as Jainism, however, there is more than one part of Jambudvīpa that constitutes *Karmabhūmi*. The salient point about the *Karmabhūmi* part of the "cosmic egg" is that it is the place of "work" or *karma*, where "penance" is done, creating the possibility of liberation from "the universe", in other words, the permanent awakening into transcendental Life and Being.

Outside *Bhārata* the rest of the *saptadvīpa* is relatively timeless. Life there is not eternal, as described in the corpus, but it is not subject to the constraints of time and suffering as we know it in the ordinary material world.

There is the idea in the corpus that what we see as stars or planets represent "abodes", the occupants of which change per *Manvantara*.[374]

Oceans Again

So Hindu cosmic time helps the argument that there is a change of order of the islands and oceans of the *saptadvīpa*, with each *Manvantara*.

If we really follow through with what the corpus says, it certainly leads to a *dynamic picture* of what is going on in "the universe", rather than a static structure.

The whole thing is essentially *alive* with cycles within cycles, and one would *expect* that as a result of that, the *saptadvipa* is not just to be viewed as a static structure, but also, as an *infinitely cycling* "structure" within which the "islands" and their "oceans" are themselves constantly propagating like waves in water.

It is just that many of the cycles in the Hindu cosmic time scheme completely dwarf the kind of time cycles we are ordinarily used to conceiving, such as the Earth day and year, or for that matter even the age of the Earth as understood by science.

What are we saying here? We are saying that all attempts at structural understanding as if this "spiritual landscape" as a material-like structure, or a "geography" of distinct parts, are basically mistaken, unless you understand that this is a *symbol*, and understand the symbolism.

The language, about water, and waters, and oceans, and so on, is not *cryptic*, and waiting to be "decoded", but rather, is *symbolic*. That is, it is a metaphor for something - the truth behind our human experience of being - that cannot be understood as an objective structure of distinct, static parts. It is not an "object" that is separate from, or other than, the actual stuff of our own experience of being and mind. And what we experience as the material world, through the principle of the brain, is all part of that experience of being and mind.

In a not wholly dissimilar the way the human brain - through which arises our experience of being, as the experience of mind, self, and the material, world - also cannot be understood as a static structure. Rather, we must understand the brain *function*. The organ itself doesn't create our experience of being. Rather, it is its functioning, that does that.

In Hinduism, oceans, liquids, and water, are in this context a *synonym* for aspects of the way in which our *experience of being* is brought about. In the Puranas there are *many* "oceans" of all kinds, not just these seven oceans.

For example, there is *the ocean of worldly existence*. And it is not surprising that many of them are, metaphorically, oceans of foodstuffs. Remember that this is *cultural*. The spiritual content of the corpus is expressed through cultural fabric. And we need to distil out of the cultural fabric, the spiritual content.

It is a cultural expression of something that is beyond all cultures, but nonetheless, has to be expressed through the fabric of the culture.

In fact, when it comes to foodstuffs, in the Linga Purana, for example, we find:

> The ocean of milk,
> The *ocean of honey*,
> The ocean of ghee,
> The *ocean of rice soaked in ghee*,
> The *ocean of fruits and lambatives*,
> The *ocean of various edibles and foodstuffs*,
> and a mountain of baked pies.[375]

These all appear around (*Śiva*), when he manifests himself as a boy.[376]

In the Varāha Purana it is *Kuśa dvīpa* and not *Kraunca dvīpa*, that is initially said to be surrounded by the Ocean of Milk.[377] But then a little later it is stated that *Kuśadvīpa* is surrounded by an ocean of curd, or *amrta* (nectar of immortality), and that it is twice the size of the milky ocean.[378]

So with no intervening explanation about Manvantaras or Kalpas or anything else, the account just changes. And now we are told that curds are equal to *amrta*, which means "nectar of immortality".[379] This is clearly a reference to the *Samudra Mathana*, or the story of the Churning of the Ocean of Milk, out of which emerges the *amrta*, but we will come to that a little later.

This passage also tells us that the ocean of curds is double the size of the milk ocean, which indicates an *expansion*. Going out from the centre, there is always described, an *expansion* of size, in the islands and their oceans.

And yet, at the same time, in terms of the *expansion of being*, but coupled with the *involution*, there is an *expansion* going on in the opposite direction. It goes from the "unmanifest" Being or *Avyakta* "outside" the "cosmic egg" of Brahma, "inwards" through the three Viśnus, through the "coverings" of the "cosmic egg", towards the centre, through the Bhu mandala, through the *Saptadvīpa*, to *Jambudvīpa* at the centre, and then on through *Jambudvīpa* to Bharata, the part of *Jambudvīpa* in which there is cyclic time, and the four Yugas.

This is a "dynamic structure" that we are looking at, in which there is eternal expansion and involution, and the entire Bhu mandala or "structure" of the "cosmic egg" is "churning" with this expansion and involution.

When we later look at the story of "the churning of the ocean", or *Samudra Mathana*, we shall see that everything in existence comes out of the churning of the ocean. And yet everything in existence is created as the Bhu mandala, and the "content" of the "cosmic egg" of Brahma.

The "ocean of milk" is *part* of the *Saptadvīpa*, but at the same time, the "ocean of milk" is everywhere, and everything comes out of it. This isn't really contradictory, at all, when we are looking at something that is infinite expansion and involution. Today, we even have a *scientific* representation of this kind of thing. It occurs in complex fractal geometry, in the "structure" of infinite, fractal "landscapes".

Later, we shall see that in the Bhakti part of the corpus, it is recognised that in the "descent" from spirit to matter, the "ocean of milk" originates in the transcendental as an "ocean of *Prema*", which is Being and the love of Godhead.

We also find an account of *Śaka dvīpa* having the salt ocean on one side and the milky ocean on the other.[380] None of this is random mistake making. The symbolism overall, holds, but it is our job to discover what the symbolism is.

The order of the islands in the Varāha Purana, some with different names, is:[381]

1. Jambu,
2. Śaka,
3. Kuśa,
4. Kraunca,
5. Śalmali, surrounded by the sea of ghee,
6. Gomeda, surrounded by sugarcane juice (molasses),
7. Puskara, surrounded by sweet water.

So if *Śaka dvīpa* has the salt ocean on one side and the milky ocean on the other,[382] as we are told, and given that the salt ocean surrounds Jambu, then we are being told that the Ocean of Milk surrounds *Śaka dvīpa*.

Should we really try to "decode" all this? Absolutely not. To "understand" the *saptadvīpa* and the oceans as a system or structure of distinct objects, is to understand nothing.

Because the meaning is about the realisation of the Divine, the realisation of God, *Brahman* or Krsna. The meaning is about the *expansion of being*. The meaning is about *involution*. It is about the true nature of the way in which there arises our own human experience of being, and what appears to us as the material world we inhabit.

The islands are described in the corpus as inhabited. The inhabitants of the "islands" are widely described as being free from suffering or "anxiety", and to live extraordinarily long lives, and so on. We might well interpret them as "heavens" or "heavenly worlds' attainable by souls, but from which souls must eventually return to mundane existence.

This is all part of what the corpus describes as "the universe". We must remember that what this "universe" *is*, is *Maya* originating from the *Brahman*. It is the illusory dream of *Viśnu*, sleeping on the *causal ocean*, but then *Viśnu* too, as we see in the Śiva Purana, is a Being created in order to allow this to happen, whilst the Divine couple *Śiva* and *Śiva* remain eternally enjoying "the blissful forest".

Like *Śiva*, *Viśnu* remains in his ultimate Identity as the *Brahman*, and His "appearance" as *Śiva* or Rudra in what is subsequently created through Brahma, is essentially his transcendental influence on what is created and unfolds in the aggregate of all that is created as Brahma.

The Bhakti descriptions of the three *Viśnus*, that we have talked about, describe the *expansion of being* of the one *Maha-Viśnu*, and they put the final form of this expansion as *Ksīrodakaśāyī Viśnu*, who lays on the "ocean of milk", or *Ksīra Sāgara*, and who 'lives in the heart of every living being.'[383]

So we can see how the "ocean of milk", which begins transcendentally as an ocean of *Prema*, the love of the Being, the Godhead, in transcendental Life and Being, becomes, eventually, through expansion and involution, the "ocean of milk" within every living being in material existence, as the basis of their experience of being and world.

Translated into modern scientific terms, this experience of being correlates directly to the *construct of brain function*, which scientifically speaking, is what we are experiencing as our conditional experience of being and world.

So the Bhu mandala and the *Saptadvīpa* within it, are essentially a conceptualised description of the principle of expansion and involution from the *Brahman*, through which arises the nature of the mind that we experience as our conditional experience of being and world. It is the Hindu version of the principle of the brain.

We can follow the expansion from the "unmanifest" *Avyakta* to the world of our own conditional experience of being. This is equivalent to penetrating from "outside" the "cosmic egg" of Brahma, through to the centre of it. The inner part of the Bhu mandala, within the "coverings" that constitute the cosmic "egg" of Brahma, is essentially described as a number of concentric spheres called "worlds" and "nether worlds", that, as it were, "lead into" and intersect with the *Saptadvīpa*. The *Saptadvīpa* then leads across its "islands" and "oceans" in towards the centre, where there is *Jambudvīpa*. Then, still travelling towards the centre, we come to to Bharata, which is the only part of this "structure" in which there are the four Yugas.

But actually, at the very centre of the whole "system", is Mount Meru, which represents the "true understanding",[384] of the whole "system". In other words, the Bhu mandala is a representation of how *time* as the cycle of the Yugas is created through expansion and involution from the Being, the *Brahman*.

It is important to note here that time as the cycle of the Yugas is not the objective time that science measures. And also, whilst the Bhakti texts refer to the whole content of the "cosmic egg" as the "material universe", this is not the "material universe" that science speaks of, and measures.

In other words, what we are really looking at here, in these parts of the Hindu corpus, is not content that is talking about the objective, material world, as understood and measured by science. Rather, it is talking about the nature, creation and content of the mind we are being, *through which* we experience the objective, material world.

To describe any part of the expansion in finite terms, say, as seven islands and oceans, is not so dissimilar to saying that there are seven colours of the rainbow. There may be, if that's what you experience, but some people can only see six, or five. And a physicist would probably say that there are actually infinitely many wavelengths of light there.

So also, the Brahmanda Purana describes what appears to be not seven, but *ten* concentric *dvīpas*, with *Jambudvīpa* at the centre. *Jambudvīpa* is said to be surrounded by the salt ocean.[385]

To remind ourselves again, measurements and relative sizes, and so on, are not scientific in the modern sense of the word *scientific*. They are symbolic, and help in building a "picture" of principles. Which are themselves symbolic.

Having nine worlds, that evolve a number of living beings, really, is again a way of talking about how our mind, as our own conditional experience of being and world, is created through many "structures" ("islands" and "oceans"), which are also mind and conditional experience of *being and world*, in their own right.

In other words, there is no such thing as a "human mind" as a separate, singular entity. Just as there is no such thing as a "neural network" in the brain, that has any meaning or capacity to give rise to any part of our experience of being, without being part of the brain as a whole. And even the whole individual brain organ has no real meaning on its own, because no brain organ ever came into existence on its own.

Symbolism

Travelling *outwards*, so to speak, from Jambu, beyond all seven (or nine) *dvīpas* and their oceans, is the transcendental realm, which lies beyond the *causal ocean*.

The Brahma Purana says that after enjoying the nectar of ruling over the kingdom (*i.e.* your self, as the earth), and after passing over the worlds [*i.e.* the worlds within the "cosmic egg"], 'you will attain my world'.[386]

We mentioned earlier how the Hindu corpus contains types of text suitable for those who can only understand physical idol worship, alongside material suitable for those who are more spiritually advanced, and beyond the need of idol worship. Often, therefore, the language is polysemic, as it is in the Brahma Purana.[387]

Other Bhakti texts explain how Krsna, in Vrndavana (which is also Balarama and an expansion of Krsna), expands Himself as the lover of the gopis, the cowherd women (who are also created through the expansion of Krsna). The gopis then become lovers of Krsna. And so too, the Brahma Purana continues speaking about the destiny of the devotee who dies, as being surrounded by celestial virgins, and musicians and dancers who will serve him and sing his praises as if he was Krsna.[388]

The only really notable difference here, is that in the Bhakti texts themselves, some of the gopis with whom Krsna enjoys pastimes (dalliances), are married rather than being stated to be virgins. But that's not a contradiction, it's just a deeper matter that some bhakti texts themselves discuss.

However, the Brahma Purana goes on to say that the devotee who has died will be reborn as a brahmin mastering the Vedas and Vedangas.[389]

A similar account occurs later, speaking of the devotee who dies after taking "the holy dip perfectly in the ocean" (meaning, not immersion in the Ganges, but the realisation of the Divine). We are told that after going to the world of *Viśnu* where he enjoys dalliances with celestial damsels, and is devoid of old age and death, he will still eventually return to be born in a noble family when his merit dwindles.[390]

Here then, the Purana is in two separate places referring to *reincarnation*, and appropriate circumstances of birth (caste).

In both cases there is a "falling", as it were, from a world of being whose description is definitely closer to transcendental Vrndavana than it is to the descriptions of the worlds of the *dvīpas.* Even though Vrndavana represents *liberation* from the cycle of birth and death, or reincarnation.

Oceans, rivers, water, liquids, what do they all mean?

In the Puranas water doesn't stand as a metaphor, it is the metaphor itself. That is, water as we encounter it, even in the material world itself, is an actual material metaphor for the aspect of transcendental

Reality that it represents. This is essentially stated in the Linga Purana, which talks about the actual water within the physical bodies of living creatures as being the watery form of the Lord *Śiva*..[391]

In other words, what the great expansion of Being creates, in creating the material world, is essentially a *metaphor*. It is a *symbol* in the limited intelligence we are being, of its own origin and status in the transcendental expansion.

Expansion of the Ocean of Milk

In the Puranic Mythology, the Ocean of Milk is associated with *everything that arises in material existence*. In the stories of the churning of the Ocean of Milk, in the Puranas, all kinds of things come out of the Ocean of Milk, both "good" and "bad", including the eight elephants who support the world in all directions.[392]

The symbolism is plainly that the *whole world* comes out of the Ocean of Milk. The whole of creation, including *Lakśmi*, the wife of *Viśnu*, the spiritual symbol of the *Prakrti* itself and material creation. In other words, the Ocean of Milk is the source emanating from the transcendental, of *everything*.

In the transcendental context an Ocean of Milk is *Prema*, the ecstatic love of God.[393] So the whole world comes out of the ecstatic love of God. It comes from the Being.

Prema, or Divine Joy, the ecstatic love of the Being, is not confined to a one-sided "emotion" felt towards a being from whom one is separate. On the contrary, there is the actual experience of *being* the Being, an unimaginable Joy compared to which ordinary human *emotions* and sensory experiences such as the beauty of fragrance, the beauty of colours, the smell of the forest, the joy of sounds such as birdsong or music, and the joy of personal relationships between separate beings, all pale into insignificance.

So *Śvetadvīpa* spoken of as being *in* the Ocean of Milk, means the pinnacle of the Joy of transcendental Being. We have to understand that the idea of a "place" or "abode" (or *dhāma*), regarded in the material world as something *separate* from the being who enjoys it, translates up into the transcendental as an aspect of Being, in which there is no such separation.

Nonetheless, because the Being "expands", then in any "abode" there is "inner" and "outer", so to speak. The "expansion" as it were, creates an "inner" and "outer". This "inner" and "outer" is not separate from the Being or the "abode", so cannot be understood as arranged in a material-like "geography". If one wants to think in terms of representing by objects, then it would be far more appropriate now to think in terms of *fractal landscapes*.

But this requires a knowledge of fractal objects that simply did not exist in ancient times. Even in these times it is only those who study them who become familiar with their characteristics. The Hindu corpus *does* relate *in its own way*, principles of *infinite cycles*, and *recurring expansions*, which are characteristics of fractals. But its communication is in terms of simpler objects that could be understood and related to, such as concentric islands and oceans.

Gosvāmī's commentary to the Brahma Samhita tells us:

> *Śvetadvīpa* is sometimes taken to mean the outer manifestation of Goloka that is predominated by a mood of opulence... however, *Śvetadvīpa* [also] refers to an area within the inner region called Gokula.[394]

Śrīla Bhaktivinoda Thākura also explains:

> That *dhāma* in Gokula (the inner region of Goloka), called *Śvetadvīpa*, is His [Krsna's] abode.[395]

Krsna's "abode" is not *separate from* Krsna. It *is* Krsna. It is an aspect of His Being. It is an *expansion of the Being*. An aspect of the Being that becomes known and enjoyable by Being as actual, *conditional experience of being*, through what the Hindu corpus calls *Śakti*. *Śakti* is the Divine power that enables this.

Śakti is an expansion of the Being, through which the play of *conditional experience of being*, arises. The materially manifested world, or the Earth, or "nature", as we know, is often regarded as female. Essentially, what is called "female" is an expansion of the Being into which the Being expands. "Maleness" and "femaleness" pertains to something beyond what we experience in the material condition as "maleness" and "femaleness". It pertains to the Divine Couple, who are transcendental Being.

The great expansion means that *Śvetadvīpa* which is the "outer covering of Goloka" is not the *Śvetadvīpa* situated *in* Gokula [the inner part of Goloka].[396] But it is not *separate* from it. Really, nothing is separate from anything else, except in the *Maya*. There is only the Being.

The transcendental "form" of *Śvetadvīpa* is poetically described in the Padma Purana, for example, in terms of an infinite lotus with infinite petals.

The inner *Śvetadvīpa* is declared to be the world of the eternal *pastimes* of *Śrī Śacīnandana Gaurahari* [Krsna in His unconditional *Being-Consciousness-Bliss* aspect], whilst the outer *Śvetadvīpa* is where Radha and the other gopis enjoy a *svakīya* (married) relationship with Krsna.[397]

As *Śvetadvīpa* expands into its "outer" region, and continues to expand into that expansion, *variety* of conditional experience of being manifests as what the Bhakti tradition calls the *pastimes* of Krsna.

These, actually, "happen" in a world of Being in which there is no past or future.[398] This is explicitly stated in the Brahma Samhita and elsewhere, so any attempt to understand these "pastimes" literally as stories *unfolding in time*, according to the ordinary human understanding of time, is clearly mistaken.

The popular Indian belief in the stories regards them as being "in the past". Actually, as the corpus explicitly communicates, they originate as eternal "stories" of being, in a world in which there is no past or future.

It is through the principle of *expansion of being* that these eternal "stories" become "archetypal models" so to speak, for the unfolding of stories in human experience, which take place in a world in which there is past and future.

Briefly, we can put it this way: We regard the world as consisting of past, present and future, but really, because it is an expression of our own experience of being, what it consists of, is the psychical past. The "what comes before" and "what comes after" aspect of it, is merely the way the *Mahamaya* expresses this past. The actuality of what we experience, all comes out of the past, and consists of past. This isn't the past of "clock time", which is part of *Mahamaya* or the objectivity of the material world. Rather, it is *psychical past*, which is the *ākāsa* (or the serpent *Ananta Śeśa*) and its expansion all the way down to materiality itself.

In the *highly personified* Bhakti representations, the Being, Krsna, expands as Balarama (his brother), and Radha and the gopis, and then so on, *infinitely*, just so there can be the Divine "pastimes" in which the *Prema* of the Love of the Being is enjoyed as infinite, conditional, yet transcendental Being.

Krsna expands literally (through Balarama) *into* a world of Being that is the *expansion of being* of Krsna. This in its highest realm is the transcendental *Gokula-dhāma* or *Goloka-dhāma*, or the Gokula aspect of Goloka 'in the highest territory of the spiritual universe'.[399]

Goloka in the transcendental abode is then further manifested in what the corpus calls "the material world" as Gokula, which corresponds to Gokul in the Mathurā-mandala (the Vraja or Braj region) in Uttar Pradesh in India.[400]

Goloka-dhāma is another name for *Śvetadvīpa*, "the white isle", so called because it is absolutely pure. It is said that those devotees who have *darśana* (absorption in, or seeing through the eyes of the Divine) experience *śvetadvīpa-tattva* (the being reality of *śvetadvīpa*) in the material Gokula (in Uttar Pradesh in India).[401]

Radha-Krsna

In Hinduism, *Radha-Krsna*, which stands for the exchange of love between Radha and Krsna, is a great *principle of Consciousness.* In Radha-Krsna, and the beautiful transcendental pastimes that emerge from this Consciousness, there is no Krsna without Radha.

And so in the Garga Samhita, *Uddhava* (who is a close expansion of Krsna) says to Radha:

> O moon-faced Rādhā, Śri Krsna is a moon, and You are His moonlight eternally. Śri Krsna is a sun, and You are His sunlight eternally.[402]

This is the language of love. Here, the *rasa* or *feeling* or "mood" in the verse comes precisely from the fact that *Uddhava* is speaking here *metaphorically*, even *within* the verse itself. As so often happens, even in modern verse.

And what it is speaking of we humans experience too. We cannot know and experience the love of the Being, until we first encounter one who reflects that love, awakening it within us. *Uddhava* then goes on to say that Krsna is the ocean of milk, and the waves on that ocean.[403]

The Ocean of Milk is the expansion of *Krsna*, the expansion of the Divine Being. In the transcendental it is Prema, the Being of Divine Joy and Love of the Being, but far out in the expansion away from the transcendental, where this Divine *Śakti* becomes the material world, it becomes the human psyche.

The Ocean of Milk is created by the Being, the *Brahman* as *Viśnu*, and so it is that in the Padma Purana *Narayana* (*Viśnu*) declares he *is* the milky ocean.[404]

And just as Radha springs from *Krsna* as His *Śakti*, and just as *Śivā* springs from *Śiva*, as His *Śakti*, so also we are told in the Padma Purana and in many other places in the corpus, that Laksmi [*Viśnu*'s consort springs from the Milky Ocean.[405]

The message here is that those whom we love are appearing in our world of being, which is still the Ocean of Milk, so that we might discover this Divine love of the Being.

The whole Milky Ocean is created through *Śakti*. The whole ocean *is Śakti*. The principle is always the same. The Ocean of Milk is everywhere in our existence, and everything arises out of the Ocean of Milk. Including, as we saw, *Śvetadvīpa*.

What Hindu Mythology calls the Ocean of Milk is none other than a feature of our psyche and being. It is a feature of the way in which our whole experience of being, as a human being, as mind and self, and the material world, comes into being. It comes into being through the churning of this ocean.

In ignorance of the Being, the modern rational mind immersed in science looks for a way in which the brain can be understood as explaining our mind and psyche and being, and experience of the world. A way in which what the Hindu corpus calls the Ocean of Milk, or what psychology called *the psyche*, doesn't feature.

But in truth, as we shall soon be talking about, it is only through *the churning of the Ocean of Milk*, that any of us will reach our full potential in understanding how the brain relates to who we are and where we come from.

The churning is the churning of our psyche. It is the churning of all the structures of our own mind and self in which we fail to understand that the world is our self. We have to understand this, and live it, before we can experience the world as the Being.

A rational mind looking at the Hindu corpus wants to ask questions like "Why is the Ocean of Milk the *fifth* of the seven oceans"? The rational mind loves to understand in an object-oriented way, by structures and numbers, about things outside itself. But that's not what this is all about.

On the contrary, like everything throughout the entire corpus, including the Bhakti part, it is ultimately about the *Brahman*. It is about the Being. And it is about the *infinite expansion* of That Being. In

Hinduism it begins in the transcendental with the infinite Ocean of Milk, which is transcendental *Prema*,[406] the emanation of Being Consciousness in love of the Being, in Joy and adoration, or bliss that cannot be "understood" through the merely evolutionary mode of intelligence and self that arises through brain function.

Where the great expansion ends, is in what science is now looking to understand as the *principle of the brain*.

18

The Origins of the Saptadvīpa

There is a story in the Puranas about how the seven islands and their oceans came into being.[407]

The story goes like this. King Priyavrata once saw that the Sun failed to illuminate the whole Earth at once, because always, half the Earth was in darkness. Determined not to allow this to happen under his reign, he used his yogic powers to fly in a luminous chariot, as big and bright as the Sun, following behind the Sun. Thus, he went around the Earth seven times. The wheels of the chariot created the oceans, and the parts in between became the *dvīpas*.

Why did he do this? It was because the Earth is continually cycling from light to darkness to light, which he wanted to overcome. That's the story. So in the Hindu corpus the *saptadvīpa* is the result of Priyavrata's attempt to overcome the darkness on Earth, under his reign.

It would be a mistake to presume this is some kind of naive, pre-scientific explanation of the planets in our solar system. It's not that.

In the great Hindu scheme of things, that the story relates to, Priyavrata is not the creator of the Sun nor of the Earth. Not even if he realises the *Brahman* as his true Identity. Priyavrata himself is only part of the great expansion.

Remember that even Brahma, the creator, as often related in the Hindu corpus, is "deluded by *Maya*". And so every being subsequently created is deluded by *Maya*, unless they realise the *Brahman*.

So the Priyavrata story is yet more of the story of beings who are deluded by *Maya*. Which is common across all the Purana stories.

Priyavrata's antics do not come anywhere near to him being able to truly emulate the Sun. It is all appearance, and delusion. What he did, in the story, is not to emulate what the Sun is doing, but rather, what the moon is doing. Which is going round the Earth. The Sun does not go around the Earth. It only appears to, from the point of view of ignorance, and *misidentification* with the rotation of the Earth on its own axis. The ancient Hindus may not have been aware of these details of modern cosmology, but the import is the same.

Modern science is not at odds with the true spiritual content of the Hindu corpus. There is only disparity between what scientific facts are *interpreted* as meaning, and what the content of the Hindu corpus is *interpreted* as meaning.

For us, the appearance of the Sun orbiting the Earth, is how it seems, from the point of view of our experience. We only transcend that "understanding" based on our sensory experience, when we start to develop understanding that goes beyond our sensory experience. Even though we may rely on other sensory experience, combined with technology, such as telescopes, in order to do so.

At the current time, our understanding goes beyond our sensory experience, through *objective* science and understanding. But eventually, our understanding must go beyond even this, by becoming *transpersonal*, which is not the same thing as being *objective*.

It is only via the extension of our understanding into the *transpersonal*, that we begin to discover, not only more and more facts about the objective, material universe in which we live, but also, the realisation and appreciation of our greater Identity as Being, or consciousness beyond the little "who I am" self-concept of *personal* self, as a mode of consciousness and being.

The contribution of the realisation of *transpersonal* consciousness to the potential of science cannot be understated. But at the moment, it would appear to be completely "off the radar" of scientific thought. For that potential to be realised, *transpersonal* consciousness needs to be combined with scientific, objective understanding. That combination is the most difficult thing to achieve, until there is sufficient establishment of *transpersonal* consciousness and being in the human network, generally.

Because, after all, human beings who come to be scientists, come into that career through the human network. And any new scientific ideas, as the history of science has adequately shown, can have a difficult birth due to the fact that the network into which the idea is released, is *not* transpersonal, but rather, is dominated by ego and political ego structures.

Today, we have had sufficient experience at science, that the "scientific community" probably has developed an instinctive recognition of the nonsense of ego and political ego structures, and that this has no place in science. But still, the full potential of science cannot be realised until sufficient of the network is actually transpersonal.

On that, we have a long way to go.

The Hindu corpus, so to speak, would be the first to recognise that the conditional experience of being we are having, in which the Sun appears to rotate around the Earth, is not our true Identity. And one of the deepest secrets in the whole of the Hindu corpus, concerning the moon, and *Soma*, is that in symbolic terms, the moon represents the creation of the mind, and the potential of the mind to reach beyond itself.

Let's put all this into a contemporary context.

One form of modern delusion, right now, today, is to not understand one's true constitution and situation. And one way to not understand that is to believe that the Sun orbits the Earth.

If you believe you already know your true situation and constitution, and who you are, but you still believe the Sun orbits the Earth, just because on superficial observation that's what it looks like, then you do not really know your true situation and constitution. And if you don't know that, then you cannot really know who you are, and where you come from.

This is true of observations in astronomy and cosmology, but it's also true of observations in general. If you still believe in how things seem, from the point of view of what is actually a construct of brain function, then you still don't really know your true constitution and situation. Because you haven't taken into account the fact that everything you are looking at, and understanding, is actually a construct of brain function.

And this applies even to modern astronomy and cosmology.

Scientific knowledge contains ignorance, but so does the lack of scientific knowledge. If you are primarily interested in God, science is not merely an embodiment of spiritual ignorance that you can just ignore because you study the Scriptures. Science is the growth of a very special kind of knowledge that in itself, can be regarded as God-given.

Science is a knowledge that pertains to the whole aggregate of human beings. A knowledge that inseparably spawns a thing called *technology*. And that's not just an accident. It's *part of the picture*. It's part of the way things are now, that makes it easier where we are now, not more difficult, to realise the truth of our constitution and situation.

If we don't understand the nature of scientific facts, if we don't understand what the scientific facts are, then we won't really understand the nature of the things that are said in the Hindu corpus that look like science, but are not. Similarly, we may incorrectly view science as somehow "anti-spiritual".

At the current time, technology may seem to some people to be essentially cold and impersonal, and a distraction from love, compassion, and our truly human potential. Especially since through the use of technologies we have been wrecking the planet that is our true home. And then there is the attendant idea that we will go off into space in search of some substitute home. Still in complete ignorance of what really constitutes responsibility, as a human being. But in all this we are only looking at a small part of the picture.

In a not unrelated way, any idea that scientific knowledge is irrelevant in human existence, compared to "ancient wisdom" *is simply mistaken*. In these times, spiritual wisdom has to embrace the truth about science. And the truth about science in these times is not simply that it is just mistaken, or that there is nothing spiritually relevant about it.

Some of the teachings of ancient Hinduism were interwoven with "observed facts" concerning the heavens, or what we now call astronomy and cosmology. The expansion of scientific knowledge and technology has been increasing in this area, pretty much exponentially.

What we now know, what we now *observe*, has improved to a staggering degree, over what was available through the naked eye. The invention of the space telescope (telescopes situated in space) has been a game changer. The availability of computers has been a game changer.

What in modern astronomy and cosmology we now know, and what we are coming to know, does not take us further away from spiritual knowledge of the kind that the Hindu corpus deals with. In Hindu terms, it doesn't take us further away from the principle that the observable universe represents aspects of spiritual understanding. On the contrary, it actually facilitates it more, if we only know how to look at it.

Science is not simply mistaken. But nor has science ever claimed to be an ultimate form of knowledge about everything. Some people believe that, but that claim is not a claim of science. Rather, it is just a claim of some individuals' personal interpretation of science.

To *not* understand the nature of what we call modern science, is to not understand the nature of the change and growth in our the human experience of being and world. *We are changing*. And *our world is changing*.

Scientific understanding is thought. And it is not science proper unless it is thought in the collective scientific mind. You can have whatever "scientific" thought you like, and be convinced that you are right, but it is of no avail unless you can convince the mainstream of the whole science network, the collective scientific mind, of your thought.

And to do that, requires *demonstration*. A kind of demonstration that in science is called reproducible, empirical evidence. Empirical evidence that can be repeated, or "reproduced".

Without that, your thought will never become science. You may convince some others, but without the reproducible empirical evidence, you may be, and most probably are, in the domain of pseudoscience. Which is stuff that "looks like" science, but is actually deluded or fake.

Science works. And as a result, it changes many aspects of the material world we live in. And, as a result of that, it is capable of manifesting great compassion. Just as it is capable of manifesting great disaster.

But the bottom line in all this is that if we don't understand the nature of both thought and science, then we don't really understand the world we are living in.

In the times we are living in, the truth about thought is that thought is synonymous with brain function. There is of course nothing in the Hindu corpus that indicates this as explicit knowledge.

In modern science, it already exists as explicit knowledge. But the collective scientific mind doesn't properly realise what this means. Because it doesn't realise that the modern scientific understanding of the brain, is still just thought in the collective scientific mind.

And that's because in modern science, there is not yet the understanding of the true relation between thought and the brain. So there is not the understanding of what either, actually *is*.

The Hindu corpus - even though it says nothing specifically about the brain - by implication, says that it is *Brahman*. Because it says that *everything* is *Brahman*. So that includes thought. But in the collective mind of modern science, there isn't much knowledge of *Brahman*.

We experience the world we live in, and we experience thought. And in general, across the whole "society" of the whole globe, we mistakenly cling to the thought that the world we live in, and thought, are two separate things.

The reason we do this, is not because of science, or because of other beliefs. It is simply because of the *idea* of "who I am", in which we do not recognise that the world is our experience of self. We cling to the idea of "who I am", as separate from the world, because we don't see the nature of our own mind. And therefore, we don't see the nature of the world in which we live.

And this is generally true, whether or not you are a scientist. Because, even as a scientist, no matter what thought you may have about the nature of thought, it is not science, until you convince the mainstream collective scientific mind, through reproducible empirical evidence.

Until we properly understand the nature of thought, we don't understand the nature of the world in which we live. Because the nature of our thought as a human being, comes out of the world in which we live. Scientifically speaking, it comes through brain function. Which is part of the world in which we live.

But you also cannot properly understand the nature of thought as something separate from you, that you then *learn about*. Properly understanding the nature of thought is *experiential*. You have to experience it, in your own experience.

And then you understand that everything you experience is thought. Not thought that the "I" in the personal *idea* of "who I am", can call "my" thought. But nonetheless, thought that *you* are experiencing. Only when we begin to understand this are we beginning to understand the nature of thought. And only when we begin to understand that we begin to truly understand the nature of the world.

But to begin to understand this we have to go beyond the all-encompassing clinging to the personal idea of "who I am". And you cannot do that just by "objective" thought of the kind that goes on in science.

It is experiential, and it doesn't happen by academic learning. It is just that some academic learning may work towards it. It may work towards a situation in which there is ripeness for it to happen. But it cannot happen in a way that is not experiential.

It takes something extraordinary to be able to even hear this. It is something that only arises, in the first place, experientially. And in general, the *process* through which it arises, is a process that in Hinduism has its own expression. In Hinduism it is called *the churning of the ocean*. And that's something that we will talk about in detail, in due course.

So the Sun orbiting around the Earth, as in the Priyavrata Myth, is certainly not part of *the material universe*, that is spoken of by modern science. Because as a matter of modern scientific fact, the Sun does not orbit the Earth. In the material universe spoken of by modern science, there is nowhere that the Sun orbits the Earth. It doesn't happen, it doesn't exist, in that material universe.

So where *does* the Sun, or *did* the Sun, obit the Earth? As described in these parts of the corpus? And, indeed, in Europe, as described by the Ptolemaic astronomy that was widely believed in before the invention of the telescope, and the subsequent growing acceptance of the discoveries of Copernicus, Galileo, and Isaac Newton?

Where was, or is, *that* "material universe"?

19

Mind and World

The answer is that it was in the mind. It was in the collective mind of everyone who believed that. Because everything about our experience of being as a human being, and our experience of the material world, and our knowledge of it, and so on, is, in one way or another, a collective. It is all, also a construct of brain function. And no brain exists in isolation, or ever came into existence in isolation.

Everything that goes on in a human mind, as thought, or as brain function, whichever way you want to look at it, comes from a collective, a network, an aggregate. It doesn't come from that individual mind in isolation, in a context in which the individual mind is self-sufficient.

So there may be some people who still believe that the Sun orbits the Earth. That belief, and the universe they live in, is in their mind. Or, if you like, in their brain function.

There are many more people, who say that the Earth orbits the Sun. That is their belief. They believe the universe they live in is one in which the Earth orbits the Sun. And that universe, is in their mind.

So also the universe that modern astronomers study is in their mind, their brain. The difference is that the universe in which the Earth orbits the Sun is the one that the most accurate *scientific measurements and observations*, support. In other words, it is based on reproducible scientific evidence that doesn't depend on anyone's individual, personal thought. And it doesn't depend on thought that exists only in a selective network of individuals. Even the network of scientists.

It is true that even when most people in Europe still believed in the Sun orbiting the Earth, that too, was based on observations and measurements. It's just that those observations and measurements were not very accurate compared to the observations and measurements that we have now. When you increase the accuracy of your observations and measurements, it can completely change your worldview. That's precisely what happened.

We call that, in Western scientific method, reproducible *empirical evidence*. It is *evidence* based on *physical measurement*, that can be reproduced. And that is what the whole of modern science - as distinct from pseudoscience - is based on.

There is, remarkably, still a feeling in some religious people that accepting modern science is to be somehow sacrilegious, and that we should just trust the Scriptures. Why? It is because when you study the Scriptures, like when you study *anything*, this study gradually changes your brain. It literally changes the brain, or certainly *can* do so, and that, in itself, is now a known scientific fact.

As the brain changes, the mind changes, the way you think changes, and your thought changes. *How* you experience and even *what* you experience, can change. Because all that, is thought, mind, conditional experience of being, and brain function.

So for many people, when they begin to study the Scriptures, actually, in any religion, they begin to develop thinking patterns and have experiences that are in line, as it were, with what the Scriptures say, and are about.

What you come to believe or experience as a result of religious studies, is a matter of how you think, and experience thought. And there may be a whole network of people with whom you mix, all studying in the same field, whose brains and experiences change in much the same way. *That much is also true of the study of science.*

However, in science, there is a the thing called *scientific method.* Which only science has. And that is a method that exists to ensure that whatever becomes established as "scientific knowledge" (which is essentially to become established as patterns of brain function, so to speak) is *not dependent on anyone's individual thought or experience.* Nor, indeed, *even on a whole network of individual minds.*

That's a major difference between religion and modern science. But in fact, in strictly neuroscientific terms consistent with what in science we now know about the brain, in terms of what the brain is doing, or what the mind is doing, it's the *only* difference.

Brain function *constructs* our experience of being, mind, thought and self, *and understanding*, as a construct. It also constructs all our experiencing of what we call the material world, that hard-science studies. Science is studying the aspect of the construct of brain function that is not dependent on any particular, individual brain.

Nonetheless, this construct is inseparable from the principle of the brain. So as our collective scientific understanding of the nature of our world changes, so, indeed, the actual nature of our world, as we experience it, and know it, is changing.

Thomas Kuhn recognised this, and more than hinted at it, in his book *The Structure of Scientific Revolutions*, but without reference to the brain. As he put it, though the world does not change with a change of scientific paradigm, the scientist afterwards works in a different world.[408] *He wasn't speaking metaphorically.* Rather, "the world" that does not change, is the objective aspect of it. Whilst the world as we know it and experience it, and understand it, does change. But even the objective aspect of it, *is part of the construct of brain function.*

20

The Sun

The apparent Orbiting of the Sun around the Earth is now well established by science to be an illusion. In point of fact, the Earth is rotating on its own axis, which gives rise to this *appearance*.

Today, in principle, if we had sufficient battery and satellite technology, if we wanted to, we could imitate King Priyavrata's antics. We could put up satellites orbiting the Earth, that continuously illuminate what would otherwise be the part of the Earth in the night time.

But this arrangement wouldn't come anywhere near changing the basic principle that the Earth *rotates on its own axis*, which is the real cause of the Sun appearing to orbit the Earth.

It wouldn't come anywhere near changing that basic fact, and all the consequences that follow from that great, cosmic principle. The consequences of it include the tides (in conjunction with the moon), the climate, the weather, and so on, and the very nature of all the life forms that science understands to have evolved on a planet that is rotating on its own axis in this way.

In the Purana story, King Priyavrata takes his own illumination, as bright as the Sun, and attempts to correct what he sees as the error in the way of things. But really, it is no error. So his legacy, Mythologically speaking, which is supposed to be the seven islands and oceans, the *saptadvīpa*, is a case of mistaken perception, and ignorance. Concomitantly, the *saptadvīpa* itself is a part of ignorance.

And perhaps that is the point, in the esoteric meaning of the Myth. King Priyavrata, just like all his "family" of progenitors and descendants, in the personalised story-telling in the Puranas, is, after all, just *Maya*, or illusion. Because *Everything* in the universe that is "created" from the *Brahman*, is only the *Maya* of *Brahman*. This is *explicitly taught* throughout the Hindu corpus.

But to this day, there is a level of understanding in human beings, that only understands our whole existence in terms of human selves called persons, and human personal relationships. Relationships of selves, and "family" relations, and so on. All of which is an expression of the ego in human beings.

So the Puranas cater for that. But it's only a catering. It's not the core of the meaning.

In the story, King Priyavrata obviously finds that he is in some way *like* the Sun. But in the corpus the Sun itself, the original Sun, does not come from Priyavrata. On the contrary, everything, including Priyavrata comes from the Sun, which in material terms, is the symbol of the *Brahman*. Let's look at this.

Of course, in modern science, we don't regard everything as coming from the Sun. But that's because the Sun that modern science speaks of, is not actually the same thing as the Sun that the Hindu corpus speaks of. Remember that what modern science calls "the universe" is not the same thing that the Hindu corpus calls "the universe". The conflating of these two things is one of the greatest errors in the interpretation of the Hindu corpus.

In the Hindu corpus, in general, the Sun that we perceive, is a representation of the *Brahman*. Everything that we perceive is only a representation. And in the Hindu corpus, because everything here comes from the *Brahman*, then in terms of what we sense-perceive, everything comes from the Sun.

So as the Brahmanda Purana states, the planets, stars and moon, and everything else and all beings, the entire universe, all come from the Sun (not from Priyavrata).

The Brahmanda Purana speaks of the Sun as the source of the stars, planets and moon. It states the moon is the Lord of all stars and the son of King of all planets. And it speaks of the five planets moving around as they please.[409]

This is geocentric astronomy, but it also highlights the importance of the Sun as the source. The Purana also regards the Sun as the source of the "three worlds", and the source of Devas, Asuras, and human beings.[410]

This isn't *meant to be* a *scientific* description. It is not even pre-scientific. It is talking about the *Brahman*, because across the corpus, it is repeatedly asserted that the truth behind everything, the origin of everything, is the *Brahman*.

Of course, some of this is still mixed up with the geocentric view point - the illusion of the Sun orbiting the Earth. But it's not astronomy, anyway. It is talking about the Being, the *Brahman*.

It is recognising that the Being from which our conditional experience of being as a human being is derived, is represented in our sensory experience - and in what we experience as a material world - by the Sun.

If you don't mind calling the Sun a "planet", which is what prescientific astronomy did, then we can indeed say in a manner of speaking that the Sun is the "king" of all the planets, so to speak. That is actually in keeping with modern scientific knowledge of the formation of the solar system. Not only do the planets Mercury, Venus, Earth, Mars, Jupiter, and Saturn, all orbit the Sun, but also, they are now considered in science to have origins inseparable from the Sun.

Unlike the distant stars, the planets Mercury, Venus, Mars, Jupiter, and Saturn, appear to "move about as they please" in their apparent rotations around the Earth, when seen from the Earth.

But this is an illusion, also arising from the fact that they, and the Earth, are orbiting the Sun, and the Earth is turning on its own axis. So actually, they move at the behest of the Sun's gravity, so to speak, in the orbit of the Sun, with no such freedom.

The moon is certainly not "lord of all the stars" in any scientific way, but rather, moves at the behest of the gravity of the Earth, and is in fact *the only one* of all these celestial bodies, that actually orbits the Earth.

This passage from the Brahmanda Purana give us a hierarchy, from Sun, to moon, to stars, but it is not science. It is an ideology, imposed upon observations, before the discovery of the scientifically understandable aspect of our world.

This is the aspect of the natural world that does not depend on anyone's individual mind, or on any particular collective mind. It is in terms of this latter that modern science describes the universe that we perceive.

The Hindu approach arises in ignorance of this latter aspect of the natural world, an aspect that definitely is part of the natural world, as we experience it. Modern science is not "wrong" in what it says about these things, but neither is the Hindu corpus, *in its own terms*.

The Hindu corpus is never talking about what modern science calls "the universe" or "the material world". Rather, it is talking about the "cosmic egg" of *Brahma*, or the Bhu mandala. And what that actually is, in modern terms, is a representation of the principle of the brain.

The idea that human consciousness arises, at least in a manner of speaking, out of the Sun, is most certainly not out of keeping even with materialist science. Because in the modern scientific view, the formation of the solar system arises out of the formation of the Sun, and the Earth and its life forms depend on the Sun. In the modern scientific view, "we are made of star stuff". And the Sun itself is none other than our closest star.

This is not what the message about the supremacy of the Sun in the Puranas is about, though. Rather, the message there, is that our conditional experience of being, as human beings, is derived from the Being, the *Brahman*. And the symbol of that in our existence is the material Sun.

The material Sun itself, that science studies, is certainly not the origin of what science refers to as "the material universe". Even though it is in more than one sense the origin of our experience of being.

As we know from modern science and astronomy, especially the relatively recent discoveries, the principles go onwards and upwards, towards something still greater.

Our Sun is just one star amongst what is estimated to be probably 100,000 million stars in our galaxy. It is now thought that most if not all galaxies are gravitationally bound by a supermassive *black hole* at the centre, millions to billions of times more massive than the Sun.

A *black hole* is a celestial object that the ancient Hindus could know nothing about empirically, and if *risis* knew anything about it in any other way, they could only communicate it abstrusely. In scientific terms, a black hole is a position in the "fabric" of space-time, at which there occurs a *singularity* in space-time.

The word *singularity* here, has mathematical origins, and refers to a mathematical combination of zero and infinity, that constitutes a *singular exception* to what mathematics is otherwise able to describe. That is actually the origin of the term *singularity*.

In short, although the mass of a black hole may be *finite* (but much larger than the mass of the Sun), the *density* of this object is *infinite*. Correspondingly, the size of the object itself (as distinct from its closely surrounding phenomena which is sometimes loosely referred to as the "size" of a black hole), is zero. Its effect is to create a point of *infinite gravity*. In mathematical terms, it manifests as an *infinite well* in the surrounding spacetime.

Our galaxy is just one in a group of galaxies. That group is just one in a *cluster* of galaxies. And that cluster is just one in a *supercluster* of, it is estimated, 100,000 galaxies, called *Laniakea*. And *Laniakea* is just one of countless superclusters.

Laniakea is oriented around the mysterious intergalactic Great Attractor, which binds it, and pulls everything towards it. And such *superclusters* of galaxies throughout the visible universe are not randomly or evenly distributed, but are *ordered* and gravitationally bound by *cosmic filaments* of what has been dubbed "dark matter". The whole structure, of vast, vast scale, in computer simulation looks remarkably similar to human brain matter.

In modern, materialist science, there already exists a kind of symbolic correspondence to what in Hinduism is the great *expansion of being*. That is, the expansion understood in science as the Big Bang, is an expansion that results in a universe that continues to expand.

Hinduism itself, however, is *not about* materialistic understanding of the kind that happens in modern science. In Hinduism everything is about the Being, the *Brahman*. In this context, the *Reality behind* what manifests as the Sun we experience through our senses, is the Being, the *Brahman*.

Hinduism, translated into contemporary ideas, basically just says that the material object called the Sun that modern science studies, must be understood as a material symbol arising in the intelligence we are being, that itself arises through the principle of the brain.

The Brahmanda Purana goes on to say that the Sun is the highest deity. It says that everything is born from the Sun, and everything gets merged into the Sun, so it is equating the Sun with *Viśnu*.[411]

Priyavrata does not really represent wisdom, because in his efforts, he doesn't recognise the true order of things. The true order of things is that the Sun is supreme, and, as far as the material arrangement is concerned, very appropriately at the centre. A fact that modern science is very clear about.

In other words, the whole point of the Priyavrata story is not really about the *Saptadvīpa*, but to tell us that the *Saptadvīpa* is the result of ignorance. Which we should know anyway, because in the Hindu corpus the *Saptadvīpa* that Priyavrata creates through his antics, is itself, all part of the Bhu mandala, which is all *Maya*, delusion, and ignorance of the *Brahman*.

The Seasons

Traditionally, in India, there are six seasons: *Vasamta* (spring), *Griśma* (the hot season), *Varśa* (the rainy season), *Śarad* (autumn or fall), *Hēmanta* (winter), and *Śiśira* (the cool season).

As seasons, in the Sanskrit these are called *rtu*, but they can also be seen as a manifestation of *Rtam* - the cyclic "law" (law of truth) that is applied through the principle of cycles or recurrence.[412]

Rtam is a word commonly appearing in the corpus, meaning "true" or "truth", which is also how the word *satyam* appearing in the corpus is usually translated. Both words tend to be translated in the same way.

However, as the Indian teacher Aurobindo points out 'there was a distinction in the Vedic mind between the precise significances of the two words'.[413] Aurobindo states that the Sun, being the Lord of Truth, has light that is *rtam jyotih*.[414] [*jyotih* is literally "light" or "spiritual Light"].

Rtam literally means "year", but also occurs throughout the *Rig Veda* generally translated as "law". However, the Brahmanda Purana equates *Rtam* with Agni [the "fire god"], and regards in some way *Rtam* as the *Samvatsara* ["year"].[415]

Who is this Deity *Agni*? Agni is a Deity in the Vedas, who, as Aurobindo tells us, *contains* and *is all* the gods of the Vedas.[416] So we can regard Agni as the Being (manifested through Soma, as far as the *risis* or seers of the Vedas are concerned).

Aurobindo also tells us that Agni is the fire of the Divine Will and the Sun of Divine knowledge.[417] Agni means not only burning brightness, but also movement, action and light.[418]

So we can see here why the Brahmanda Purana says *Rtam* is Agni, *and* is considered to be the *year*. *Rtam* means truth, law, and signifies the means of working of that law, in a cyclic thing called *time*, not least in what we see as the movement of the Sun. In that, *Rtam* is inseparable from *cycles* of *time*.

Samvatsara, the year, is a cyclic period of time. The day and night, the rotation of the Earth whose effects Priyavrata tried to overcome, is a cyclic period of time well "beneath" or "further out" in the great expansion, than longer cycles of time, such as the Manvantara.

Time

Time in Hinduism is not so much a *dimension* - as modern science considers it - as an *illusion* (which actually now, some quantum physicists also consider it to be) created through the expansion of Being.

Hinduism is very explicit about the hierarchical nature of time. All time is based on cycles of Being. For example, a cycle of "waking and dreaming" of *Nārāyana* (*Viśnu*) is much longer than the "lifetime" of Brahma, who emerges from, and is an expansion of, *Nārāyana*.

But on what absolute "scale" is this all measured?

There isn't one. There is no "scale" of "time", separate from the *beings*. And *they* are not separate from the Being, the *Brahman*. They are all an *expansion* of the Being.

What is the "length of time" of the *Being* of the *Brahman*? Or Krsna? There isn't one. The Being is eternal. "Time" is an illusion arising from the *expansion* of the Being.

The interactions of beings can be "measured" as "time lengths" only relative to each other. And ultimately, they are all *expansions* of the one eternal Being. That expansion doesn't happen *in* anything called "time" that is separate from the Being. Hence time is an illusion, whilst Reality is the Being.

The year, the *Samvatsara*, which is one orbit of the material Earth around the material Sun, consists of the six periods of time that are the seasons, or *rtus*.

The reason that *Rtam* as "truth" is also both *Agni* and *the year*, is because *Agni* - culturally represented by fire - is a Being, or part of the expansion of the Being, that appears as the cyclic period of time we know as *the year*.

The whole *great expansion* of the Being becomes what we experience as cyclic periods of time, in our own experience of being.

The year, the *Samvatsara*, is not a cycle or change in the Sun. And what we materially experience as a year, is not a change in the material Sun. Rather, the year is due to *the orbit of the Earth around* the Sun.

In the Brahmanda Purana everything originates from the Sun,[419] and the Earth too, is recognised in the Purana as originating from the Sun. This isn't a modern scientific statement. It is saying that the Earth Being is an expansion of the Sun Being. The static Being of the Sun expands as the "moving" Earth Being, whose rhythm, vibration or frequency, is the *Rtam* that is the year. And in turn, the seasons, the *Rtus*, are born of *Rtam*.[420]

So here we can see how to make sense of the way the Puranas see human beings, all of whom are an expansion of the Being. Everything, for us, is a matter of time. And time, for us, is a matter of *Rtam*, the rhythms or cycles of truth. And the primary rhythm or cycle, for us, is the year.

The message is that "time" consists of cycles, which are cycles of *being*, cycles of conditional experience of being, within the eternal nature of our own true Being.

Through this, the ignorance of the truth of our constitution and origins works itself out, *in* "time", in the work called *karma*. And as this ignorance works itself out, in a play of being or *lila*, and what it works towards, is liberation from this ignorance, or in other words, the awakening of knowledge or *vidya*.

The principle of cycles appears everywhere in nature, not least in our own cycling of the blood, heartbeat, breathing, sleeping and waking. It is called *prana*. What Hinduism calls "the universe" is not separate from our own existence, but rather, is the aggregate of all *cycles of being*.

From the Earth, we see the Sun as the *moving* Sun. We see it as the Sun moving around the Earth. But, as we know, that is an illusion. In Hinduism this illusion is the Sun *chariot*, to use the Puranic terminology. The Brahmanda Purana also speaks of the Sun as the chariot of the Lord, whereby the Lord goes to his abode.[421]

So given that the Purana says the Sun is the Divine source of all, we can see here that the "chariot" or moving aspect of the Sun is secondary. The chariot is only the *apparently moving* Sun that we see, the material Sun, the Sun as seen from the material Earth. It is the illusory chariot presided over by all those other beings, whilst in truth, because in terms of Being *everything* originates from the Sun, all those beings are presided over over by the Sun.

The language can be confusing because sometimes "Sun" refers to the object we perceive through the senses, and sometimes it refers to the Being. The Hindu corpus itself doesn't necessarily *distinguish* between the two. And in its own sphere, this is *perfectly correct*. Because, in the first instance, everything is the *Brahman*, the Being, whether you are talking about the manifest, or the unmanifest.

To put this in modern terms, it is not that what we perceive through our senses is *separate* from the Being we already really are. Rather, everything we perceive through our senses is a symbolic manifestation of the way in which that thing comes to be how we perceive it.

In Hindu terms, the way it comes to be, is through the *expansion of being* of the Being, the Self, we already really are. But the expansion of being never creates anything that is separate from, or other than, the Being, the Self, we already really are.

21

The Bhu Mandala

The Indian Puranas speak of the "cosmic egg" which contains what Hinduism refers to as "the material world" or "the universe".

The "cosmic egg" or *Brahmanda*, which literally means the "egg of Brahma", *constitutes* Brahma. In the depiction, the "outside" of the "egg", equivalent to the "shell", is referred to as "coverings".

In this representation, we might say that "outside" the "coverings" that form the "cosmic egg" is the *Brahman*. The *Brahman* in itself, is not these "coverings". But it *creates* these "coverings" from the involution that takes place in the great expansion, the emanation of Prema from the splendour of the *Brahman*.

Taking into account also the Bhakti part of the corpus, if the "arrangement" was something that could be seen with our eyes, our position would be like being at the centre of the "egg", and looking towards a bright light in the distance that is coming from something.

You cannot see it because of the "coverings" around the world in which you are standing. And finally, when you overcome the effect of these "coverings", then you see the light, but the light itself is so bright that it is still a "barrier" to what is beyond.

This light of the *Brahman* is not "there" in the sense that it is separate from us. These "coverings" are in *us* because we are created through the expansion and involution of the *Brahman* radiance.

The "cosmic egg" of Hinduism is said in the corpus to contain "the universe". But this is not what modern science calls "the universe". It's something different.

We only encounter what science calls "the universe", we can only see it, with the naked eye or through telescopes, because first, we have this conditional experience of being that we are having, as human beings. In material terms, we only encounter it in the first place, through brain function.

So the Hindu "cosmic egg" is not a representation of any "universe" considered to be separate from us, or separate from this experience of being. Rather, it is a representation of the way in which our *experience of being and world* arises as a human being. In relation to science the "cosmic egg" is essentially the Hindu representation of what - in the view of brain science - is a construct of brain function.

Part of our experience of our world is what we call "the planets". And sometimes, even in science, these are referred to as other "worlds".

"Planets" or "worlds" also appear inside the "cosmic egg" as part of what the Hindu corpus calls "the universe". What *it* calls "the universe" inside the "cosmic egg" is all about the set-up of our experience of mind and being and world. All as one thing.

It is essentially a "model" of how our experience as self and world, is created. But it is not a scientific expression and not in that language, so to speak, at all. We must remember that when people in general, from any time, culture or place, use the word "science", they do not necessarily even understand what the modern word *science* means, applied to what actually constitutes modern science.

The constitution of "the cosmic egg" in Hinduism is otherwise known as the *Bhu mandala*. The "outer part" of the "egg" itself, equivalent, as it were, to the shell of an actual egg, consists of what the corpus calls "coverings", like concentric layers.

These "layers" called "coverings" are essentially parts in the infinite expansion of being where *Prakrti* arises. We will see later, explicitly from the corpus itself, that these "coverings" are not nice and neat, easy to understood finite layers, like the layers of an onion, but rather, are *infinite* and *interpenetrating*.

Inside the "coverings" are then more concentric "spheres" continuing on towards the centre of the mandala. These are three in number in the early part of the corpus, developing eventually in the later corpus, to seven in number.

These seven spheres are then considered as upper and lower hemispheres, constituting fourteen "worlds". And again, although they are widely characterised as fourteen in number, they are also, in the corpus itself, acknowledged to be infinite.

Inside the "cosmic egg" are also the seven islands and oceans, known as the *saptadvīpa*. We have already talked about this. Both the islands and the "worlds" are sometimes interpreted as "planets". The whole "cosmic egg" is even called "the universe" in the corpus. All this makes it *look as though* the Bhu mandala is a kind of *metaphysical representation* of what science calls "the universe". But this is simply not so.

In actual astronomy we can of course see "planets". But what we are looking at is not the "planets" in the Bhu mandala. And the "planets" in the Bhu mandala are not the "planets" that we look at through telescopes, today, and can measure objectively. The confusion arises because there is a *correspondence*.

Rather, the "planets" or "worlds", and indeed the "islands" or *dvīpas* of the *saptadvīpa*, which are also sometimes called "planets", are something different. They are the representation in the Bhu mandala, of the various parts of the means through which we come to see the "planets" that we see, when we study the heavens.

In Hinduism the Bhu mandala is the means by which our experience arises. In modern science, we call this means the brain, or brain function.

In earlier times, Mercury, Venus, Mars, Jupiter, Saturn, the moon, and the Sun, were all visible to the naked eye, and were in general, regarded as seven "planets". Of course this is different to how modern science considers things.

Planets - whether referred to by modern science or ancient astronomy - differ in the way they are observed from the Earth, to move in the sky, to the way the distant firmament of stars appears to move.

This difference in the way they move, is because Mercury, Venus, Mars, Jupiter, and Saturn are all orbiting the Sun, the moon is orbiting the Earth, and the Earth is orbiting the Sun. Whilst the distant firmament of stars are completely independent of all of these orbits. Due to the rotation of the Earth on its own axis, from the Earth they simply appear to rotate around the Earth, on a fixed "sphere". There are seasonal variations, but they never change position in relation to each other.

Everything appears to rotate around the Earth, because the Earth is rotating on its own axis. The moon is the only one of all these things that actually does, also, rotate around the Earth.

Because of this, the firmament of distant stars always appears to rotate around the Earth, steadily, together, as a mass whole. Whilst all the other "planets" that we just mentioned, do not. They appear to have *independence.*

So in early astronomy there is no real distinction between stars and planets, of the kind that there is in modern astronomy. There is no recognition that the Sun is in fact, a star. Or, for example, that some of what appeared to be stars, in the night sky, are in fact galaxies.

Rather, in the early view the only thing that distinguishes the "planets" from "stars" in general, is that the "planets" are "stars" who have this independent, freedom of apparent movement. In fact, the word "planet" means "wanderer".

This led to all kinds of interpretations as to why this should be. After the invention of the telescope, and observations became more accurate, what is now the modern scientific fact, began to become established.

The modern scientific fact is of course that Mercury, Venus, Earth, Mars, Jupiter and Saturn, all revolve around the Sun, the moon revolves around the Earth, the Earth turns on its own axis, and the rest of the firmament of stars are relatively static.

Of course when we dig even deeper, then more features arise. Such as the fact that the entire universe of "static stars" is in fact expanding. And way out there, in the firmament of "static stars", there are more rotations going on, and so on.

In terms of evolving scientific knowledge, the earlier understanding consisted of observed facts and theory. Which is also what modern science consists of. The observed facts reasonably fitted the theory. But scientific knowledge evolves. Observations became more accurate, until the theory no longer fitted the facts.

In "spiritual terms" the earlier understanding was not "wrong". It was based on the principle of understanding how things appear, from our human point of view, according to the principle that the universe is *not* something separate from us, that has nothing to do with us other than that we happen to have arisen in it.

In "spiritual terms" the current, *modern scientific understanding* is not "wrong". To consider it "wrong" because it appears to disagree with something in spiritual texts, is to not understand the situation. And to think that anything in spiritual texts is a scientific statement, is also to not understand the situation.

In "spiritual terms", the scientific understanding is mistaken only in one essential way. And that is because it is generally being assumed that it is all about a universe that is separate from us, and has nothing to do with us other than that we happen to have arisen in it.

In fact, that interpretation is simply not consistent with the basic modern scientific facts themselves, about brain function. It attempts to avoid the scientific fact that our whole experience of being and world, as human beings, consists, in material terms, only of biological brain function.

So the effulgent, "golden egg", or "cosmic egg" described in the Indian Puranas, was never meant to be an object, of the scientific kind. It is, we could say, the Being-effulgence of the Being. And the description of it as a "golden egg" is figurative.

And unless this, at the very least, is realised, then the whole point of the Puranas is being missed. And yet, once it is realised, the Puranas are an incredibly rich resource that can speak even to a modern, Western mind, educated in science.

The Puranas go into considerable detail about this "egg" in a way that appears very structural. We have said, in addition to the *saptadvīpa* (the seven islands and their oceans) the corpus also describes up to fourteen "worlds" which are within the "egg". Across the corpus we generally glean that these "worlds" are like spheres, within the "egg". And then they are conceived as divided into upper and lower hemispheres.

The "coverings" of the "golden egg" both obscure the *Brahman*, and allow the realisation of the *Brahman*. The "golden egg" shining as the bright side of Lokaloka, is the *Brahman* as it appears through the "coverings".

So the "coverings" of the "golden egg" - which is *Brahman* as realised from the point of view of ignorance arising *within* the Bhu mandala - are "layers", so to speak, which continue on inwards, *into* the "egg", *as* these "heavenly worlds".

Remember that these are "worlds" that have been created through the "layers" or "coverings" on the "outside" of the "egg". If we want to imagine this in visual terms, then the *great expansion of being*, is expanding *inwards*, from infinite space, towards the centre of the "egg". But remember, that this is only a *visual* and therefore partial representation.

So as we have mentioned, earlier texts commonly refer to what is "inside" the "egg", above and below, and intercepting with the seven islands and oceans of the *saptadvīpa*, as just "the three worlds". Part of the Brahmanda Purana refers to "the four worlds",[422] which later become the seven worlds, and in the full development of the idea in the corpus, there are the fourteen worlds.

The fourteen "worlds" are usually described as arranged like seven concentric spheres around the *saptadvīpa*, the upper hemispheres constituting seven worlds "above", and the lower hemispheres constituting seven worlds "below", generally called the "nether worlds".

It is also important to realise that the "nether words" are not hells. On the contrary, the Śiva Purana tells us they are more beautiful than heaven.[423] We are told that even liberated souls like the nether worlds.[424]

In the corpus, there are hells spoken of, but they are *above* the nether regions, and the Śiva Purana lists nine of them.[425] However, these are not the seven worlds or planets (Bhurloka, Bhuvarloka, Svarloka, Maharloka, Janaloka, Tapoloka and Satyaloka), that are the upper hemispheres.[426]

The Brahmanda Purana tells us that everything, including Lokaloka, is well established in the cosmic egg. This includes the seven continents and oceans, the moon, the planets, and the stars.[427] We met Lokaloka, before. So we don't need to say any more about it now.

Remember, again, that here, what is called in the Purana "this universe" is not what science calls "this universe". Rather, it is the Bhu mandala. And the passage is saying that the Bhu mandala is "within the cosmos".

Again, if we like, we can translate this into the partial, visual image, of the expansion of the Being, inwards, from infinite space, towards the centre. As it is described, what is "outside" the "cosmic egg" is "the cosmos".

So following everything we have said, it is perhaps too easy to conflate what a text such as the Śrīmad Bhāgavatam regards as the "material world",[428] with what we would call the material world in the everyday sense, or in the scientific sense. But they are actually not at all the same thing.

None of what is described in the corpus as inside the "cosmic egg" corresponds to what modern science regards as the "material world", except arguably *Bhārata*, which is a small section or *varsa* of Jambudvīpa. Even Jambudvīpa, the island at the centre, is literally *ideal*, and described in one way or another as wonderful and free from suffering, compared to the world of actual human, material, existence.

At the very centre of the *saptadvīpa* (the seven islands and oceans) stands Mount Meru, sometimes called Sumeru, which actually, is not just part of Hindu cosmology, but is at the centre of most Indic cosmologies.[429]

The land containing Mount Meru is Jambudvīpa itself, and in the Brahmanda Purana, for example, it is indeed referred to as "this Earth".[430] But from its descriptions in the Puranas it is most emphatically not the actual material planet that we experience living on. It doesn't represent human existence as we ordinarily know it.

Bhāratavarsa (*Bhārata varsa*) is the only place that arguably does correspond to the actual material world we are familiar with, and it is only a tiny *varsa* of Jambudvīpa. And at the centre of Jambudvīpa in all accounts is Mount Meru.

Bhārata, however, is recognised as "the most excellent". It is the land of "work" (*karma* and "penance") whilst all other lands in the *saptadvīpa* are "lands a pleasure".[431]

Very importantly, *Bhārata* is the only land that is subject to the cycle of the four Yugas, the four "great ages" of Hinduism during which there is a decline of virtue, and descent into greater and greater ignorance. The saptadvīpa as a whole, including Jambudvīpa (other than the small part of it that is *Bhārata*), is not subject to the Yugas.[432] In other words, it is not a place where *material time* (as measured by clocks) operates.

The Śiva Purana's *Sanatkumāra* says about *Bhārata* that it is a place where rarely is a man born, and then, due to hoarded merits.[433] Because it is the pathway leading to salvation it is a blessing to be born there.[434]

So *Bhārata* - an ancient name of India - is in the Hindu spiritual scheme the very *key* to the realisation of what is *beyond* the *saptadvīpa*. Which these verses refer to as "heaven and salvation".

In other words, we are talking about transcendental Life and Being before the part of the great expansion in which *Prakrti* arises, which includes the "worlds" that are "inside" the "egg", and the *saptadvīpa*. Although the *dvīpa*s or islands in the *saptadvīpa* are extensively described in the Puranas as idealised places, of great longevity and no suffering, they are not generally referred to as "heaven".

In the total "picture" the Bhu mandala is the part of the great expansion that takes place in *Prakrti*. It is a vast *Chakracāra*, in which there is endless *Kauṭika Syandana* ("trapped circulation") that can only be awakened from in the *Karmabhūmi*, which in texts such as the Śiva Purana is *Bhārata*.

Mount Meru is *literally* the central symbol. The Bhu mandala is the "contents" of the "egg", realised from the point of view, as it were, of Mount Meru, at the centre. What the Bhu mandala *is not*, is what modern science calls "the universe". And it is not what we see and experience through our senses, as "the universe" or "the material world". Rather, in the Hindu picture, the Bhu mandala is what *gives rise to* that.

The Indian Puranas are not merely a cultural belief system, but through their cultural fabric, they express the Hindu cosmological picture, which is not a scientific, but a spiritual understanding. The cosmology is literally centred on Mount Meru.

Mount Meru represents things as seen from the "position" of spiritual illumination or *vidya*, "looking out", as it were, across what Hinduism calls "the universe", from within it, *but from an enlightened point of view*. So Mount Meru is what the Hindu scholar Manmatha Nath Dutt in his translation of Harivamsha calls "true understanding".[435]

The *whole point* of the Hindu descriptions of what it calls "the universe", is that they are described *from an enlightened point of view*. And actually, the descriptions of Mount Meru itself, in the corpus, as the awesome, effulgent "golden mountain", clearly indicates this symbolically.

A great deal of confusion and conflict seems to arise between the way many Hindus want to understand "the universe" based on the Scriptures, and the way modern science understands what *it* calls "the universe". This sometimes then overspills into the attempt to dispute modern science.

The confusion arises because, to emphasise it again, what the scriptures describe as "the universe" is not at all the same thing as what modern science is talking about, when it talks about "the universe".

That is fundamentally why the two accounts are different. And the same thing applies to, for example, the concept of a "planet".

In the Bhu mandala Mount Meru is generally thought of as being at the centre. But actually, it is not always at the centre. In the Brahmanda Purana, for example, it is mentioned as being on *Sakadvīpa*.[436] Essentially, it is simply that the Bhu mandala doesn't refer to what you think it refers to, if you just take it literally, as an object, or an objective "geographical arrangement".

In the *imagery* of spatial arrangement, what is "outside" the Bhu mandala, is the Being, the *Brahman*, whilst the Bhu mandala itself is an *expansion* of the *Brahman* in *Prakrti*.

The Bhakti scriptures such as those relied on by the Hari Krsna movement eschew what they call the "impersonal *Brahman*" as the absolute Truth, but let us be absolutely clear about something here, too:

It's not that what the Bhakti texts talk about as the transcendental Life and Being, is not the *Brahman*.

On the contrary. For Bhakti, Bhagavan (Krsna) is the *parabrahman* (Supreme *Brahman*).[437] *Svayam Bhagavān*, God Himself, is the full and complete Brahman,[438] and the embodiment of *Brahman*.[439] Even the *Brahman* realised impersonally from "within the egg" as it were, is still the glory of God.[440] *Brahman* is indeed the Absolute Truth.[441] It is just that what *Brahman is*, goes beyond what it is realised to be, when first realised from ignorance "within the egg".

The whole idea of approaching what the Puranas are saying, by visualising "structures" and "hierarchies" in linear and simplistic ways, as if we as interpreters are cosmic engineers of some kind determining how the cosmos is "put together", *is mistaken*.

It leads to an understanding that is both perhaps true in one sense, in terms of imagery, but is also mistaken. It effectively says that God can be understood as a structure. A structure of objects. And quite simply, that is a mistake.

22

The Arising of Prakrti

The Brahmanda Purana says:

> All around this *Anda* (Cosmic egg) is situated the *Ghanodadhi* - sea of solidified waters.[442]

We are not talking about ice, here. The *Ghana* part of the word *Ghanodadhi* here means compact, solid, material, hard, firm, dense, coarse, gross, viscid, thick, inspissated (thickened or congealed), full of, densely filled with, uninterrupted, dark, deep.[443] It is easy enough to get the idea.

The *Dadhi* part of the word actually refers to coagulated or thickened milk.[444] So here we can even see the *causal ocean* around the "golden egg" as none other than a "dense" Ocean of Milk. We will be talking more about what the reference to "milk" actually *means*, in due course.

In Hinduism there are generally five "elements" which are Earth, Water, Fire, Air (or sometimes wind) and Ether or Space (*Ākāśa*). These actually follow a "descending order" from the transcendental or "unmanifest" to the "material", which is: Ether or Space (*Ākāśa*), Air (or sometimes wind), Fire, Water and then Earth.

The "unmanifest" doesn't refer to something that has no being. It merely means that it is unmanifested in human, sensory experience. In the Bhakti context it refers to transcendental Life and Being. In other words, transcendental Life and Being descends into the manifest material world, through these various "stages". And it turns out that these "stages" are not separate, or finite.

So essentially, in terms of the great expansion, Ether or Space (*Ākāśa*) "turns into" Air (or sometimes wind), which then "turns into" Fire, which then "turns into" Water, which then "turns into" Earth.

This is not the material things by these names, turning into the next material thing on the list. It is not a claim literally that what we ordinarily call fire, turns into what we ordinarily call water.

As we shall also see, the idea of "elements" is not to be confused with the scientific concept. Here, as we shall come to see, the "elements" are *infinite* and *interpenetrating*.

The Brahmanda Purana says that the "solidified water" is surrounded by fiery matter, which is like a "ball of iron". This is then surrounded by "solidified air". This, in turn, is then surrounded by "ether".

Surrounding the ether is then the *Bhūtādi* (the cosmic Ego), and then there is *Mahān* (the great principle) and finally *Avyakta* (the unmanifest one).[445]

Avyakta is unmanifest Being, not separate from our own true Identity. So here, outside the "sphere" of "fire" is "solidified air". Around that, is something called *ether*. This is sometimes alternatively called space, or *ākāśa*.

So the "solidified air", sometimes just called "air" or "wind", is the *expansion of being* of the ether or *ākāśa*. Note that here, "expansion" does not result in something less "dense", but something more "dense".

Ākāśa means "space". But it does not refer to "physical space", of the kind that modern science talks about. These are all psychical descriptions in relation to which, the physical things science might talk about, like "space" and "fire", are manifest *symbols*.

Ākāśa means "space" or "ether", but it is also essentially the same thing that other parts of the Mythology represents as the infinite serpent, *Ananta Śeśa*. Essentially, the serpent *Śeśa* represents the ignorance of *Brahman* that keeps recirculating in the churning of the ocean, or mind of *Viśnu*.

As we already briefly mentioned, we should remember that the *expansion of being* isn't the same kind of thing at all, as the expansion of something "material" in the scientific sense. When what science calls "material" things expand they generally become less "dense". Figuratively speaking, the opposite is true of the *expansion of being*.

So when the Purana speaks of "solidified water" or "solidified air", it is referring to something that has become, as it were, more "dense" as a result of the expansion and involution of the Being. It is an *expansion of being*, of the part of the great expansion of being that it has *come from*.

Surrounding everything, we are told here, is the *Avyakta* ("the unmanifest one"). As the "waters" of the great expansion of being from the transcendental becomes the *causal ocean*, it become more "dense". Or, as the Purana describes it, it is "solidified".

In the visualised "model", this reference to "solidified" is a reference to the way in which the *Avyakta* (the unmanifest one) surrounding all, is expanding *inwards*, as it were, from infinity towards what Hinduism calls "material world" which is the contents of the Bhu mandala.

In all accounts of this *Pradhāna*,[446] the *Avyakta* (the unmanifest one),[447] gives rise to Mahat (the Great Principle),[448] and Buddhi, the "cosmic intellect", which then itself gives rise to *Ahamkara* or *Bhūtādī*, which is the "cosmic ego".[449] This then goes on to give rise to the "elements" in their descending order that we have already mentioned, which is Ether or Space (*Ākāśa*), Air (or sometimes wind), Fire, Water and then Earth.

Let's start at the very top. Who or what aspect of the expanding Being is *Avyakta* here, (the unmanifest one)?

The Brahmanda Purana goes on to say that it is and manifest and infinite ("endless" and "boundless"), and without beginning or end. However, it also says that compared with the supreme Being, it is not permanent.[450]

So in other words, it is an aspect of the Being that is infinite (it is boundless and has neither a beginning nor an end), but it is not eternal. Because "compared with the supreme Being", we are told, it is "non-permanent". So by the more well known imagery of *Viśnu* and Brahma, this unmanifest one is Brahma that we are talking about.

The outermost island of the *saptadvīpa* according to the Śiva Purana is Puskara. Puskara is adjacent to the "coverings" we have been talking about. More specifically, Puskara is surrounded by its ocean of sweet water, which is next to Lokaloka, and around Lokaloka is the *causal ocean*. Speaking of Puskara, the Śiva Purana says that brahma resides there and that Puskara is surrounded by the ocean of sweet water.[451]

So Brahma "extends" from being unmanifest, as *Avyakta*, down to Puskara, and this "extension" is more *expansion of the Being*. This *expansion of being*, taking place through Brahma, and is not *separate from* the *expansion of being* of *Viśnu*. Just as *Viśnu* is not separate from the *expansion of being* of the *Brahman*.

The great expansion is *being*, always as some aspect of the consciousness that is the Being, the *Brahman*. It is the expansion and involution of the Consciousness of the Being. But the great expansion is not all consciousness that is conscious to the degree that it realises its own nature.

So when we say that Brahma "extends" in the great expansion, "down" as far as Puskara, what this really means is that Puskara is where, in the great expansion, consciousness is Brahma knowing Brahma as Brahma. Brahma being a manifested aspect of the Being, the *Brahman*.

Beyond this, in the great expansion, it is also true that everything "subsequently" in the great expansion is also Brahma, because it is an expansion of Brahma. Just as it is also true that everything is *Śiva* "on the outside", as we have already talked about. The great expansion of the Being does not finish with Brahma, or at Puskara.

Another great part of the Hindu corpus that here we are not focusing so much on, is the Upanishads (mystic doctrines). The Taittrīya Upanishad, for example, teaches through the path of realising that everything is Brahma, leading to the realisation of the Being, *Brahman*, through the realisation of Brahma.

* * *

Although Brahma is indeed an aspect of the infinite Being *Brahman* (and indeed in Hinduism there are infinitely many Brahmas), it is *Viśnu* who in the Hindu imagery eternally "floats on the waters", whilst Brahma is caught in an eternal *cycle* of creation and dissolution through the other two members of the Trimurti. In other words, Brahma emerges from *Viśnu*'s navel, and is sustained during the creation process, as long as *Viśnu* is asleep. But then, everything is dissolved by *Śiva*. And then the whole cycle starts again, as described in the Śiva Purana.

This is why we have been told that the "unmanifest one", *Avyakta*, when compared with the supreme Being, is non-permanent.

Essentially, Maha-*Viśnu* (*Kāranodakaśāyī Viśnu*) expands as *Garbhodakaśāyī Viśnu*, and *Garbhodakaśāyī Viśnu* expands to create and become the "layers" around the infinitude of "eggs", each of which is a Brahma.

This cyclicity is the foundation of cyclic *time*. We have to understand that it is not just Hinduism that views time as cyclic. So often we hear that the West views time as "linear". But this isn't really true.

Even in terms of the modern West, time is *cyclic*. Not in the sense that what happens "in time" is a "loop" like a video loop. But we always measure *time* by some *cycle* of something, whether it is the rotation of the Earth around its axis (the day), or the orbit of the Earth around the Sun (the year), or a certain number of vibrations of a caesium atom (the second).

You might look at a digital clock and say that it is not cycling like the hands of an analog clock, but in fact, it is. Because the numbers themselves follow cycles. Any way that we have of measuring what we called *time*, directly, involves counting cycles.

In contrast, the Krsna-Bhakti texts speak of transcendental Life and Being as transcending this "time" feature of our material existence. In

Vrndavana is the Reality of Being in which there is variety of being but no past or future.[452]

The first eternal cyclic "process" in the Mythology is the "waking" and "sleeping" of *Viśnu* who is also known as *Nārāyana*, laying on the *causal ocean*. *Nārāyana* Himself is already an expansion of the transcendental *Brahman* Being.

When *Nārāyana* is *awake*, then *Nārāyana* is consciously one with His Identity, which is the *Brahman* Being. Which never sleeps. And so *Viśnu* (*Nārāyana*) says he is the creator, sustainer and destroyer. He knows that he is the supreme Brahman, and the great Ātman.[453] However, in terms of the way we have been speaking of the expansion of being, he is an *expansion* of Brahman.

So let us now reiterate.

The Brahmanda Purana says that the "coverings" of the cosmic "egg" consist of the "waters" surrounded by the *Tejas* (fiery element), which is surrounded by the air or *Vāyu* (wind), which is then surrounded by the *Nabhas* (Ether), and each layer is ten times bigger than the previous one. The ether is then surrounded by *Bhūtādi* (the Ahamkara or ego).[454]

The *Bhūtādi* is enveloped by Mahat and the Mahat is enveloped by *Pradhāna* (the primal *Prakrti*). The cosmic egg is thus enveloped by the seven *Āvaranas* (coverings) which are the Prakrti.[455]

Going *inwards*, the full set of seven "coverings" represents seven "descending stages" in the creation of the Bhu mandala. These stages (*Āvaranas* or coverings) in "descending" order, from the "outside" inwards are:[456]

1. *Pradhāna*,[457] or *Avyakta* ("the unmanifest one"),[458]
2. Mahat (the Great Principle "I am Brahman"),[459]
3. Cosmic Ego (*Ahamkara* or *Bhūtādī*),[460]
4. *Nabhas*, ether,[461]
5. *Vāyu*, wind (air or gaseous element),[462]
6. *Tejas*, fire,[463]
7. The waters of the causal ocean.[464]

Across the Puranas these "layers" are said to have sizes, in one way or another, that are always "ten times" the size of the layer inside it. We should be aware that the number "ten" in ancient texts often refers to infinity, and the phrase "ten times" may also just mean "much greater" or "infinitely more".

So the references to the "sizes" of these "coverings" relative to each other, indicates an *expansion* across the "coverings" going outwards towards "the unmanifest one" or *Pradhana*, whilst at the same time, the continuing *expansion of being* from the transcendental is in the direction towards the centre of the Bhu mandala.

Earth

Given that in Hinduism the "elements" are widely reported to be *Ether* (or space or sky or *ākāśa*), Air (or wind), Fire, Water, and Earth, then the element "Earth" is missing from the list we have been looking at.

Why is this?

This is because "Earth" is "inside" the "egg", as the main part of the Bhu mandala.

This is occasionally a bone of contention, so there is a little more we need to say about it.

In the Śrīmad Bhāgavatam, King Citraketu, speaking to Krsna, also says that every universe (there are infinitely many created by Brahma has seven layers, the outermost being false ego, each ten times bigger than the previous one.[465]

Here, the Purana says that the universe is "covered" by "layers" including *Earth*. But this is not actually contradictory to what the Brahmanda Purana says, or what we are saying about this.

We should not be surprised to find the idea that "the Earth" in this scheme of understanding, is a world that is "covered" by the Earth "element".

The seven "coverings" constitute a "descent", as it were, from spirit to matter in what the corpus calls "the material world". The word translated as "coverings" in the Brahmanda Purana is transliterated as *Āvanaras*.[466] The meaning here is indeed "covering", but in the sense of hiding and concealing. It also refers to an obstruction or interruption, and in Jainism to veiling the real nature of things.[467]

So we can see here the *import* of these "coverings" is not in the image of a geometric structure in geometric space, but rather, in the *function* of these "coverings". Which is that they are the means by which our sentient experience of being comes about, that also necessarily obscures the truth behind this conditional experience of being.

In other words, our sentient experience of the world, as material beings, "covers up" the truth of the origins of our self and world.

In modern scientific terms this "covering" is what we call *brain function*. What we *experience* as the objective, material universe, amounts only to a construct of brain function. But brain function is itself part of this objective, material universe. This is the "covering" that we are confronted with.

The way in which our "consciousness" arises out of *matter*, or "the Earth", is literally hidden from us, because what we are "looking at" or experiencing, as the material world, is in fact, the "covering" itself - brain function.

As we have already said on numerous occasions, what the Hindu corpus calls "the universe", is not what modern science calls "the universe". What modern science calls "the universe" is the objectivity of the material world in which we live. In contrast, what the Hindu cup is called "the universe" is the Bhu mandala.

What modern science calls "the universe" is mostly separate from our body. Even though our body is part of it. Our brain function creates an experience of being the body, in a world that is mostly separate from our body. But it is still a construct of our brain function.

Correspondingly, the Bhu mandala is not something separate from us, but is *within us*, as the way in which our limited experience of being as a human being, is arising.

In terms of the Hindu "cosmos" and the Bhu mandala, this experience of being arises through the great expansion of being from the *Brahman* into *Prakrti*, like a "descent".

This is:

1. *Pradhāna*,[468] or *Avyakta* ("the unmanifest one"),[469]
2. Mahat (the Great Principle [of material creation]),[470]
3. Cosmic Ego (*Ahamkara* or *Bhūtādī*),[471]
4. *Nabhas*, ether,[472]
5. *Vāyu*, wind (air or gaseous element),[473]
6. *Tejas*, fire,[474]
7. The waters of the causal ocean.[475]

Together these "stages" finally arrive at the "element" Earth, which is the world we experience ourselves as occupying.

However, these are not really *stages* at all. Why?

Because the Brahmanda Purana tells us that this all happens "unpremeditated" and instantaneously, like lightning.[476]

Infinity and Interpenetration

So the Hindu "elements" of *ether*, *wind* (or *air*), *fire* and *water*, are *not* separate "elements" in the modern sense. They are not an "explanation" of the world in terms of simpler substances. They are mixed, as the Brahmanda Purana tells us, like intertwining threads and are enmeshed in each other.[477]

This is because we are talking about expansion and involution. The "elements" are *mixed* like the components of any complex sound, and each "element" is itself, already a complex mix.

We are specifically told that the five "elements" (Earth, Wind, Ether, Water, Fire) are constituted of *infinite ingredients.*[478] Furthermore, all seven of the "coverings" or *Prakrtis* or "elements" *mutually penetrate.*[479] In other words, to use Buddhist terminology, they are *interpenetrating*. The Brahmanda Purana also tells us that the seven groups of elements *mutually interpenetrate.*[480]

Although the corpus in general *describes* the "transformation of the *Pradhāna*"[481] ["the unmanifest one"] in just seven zones, the the *Prakrtis* themselves are actually innumerable (infinitely many). The Brahmanda Purana tells us that these *Prakrtis* are impossible to enumerate in "extent and dimensions",[482] and they are themselves, *innumerable.*[483] In other words they are infinite, and infinitely many.

They are then *represented* in the intelligence we are being. In other words, these transformations appear to us, in the *conditional experience of being and world* that we are being (as sentient beings who arise out of the result), in a particular way.

They appear as something that we can *see*. And as something that we experience, through the senses, as the sentient beings that have arisen through this process. They are what we encounter as the visible heavens and the form of the Earth:

> The *Prakrtis* are innumerable, above, below and at the sides. The situation of the constellations is in the firmament in different zones and regions. The situation of the Earth is thereafter in the form of circle or globe.[484]

What do these innumerable *Prakrtis* consist of, from the point of view of our own conditional experience of being?

As we know, *Prakrti* is none other than the *Gunas*. They can be described as goodness, ignorance, and passion. Really, as we have been explicitly told in the Brahmanda Purana, they are innumerable. They are the infinite expansion and involution of the Being through which is created our own conditional experience of being and world. Our experience of self and world.

And because we cannot comprehend this infinite expansion and involution in the fullness of its infinity, Hinduism explains it as a combination of just three things. The three Gunas. And from our *experiential* point of view, this is adequate.

23

Kaleidoscope

Let's talk about "Brahma's egg" again. The seven "coverings" (*Āvaranas*), beginning with the *Pradhāna*, as we have said, are also referred to in the Brahmanda Purana as *the seven Prakrtis*.[485]

Basically, *Pradhāna* signifies a more primal form of *Prakrti* before it develops into "agitated" *Prakrti*, or *Prakrti* "in disequilibrium", and the creation of what Hinduism calls "the material world".

We shouldn't make the mistake of presuming that what we are talking about here, is something separate from us. It is not. *Pradhana*, or *Prakrti* "in equilibrium", is in us. It resides in us at the root of our mind and experience of being. Essentially, when *Prakrti* is brought "into equilibrium", the three *Gunas* that it is composed of, do not cease to be. That's not what is said to happen. What is said to happen, is that they are "in equilibrium".

And yet at the same time, the three *Gunas* "in equilibrium" is also said to be the state of the dissolution of the universe. But, as we have said all along, "the universe" referred to in the Hindu corpus is not the same thing as what modern science calls "the universe". What modern science calls "the universe" will not go into dissolution just because somebody brings their three *Gunas* into equilibrium.

It's not that what science calls "the universe" is separate from us. It's not that it is other than a construct of brain function. Everything we know and experience as a construct of brain function. But still, any individual human, or network of humans, bringing the Gunas into equilibrium, will not dissolve what science called "the universe". You cannot make what science calls "the universe" dissolve, by meditating. But you can make what you *experience as* "the universe" dissolve. However, you can also do that, just by going unconscious.

What does it *mean* to bring the three *Gunas* into equilibrium? The three *Gunas* are what *Prakrti* is. This is explicit. It is what we, as human beings, are made from, in the Hindu picture. Except that we also have Purusa in us, as our own being. Because Purusa has entered the *Prakrti*.

If the three *Gunas* are in equilibrium, and we are alive in the body, then *we* are in equilibrium. As an individual. What it is talking about is what is otherwise called "spiritual equilibrium".

If the three *Gunas* are brought into equilibrium, which in the first instance an individual can do through the practice of meditation, then that is the natural state of our *transpersonal consciousness*, the natural ego, or "I" that arises *impersonally* through the principle of the brain as the experience of self.

This is none other than the Purusa that is in us. Or, in other words, *Ksīrodakaśāyī Viśnu* "in the heart of every individual", that we have repeatedly spoken of, as mentioned in the Bhakti texts.

This *Ksīrodakaśāyī Viśnu* is not the Maha *Viśnu*, the great *Viśnu*, as we have already explained. It is an *expansion* of Maha *Viśnu*. So to be in transpersonal consciousness and being is not the same thing as the realisation of *Viśnu*, or the realisation of the Being, *Brahman*. But it is the place from which this "expanded" and still conditional experience of being, can be reabsorbed into the *Brahman*, just as in the Mythology, *Viśnu* is reabsorbed into the radiant consciousness of the *Brahman*, which is His true Identity anyway, when He awakens.

Viśnu's awakening, in the Mythology, refers to *our* awakening. It refers to *our* realisation of the *Brahman*. As an individual. But whereupon, that separateness of self-conception, is dissolved. What the Hindu corpus calls "the universe", is none other than the Bhu mandala.

And the Bhu mandala is none other than the means by which we come to be having our conditional experience of being, as a human being. Our perceptions and experience and understanding of what a modern science calls "the universe".

Which, if you want to talk about it in modern terms, rather than in terms of the Mythology, is the principle of the brain. The Bhu mandala is none other than the Hindu representation of the principle of the brain. But it is a representation *in ignorance of* the brain.

It is *from* this state of equilibrium that we can go back into what is prior to it, or, in terms of the Mythology, back into what is "outside" the "egg". Which really, is "inside" us, because it is within us. We can "cross the causal ocean", and discover the *Brahman*. Which all along, is the true Self we already really are, and always have been.

In other words, if we reside where the *Gunas* are in equilibrium, which means we *bring* our *Gunas* into equilibrium, then we reside in transpersonal consciousness, and it is from there that this consciousness also may begin to sink back into the Self.

In Buddhist terms, we "remain as pure awareness", from which it is possible for this transpersonal state of being to dissolve into the pure Consciousness of the Self, in which it is realised that everything is the That.

Transpersonal Consciousness

As we have said, many times, what the Hindu corpus calls "the universe" is not at all the same thing that modern science calls "the universe".

Science understands things in terms of what is measurable. But science doesn't really know how the universe comes to be experienced. It knows it happens through the brain, but it doesn't really know how.

The Hindu corpus presents a narrative on *how* it comes to be experienced. But it doesn't really know anything about the brain. And eventually, science will present its own narrative on how it comes to be experienced, in a way that doesn't naively assume it is separate from the brain.

The consciousness we are being now, that consciousness itself, isn't personal, or self-conscious. Buddhists call it "pure awareness". It is divested of the "I" in the personal experience of being, of personal self.

So if our personal "I" is not the one who is conscious, then who is it who is conscious? It is the consciousness itself, as a human being, arising through the principle of the brain. This consciousness is not personal.

The peak of transpersonal consciousness and being in human beings is self that is arising as everything. Beyond the mind and the idea of "who I am". It is actually the truly natural condition of human beings. Once the personal "who I am" idea is fully transcended.

Transpersonal consciousness, at its peak, is in harmony with its own, true Source, which it knows to be the Being, or the Self, or God. It is not separate from That, it is That. But it is still not the Self fully awakened or realised. It is an aspect of what, in the Hindu corpus, is called, by the Bhakti texts, "the impersonal Brahman", related to Brahma.

So harmony is there, in fully transpersonal consciousness, in the oneness with everything, and with the Source that it knows itself to be. And in that, is the love of the Being that it is. But this harmony is itself just a play of a still greater harmony. The harmony in That which the Bhakti texts say is beyond "the impersonal Brahman".

Even in the realm of scientific knowledge, we should never mistake what we *sense-perceive* as the universe, for what science understands a good deal about, and calls "the universe". Science does not yet understand how the sense-perceived basis of our experience of being comes about, because it does not have sufficient understanding of the brain.

Mainstream scientific thought usually considers "the universe" to be separate from human consciousness. Or separate from brain function. But the realisation of *Brahman* reveals it is actually a world in which there is already our oneness with everything. Even materially, this is so, because it is all a construct of brain function, which is the hypostasis of the self we are being. It is also the Self as realised in the *impersonal* realisation of the *Brahman* (or Buddha mind).

The full Hindu picture is still greater than this. It is a picture in which the impersonal realisation of the *Brahman* itself awakens into a still higher realisation in what it calls "beyond the fourth". Where "the fourth" or *Turiya*, is the consciousness and being of this impersonal oneness, or non-duality.

Beyond *Turiya* is said to be the realisation of transcendental Life and Being. This is the overall message of the Hindu corpus considered as a whole, including the Bhakti texts.

The Coverings

The Brahmanda Purana states something very important about the seven *Prakrtis* or *Āvaranas* or "coverings" of "the universe", something that we briefly mentioned before.

This is that they are not independent, but *sustain one another*, and cannot be enumerated with reference to their extents and dimensions.[486]

In other words, they are *infinite*. And saying they "sustain one another", is a way of saying they have what Buddhists call *dependent arising*. Not only this, but they are also constituted of *infinite ingredients* and they are *all-pervading*.[487] So this is not a straightforward, simple, finite *structure*.

Whilst what we are looking at in this part of the corpus may *seem*, shall we say, "conceptually developed", it is actually just the way something has come to be transmitted, and talked about, that pertains to the *inconceivable*.

The fundamental nature of it is not mentally "heavy" or "dense" but more like the "ether" (or Space, *Ākāśa*) itself that the corpus speaks of.

The whole point of the Hindu communication here, really, is to try to show how what it calls "ether" or "space" becomes "Earth", something as "dense" as what we call *matter*. Or indeed, our "Earthly" existence. In a very complex, specific, and "dense" form of *svarūpa*, that is the human body-mind.

So these Prakrtis, *include* the "elements" Ether (or Space, *Ākāśa*), Air (or sometimes wind), Fire, and Water, which then combine to create "Earth". It is a sequence of things becoming more and more "dense". We are using the term loosely.

The "elements" that the Hindu corpus talks about are not at all "elements" in the way the modern mind thinks about "elements". The Hindu mind in the corpus simply was not thinking in that way. Scientific reductionism is a *modern* trait. Not an ancient Indian one.

This is *extremely important* in understanding what the corpus is actually saying. It cannot be emphasised too much. Let's say it again. What is described as the "coverings" of what the corpus calls "the universe", is actually recognised in the Brahmanda Purana as *infinite* "layers" of *infinite, all-pervading, interpenetrating* ingredients.

These are arising instantaneously now, to create what we are experiencing as self and world, in human form. The Bhu mandala, or rather, what it represents, is not separate from us. It is the Hindu description of the basis of the experience of being of each one of us. It is the Hindu equivalent of a description of the principle of the brain, that modern science currently does not have.

The Hindu "universe" is the Bhu mandala. What science refers to as "the universe" is the material phenomena that science can measure. The Bhu mandala is not that. Rather, in the Hindu teaching - which is just one teaching in one particular cultural fabric - the Bhu mandala is what *gives rise to* us, and to what science calls "the material world" or "the universe". Whether we are talking about the brain or the Bhu mandala, we must also talk about something we call "the universe". There is not one before the other. The two arise together.

Speaking of the seven "worlds", which in the Hindu picture are like concentric spheres *within* the "cosmic egg", the Brahmanda Purana tells us that there are seven worlds as well as the Earth with its seven continents [the *saptadvīpa*] all within the cosmic "egg". They are called

Bhurloka Bhuvarloka, Svarloka, Maharloka, Janaloka, Tapoloka and Satyaloka and form the shape of an umbrella. [They are the upper hemispheres of the seven "world" spheres. The lower hemispheres are the "nether worlds"].

We are also told that these are each held by their own subtle coverings. Around the cosmic "egg" is then the "solidified ocean" [*the causal ocean*].[488]

So here we see the "world" spheres *inside* the "cosmic egg", as part of the Bhu mandala, and that *they each and all have their own* subtle covering. Whether or not this refers to the "coverings" of the "cosmic egg" is not clear. But the general picture is clear.

In this "visualisation" the *expansion of being* is in the direction from the infinite Pradhana, or "unmanifest one", in towards the centre of the "egg". And the reference to "sizes" of the "coverings" outside the "egg", and to the "worlds" within the "egg", is one in which each of these "layers" is a fraction of the surrounding "layer".

Remember this is not a scientific statement. It has nothing to do with modern science. The principles of modern science had not been discovered then. But we are so used to the scientific attitude now, that we easily misinterpret such texts when they speak of *quantities* or *measurements.*

So in a manner of speaking the expansion *in towards* the centre of the Bhu mandala is one in which the "stuff" of the expansion becomes more and more "compressed" or "dense". This is precisely the opposite of the effect of expansion of material things.

What is happening is that each "layer" is created from its surrounding "layers". In this way, the expansion and involution continues. The coverings are *subtle*, which means they are *psychical* and not physical or *material* in the modern scientific sense of the word.

As we have seen, we are told that these "layers" are "filled with characteristics" that *originate mutually*. So these "coverings" which include the "elements" are not separate, distinct things.

All in all, they have arisen *instantaneously* ("like the lightning"), and they have *dependent arising*.

In modern scientific understanding there is an analogy to this. It is the nature of *sound*. So it is not surprising to find some Hindu teachers teaching that the universe is "made of sound". They don't mean it literally, in the modern, scientific sense.

In the ancient Hindu culture, sound, as utterance, and chanting, has its own particular meaning. Vowel sounds, and the particular dimension of the Sanskrit language that is about pronunciation, is all part of that. There are four different "levels" of language use, from that which communicates aspects of the transcendental, down to that which is mundane. We won't go into that here. That is a whole field in its own right. But we can say this:

Sound is waves or cycles, and it is possible for a given sound to be constituted of theoretically infinite components, each of which is a wave or cycle. In one way, these components are "separate". But in another, they are inseparable. This is well understood in science and mathematics, and sound engineering, and the manner of understanding it in modern science is mathematical. But it uses mathematical concepts (such as, for example, the Fourier transform), an understanding that simply didn't exist at the time the Puranas originated.

This is very much connected with *time*, which we can only directly measure anyway, by counting *cycles*, of one kind or another. Hinduism presents time as eternal cycles. But this doesn't mean that there is no linearity (moving along a line in one direction) at all, in time.

In our experience, time moves in one direction. You might be able to go "back in time" in your mind, but you cannot do it in the objective world. Because the objective world has no dependence on your individual mind. The objective world "moves in time" in one direction. And that's why science "moves in one direction", always towards "scientific progress". Precisely because it is the study of the objective world.

We tend not to see the link between the two, the nature of the objective world, and the nature of science, quite as it is, if we think of time and the objective world as a separate from us. But they are not separate. Time and the objective world are all part of the way our own mind and experience of being arises.

The Kaleidoscope

A good analogy exists in the thing called a kaleidoscope. This is an optical instrument invented in the early 19th century, which was produced for many years as a children's toy. But of course, in an age of modern electronics, it has fallen out of popularity.

The kaleidoscope basically consists of a cylindrical cell that can be rotated around its own axis, inside which are two mirrors facing each other at an angle, together with many tiny pieces of coloured glass or other translucent material, which are "churned" as the cylinder is rotated. The contents of the cylinder is then observed from one end, rather like looking into a telescope.

As the cell is rotated, inside it can be observed an ever-changing world of beautiful, emergent, complex patterns, of great fascination. Occasionally, a pattern may emerge that seems to be a re-arising of something similar from a previous turning of the cell. But really, because the number of coloured parts is very large, no two arising patterns are ever truly identical. However, there are *principles* and *features* of the patterns, that continually re-arise.

The arising of the patterns is based completely on the cyclic principle. In one sense, there is no particular "one direction", so to speak, that the arising changing patterns must make. In modern scientific language, the effect is *nonlinear*. And yet, in principle, if you began with your attention immersed in that wonderful emerging world, it might be possible to "work backwards" from the arising patterns, if that was all you knew about, to the deduction that you were looking through a rotating cylinder containing two mirrors.

In a way, time and the progress of science is somewhat like this. The origin of time is like the rotating cylinder. Out of it comes continuously emergent patterns of phenomenal complexity. But these patterns don't "jump around" discontinuously from one pattern to the next. The glass bits bump into one another, and affect each other, and are affected by gravity. So each pattern leads to the next through direct cause and effect, of all its parts.

In this analogy, our world is these emergent patterns. And our world isn't something separate from us. Science is part of the world, and science is part of us. Science is basically studying those laws of cause and effect. And they are "one directional". And because science itself is part of this, it too, is "one directional".

In terms of the analogy, this "one directional" aspect arises because of the *cycling* of the cylinder. Which isn't actually "going anywhere", so to speak. It's just going round and round. In an analogous way, the "one directional" aspect of time that we experience, from "past" to "future", arises because of the way all the phenomena of our world changes "one directionally" through what we call cause and effect, from one condition to the next, as do the patterns in the kaleidoscope.

The patterns arising in our world are far more complex than anything in the kaleidoscope. Furthermore, in the nature of our mind, things get more complex as the turning continues. But the principle is similar. It is all cycles within cycles within cycles. And some of the cycles are so large that they don't seem like cycles. This general principle is already formulated in science and mathematics in what is known as the Fourier transform. Mathematicians have invented things called *pathological functions*, that appear to break this principle. But that appearance is because there is something missing from the picture.

What is missing from the picture, is what is missing from our understanding of what science is, as a whole. What is missing from the picture is the mirrors. And the one who looks into the mirrors. The kaleidoscope is only a rough analogy. Our world is one in which there are not mirrors *separate* from the rest of the content - the "phenomena" of all those coloured pieces of glass, so to speak. Rather, in our world, the phenomena of it *is* the mirror, as well as the phenomena. In our world, even the one who looks into the "kaleidoscope" is not separate. That one, too, is part of the kaleidoscope.

The equivalent of the kaleidoscope in our actual existence, is a thing we do actually already know about. It's called the brain. The kaleidoscope of our existence is far more multidimensional than a simple kaleidoscope toy. As we said, it's only a rough analogy. The kaleidoscope of our existence is also something that, as we are looking into it, and because it consists of the experiential, can bring us to the realisation of what it is that is really going on. And then we can see that it is not separate from us, but that as a human being, we *are* the kaleidoscope.

The Hindu corpus has its own description of the magnificent cosmic kaleidoscope that we are being, as human beings. It's called the Bhu mandala.

24

The Creation of the Senses

The *saptadvīpa* is part of the Bhu mandala. Sometimes the whole *saptadvīpa* is referred to as "the Earth",[489] and sometimes Jambudvīpa, the central island" is referred to as "this Earth".[490] And as we have seen, sometimes the whole sphere comprising the "inside" of the "cosmic egg" might be argued to be the Earth.[491]

The Brahmanda Purana goes into much more detail about the arising of Pradhana, and the "gradual" development of *Prakrti* as disequilibrium in the *Gunas*, in terms of Being or beings.[492] But the main point to remember is that this all happens "unpremeditated" and instantaneously, "like lightning".[493]

The descriptions are "methodical" representations of the way in which infinite expansion and involution of the *Brahman instantly* turns ignorance of the Being into time and material evolution, and our own conditional experience of being as self and world.

The Senses

Here is that list of the seven *Prakrtis* again:

1. *Pradhāna*,[494] or *Avyakta* (the unmanifest one),[495]
2. Mahat (the Great Principle),[496]

3. Cosmic Ego (*Ahamkara* or *Bhūtādī*),[497]
4. *Nabhas*, ether,[498] often *Akāsā*, or space, instead,
5. *Vāyu*, wind (air or gaseous element, and later prana),[499]
6. *Tejas*, fire,[500]
7. The waters of the causal ocean.[501]

According to the Brahmanda Purana, the "sages" in the Mythology are beings who have knowledge of particular *Ātmans* (souls). These different "knowledges" of particular *Ātman*s means different levels of *realisation* of the Being.

Specifically, we are told there are five classes of "sages" whose knowledge of the Being corresponds to the following:[502]

1. The unmanifest *Ātman*. The primary instance is of course the *Brahman*.
2. The *Mahān Ātman* of the Soul (the Great Principle) called Mahat. It is sometimes followed in descending order by the Cosmic Intellect, or *Buddhi*. It can otherwise be called the principle "I am *Brahman*".
3. The *Ātman* of the Cosmic Ego. This is basically the primary way through which ignorance is capable of realising its Source, and its true Identity, as the *Brahman* or Being. The cosmic ego is *Ahamkara*.
4. The *Ātman* of what the Purana calls the "living beings" that are the "elements". These "elements" we have also been told are of infinite ingredients. So these "ingredients" are all aspects of the expansion of the Being. This *Ātman* is related to the *aggregate* of the conditional experience of being that arises in nature through which it arises.
5. The *Ātman* of the Sense-Organs (*Indryātman*). This refers to the *natural ego* or experience "I" as sentient self, arising through the body and the brain, which is *impersonal*. This is more fundamental than the personal *idea* of "who I am", or "me",

arising in the mind, which is the complex composite of the *personal ego*.

The Sense-Organs are therefore an expression of *Ātman*. In us, our organs of perception and experience, only really have any meaning in as much as there is the one who perceives and experiences. This is the *Ātman* of the Sense-Organs, or *Indryātman*.

By "Sense-Organs" the Purana is referring to a standard part of yogic understanding. This is not just the usual idea of "the five senses". It doesn't just mean the ability to touch-sense, see, hear, smell, and taste.

In the Hindu understanding there are *ten* "senses" associated with the body, considered as distinct from the mind. They are generally thought of as five "inward going" senses, plus five "outward going" senses, which means, respectively, going *into the body*, or exiting *from the body*.

So the five "inward going" senses are the standard five of seeing, hearing, sense of touch, sense of taste, sense of smell. The five "outgoing" senses are generally said to be associated with the *organs of action*, which are said to be the mouth, the hands, the feet, the anus, and the genitals.

So the "outgoing" senses are called the *senses of action*, and the "inward going" senses (seeing, hearing, touch, *etc.*) are referred to as the *senses of knowledge*. In modern terminology these ten components combine and interact to contribute to the human experience of self, and the experience of interacting with the material world other than the body.

There are many yoga methods that call these ten senses or "Sense Organs" *Indriyas*. *Indriya* means "belonging to or agreeable to Indra [the main Being in the early Vedas]".[503]

In Hinduism, everything, including our "senses" is created through the great *expansion of being*. Indra is just the name of a primary Being, an aspect of the Divine Being, the knowledge and realisation of which, has its roots in the Vedas.

In the early Vedas *Indra* is the primary deity, and associated with *Indra* is an important idea that comes to full fruition later in Buddhism, and especially in Hua Yen Buddhism. This is the principle called *Indra's net.*

Indra's Net

Buddhism arose out of Hinduism, and an important feature of Buddhism in general, that reaches full expression in Hua Yen Buddhism,[504] is this concept of *Indra's net.*

Indra's net, essentially, refers to the infinite expansion of the Being called *Indra*, and this "net", as it is called, of Indra's expansions, epitomises the nature of the principle of the *expansion of being*.

The earliest reference to *Indra's net* is in the Atharva Veda,[505] but similar references to the net of Agni, and indeed of Visva or all the gods, occur in the Rig Veda.[506]

The word "net" (in translation) that appears originally in the Vedas, is superficially a reference to the way in which a "net" can be used to "capture" things.

In essence, everything created through the principle of the *expansion of being*, is "captured" in that principle. So Indra's net captures everything.

And so, in the general picture, the affairs of human beings are culturally believed to be, as it were, in the "net" of the gods, through whom human beings have been created. That's the general meaning. But there is a deeper meaning to this, too.

Because the "net" here, is not a *network* of separate, distinct things. It the *expansion of being* of Indra. And the arising of the appearance of distinct things, is an illusion created by the "net".

In Hua Yen Buddhism there is an infinity of beings in various conditions of Buddhahood, or approaches to Buddhahood, all of whom are part of this *Indra's net*. But all parts of *Indra's net* have what Buddhists call *dependent arising* and *interpenetration* (*Pratītyasamutpāda*). This is because although there are infinitely many Buddhas, all, in the Hindu sense, are *expansions* of the one Buddha.

In this nature of *Indra's net* is precisely those features that, as we saw a little earlier, the Brahmanda Purana describes as features of the Hindu "elements".

Here again is the list from above, of the *Ātmans* as known by the various classes of sages:

1. The unmanifest Ātman (the Self or *Brahman*),
2. The Mahān Ātman of the Soul (the Great Principle) called Mahat,
3. The Ātman of the cosmic ego,
4. The Ātman of the living beings that are the elements (which, remember, are not truly just five, but are infinite),
5. The Ātman of the Sense-Organs (*Indryātman*).

Note that (in 4) the living beings *are* the elements. The elements that Hinduism speaks of are all life. Not something distinct from life.

Similarly, the "Sense-Organs" are not *biological* organs, as would be understood by modern science. They *have* biological organs associated with them, indeed, but they are not just biological organs.

Rather, they are components of our *experience of being*, as a body, in the material world. And so it is also that in the Hindu corpus *the mind* which is also not in itself material, is considered to be the eleventh Organ.

Note that the "eleventh Organ" in Hinduism is not the brain. It is the mind. The idea of an "Organ" is not about the material or the biological. It refers to a *psychical component* of our total conditional experience of being.

How does this fit together in the light of modern neuroscience?Contrary to the illusion, we don't feel the hand in the hand, and the eye doesn't see. Not just all *sensory* experience, but *all experience*, completely, takes place, biologically, *in the brain*. It is *a construct of brain function*.

And it is true that there are components of our conditional experience of being, including the ten "Sense Organs" that Hinduism speaks of. But in terms of modern neuroscience, there is much more to it, than that. It all arises through the supreme complexity of the brain.

In Hinduism when the mind (*manas*) is considered as an eleventh organ then there are *fourteen* components or principles in our experience of being, when the mind is considered as being made from the four principles *manas*, *buddhi*, *ahamkara* and *citta*.[507]

In terms of modern neuroscience our experience of being as human beings could not be divided up simply into fourteen components. The brain itself is not modular, in this way, despite that there are areas of the network of it, that "specialise" in particular functions, such as hearing or seeing.

The basic *modus operandi* of the brain in this respect, is that it is an interconnected super-complex network. We could even say that the principle of *dependent arising* which is so much a part of Buddhism is exhibited in brain function itself.

The Brahmanda Purana gives our ten "Sense Organs" names as *beings*, and identifies them as "mentally born of god Brahma".[508] Across the corpus the *mental sons* or *psychic sons* of Brahma are the first amongst beings created by Brahma in the process of creating the universe, *after* the initial stages of creation.[509] But actually, the initial stages of creation *includes* the creation of the senses and sense organs.[510]

Recursion is perfectly evident in the Brahmanda Purana's account of creation,[511] beginning with the recursion of Brahma's re-creation of the initial stages of creation, at the beginning of every *kalpa*. The account also clearly talks about the *evolution* of *emergent* stages of being, *manifesting themselves*.[512]

This self-manifestation is not so unlike the current mainstream scientific view of the evolution of the species. This essentially boils down to statistical probabilities under the principles of *adaptation and survival of the fittest*. Evolution takes place, as it were, "by itself".

Importantly, in Brahma's creation process, variety *also evolves by itself*.[513] But unlike the contemporary understanding of the evolution of the species, the whole process comes about *because of* Brahma's "action of creation" in the first instance. The creation *is* created *by* Brahma, but it is a "mental" or psychic process, which is *actuated* through mechanisms that happen by themselves.

We must remember that this is the account in the Mythology where there is *personification*. However, we must also remember that the Brahmanda Purana tells us that it all spontaneously happens *instantaneously* "like the lightning" and without premeditation.[514]

In the Brahmanda Purana's account it is only *after* all the initial stages of creation are described that Brahma then creates his "mental sons" who are referred to widely across the Puranas, and who are beings "on a par with himself".[515] These sons then renounce the world because they have knowledge of *Brahman*.[516]

In the Brahmanda Purana the evolution is described as developing from plants to animals to human beings, as it does in modern evolution theory.[517]

The difference is that it is not the case for Hinduism that the universe comes first, and then human beings evolve in it, and develop these "senses" with which to interact with the universe. Rather, the total world we actually live in, as we experience it, springs from the creation of the senses.

The mainstream contemporary idea is that the universe begins with the "Big Bang", a singularity of infinite energy, which expands and cools, thus creating initial quantum fields, or quantum particles, space, time, and gravity. And then from this the evolution of the universe continues, resulting in the formation of stars, and then the Earth with the potential for life forms. And then life forms on Earth begin to evolve. And then out of these life forms evolves higher apes, and then our own bodies and brains.

All of this is "correct" in the material picture, but in the Hindu picture the material itself, without being anything different from what it is, is nonetheless an illusion. It only comes to be known by us, because first, we are being. The material even forms the basis of that conditional experience of being. But it is also possible for us to awaken out of the whole limitation of this conditional experience of being, into the realisation of Reality or Being beside which the former is an illusion.

So science's understanding is correct in the material picture. But the material picture as we understand it, is only true relative to the intelligence we are being, as it arises through the brain. Our ideas about the nature of this picture in a time when there was no human brain, are merely a representation of a condition of the universe without the brain, *as if* the human brain still existed as part of that picture. But it's only a *representation* that ignores the fact that the material world itself as we know it is actually a construct of brain function. So "the universe" that we are talking about here is none other than the structure of our own intelligence, the intelligence that we are collectively being.

Much of Buddhism concentrates on the disappearance of illusory identity that arises in identification with the material. It often speaks of "pure awareness". But it doesn't always take the next step into the realisation of the Reality of Being or the *Brahman*, as God, at the higher levels that we have spoken of, and that Bhakti speaks of, that this "pure awareness" leads into. And as a consequence it has become known as an "atheistic" religion.

The current mainstream idea in science, about the brain, is that it has arisen in a world that has nothing to do with us other than that we happen to have arisen in it. But this world is a world that we can only contemplate in the first instance, because we experience it, in an experience that is inseparable from the experience of self. All of which is *a construct of brain function*. The biological functioning of something that itself only arises in this world, that is a construct of brain function.

The *meaning* of it, the *knowledge* of any of it, the *experience of* any of it, that we have, requires the brain. And that *meaning*, that *knowledge*, that *experience*, is a *construct of brain function*. Which itself, is something we only know about through our *experience of being*. Which itself is *a construct of brain function*.

This is *meta*. Of course it is. It is self-referential. It is a "circular reference". What science calls "the material world" is a world only known and encountered through the construct, or many constructs, of brain function. And there is no way of demonstrating *what* there is, or *that* there is anything other than this construct of brain function. It is only *in* the constructs of brain function, that material brain function itself comes to be known.

Essentially, the expansion of the *Brahman* can be seen in the same way. The expansion, as *Indra's net*, is nothing but Indra. The expansion of the *Brahman*, is nothing but the *Brahman*

Or, as the Nirālamba Upanishad that we looked at earlier, says:

> That *Brahman* is Brahma, Viśnu, Rudra and Indra, Yama, Sun and Moon, *Devas*, *Asuras*, *Piśachas*, men, women, beasts, etc., the fixed ones, Brahmans [a caste of Indians] and others. Here there is no manyness in the least degree: all this is verily *Brahman*.[518]

25

The Churning of the Ocean

In our current, mainstream, collective scientific thinking, naivety leads us to presume there is some kind of "mechanism" in nature whereby we are provided with experience of being a body, in a world that in itself, has nothing to do with us, or our existence in it, other than that it has given rise to us.

This presumption is indeed naive, especially in the face of the actual scientific evidence to the contrary. Because the scientific evidence is that there is nothing we know or experience, including all our scientific knowledge, that is not in fact a construct of brain function. And the idea that the material world cannot be a construct of brain function because it is "objective", is also naive.

The main obstacle that we face in realising what it is our true prerogative to realise, about ourselves and our situation as human beings, is not in fact about data or computing power. Rather, it is in the psychology of the mind. It is in the entanglement of our experience of being with the personalised mind.

Subtly woven into scientific thinking, is something deceptively simple, something that has long been tacitly assumed to have nothing to do with the progress of science. This thing is simply the idea of "who I am".

The reason is that for a long time, it hasn't mattered. In fact, the whole point of the objectivity of science has been that it has nothing to do with the idea of "who I am". But now that we are turning the scientific spotlight on the human brain in a newly invigorated way, it now has everything to do with scientific understanding.

So far, up to this point, the psychology of the mind doing the science hasn't seemed to matter too much, as long as objectivity has been adhered to. But things change, and evolve, and that is not where we are, anymore.

It is through the human brain that our *experience* of "who I am" is being delivered, so it is no longer the case that the *idea* of "who I am" remains irrelevant to science other than in the science of psychology.

On the contrary, if we are to realise our potential, then it is utterly necessary that "scientific thought" does not remain merely *objective*, and using objective mind and thought, but also awakens into *transpersonal* mind.

The two are not the same thing. And merely understanding increasing quantities of data objectively, is not sufficient to bring us to the understanding we need.

It is perfectly possible to be very good at objective thinking, and yet not to be *transpersonal*. And transpersonal mind and being is not something that can be understood through reasoning based only on objective thought structures and systems.

There is no way into a true understanding of the brain and its role in our overall human situation, unless we are *transpersonal*. And there is no way to become transpersonal just through objective understanding.

The way the awakening of transpersonal being and consciousness happens in human beings is the way it always happens. Which is not through mental understanding but through *experiential* metamorphosis.

When the metamorphosis happens, then all the standard anchor points and foundations of the widespread human "attitude" to our life and experience of being, are shaken down.

All the presumptions about good and bad, and right and wrong, and about birth, and death, and especially who is responsible, are all shaken down. In some people it is just a little bit. In others, it is more. Ultimately, the whole play of personal nonsense is burnt down and from the ashes arises none other than what Hinduism, deep in the meaning of its corpus, calls *Śiva*. It is completely beyond anything that being merely *objective*, as we are in science, can arrive at. But within it, is the possibility of a completely new application of *objective understanding* in science.

The story in the Hindu corpus is called the *Churning of the Ocean*. So right now, this is what we are going to look at.

The Churning

An account of *the churning of the ocean* is a standard part of all the Puranas. So in the corpus there are many accounts of it, some of them more elaborate than others.

The Śrīmad Bhāgavatam devotes four chapters to the story as a whole, and we will be basing at least some of our outline here, on that account. Like most stories in the Puranas the story of *the churning of the ocean* tends to differ somewhat, in different sources. But the essence, and the key elements, remain the same.

The initial setting for the story is an ongoing battle between the *Suras* (devas, sometimes called demigods) and *Asuras* (demons). Of course the materialist, rational Western mind would find this to have the appearance of myth as fiction. But it is not that. It is Myth, indeed, but then, so is our own existence, in the context of the Hindu corpus. It is all *Maya*. So it shouldn't be so surprising to find that there are Hindus who take it all to be literally true.

The point is that whether you take it to be literally true, or just a story, it has a very meaningful content, beyond the surface story.

So the *Suras* are the *virtuous beings*, beings who are seeking Divine knowledge and wisdom. The *Asuras* are *ignorant beings*, or demons, or those sometimes referred to as "atheists".

The story involves multiple personalised characters, but its deeper meaning is aimed at the reader, and like so much of the corpus, its secret is that it speaks directly to the reader.

It is about what happens in the *individual*, when the awakening of consciousness of the Being begins to enter self.

The churning of the ocean is the result of *Mahat*. Appearing in an individual human being, it is the churning of the self and mind, the churning of the mind and the emotions that is necessary in order to consciously pass through and transcend identification with the ego.

So let's begin retelling the story now (the account is paraphrased):

> In the midst of their ongoing battles with the *Asuras*, the *Suras* are told by *Viśnu* (or Krsna) that they should make a truce with the *Asuras*.
>
> They are told that they should endeavour to churn the Ocean of Milk, in order to produce from the churning, *Amrta*, the "nectar of immortality".[519]

We have to understand the meaning of the scenario as a whole, here. To begin with, the whole scenario of *Suras* and *Asuras* represents not only a Mythological account of the origins of the human condition, but also what is *right now* the struggle *in an individual*, the struggle of individual human consciousness and being, with the *self.*

Remember that we are not here talking about the overly simplistic Western idea of good versus evil. Rather, we are talking about *goodness*, *passion*, and *ignorance* - the three *Gunas*.

The *Suras* represent goodness, and the endeavour to *overcome attachment to the Gunas altogether*, in order to attain transcendental realisation - the realisation of the Being.

The *Asuras* represent ignorance. And the battles in which the *Suras* and *Asuras* engage, are of course full of passion, united predominantly with ignorance or goodness. The *Asuras* represent the fighting nature of greed for power and possession, they represent the pursuit of ego. They represent the egoic way of seeing the world. The egoic way of being.

Whilst the *Suras* represent the fighting spirit and the pursuit of love and truth. Both the *Asuras* and the *Suras* engage in battle with each other. Because both kinds of being are born of *Prakrti - goodness, passion*, and *ignorance*. The fighting spirit of the Suras is driven by goodness and passion, but nonetheless happens in ignorance. The fighting nature of the *Asuras* is driven by ignorance and passion, but nonetheless happens in an environment in which there is goodness.

These very battles are played out repeatedly, in human existence. Everything played out in human existence can be seen in terms of *goodness, passion*, and *ignorance*, if you know how to look at it. But you have to look at it from beyond the ego. From beyond the idea of "who I am". From beyond *Ahamkara*.

The *Asuras*, essentially, are demons. And the underlying message about them, in the Puranas, is that ultimately, they are are *Maya*, illusion. But then ultimately, so are the *Suras*. Already beyond both the *Suras* and *Asuras* is the *Amrta* that both *Suras* and *Asuras* become engaged in the churning of the ocean, in order to try to obtain.

What comes out of the Ocean of Milk, is what the churning of it produces. And what is produced from the churning is what the Ocean of Milk already has the potential to make from itself. What it produces are things that aren't "hidden" in the milk, as something separate. In much the same sense, butter comes out of the churning of cow's milk, and so butter is in some sense already "in" milk. And yet there is no butter, until the milk is churned.

In Hinduism, the "butter" of our world, so to speak, comes out of the churning of something that does not have this world "in it" until it is churned. What that "milk" is, out of which the "butter" comes, is the Being.

The original "milk", as we have already mentioned is described in the Bhakti texts as *Prema*, or Divine Love. And basically, the churning is in the great *expansion of being*, vastly, unimaginably, and infinitely, into the creation of time itself, which is none other than this churning.

So here we are at the very crux of the matter. Because before we understand what is going on, we have to understand the very nature of the Ocean of Milk.

This is not a scene in some mythical or magical place separate from us. It is not just an entertaining story with mythical or magical beings, separate from what we, ourselves, are being. Because we, ourselves, come out of this *churning of the ocean*.

So it is not just a whimsical story. On the contrary, the Puranas, as always, speak directly to the reader. The Ocean of Milk, the *Asuras*, the *Suras*, and the whole scene, is *within us*. Within each and every one of us. And the churning, is the churning of the self. The churning of the mind and the emotions.

So first, the Ocean of Milk itself. As we have spoken about, previously, the Ocean of Milk is everywhere. As far as an individual is concerned, it is within and without. Even though it also has its rightful place in the Mythology, in the *saptadvīpa*.

The Ocean of Milk begins as the ocean of transcendental love, or *Prema*. And then, through the great *expansion of being*, of the Being, through *the great expansion* and involution, it becomes everything. Everything in existence comes from that Great Principle called Mahat, the great Cosmic Intellect, which is no less than the entry of Cosmic or Divine Consciousness into its own radiance, the *Brahman*.

"Outside" what Hinduism calls the "cosmic egg", or "golden egg" or "egg of Brahma", before the "cosmic egg", in the unmanifest, or *as* "the unmanifest one", *Avyakta*, the Ocean of Milk is not yet manifested as material existence, or "the universe". That manifestation has to happen through the "coverings" that we have spoken about.

These "coverings" are more of the *great expansion*, through *Ahamkara*, through its becoming what Hinduism calls the *ākāśa*, then "air", then the "fire", then the "water", and finally material existence itself, as the Earth. Which is only knowable, only a world of being, only experienced and known by us in the way that we experience and know it, in the first place, through the brain.

The "egg", the *Hiranyagarbha*, the "golden womb" of Brahma, gives birth to our conditional experience of being, as a human being, which comes through *Mahat*. And the process of expansion continues on, and on, in this finite material world. It continues on, in what we call time, through what we know as our own procreation in the cycles of material time.

So the Ocean of Milk contains everything, because everything comes out of it. Everything that constitutes the world, for we human beings. In one way or another, what comes out of it, comes from what Hinduism depicts as the cosmic churning of it.

But it is also what is within us. It is the constitution of the human self, the human mind. It is the human psyche. The human psyche, mind, and self, *is* the Ocean of Milk. And there is even a modern, equivalent understanding of this, too.

Which is simply that everything we experience as "the world", is a construct of brain function. And the *prima facie* function of the brain, is the creation of our conditional experience of being, as a human being. Our self. As human self, human mind, human psyche. And as the human body whose arising is all part of this condition. Our entire experience of being this body, everything we experience about it, happens in the brain. It is a construct of brain function. That is the now known and established scientific fact.

All of this, in Hindu terminology, is the Ocean of Milk. It is what the Ocean of Milk, which begins as a transcendental current of *Prema*,[520] or an ocean of Divine Love, has become, through the great *expansion of being*.

In the *Samudra Mathana* story in the Puranas, the Ocean of Milk is so vast that it must be churned by using Mount Mandara as the churning rod. The task requires uprooting Mount Mandara and bringing it to the Ocean of Milk. This part of the story is common to all the accounts.

As the great but not so well-known known Hindu scholar Manmatha Nath Dutt points out in his prose translation of *Harivamsha*, Mount Mandara symbolises true understanding.[521]

So the story is telling us that true understanding has to be brought to the Ocean of Milk, which is the stuff of our own self, mind, and psyche. And the Ocean of Milk then has to be churned.

In all the accounts, the churning turns out to be too difficult for the *Suras* and *Asuras* to carry out by themselves. The Mount Mandara will just sink in the ocean. It requires Divine intervention.

Divine help comes from *Viśnu*. *Viśnu* takes the form of a tortoise (turtle) on whose back Mount Mandara is easily supported, its turning being just a pleasant scratching for the great omniscient *Viśnu*.

So the *Suras* and *Asuras* must throw all kinds of herbs and creepers into the ocean, and then churn it, in order to obtain the *Amrta*. As Manmatha Nath Dutt also points out these herbs and creepers that we must throw into the churning of the ocean are bodily attachments. The attachment to the things of the world that we experience through our bodily being.

So the next question is, what is this *Amrta*?

Amrta

Amrta translates as "immortality" and "nectar". In other words, it is the "nectar of immortality". It occurs widely in Mythology, not just in Hinduism. It is often *symbolised* as a drink, and is sometimes portrayed in that way in Buddhism.

But behind the mythical symbolism it simply refers to an aspect of spiritual awakening. Specifically, a profound awakening of consciousness of being, which in terms of Hinduism is an initial degree of realisation of what is called *Brahman*. It refers to the *realisation*, the actual awakening into an aspect of the Being, through illumination, rather than faith. It constitutes the beginning of direct knowledge of our true constitution and situation, as human beings, to whatever degree that awakening happens by Grace.

So although it is invariably portrayed symbolically as a "drink" that can be *acquired* like material gold can be acquired, it is not an acquisition. And really, this is reflected in the difficulty of "obtaining" it portrayed in the mythical accounts of it.

Behind all the mythological imagery it is simply the reality of the nature of *the being we already are*, that is *realised* when false ego and identification with the body is transcended. It is a stage in the realisation of the Self.

The realisation of being beyond identification with the body *does not mean* becoming immortal as a person, or realising oneself to be immortal, *as a person*. The idea that the realisation of immortality must mean the latter is probably the greatest misunderstanding which leads to the dismissal of the "nectar" as "myth" of the kind that is just fiction.

It doesn't mean that a *person* identified with personal ego and the personal idea of "who I am", becomes immortal, invincible, or perfect. There is no such thing as a perfect person, or an immortal person, if the personal ego and idea of "who I am" is what we mean by "person".

We are talking about consciousness of *being*, still as a "who I am" experience, but not loaded with what the *idea* of "who I am" is built on. Not loaded with what gives rise to the idea of "who I am". Which is the self. Which is the sum of all experience being delivered through brain function.

The truth of our constitution and situation is not uniquely Hindu, or uniquely of any other particular religion. It is of the *human being*. It is a universal truth behind what it is to be a human being. Although it is possible that the mind may subsequently contextualise it according to some particular fabric belonging to a specific religion.

Plotinus speaks of it outside of any such context, at the beginning of the eighth Tractate of the fourth Ennead, where he says:

> Many times it has happened: lifted out of the body into myself; becoming external to all other things and self-encentred; beholding a marvellous beauty;
>
> Then, more than ever, assured of community with the loftiest order; Enacting the noblest life, acquiring identity with the divine...[522]

There is no way that this realisation is synonymous with any kind of intellectual or mental understanding. Its reality is in the *realisation* of it, as consciousness of *being*. Which means to *awaken as* that level of *being*, literally, as "who I am".

Behind the mind, and its endless thought, and the personal *idea* of "who I am", beyond the self, as the "I am" experience that is dependent on the body, created through the brain function, is where this *being* that is who we already really are, begins.

As a newborn, we may be already in touch with this level of being, as the experience and psychical knowledge of *conscious being* as "I am", devoid of any self-conception, or idea of "I". It is not that we are floating around separate from the body, because this consciousness is arising *through* the body and the brain. Actually, it happens in the brain. But the brain itself is not an object arising in some world that has nothing to do with us, other than that we happen to be in it.

The world is our world. It is the world in which our brain arises. It is the world in which our mind, and conditional experience of being arises. It is inseparable from that. And our conditional experience of being is inseparable from it.

How come we might have this consciousness as a newborn?

As a newborn, our identification with the breathing body is still not necessarily concrete. In the womb we don't have that identification, because our body is not breathing. Once the body starts breathing, our experience of being is different.

So now we have an identification with the breathing body, but it is certainly not concrete at this stage, not if we are at a certain stage of advancement in the potential to realise the truth of our own being. And in any case there is, naturally, no personal self-conception. That develops later.

The ignorance in the surrounding adults may psychologically and emotionally project the idea of personal self-conception onto the newborn, and imagine they see it there, but that is all just illusion of mind. That just happens in the ignorance of the adults around, not in the newborn.

In the newborn the true root of the "I" experience is not yet entangled in self conceptualisation of the kind that adults are attached to. The personal *idea* of "me" and "who I am". In the newborn the being is not attached to the thinking, conceptualising mind, because that hasn't been developed yet. There is self, indeed, because there is experience delivered through brain function. But that's not the same thing as the personal idea of "me" and "who I am".

So the experience of being may naturally move into the pristine consciousness of *being* beyond identification with the body, even in this new bodily conditional experience of being. In terms of Hinduism, it is the consciousness in the brilliant *Prakrti* that we have been talking about earlier, just after the entrance of the Purusa. So it is now imbued with all the higher past. But the body and the brain is imbued with all the lower past. Everything that in terms of evolution theory we would call the evolutionary past.

If the unadulterated consciousness of being arises, it will invariably become relatively quickly lost. But it may be rediscovered later in the life. The rediscovery of it is a profound awakening of consciousness. The ordinary mind may try to conceive it as "memory", but that is only because the true nature of memory in human beings is not being properly understood.

Everything about our existential experience of being, as a human being, is essentially a form of memory. As far as the brain is concerned, it is all *neural memory*. It is not personal. It is not fundamentally the personal memory of "me" and "I" and the idea of "who I am", based on self conception, and the illusory ego's desire to preserve itself. It is just neural memory.

The essence of memory in human beings isn't about what "I" the *person* "can remember". It is not even confined to the individual brain organ, since no individual brain organ ever arose in isolation, and its ability to create our conditional experience of being isn't achieved by itself, in isolation, in some world that has nothing to do with the brain, other than that the brain happens to have arisen in it.

The essence of memory doesn't become lost just because the brain "rewires" itself. As it does at various stages in growing up, that neuroscientists call "pruning". And the memory principle in the brain is not absent, just because as a newborn the way in which memory works later on has not yet been established.

But nor is this essence what "I" say "I can remember", where this "I" is of the personal "who I am" idea. It's not something that can be *interpreted* by the ego, according to the ego's idea of "what happened to me". All that is just the nonsense of the ego and its constant interpretation of experience according to its desire to maintain it idea of itself.

So "memory", the root of what it is, operating as brain function, is not about what "I" can "remember" through "my" mind processes. Based on the idea that "I am the body". Or that I am my *idea* of "who I am". On the contrary, the foundation of everything here, in our existential experience of being, is essentially a form of memory, *but it's not personal.*

Rather, it is created from vast, *fundamental memory*, that you cannot understand in terms of the personal *idea* of "who I am". The Hindu corpus refers to this as the *ākāśa*. Or sometimes "ether" or "space". And in the wider known imagery, it is depicted as the serpent, *Ananta Śeśa*, on whom Viśnu floats, on the ocean.

And so it is perfectly possible for the "memory" of being born, to reawaken. It is possible for that experience to be *re-experienced* in the adult body and brain. But it's not a personal "remembering". The personal "I" as the one who would remember it, wasn't even there at the time.

In that "memory" is the full experience of being, as a newborn. Because it isn't "in the past" as any "distance" away from *now*. It is still at the root of our experience of being, *now*.

Brain scientist used to say that it was impossible to remember "being born", because of the lack of development of the hippocampi in the brain. And so forth. The hippocampi are the parts of the brain that are active in "laying down memories". But all that, is as much ignorance, as it is fact. It is based on knowledge of the brain in ignorance of *how it is in the first place*, that brain function equates to what we call "consciousness".

In fact, we now know scientifically, that memory is "distributed throughout the brain". Even though the hippocampi still have their role. The "memory" we are talking of here, the "birth memory", is not a memory that is "laid down" in the way that later personal memories are. It's not an integrated part of the personal *idea* of "who I am", that later forms. *It's not personal*. So it's not a necessary part of the personal idea of "who I am". But it is nonetheless a profoundly intimate experience as "I".

"Being born" is a profound experience of being. But it's a *conditional* experience of being. And as such, it is not the truth of who we are. So in terms that we have been talking about, of which Hinduism is an expression, it is not the full-blown realisation of the Being. Rather, it is part of the *immortal condition* of the *being* in the human being. Contained within it, is the *Amrta*.

It is only the immature, restless mind, full of self-conception, the idea of "who I am" and "me", the noise of the mind and personal ego, that makes a fuss about talk of immortality, either by dismissing or ridiculing it, or joking about it, or believing in it. Our prerogative as human beings is not to dismiss it or believe in it. Both are just expressions of ignorance. Our prerogative is to *realise it*.

The truth is that many, many people on Earth realise the *Amrta*. It is a fact of human life. In the Christian religion, for example, faith itself can eventually merge into it. Many people may realise it to a degree, in a way in which they don't even realise that they have realised it. Just to be at peace with dying - no matter what the mind thinks and says about it, no matter that it might say there is nothing, and that it is the end - is the beginning of the realisation.

In the Mythology, and not just in Hindu Mythology, it appears represented *symbolically*, and generally as *a drink*. And it is possible in some contexts that it does indeed *relate to* an actual drink constituting the ingestion of a psychoactive substance such as *Soma*. A substance through which aspects of the Being that we already really are, are realised. That is why in the scientific studies of the effect of substances such as DMT that we spoke of earlier, some people report that as a result they have lost their fear of death.

So it is also that in the Hindu Mythology, and in particular, in the story of *the churning of the ocean*, there is *Amrta*, which is the "nectar of immortality". And we have now just explained what *Amrta* actually means. The story of *the churning of the ocean* is not just part of some ancient Indian Mythology, without relevance to the modern, Western, human being. On the contrary, it is completely relevant. Because whilst *Amrta* is something that only exists in mythology, it is a mythological *symbol*, for something that it is the prerogative of all human beings to discover.

There are many things about the expression of spiritual truth through this Eastern medium, that to the modern, Western mind, otherwise perhaps inclined to reject religion, are a suitable doorway into spiritual realisation. And in these contemporary times of secular society, the rise, in the West, of interest in Eastern spirituality, is no accident.

So let us continue with the story:

> The *Asuras* are then told that in order to obtain *Amrta*, the nectar of immortality, they must cast into the Ocean of Milk

> all kinds of vegetables, grass, creepers and herbs. Then, with Divine help they must churn the Ocean of Milk using the Mandara Mountain as the churning rod, and the snake *Vāsuki* whom *Viśnu* wears around him, as the rope for churning.
>
> They must churn with undivided attention, and they must cooperatively engage with the *Asuras* (the demons) in the churning process. However, the *Suras* are told that *only they* will gain the result of the churning, which is *amrta* - the "nectar of immortality" produced from the ocean.[523]

This churning of the ocean is clearly not going to be easy. Most notably, for the *Asuras* it is going to require not *battle* with the *Asuras*, but rather, working *with them*. The *Suras* are instructed to remain calm, and to accept the demands of the *Asuras*, in order to work with them. They must not become angry.[524]

> The Suras are told that they should churn carefully, and that the Asuras Will share the labour, but the Suras will obtain the nectar produced from the ocean.[525] The Suras are told that they should accept the demands of the Asuras without becoming angry. Their success depends on remaining at peace.[526]
>
> The Suras are also told not to be afraid of the *kālakūta* poison that will appear from the ocean of milk, and that as things are manifested from the churning of the ocean, they must not become greedy or lustful or angry as a result.[527]

Out of the churning of the ocean, is going to emerge all kinds of things. And out of the churning is then going to emerge the *Amrta*. But also, out of the ocean, is going to arise a "poison", called *kālakūta*. Sometimes, in some accounts, the poison is called *halahala*. In most accounts the churning causes *kālakūta* to be released from the ocean, before the nectar is obtained.[528] However, this is not an inviolable rule.

The ocean being churned is the ocean of milk that is within us, and that makes us. It is what our human nature consists of. It is everything that is within us, as our subconscious and unconscious, and as all our emotions. It consists of the past, the "memory" within us. Not the *personal* "memory", associated with the personal idea of "who I am", but the psychical stuff of "memory" about which we have already spoken.

It consists of all our attachments to existence, and to the idea of "who I am". The churning of the ocean of milk within us is the part of the spiritual path that produces the realisation of transpersonal being - the "nectar" or *Amrta* that is the Joy of realising that who we are, and always have been, is not at all dependent on any of the stuff of this existence in which we arise in this illusory condition of being called a "person".

It produces the realisation of identity that transcends all this attachment, all this stuff of self, and the idea of "who I am", that modern, Western mainstream society, puts on a pedestal and ideologically worships as who "we" are.

The journey begins when we are inspired or driven to come to know what is in there, what is in this ocean, which is the stuff of our self. And the process is not something we can undertake without Divine assistance. In the Purana story that Divine assistance comes in the form of *Viśnu*, who assists the churning by taking on the form of the tortoise (turtle).

The process of coming to know the self, or self-knowledge, is central to the spiritual path. But it is not at all the same thing as the personal idea of "who I am" or "what I am like" or "what kind of person I am". All that, is just the mind, the idea of the "person", and the ego, together with its *idea* of the self, and "me". There is no shortage of "I know who I am", or "I know what I am like", and so forth, in the world. Which is all the mind, the ego.

It is actually impossible for the mind to fully know itself. The knowledge of the mind has to come from beyond the mind, it has to come from the being. And it is from the being, that the nectar comes.

The nectar *amrta* that we have already described the meaning of, is also known in the Hindu corpus as *samudranavanita* or *samudranavanitaka*, which are respectively, *the nectar produced by the churning of the ocean*, or the moon, and *ocean ghee*, or the moon.[529] Why does the word for the nectar (*Amrta*) produced by the churning of the ocean, also mean the moon?

In many accounts the "cool-rayed" moon is notably one of the things that comes out of the churning of the ocean. Earlier on, we talked about *Soma*. In Hinduism *Soma* is the moon, and as we talked about earlier, the corpus suggests that in ancient India, ingestion of the psychoactive plant *Soma*, which was made possible by crushing out its juice and mixing it with milk, provided access to the levels of superconsciousness from which at least some of the content of the Vedas arose.

Now of course spiritual wisdom is not something that can be literally "acquired" just by ingesting a drink, even if it is psychoactive. Nevertheless, there is a very good reason why it is associated with spiritual knowledge in shamanism, and Vedic wisdom, and so on.

In modern scientific terms, that reason is, of course, about the brain. The psychoactive substances remove "constraint conditions" on the way the brain is working. Constraint conditions that ordinarily, arise from the natural principles of neuroplasticity, and the brain's tendency to "rewire" itself according to its functioning.

Removing the constraint conditions on existing pathways of connectivity within the brain, can result in *experience of being* and the arising of *world of being*, whose full import cannot be understood, or related to, by mind and experience of being that has never had its constraints removed.

But you'll notice that no matter what anyone might experience under the influence of a psychoactive, no matter how the world of being might change, no matter how their experience of being might change, it doesn't change the actual objectivity of the world. Just like when you are asleep in bed dreaming, it doesn't change the actual objectivity of the world.

If you are under the influence of a psychoactive, or just sleepwalking, and you think you can walk on air off the edge of a cliff, you will still actually fall. The objectivity of the material world doesn't depend on what is going on in anyone's individual brain. But your experience of being and world, does depend on what is going on in your individual brain and mind.

There are any number of things that might change the way the brain is working. For example, psychological trauma, or autism, or schizophrenia. Or even artistic or scientific genius. Another one is what is now called *spiritual emergency.*[530] Which is part of the path of spiritual awakening, that can range from "emergence" to "emergency", in the ordinary senses of those words.

And it is not always easy to distinguish between the kind of thing experienced in schizophrenia, and the kind of thing experienced in spiritual emergency, or, indeed, under the influence of certain psychoactive substances.

What all these things have in common, is that they undermine the commonplace but mistaken belief that the world in which we live is independent of our experience of it. It's not. It's just that it has an objective nature that is independent of anyone's individual experience of it.

It should be easy to see that scientifically speaking, the principle of the brain is neither separate from the brain, nor separate from the nature of the world. And it should be obvious that it is also not separate from our experience of self. After all, the *prima facie* thing about the brain is that it creates this experience.

It is our *experience of being* together with our *world of being*, that Hinduism speaks of as arising out of what it calls the Ocean of Milk.

The fact that the moon, specifically, is described as emerging from the Ocean of Milk, is perhaps not surprising. The moon, in Hinduism, is called *Soma*. So there is clearly an entanglement between the entheogenic plant *Soma*, apparently used as an entheogenic to access higher states of consciousness, and the Hindu spiritual cosmogony and cosmology in which the moon is a Being.

In the cosmology of the *Bhu mandala* which is essentially geocentric, *all* the "planets" or "worlds" within the "cosmic egg", not just the moon, are Beings. But it is through *Soma*, as both a substance and the moon Being, that access to spiritual knowledge was being obtained by the *rsis*.

The substance *Soma* that appears to have been made by crushing the juice from a plant and mixing it with milk, was not the *Amrta* that comes from the churning of the ocean, that the symbolism refers to. Because *Amrta*, as we have said, is not a *drink*. Spiritual realisation is not a *substance* that can be acquired. And *Soma*, the entheogenic substance, that *can* be acquired, by all accounts came from a plant, not an ocean of milk.

But nonetheless, if it had effects similar to those DMT has on some people, we can surmise that it assisted in the route to attaining *Amrta*. And so it is that we find "the churning of the ocean" and "the moon" are both connected in the words *samudranavanita* or *samudranavanitaka*.

The moon is just one of many particular things that are repeatedly said in the Puranas to come out of the churning of the ocean. The Śiva Purana states:

> There also emerged—Dhanvantari, the moon, the Parijata tree, the horse Uccaiśśravas, the elephant Airavāta, wine, the bow of *Viśnu*, the conch, the cow Kāmadhenu, the jewel Kaustubha and the nectar.[531]

These are just some of the things that emerge. The various accounts have many things in common, but also differ. One of the things that comes out of the Ocean, is *Viśnu's* lover, the goddess of heaven.[532] *Viśnu's* lover is of course *Viśnu's śakti*, when *śakti* is understood as the Divine potency, or creative power.

The principle is that Divine Being enters its own effulgence, its *śakti*, in order to enjoy the Divine creative pleasure potency, and this principle is infinitely recurrent and reiterated.

Eventually, in the expansion, it appears as the Purusa entering the *Prakrti*, the *Sthanins* entering the "abodes", the creation of the *Prajapati* and the means by which *Prajapati* further creates. This is all in the nature of the great *expansion of being*.

As we have already said, the Ocean of Milk begins as the transcendental ocean or current of *Prema*, the ecstatic Love of the Being, the Divine. Through the *expansion of being* in transcendental Life and Being it eventually becomes *Pradhana* or *Mulaprakrti*, which comes to life as the *Prakrti* when the Purusa enters it and "agitates" it. But then the agitation, the churning, continues on.

In the cultural picture, the agitation that constitutes churning actual milk by turning a churning rod, also involves the repeated *cycles* of the churning rod, which results, as a gross mechanism, in the repeated *involution* of the milk into itself.

Out of this churning literally emerges, eventually, butter. And then the butter itself, can be further changed, into "clarified butter" or ghee, through the application of the "fire element", in other words, by heating.

By the churning, something "solid" literally emerges from the milk, from what was otherwise the unsolidified constituents of the milk itself. And it's not only butter that can emerge from milk.

In India *chaas* is made by churning yoghurt, and adding herbs and spices. And yoghurt itself can be made by adding acid ingredients such as lemon, to milk that has been appropriately heated and cooled.

The allegory of milk, and what can be created from milk by churning and adding herbs and other ingredients to it, is a good one. It is a symbol for the whole idea of Divine *Prema* that when churned (repeated agitation, cycles, and involution) starts to create things out of itself.

The Hindu corpus contains the message that through this very same process the transcendental reality of the Sun becomes the material Sun in what the corpus calls "the universe" or "the material world". The cultural symbolism continues.

When, from the churning of milk, butter is made, then butter can be further changed. It can be changed by heating through the Sun, or its associated "element" of fire. It becomes *clarified* butter. And the idea of *clarity* here, is significant.

And then, furthermore, when the clarified butter is thrown into the fire, as in the early ritual fire sacrifices, it *becomes* the fire. All of this is allegory for spiritual catharsis and realisation - the churning produces the butter, the "fire" turns the butter into clarified butter, and finally it returns to and becomes the "fire".

The churning of the milk is the symbol for the churning of the human self and mind. Whether that happens inwardly, energetically, psychically, as it does in stages on the spiritual path, or whether it happens by the trials and tribulations of actual circumstances that one must "rise above".

So what comes out of the Ocean of Milk, through its churning, is everything in existence. Or more accurately, everything that appears to exist. Because really, it is all *Maya*.

And so it is that the Śrīmad Bhāgavatam tells us that what emerges from the churning of the ocean includes the eight elephants who support the world in all directions.[533] The whole world - "the universe" or "the material world" - and its supports, comes out of this ocean. Just as it is all a construct of brain function.

26

Beyond the Poison

In the context of the Hindu corpus, what an ocean consists of, whether we are talking about the milk ocean, the salt ocean, the ocean of curds, or the ocean of worldly existence, is the stuff of our mind and self. Which itself, comes out of this "ocean". As we have already illustrated, there are many kinds of "oceans" spoken of in this way, in the corpus.

Let's go right back to the beginning, according to the Śiva Purana. There we can see the beginning of it all. There, at the beginning of creation, even before the creation of Brahma the "creator", we can see the churning of the ocean of *Śiva*'s mind:

> With the consent of *Śiva* the supreme lord spread the liquorine essence of nectar on His left side, on the tenth limb, nectar which was the outcome of churning the ocean of His mind wherein Thoughts were the waves, the Sattva Guna was the precious gem, Rajas being coral and Tamas - crocodile. Thereupon a person came into being who was the most charming one in the three worlds, who was calm with Sattva Guna being prominent, and who appeared to be the ocean of immeasurable majesty.[534]

The "person who comes into being" who is spoken of in the last part of the passage here, is of course *Viśnu*.

The supreme lord spoken of here is the Being, the *Brahman*, spoken of in the same chapter, at the outset.[535] Or, if we wish to interpret the text from the point of view of the Bhakti tradition, we might prefer to say that the supreme lord spoken of here, is transcendental Krsna. Both would be true.

Śiva's "tenth limb" here is outside the usual depiction of Śiva as having four arms, and possibly refers to his infinite influence. The nectar, however, is the source of the nectar that comes out of the churning of the ocean of milk. Here it *originates* by first coming out of the churning of the ocean of *Śiva*'s mind, as depicted in the passage above.

The churning we see here is the creation of *the waves*, the *thoughts*. The *Sattva Guna* (goodness, also stillness, calm, and equilibrium) is the precious gem, because when that is discovered, it is the means of our homecoming back into the Reality of the Being.

It is only in the course of the expansion and involution that the emotionally negative, the "poison" in the "milk ocean" of our psyche is created. And that is only created by first creating the emotional. And the emotional is created through the brain. And the brain is created out of the past. And the past isn't something belonging to some world separate from us, that we just happen to be experiencing. It is all, both material world, and self, a *construct of brain function*.

The only past in time, for us, is the fabric of our conditional experience of being and mind. The only past in time is the fabric of our emotional self. And the emotional self is created out of the past. Which is created out of the continuing expansion. And the continuing expansion is created out of the past.

The secret of living in the churning of the world in which we live, the secret of wisdom within it, is still in the *Sattva Guna*. The key is in the discovery of it, and the adhering to it, as much as possible. To "stay calm in a crisis", or as Kipling said, to "keep your head when all around are losing theirs and blaming you", is a Western rendering of this same principle.

Except that you cannot always stay calm, until you do always stay calm. Nevertheless, even in the midst of terrible emotional turbulence, and reaction, in the midst of that *Tamas* and *Rajas*, there is still *Sattva* if there is *seeing*. Conscious *seeing*. And therein lies the difference between the personal and the transpersonal. The personal never sees. The transpersonal always sees.

If we are to discover the *Amrta*, there will be much more churning for reasons that often, to the world are inscrutable, than there is for someone who is already naturally calm by personal disposition, or by training.

In this churning of the mind of *Śiva*, which is in any case who we already really are, *Raja* (passion), we are told here, is the coral. In India red coral (*moonga*) is associated with strength, both in marriage, and against one's enemies, and is believed to ward off lethargy (associated with *Tamas*).

The text says the crocodile in this ocean is the *Tamas* (ignorance). In Hinduism the crocodile is sometimes venerated as the embodiment of many gods, including the god of love and desire, *kāma-deva*.[536] Nevertheless, any *embodiment* of the Divine in material form is essentially an embodiment of the Divine in the ignorance of material existence.

So the depiction of crocodiles as symbolising ignorance, and the ill effects of ignorance, is common in the Puranas. And crocodiles are commonly depicted as ignorance, or the effects of ignorance, in lakes or oceans of experience of one form or another.

The Skanda Purana speaks of the crocodile that assumes the form of *Kali* (goddess of time, death, and destruction).[537] The crocodile symbolises the hazardous effects of *Tamas* (ignorance). We are told that to cross the ocean of worldly existence requires avoiding greed, otherwise we will be swallowed by the crocodile.[538]

Lord Hara, we are told, saves one from the ocean of worldly existence, where there is terrible misery, and *Adharma* [the practice of self pursuit only, resulting in negative karma] as its very waters, greed, arrogance, inebriation, and false pride. But this world is also adorned with the *Sattva Guna*.[539] So there are also "crossing places" that can take the devotee across the ocean of worldly existence, even though it is full of crocodiles.[540]

* * *

As we have said, in the Hindu corpus there are many kinds of oceans that are spoken of. Even the Scriptures themselves are described as constituting an ocean of knowledge. And that ocean, too, must be churned, in order to produce the nectar.[541]

The idea of churning is prominent in the corpus, and generally *alludes* to the churning of the ocean of milk, even if not explicitly about that. It is something that applies to the way in which "the universe" is understood to have come into existence, a principle *within which* at the very outset arises, as we just saw, *Viśnu*. And it is something that applies to the individual, in the search for the truth of our origins.

The churning of the ocean, arising in our experience as an individual, in one way or another is always the churning of the stuff of our mind, psyche and self. It is a coming to know our mind and psyche and self, by *consciously passing through* the stuff of it, and awakening from misidentification with it.

We have already talked about how the *Brahman* is the Being even in the Bhakti tradition of Divine realisation, whose parts of the corpus speak of going beyond the "impersonal" realisation of the *Brahman*. We have seen how the Bhakti texts such as the Brahma Samhita still speak of what is beyond that impersonal realisation, as both Krsna and *Brahman*.[542]

Whichever part of the corpus you want to look at, in the Puranas there is always the churning of the ocean. It is depicted in the actual story in terms of personified beings, but is nevertheless the churning through which "the universe" arises. Purusa enters the *Prakrti*, or *Pradhana*, or *Mulaprakrti* (depending on the particular source you look at) to create what parts of the corpus call the "disequilibrium" or "agitation" of the *Gunas*, which are of course, *Prakrti*.

But if you look carefully, the Puranas themselves speak directly to the individual, and even explicitly declare as much. And so the story of the churning of the ocean speaks directly to the individual reader, too.

In the awakening into transpersonal and then transcendental consciousness, the churning occurs as an inner churning, that may even have no particular outward circumstances to indicate to the world at large what is going on in that individual.

In the terms talked about by Saint John of the Cross, it may be a *dark night of the soul*. Or it may be *manifest* as adverse circumstances that anyone could recognise. It may be the everyday trials and tribulations of living in the world. In one way or another, the self, the mind, must be faced, rather than just defaulting to the commonplace attitude. Which is to blame the world, to finger point, and to hold others responsible.

Progress is made through the practice of self-responsibility. Which is, very simply, responsibility for one's own mind and emotions. Responsibility that is not *personal*, but rather, is *transpersonal*. It doesn't mean that you don't *have* mind, or don't *become* emotional. It just means that you, and you alone, are consciously responsible.

And that is what is meant in the story by the direction given to the *Suras* that they should work *with* the *Asuras*, but remain "peaceful". The *Suras* are us. The *Asuras* are the stuff of our own ignorance, the content of our own emotional self. Which gets literally stirred up by the churning.

Sometimes the churning is not the churning of difficulty or adversary, or inner, psychological and emotional pressure, but rather, is the more tantric churning simply of conscious entry into the stuff of our own unconscious self, the "shadow self" of Jungian psychology. What is in there, is what "comes out" into the light of consciousness, and so it is that in the story the Suras are told not to at any time become greedy or lost or angry, for any of the things that come out of the churning of the ocean.[543]

What comes out of the churning is also everything or anything in the world that the world at large would normally desire or lust for. Such as improvement in material circumstances, improved status, money, fame, and so on.

But it also applies to what comes out of the churning, as "higher experience", or "peak experience", which are experiences of higher beauty and knowledge and being, which cannot be grasped.

Contemporary Western society, particularly in the faction that considers itself "liberal", is currently engaged in trying to create a world, a society, which will not churn us, on the basis that we have the "right" not to be churned. This false ideology arises out of the otherwise very real need of society to improve expectations of standards of behaviour.

But as much as we stop the churning coming from one place, it crops up in another. Because it is an ideology in ignorance of the truth.

The current Western ideology is based on *hyper-personalisation*. It is the pursuit of the idea of *personal* freedom, for "me" and "my" idea of "who I am", for *personal* mind and self, in which the only responsibility is *notional* responsibility as this idea of *person* in the world.

While true responsibility for the self, which is our mind and emotions, is held whenever it suits, to be the responsibility of the network and others outside and separate from our own being.

This ideology is of course based on the notion of freedom without responsibility. Which is also, of course, a childish, idealistic dream, that never has been, nor will ever be, part of the truth of human existence.

There is, in truth, no freedom without responsibility. And if there ever appears to be, temporarily, the mighty leviathan of time itself, will eventually turn the tide.

Let's look again at what, in the story, the *Suras* have been told.

They have been told to check carefully and without distraction. They have been told that the Asuras (demons) will share in the labour, too. However, the Suras will gain the nectar (*amrta* - the nectar of immortality) produced by the churning.[544]

They have been told to accept the demands of the Asuras, without anger. Success, they are told, will come through peaceful effort.[545]

They have been told not to fear the terrible *kālakūta* poison that will manifest from the churning. And lastly, they are told that as other things are manifested from the churning, perhaps desirable things, they must not become lustful or angry for them.[546]

The Suras, our own negative tendencies and emotions, share in the labour. We cannot just instantly suppress these, but rather, have to work with them, and *see* them. This is the "accepting the desires of the *Asuras*", and the "peaceful execution".

We cannot just "throw a switch" and overcome these negative tendencies, these attachments, or *vasanas* as they are called both Hinduism and Buddhism, just by withdrawing from them or attempting to remain aloof. As often as not, we have to *awaken* from them by *consciously passing through* them.

But we have help. The Divine assistance portrayed in the story of *the churning of the ocean*, is *Viśnu* taking the form of the Divine tortoise, to support the churning rod, Mount Mandara, which otherwise sinks in the ocean. Mount Mandara, as we have already mentioned, is true understanding.

So putting all this together, we must *work with* what is within us. And in this way, we come to know what is *in* this ocean that we are churning. And we don't do it alone. We have help.

It is through the churning that *self-knowledge* arises. It doesn't arise from pretending to be morally superior, or noble, or perfect, or Divine. It arises from being the self, but *seeing* the self.

Eventually, the nectar comes out. Which is the nectar of the realisation of the *Being* that is our true Identity, that depends on none of it. Not even on Laksmi, the Divine goddess of "the universe", *Viśnu's* lover, who in the accounts also comes out of the ocean.

Because the Self depends on none of it. Rather, as the Puranas state, it is on the contrary - everything in the universe comes out of the Being. Everything in the universe *is* the Self. And the realisation of the Being, the Self, that emerges from the churning, is the nectar, *Amrta*.

How can you work peacefully with your own emotional pain or agitation? How can you work peacefully with anger, resentment, jealousy, envy, or hatred?

The answer is in *seeing*. It's not a question of *not being* churned or "churned up". It is a question of *transpersonal* observation. Transpersonal seeing is always peaceful, even if what we are seeing is our own perturbed behaviour. It is in the nature of the way transpersonal consciousness and being arises. It comes out of our consciously *passing through*, and then *awakening from*, what is within our own mind and emotions, our own *ocean of milk*.

This process is the process of the higher consciousness entering the lower. Not some higher consciousness separate from us, but our own higher consciousness. It is a profound process that the world at large in the daily News knows nothing of.

As the higher consciousness pushes into the lower, the churning takes place. But the churning itself, of our own mind and emotions, causes our awakening into the higher.

The Śrīmad Bhāgavatam describes the *higher* consciousness entering the lower, saying that Lord *Viśnu* entered the Asuras as the passion *Guna*, and the *Suras* as *Sattva* or goodness, and *Vāsuki* [the serpent] as *Tamas* or ignorance, in order to encourage them in their various types of strength.[547] It also tells us that the alligators in the ocean were disturbed but the churning continued nonetheless.[548] The alligators as we have already seen are the ignorance that is within us and the world.

As the *Amrta* comes out of the ocean, so does the *kālakūta* poison. And as the Puranas relate, there is going to be Divine help with that, too. Because, what happens, in the story, as it is recounted in so many versions, is that *Viśnu*, who has been supporting the churning in the form of the tortoise, *then drinks the poison himself.*[549]

What is this poison, the *kālakūta*?

Different cultures, different religions, different spiritual disciplines, express this in different ways. And the poison itself has two facets.

First, there is "the poison of the serpent". The poison of *Avidyā*, or ignorance, which is driven by emotional energies. Ignorance in the form of personal tendencies, towards gross experience, especially excitement, anger, resentment, and certain kinds of things to which we are attracted and desire. Things that we seek the experience of, but do not perceive the effects of.

Emotional pain, in human beings, is something human beings in general have very little self-knowledge of. Invariably, because most people live according to the principle of the avoidance of self-responsibility. They are always looking outside themselves, for the causes of their pain, in the form of blame.

Not knowing, for example, that anger, resentment, and hatred, is emotional suffering itself. Emotional suffering for which the power of liberation from it, is in oneself. Simply, through the principle of self-responsibility.

So this is one form of the poison that comes out of the Ocean, from its churning. The poison of the serpent. The serpent of ignorance. But there is another form, too.

This is the form locked up in the very nature of our existence as material beings. This form of the poison is something that different religions, cultures, and spiritual disciplines, express in different ways. Not just in the East, but in the West too, it is sometimes expressed as the *pain of separation*. Not separation from another person or material being. But rather, just the pain, that may or may not be realised, of our apparent separation from the Being (or God). Some cultures call this the *separation from the Beloved*.

Our experience of being as human beings is dominated by separation. We have separate bodies, separate minds, separate personalities. Separate families, separate networks, separate nationalities. And now there is the attempt to overcome all that separateness, through the idea of a global "us", simply by saying "we are all human beings", and "we are all in this together". But it simply won't cut it, in overcoming that separation.

We arise in this condition because we arise in *matter*. And the most fundamental thing about matter is separation. This is built into the fact that matter consists of distinct objects. Objects distinct in time and space. And so we have separate bodies and live in the world of separate objects.

We may unconsciously long for the oneness we knew in the womb, before we took our first breath. But even that oneness was a limited, partial experience, already absolutely dependent on the arising of separateness, because the human womb is part of that world of separateness.

This whole condition of separateness actually arises through the principle of the brain. Ours is not really a world of separate beings and things, that is separate from us. Our experience of being a separate body in a world where things are separated in space and time, is all a matter of the principle of the brain. It is all a construct of brain function that we are experiencing as our self and world.

Without realising this, we have come to considerable scientific knowledge of this world, and have started to reformulate it through what we call technologies. We are doing this whilst immersed in a mixture of our growing scientific knowledge of this material stuff, and our ignorance of our own underlying constitution and situation as beings.

The only way to realise the oneness we are really looking for, is to overcome what makes us separate. And the only way you can truly do that, is by realising your true Identity above all this appearance of separation. And the only way you can do *that*, is by realising that your *idea* of who you are, and your identification with the experience of self that arises through the principle of the brain, is *not* who you are.

And that, really, is the whole message of the Hindu corpus. The Hindu corpus calls our true Identity the *Brahman*. And because it is our true Identity, it is also called the Self. But it's not the little emotional self of separation, around which is wrapped the personal "who I am" idea.

So sometimes, as the higher enters the lower, as we were talking about, which is the Great Principle called *Mahat* itself, a new kind of separation is discovered. Even as the illusion of separation is being expunged through the entering of the higher into the lower, and the consequent churning, the very root of all our separation, previously hidden, is something we become acutely *conscious of.*

This experience is sometimes called *separation from the Beloved*. But the Beloved isn't a person, or a human being. *The Beloved* is something far greater, far more profound, of which our greatest personal love of any other person is a part, and from which it has been derived. It is separation from the Being, separation from the realisation of the Self. Or separation from God.

There are stages in the churning at which the more the Being is realised, and the more we realise the truth of our own Identity, the true Home of the being we already really are, then the greater and more acutely felt is this *separation from the Beloved*.

This process is a catharsis, a dissolving of the "poison of the serpent". Which really, is what separates us from our own, ultimate Homecoming into the Self, the Realisation of the Being.

One drop of the profoundly awakened consciousness of the true nature of the Being we already really are, and that everything is, is sufficient to begin the transcendence of the illusion of personal love. But the world will not understand it.

The Bhakti tradition in the East, when speaking of God as Krsna, expresses this in the Caitanya-caritamrta, as the love of Krsna, and an ocean of happiness, a single drop of which can drown the whole world. It also states that this Divine love or ecstasy is something that is really impossible to speak of, and the one who is in the state may appear like a madman.[550] There are parallels in the description with the references to Divine frenzy spoken of in Plato and in the writings of the Neoplatonist philosopher and priest, Marsilio Ficino.

The Caitanya-caritamrta also states with tacit reference to the *churning of the ocean of milk*, that such love of Godhead can be compared to hot sugarcane. Even though the mouth burns, one cannot give it up. It can sometimes be compared to a mix of both poison and nectar.[551]

The *nectar*, as it is called in the East, is sometimes called *exaltation* in Western Christianity. Its purpose is not for the individual to be walking around all the time in the state of ecstasy. Divine realisation is not a personal acquisition.

The *nectar*, as it is called in the East, or *exaltation* as it is known in Western Christianity, has another purpose. Which is simply to catalyse the extinguishing of ignorance from the individual, in the form of attachments and tendencies, or *vasanas*, as these are called in the East.

Eventually, it is seen that these *vasanas* are what causes the material being to arise in the first place. So Divine realisation is not a personal attainment that distinguishes one person from another. And it's not something that can be grasped, as a source of pride. The Caitanya-caritamrta says that the poisonous effects of the love of Godhead defeat the serpent [ignorance and the *vasanas*], whilst the transcendental bliss defeats the pride of having attained the nectar.[552]

27

The Core

We human beings come into existence through sex. Concomitantly, sex is at the core of our limited self. And so arises the idea that the realisation of the spiritual aspect of our being which is beyond this self, is only accessible outside the sphere of sex. Out of that comes the ideas that sex is intrinsically "sinful", and that celibacy is necessary, and so on. Some of the later scriptures, the *tantras*, reversed this idea.

Whichever way you want to go on that, the deepest knowledge available to human beings must include the knowledge of who we are, and where we come from. In other words, how we come to be in existence, as human beings. But we can't separate that from the knowledge of what sex is, where it comes from, what it means, and so on.

The scientific mind that is objective, but not necessarily transpersonal, will "explain" it in terms of evolution. But the scientific understanding of this evolution isn't an understanding of how our actual experience of being, as mind, self, thought, and experience of the material world, comes about in the first place, as a construct of brain function.

Let's put that in the context of sex. Science doesn't currently understand "consciousness". It doesn't understand how anything of our actual experience of being, as sexual mind, sexual self, sexual thoughts, the whole gamut of human sexuality, and our experience of the world and each other in the context of sex, comes about in the first place, through brain function, as a form of "conscious being".

And yet even without science, and without knowing how this comes about as a construct of brain function, we are capable of coming to the knowledge of *all this*, as *self knowledge*. Because we are already *being* this self, that all this is arising as.

The human experience of sex and love, and the relation between the two, falls across a whole wide spectrum. This spectrum in its entirety exists to some degree, in every culture. But every culture is a collective, that consists of everyone who is "plugged into" that culture, and contributing to it.

The modern, popular culture of the West, is no exception. And in every culture most of that spectrum consists of ignorance of the true relation between love and sex. The mainstream Western culture puts out the message that love and sex is all about survival, the creation of new generations, and the maintenance of the culture. On a personal level it is viewed as being for the purposes of recreation, cementing personal relationships, having children, and just sheer sexual experience.

And so the "attitude" to love and sex becomes woven into the fabric of the culture, and most people in that aggregate are *kept away* from actual *self knowledge* by their cultural conditioning. Religions often have their own view on it, which invariably becomes part of that cultural fabric.

The West is living in times now that is endeavouring to promote tolerance of multiple religions and cultures under the one umbrella of the one "Western culture". Within that cultural fabric, is just more cultural fabrics. And every cultural fabric still has woven into it, this ignorance of the true relation between love and sex.

How can you know the true relation between love and sex, until you know the truth about the origin of love, and the origin of sex? We cannot get to the true origin of anything, through just cultural conditioning. You cannot get to it through a personal idea of "who I am" that is born of cultural conditioning.

The backstory to where the West is now, is that sometimes alternative, bohemian societies, spring up beside mainstream society, as networks of people who are resistant to simply sacrificing their individual consciousness to the cultural fabric of mainstream society. So such networks typically consist of artists and writers and philosophers, and so on. And invariably, such "bohemian societies" are eschewed by mainstream society, usually not least because of their sexual freedoms.

The "liberal" part of mainstream Western society now, of course considers itself "liberal". But actually, it is no such thing. It is only "liberal" within a strict framework of new rules which are themselves basically illiberal. Rules which are all about preserving the idea of the freedom and liberty of *the person*, but without self-responsibility, which means responsibility for one's own mind and emotions.

Wherever there is ignorance of the true relation between love and sex, there is always prejudice and judgement and reaction, and finger-pointing, self-projection, discontent, and the complete inability to find love that doesn't in the end fail, or end in grief or anger or resentment.

So for all its "liberal" attitude, the "liberal" part of mainstream Western culture, for all its ideals of "freedom" of sexual expression, is no closer to being free in matters of love and sex, than any former society or culture. In this respect, it lives in an illusion created by the personal mind.

Beyond cultural fabric and cultural conditioning, love between human beings is not about personal, emotional attachments, built on personal self, and the personal idea of "who I am", and "me" and "mine". And sex between human beings is not about that either, nor is it about personal recreation, self-indulgence, or the propagation of the species or the stability and survival of society.

In the context of both Buddhism and Hinduism all that is just interpretation by personal ego, the mind's idea of "who I am". The discovery of the Being, or in Hinduism the *Brahman*, dissolves all that, and also, in the dissolving of all that, is the discovery of the Being. Trying to understand love and sex in terms of the material and personal idea of "who I am", is a hopeless endeavour, because of the way in which the material and the personal comes about, in the first place. Which is through the play of ignorance and *Maya*.

Our existence comes into existence, so to speak, through what we, *in* our material existence, experience as sex. But also, what comes into existence, whether realised or unrealised, is the love of the Being.

The Śiva Purana describes the love of the Being coming into existence in this way, through the churning of the ocean:

> From the sprays and drops that sprang up at the outcome of nectar, many damsels of wonderful beauty were born.
>
> Their faces resembled the full moon in the Autumn; their lustre was as glittering and dazzling as fire, lightning or the sun and they were bedecked in divine jewels, necklaces, bracelets and bangles.
>
> Sprinkling the ten quarters by the water of nectarine beauty they seemed to madden the world by their beauteous glances. They emerged in crores from the nectar sprays.[553]

Why do the Divine damsels "madden the world by their beauteous glances"? This is all about the attraction of the Divine Beauty that lies behind what we experience as the beauty of each other, and attraction to each other. And it is of course, also about sex, through which we come into existence.

The maddening glances of the damsels is also in the depth of beauty and attraction in human damsels, and of course we would also say it is there in the glance of the male, too.

It is at once both the pull into attachment to the senses and material being, but at the same time, it is also the pull back towards the transcendental, the Divine, and the awakening from the illusion, the *Maya*.

Superficially, *glances* in Hindu scriptures, literature and arts, between male and female, such as those described in the pastimes and dalliances of Krsna, have much the same superficial meaning as they do in the West.

They infer, for human beings, love, but also without a doubt they also infer sexual attraction and desire, and inference. They imply admiration, the loving desire for relationship, and the promise of something not yet explored or discovered.

The Caitanya-caritamrta speaks of Krsna coming back from the forest of Vraja, worshipped by the gopīs on the roofs of their palaces, and surround him dancing on the path with glances and smiles. The Caitanya-caritamrta refers to the corners of Krsna's eyes wandering, "like a large black bees, around the gopīs' breasts".[554]

Superficially, as is the case with much Bhakti literature about Krsna, this may look like just a crude reference to sex. But the whole point of these texts that deal with Krsna as lover, is that they are a spiritual teaching about the transcendental origins of what in human beings manifests as a sexual attraction.

In human experience, in matters of love, a single glance can seem to contain all the energy of the universe. Because that is how we are made. In the Bhakti texts the agitation of the *Gunas* is created by the Divine glance. And in human existence this is none other than the glance of someone to whom you are sufficiently attracted, and who is attracted to you.

In that glance is the whole energy of the universe and the pull into the exploration of existence as separate, material bodies. But also in it, is the pull back into the transcendental, in which there is no separation to begin with.

What we have seen is that in the Hindu Scriptures the *Ocean of Milk* originates as an ocean of transcendental Prema, the love of the Being. The churning begins immediately as the churning of the mind of *Śiva*. The "thoughts" therein are what Hinduism calls *Rasa*. This is the transcendental origin of what in we humans, are the ingredients of our own conditional experience of being and world.

We have our senses, with which we see, and hear, and taste, and so on, through which we know "taste" and fragrance, and beauty, and love, and joy. And so on. And then, in connection with that, what we know as "atmosphere" and *ambience*, and "energy", and "story", and so on, which seems to be more subtle, but really, is more fundamental.

Really, all this is just a "translation" into the stuff material existence, or *Prakrti*, of transcendental *Rasa*. Which begins with the entry of *Viśnu* into *Śakti*, and then through Brahma, into the vastly expanded *material* "Ocean of Milk", from which springs our own existence, our own mind, our own psyche, in which there is lostness, and ignorance of our origins.

The Purana is saying that it is because we become lost in this Ocean of Milk, lost in the stuff of our mind and psyche, in the material condition in which we live, that the great expansion of which we are a part, goes on to create all the trouble.

Especially all the trouble in the world that is created through human ignorance of the true origin, and *experiential meaning* of sex. Without which, we don't know the true origin and experiential meaning of our own existence.

Which is why, after describing the emergence from the churning of the ocean, of the Damsels "of wonderful beauty who seemed to madden the world by their beauteous glances", the Śiva Purana goes on to describe how the *Viśnu* immerses himself and becomes lost in what the churning has created out of the ocean of *Prema*:

> In the meantime *Viśnu* saw those damsels born of nectar sprays who were haughty due to their divine beauty and whose faces resembled the full moon [the moon symbolises the mind and the past, and attachment to the mind and the past].
>
> Fascinated by the Cupid's arrows *Viśnu* attained highest pleasure only there. He began to indulge in sexual dalliance with those women of exquisite beauty.
>
> *Viśnu* begot of them sons of great exploits and valour, experts in various kinds of warfare, shaking the entire earth.
>
> Those sons of *Viśnu* of great strength and valour wrought great havoc both in heaven and earth causing misery to all.[555]

This "havoc" that has been created through this expansion and involution of the Being, the fall of *Viśnu* into what comes out of the ocean, refers to the human condition. The message here is that this is the sexual ignorance in human beings. And that, itself, is synonymous with the ignorance of who we are, and where we come from.

It's not that sex, in itself, is a sin. Rather, it is just a question of ignorance. It is that in our materialistic ignorance of what sex is, and where it comes from, in relation to the Being, we don't know how to engage with it. Without it churning out unexpected trouble from the ocean of psyche that it comes out of and perpetuates itself through.

Some scriptures (*sutras*) suggest that the best way out of it, when an aspirant is ready, is celibacy. And perhaps withdrawal from the world, or even asceticism. And that is why, in more than one religion, being a monk has often been associated with being celibate.

But there is another part, associated with the *tantras*, which are texts suggesting that the best way out of it is by *consciously* engaging with it. So that in that way we can awaken into the conscious knowledge of its origin, true purpose, and the Reality of the Being from which it has originated.

Whichever way you go, the *churning of the ocean* is more fundamental and universal. It underlies both ways. The *churning of the ocean* is something that applies whichever path you take, *sutra* or *tantra*. Even if you withdraw to a monastery or a cave, or to the desert, or the wilderness, in one way or another there is still going to be the churning. Or, if you are a Christian, the forty days and forty nights.

Because we have been created *from* the churning of the ocean, then without *conscious engagement* in the churning, as depicted in the Purana story, the ocean just churns anyway, and produces out of it, what it produces, without the higher purpose of *working with* the "Asuras", which leads to the *Amrta*.

The *churning of the ocean* of the Mind of *Śiva*, that is spoken of in the Śiva Purana, originates in the transcendental, and then becomes the churning of the "ocean of milk". It then creates us, it creates our experiences, of self and world. But it also provides the key, the necessary *yoga* through which we can realise who we already really are, and where we come from.

And if we are engage in that then we are bound to discover what is at the core of our material existence, in the first place, which is sex. We are bound to discover the way in which, in the story, *Viśnu* became "lost in his dalliances". Because that is how we *come into existence.*

Another way of putting it is that the material world is a shadow world, just as Plato said, in the *allegory of the cave*. It is a symbol of how it comes to be arising in this moment now, as our experience of being. But it's only a symbol. A symbol based on time. Which itself is the basis of the whole illusion, or what Hinduism calls *Maya*.

Our whole scenario only arises because we have created it so. We did it in a "past" that science knows absolutely nothing about, a *psychic past* that is not a matter of objective time, as measured by clocks. It is nonetheless *discoverable* by us, in our own self-knowledge, because it persists on, in us, in the stuff of our self and mind, as what Hinduism calls our *samskāras*.

These are none other than our attachments to the content of mind stuff or psyche, the stuff of psychic past through which arises our sexuality and wanting and thought and belief, and all personal mind and self in general. Which is then all rounded up together and conducted and interpreted by the illusory "who I am" idea.

28

Yogamaya and Mahamaya

It is sometimes said now that science is awaiting a new scientific revolution, probably the biggest revolution in the history of science.

Scientific knowledge has been moving inexorably forward, and our technological abilities that come out of it, have been increasing, it seems, exponentially. But we are now at the point where it sometimes seems we are raising more questions than we are answering.

One of the things that has happened is a change in the nature of the way our scientific understanding regards nature or the universe. For example, we have moved on from being able to describe nature as predictable in terms of mathematical formulae, as we did in the rise of modern science, into the understanding of *complexity* and *nonlinearity*. And our understanding of what we now call *networks* is relatively recent, in the history of science.

Complexity, nonlinearity, and causal networks, are features of nature that cannot be efficiently encapsulated and described in the old way of using mathematical formulae. And it now looks as though these features constitute the greater part of nature. Entering into the realm of understanding this aspect of nature, would have been impossible without first, the invention of computers.

As ever, as our observations and measurements become better, the old ways of understanding becomes challenged again. Despite this, the enthusiastic reporting on advancements in scientific knowledge often gives the impression that we are already "on top of this", so to speak, and that we can just carry on exploring in the way that we have been. Both in practical, and intellectual terms.

But this is not really the truth. Because our greatest area of ignorance *in science*, is not ignorance of such things as quantum particles and the beginning of the observable universe, or dark matter and energy.

We do have ignorance in that area, but our greatest ignorance is our ignorance of the nature of our own intelligence, the intelligence we are being, that is *doing* the understanding in science. We are easily mistakenly convinced that what we are studying is separate from the intelligence we are collectively being.

If we were to accept the fundamental fact of modern neuroscience, which is that everything we know and experience is a construct of brain function, then our view of the world, the universe, and nature, in which we live, would change appropriately.

The idea that we are living in, and scientifically studying a world, that because it has an objective aspect to it, essentially has nothing to do with us other than that we happen to be arising within it, is quite simply mistaken.

The objectivity of material nature simply means that as a construct of brain function, it does not depend on the functioning of any individual brain. It does not mean that nature as we know it and experience it, cannot be a construct of brain function.

The way we ordinarily think about this, in terms such as "inside the brain", "outside the brain", self and not-self, and of course the idea of "who I am", is a feature of the psychology of the intelligence we are employing, rather than a matter of scientific fact. It comes about through a level of intelligence that identifies the individual idea of "who I am" with the sentient experience of the world that arises through individual brain function.

We cannot rise into the level of understanding that it is our human prerogative to rise into, until we realise that nature herself is *our* nature.

We cannot do it until we realise that the *prima facie* thing about the human brain is not that it is some kind of machine for perceiving the material world, but rather, that it is the means through which arises our experience of self.

We cannot do it until we realise that this experience of self as it arises through nature, is inseparable from the arising of the world that we experience.

We cannot do it until we realise that the world we experience, including its objective aspect that science studies, is inseparable from this experience of self.

We cannot do it until we accept the already discovered scientific fact that both what we experience as the material world, and what we experience as self, come through the same principle, specifically, the functioning of the brain.

Everything that we have been talking about in this book boils down to saying that our conditional experience of being, as a human being, in other words, our experience of self and world, arises from the Self. In Hinduism this is called the *Brahman*.

In order to come to this realisation, we first have to be weaned off the idea that our world, the whole universe that science studies, has nothing to do with us other than that we happened to be arising within it. On the contrary, it is our prerogative to realise it has everything to do with us, because it is us.

We have to be weaned off the idea that we are in our world as some kind of separate entity called "consciousness", or human "being" or self, that is other than what this world is.

We have to be weaned off the idea that our responsibility as a human being is to something separate from our self, an idea that we only hold in the first place because we mistakenly believe the world to be separate from our self.

Without the Self - or what Hinduism calls the *Brahman* - there could be no experience of being here. The fact that our conditional experience of being, as a human being, arises through brain function, makes no difference to this.

We are saying that human brain function, and what it constructs as our *conditional experience of being* - which is what we encounter as our experience of self and mind and world - is a play of the Self. Our conditional experience of being as a human being is not something that arises in its own right, separately from the Self, or the *Brahman*.

Everything in our human experience of being arises because in the first instance, of course, it is a possibility. The whole of what we call "the universe" in science, is just, as it were, the representation in our conditional experience of being, of this possibility.

It has become what it is, it is activated in this way, only because the Self is already here, playing in this possibility. If you pull it apart, and drill down into it, and go down into the smallest things from which it is constructed, you just find quantum particles, that actually don't have any material existence independently of them being part of the play of our own experience of being. Rather, they are always just a possibility, and the nature of the way that plays out, is through what we understand scientifically, as probability.

There is no such thing as a modern scientific concept of "reality". The question of "reality" is treated as a question for disciplines outside science. Nevertheless, we are saying that what science refers to as "nature" is not Reality. We are saying that discursive thought and objective understanding is actually a kind of decoy, when it comes to realising the truth of our constitution and situation.

We are saying that the truth of our constitution and the situation, the truth of our very existence as human beings, is a matter of the self that we, in the first instance, experience ourselves as being. It is not that the truth of us *is* this self, but rather, that the whole context of our existence, including our scientific understanding, is about this self. And not about something, some universe, or nature, that we mistakenly presume has nothing to do with it.

We are saying this: The only Reality is the Self that is playing at being this nature, and the Self does not depend on it, in the least. Again, this Self - or *Brahman* as it is called in Hinduism - is not separate from us, but on the contrary, is already our own true Identity.

The message in the Bhakti part of the corpus, and indeed, hinted at in the Śiva Purana, is that our true home as *experience of being*, as the play of the Self, is not here, in this material phenomena, that we now know scientifically arises through the principle of the brain. Our true home, as the Self that we already really are, is in transcendental Life and Being that is unimaginable and unknowable to the limited mode of intelligence that arises through the principle of the brain.

The barrier to our contemporary realisation of this is not a lack of data or computing power. The blockage is in the nature of our own mind and being. Just as it is. If we realise even just a glimpse of the limited nature of our conditional experience of being here, then the whole nature of our comprehension of this conditional experience of being that we are having, changes.

This, really, in its own language, culture, and way, is what the Hindu corpus teaches. But the knowledge that it expresses through its own cultural fabric, is actually the knowledge of something - a truth - that has no dependence whatsoever, on *any* cultural fabric. Even in Hinduism's own terms, any cultural fabric is illusory, it is *Maya*.

The underlying Hindu message is that the root "cause" of the whole *play of being* in which we are living, is ignorance of the Self that we already really are, and of the way in which the Self we already really are, gives rise to this scenario.

So that at the root of the scenario in which we find ourselves, is not a separate thing called the Big Bang, or a separate thing called "consciousness", or even a separate thing called God. At the root of the scenario in which we find ourselves, is the Being - the *Brahman* - we already really are.

Mahamaya

This, really, is the fundamental story in the Hindu corpus. Essentially, the objective nature of the material world, the aspect of our world that science studies and is coming to understand, is what Hinduism regards as *Mahamaya* (the great illusion). But when Hinduism talks about *Mahamaya*, it doesn't really know what the modern scientific meaning of *objective*, applied to the material world, is. Because the Hindu corpus is *prescientific*.

The objectivity of the material world is simply the aspect of brain function through which our experience of self and world is created. It is simply that aspect of it that does not depend on any particular, individual brain function, or any particular network of brains. Just as the laws of quantum correlations do not depend on any specific quantum particles. But there are, nonetheless, no actual quantum correlations without quantum particles.

Yogamaya

Yogamaya is something different. *Yogamaya* is about what we experience. It is about our subjective experience of mind, and self, and world. It is about our individual psyche. The Christian version of it would be what Christians call the individual's "relationship with God". And in terms of scientific materialism that's down to the individual brain. But then again, this individual brain is not *separate*, or isolated. It's just an individual instance, of the *one principle*, the principle that is instantiated here, where this individual brain organ is. Just as what we call the material world is actually inseparable from brain function, so also *mahamaya* is inseparable from *yogamaya*.

The realisation of the truth of it all is beyond the personal idea of "who I am". Society as a whole, in contrast, clings to the idea that you must remain involved and invested in the personal idea of "who I am". Because society is a *network mind*. It is thoroughly and totally identified, essentially with *brain*, essentially with what unconscious brain function is doing.

The process of becoming free from psychological and emotional involvement in that, is part of the most beautiful thing that can happen to a human being. It is the discovery of our own true nature, the true nature of our own being, that is what and who we already really are, here, even in this limited, *conditional experience of being* as a human being.

What we are being here, in Hindu terms, poetically speaking, but also in completely up to date, contemporary terms, is *Śiva*'s brainchild. It's a play of being, created through the principle of the brain. We can only realise this by realising who we really are, which Hinduism calls the *Brahman*.

We don't have to do it through Hinduism, though. There is no limit to the ways in which we can do it. It's not confined to a particular culture, or particular religion.

In Hindu terms our human experience of being arises because we are *Viśnu*, the Purusa, having accepted this mode of conditional experience of being. Our conditional experience of being arises out of this *Prakrti*, which gives rise to its own principles, but *Prakrti* arises originally from the Self.

This is basically what the Śiva Purana means when it says that all the principles originating from *Prakrti* are insentient, whilst the Purusa [the Self] is not. It is why it says that *Viśnu* accepted all these principles according to the will of *Śiva*, and then started to "sleep in the *Brahman*".[556]

We only know of material phenomena, we only experience it, we can only scientifically measure it, because first, we are already being this sentient being, arising through brain function, which in Hindu terms arises through *Prakrti*.

In Hinduism it comes into being through Mahat, the Great Principle, that is the principle "I am *Brahman*" in the great expansion, and the principle of the expansion itself. And so the Śiva Purana says that the Great Principle is the perfect knowledge and the consciousness that "I am Brahman", which belongs to the cosmic intellect where nothing else is remembered.[557]

The *ākāśa* - the universal past or psychic memory - is behind everything that emerges in us as experience of being, mind and world. But as the Puranas describe, it is "beneath" the cosmic intellect, the Buddhi, through which the Mahat is realised. All our experiences of being, and stories of being, are essentially a reflection in the mirror of this one cosmic intellect that is in all of us.

Whilst this perfect knowledge of Mahat is the consciousness "I am Brahman",[558] the *ākāśa*, the "space" or "ether" which becomes "air" or "wind" is the great "memory". It is the great "memory" of everything under the Sun that maintains the possibility of the stuff of our mind and conditional experience of being.

But it's only a possibility. It's not Reality. It doesn't exist by itself. It just becomes known by the Self entering into it, or as Purusa entering *Prakrti*. The Self, the *Brahman*, has absolutely no dependence on it, whatsoever. The true home of the Self - the *Brahman* - is transcendental Life and Being, in the "blissful forest".

To borrow from the language of the corpus, the infinite lotus of infinite transcendental Life and Being, becomes the infinite lotus of infinite dreaming. And that infinitude is infinities of infinities within infinities. Which we experience as our world of time and material being, the stuff of our own mind stuff. And we don't yet know how to understand that in terms of recursive infinities, or infinite recursions, because we do not yet even understand material phenomena in this way.

What it all *is*, is what it comes from. What it all *is*, as described in Hinduism, is *Maya*, and *Śakti*. What it all *is*, is *Śiva*, *Sivā*, *Viśnu*, and *Lakśmi*, all created through Brahma, as infinite expansion and involution.

In the Padma Purana and Brahma Samhita the infinite expansion of transcendental worlds of being are described in terms of infinite lotuses within lotuses.[559] And so it is that in the imagery *Lakśmi* - the *Śakti* lover of Viśnu - is invariably depicted emerging from a lotus, and holding a lotus. And all is created by Brahma emerging from an infinite lotus emerging from the navel of *Viśnu*.

And in the Puranas, in the story of King Punyanidhi, the king sees his own adopted daughter - who is really *Lakśmi* - in a dream about Hari (an expansion of *Viśnu*). We see the expansion where she stands in a full blown lotus, and in her hand, is a lotus flower.[560]

Our lives are stories of being, made from infinite expansions and involutions of the *Brahman*, expansions and involutions that are still churning in the ocean of our experience of being.

Whilst literally all the time, the Being, the *Brahman*, is untouched. And our realisation of That Being, is also something that emerges from the churning of the ocean, the churning of the ocean of our own life and circumstances, our own conditional experience of being, as a human being.

The universe doesn't exist without us, any more than we exist without the universe. The hypostasis of both the human experience of being and the world in which we live, is not something separate from us, or other than who we are. It is nothing material or mathematical or that science itself can understand or explain. On the contrary, it is the Self, the *Brahman*, which is none other than our own true Identity.

Bibliography

Papers

Steven A. Barker, "N, N-Dimethyltryptamine (DMT), an Endogenous Hallucinogen: Past, Present, and Future Research to Determine Its Role and Function", *Front. Neurosci.*, 06 August 2018 | https://doi.org/10.3389/fnins.2018.00536.

Anjana Chakraborty; (Guide: Das Roy, Snigdha), *A Study of the Evolution of Soma in Vedic Mythology and Ritual*, 2017, Assam University, Department of Sanskrit.

Corbett, Lionel et al. "Hallucinogenic N-Methylated Indolealkylamines in the Cerebrospinal Fluid of Psychiatric and Control Populations", *British Journal of Psychiatry*, 132 (1978): 139-144;

Davis AK, Clifton JM, Weaver EG, Hurwitz ES, Johnson MW, Griffiths RR. "Survey of entity encounter experiences occasioned by inhaled N,N-dimethyltryptamine: Phenomenology, interpretation, and enduring effects", *Journal of Psychopharmacology*, 2020;34(9):1008-1020. doi:10.1177/0269881120916143;

Andrew R. Gallimore, Rick J. Strassman, "A Model for the Application of Target-Controlled Intravenous Infusion for a Prolonged Immersive DMT Psychedelic Experience", *Front Pharmacol*. 2016; 7: 211. Published online 2016 Jul 14. doi: 10.3389/fphar.2016.00211.

Jiménez-Garrido, D.F., Gómez-Sousa, M., Ona, G. et al. "Effects of ayahuasca on mental health and quality of life in naïve users: A longitudinal and cross-sectional study combination". *Sci Rep* 10, 4075 (2020). https://doi.org/10.1038/s41598-020-61169-x

Griffiths RR, Hurwitz ES, Davis AK, Johnson MW, Jesse R. 'Survey of subjective "God encounter experiences": Comparisons among naturally occurring experiences and those occasioned by the classic psychedelics psilocybin, LSD, ayahuasca, or DMT.' *PLoS One*. 2019;14(4):e0214377. Published 2019 Apr 23. doi:10.1371/journal.pone.0214377

Don N. Page and William K. Wootters, *Evolution without evolution: Dynamics described by stationary observables*, Phys. Rev. D 27, 2885, 15 June 1983.

Michael Pascal, Luke David, Robinson Oliver, "An Encounter With the Other: A Thematic and Content Analysis of DMT Experiences From a Naturalistic Field Study", *Frontiers in Psychology*, Vol. 12, 2021, https://www.frontiersin.org/article/10.3389/fpsyg.2021.720717. DOI=10.3389/fpsyg.2021.720717. ISSN=1664-1078.

Michael Winkelman, "Introduction: Evidence for entheogen use in prehistory and world religions", *Journal of Psychedelic Studies* 3(2), pp. 43–62 (2019) DOI: 10.1556/2054.2019.024

Online

Mahabharata, Shanti Parva, Mokshadhāma Parva, Section CCCXXXVII. (https://www.sacred-texts.com/hin/m12/m12c036.htm, accessed April 17, 2022).

Hindu Source Translations

Atharva-Veda: *Atharva-Veda*, Tr. Dr. Tulsi Ram M.A., Ph.D., Delhi, 2103.

Bhagavad Gita: HDG A.C. Bhaktivedanta Swami Prabhupāda, *The Bhagavad-Gītā As It Is*, The Bhaktivedanta Book Trust, 1985; Tr. Laurie L. Patton, *The Bhagavad Gita*, Penguin, 2014.

Brahma Purana: *The Brahma Purāna*, 'Ancient Indian Tradition and Mythology', Tr. A Board of Scholars, Ed. Prof. J. L. Shastri, Vols. 33 *ff.* 1957-2003.

Brahma Samhita: Śrila Jīva Gosvāmī; Śrila Bhaktivinoda Thākura; Prabhupāda Śrila Bhaktisiddhānta Saravatī Gosvāmi Thākura; Śri Śrimad Bhaktivedānta Nārāyana Mahārāja; Śri Śrimad Bhakti Prajnāna Keśava Gosvāmī, *Śri Brahma-samhitā*, Gaudīya Vedānta Publications, Vrndavana, Uttar Pradesh, 2003. ISBN 81-86737-10-3.

Brahma Sutras: *Brahma Sutras*, Swami Vireswarananda, Mayavati, Almora, 1936.

Brahmanda Purana: *The Brahmānda Purāna*, (4 Vols.) Parts 1-2, Montilal Banarsidass, Delhi, 1958.

Brihad Bhagavatamrta: ark:/13960/t0004tx86; Alfred J. Valerio, *Brihad Bhagavatamrta*, Chennai (Notion Press), 2019.

Caitanya-caritamrta: His Divine Grace A. C. Bhaktivedanta Swami Prabhupāda, *Srī Caitanya-caritamrta*, Ādi-līlā, 2012, ISBN 978-91-7149-661-4.

Caitanya-caritamrta: His Divine Grace A. C. Bhaktivedanta Swami Prabhupāda, *Srī Caitanya-caritamrta*, Madhya-līlā, 2012, ISBN 978-91-7149-662-1.

Caitanya-caritamrta: His Divine Grace A. C. Bhaktivedanta Swami Prabhupāda, *Srī Caitanya-caritamrta*, Antya-līlā, 2012, ISBN 978-91-7149-663-8.

Devi Bhagavatam: *Sri Devi Bhagavatam*, Tr. Swami Bhagawatam, 1921-1922.

Garga Samhita: *Srī Gārga Sāmhita*, ark:/13960/t42s4634q.

Gopala-tapani Upanishad: *Gopāla-tāpani Upanishad*, Tr. Swami B. V. Tripurāri, Audarya, 2003.

Harivamsha: *A Prose English Translation of Harivamsha*, Tr. Manmatha Nath Dutt, Calcutta, 1897.

Krsna Karnamrta: Tr. HH Bhānu Swāmī, *Śrī Krsna Karnāmrta of Śrīla Bilvamangala Thakkura (Līlāśuka) and Sāranga-ranga-dā Tīkā of Śrīla Krsna-dāsa Kavirāja Gosvāmi*, 2016.

Kubjikāmatatantra: *The System of Five Cakras in Kubjikāmatatantra 14-16*, Dory Heilijgers-Seelen, Egbert Forsten Groningen, 1994.

Kurma Purana: The *Kūrma-Purāna*, Motilal Banarsidass, Delhi, 1951-1998.

Laghu Bhagavatamrta: Śrila Rūpa Gosvāmi, *Laghu Bhagavatamrta*, Tr. HH Bhānu swāmī, Com. Śrila Baladeva vidyābhūsana, 2012.

Linga Purana: *The Linga-Purāna*, Motilal Banarsidass, Delhi, 1952-1990.

Maitri Upanishad: Hume, *The Thirteen Principal Upanishads*, OUP, 1921.

Matsya Purana: *Matsya Purana - A Study*, Vasudeva S. Agrawala, Varanasi, 1953.

Natyashastra: *The Nāṭyaśastra ascribed to Bharata-Muni*, Calcutta, 1951.

Nirālamba Upanishad: Tr. K. Nārāyanasvami, Aiyar, *Thirty Minor Upanishads*, Madras, 1914.

Padma Purana: *The Padma Purāna*, 'Ancient Indian Tradition and Mythology', Tr. A Board of Scholars, Ed. Dr. G.P. Bhatt, Vols. 39-48, Tr. Dr. N.A. Deshpande, Parts I-X, Montilal Banarsidass, Delhi, 1988-1992.

Prīti Sandarbha: Śrīla Jīva Gosvāmī, *Prīti Sandarbha*, Tr. HH Bhanu Swami, 2018.

Radha Tantra: *The Rādhā Tantra*, Tr. Måns Broo, Routledge, 2017.

Satapatha Brahmana: *The Satapatha Brahmana*, Tr. Julius Eggeling, (5 Vols.) Parts 1-5, Montilal Banarsidass, Delhi, 1882-1993.

Śiva Purana: *The Śivapurāna*, Motilal Banarsidass, Delhi, Vol. I; Vol. II, Ed. J.L. Shastri, 1970; Vol. III; Vol IV, 2002.

Skanda Purana: *The Skanda-Purāna*, (20 Vols.) Parts 1-20, Montilal Banarsidass, Delhi, 1950.

Śrīmad Bhāgavatam: His Divine Grace A. C. Bhaktivedanta Swami Prabhupāda, *Śrīmad Bhāgavatam*, 2011. (12 Cantos).

Tantrāloka by Abhinavagupta, Tr. Professor Satya Prakash Singh, Swami Maheshvarananda, *Abhinavagupta's Śrī Tantrāloka and Other Works*, Vols. 1-8, New Delhi, 2015.

Upanishads: Tr. Robert Ernest Hume, *The Thirteen Principal Upanishads*, OUP, 1921; Tr. K. Nārāyanasvami Aiyar, 1914, *Thirty Minor Upanishads*, also published as *Yogic Philosophy and Practices* (*Thirty Minor Upanishads*).

Vaimānika Śastra: Maharshi Bharadwaaja; Subbaraya Shastry, Tr. GR Josyer, *Vaimānika Śāstra*, Mysore, 1973.

Varaha Purana: *The Varāha-Purāna*, Tr. & An. S. Venkitasubramo-niaiyer, Motilal Banarsidass, Delhi,1985-2003.

Viśnu Purana: Tr. Manmath Nath Dutt, *Vishnu Purana* (*A Prose English Translation of Vishnupuranam*), Calcutta, 1896.

Vedas: Ralph T. H. Griffith; Arthur Berriedale Keith; Ed. Jon William Fergus, *The Vedas*, 2017, ISBN: 978-1541294714

Yoga Vasishta: *Yoga Vasishta by Valmiki*, Tr. Vihari Lala Mitra (1891), Ed. Thomas L. Palotas, 2013.

Other Books

Sri Aurobindu, *The Secret of the Veda*, Pondicherry, 1998.

Arthur Avalon, *The Serpent Power,* New York, 1974.

Śrila Visvanatha Cakravarti Thakura, *Sri Vraja-riti-cintamani*, Tr. Kusakratha dasa, ark:/13960/t4mm4c24k.

His Divine Grace A. C. Bhaktivedanta Swami Prabhupāda, *Teachings of Lord Caitanya*, The Bhaktivedanta Book Trust, (New Edition), 1985 (ISBN 0-902677-01-2).

Sudarshan R Iyengar, *Meditations on Sri Jayadeva's Gita Govinda*, GIRI, 2021.

Tejaswi Katravulapally, *Journey Through the Vedic Thought*, 2020.

Thomas S Kuhn, *The Structure of Scientific Revolutions*, 3rd Ed., Chicago, 1996.

Alexander Lipski, Ed. Joseph A. Fitzgerald, *The Essential Śri Ānandamayī Mā*, Delhi, 2007

Arthur Anthony Macdonell, *A Vedic Reader*, OUP, 1917.

Vettam Mani, *Purānic Encyclopaedia*, Montilal Banarsidass, Delhi, 1964-1974.

Sr. Edward C. Sachau, *Alberuni's India*, London, 1910.

C. Sivaramamurti, *Nataraja in Art, Thought and Literature*, National Museum, New Delhi, 1974

Monier-Williams, *A Sanskrit English Dictionary*, OUP, 1899.

References

1. Ralph T. H. Griffith, ; Arthur Berriedale Keith; Ed. Jon William Fergus, *The Vedas*, 2017, ISBN: 978-1541294714, *Foreward.*
2. *Yoga Vasishta by Valmiki*, Tr. Vihari Lala Mitra (1891), Ed. Thomas L. Palotas, 2013, Ch. 190, 8.
3. Because, as explained in Caitanya-caritamrta, 20.289-295, the Supreme Personality of Godhead in the form of Viśnu (20.289) expands into Garbhodakaśayī Viśnu (20.292-293) and then into Kśirodakaśayī Viśnu (20.294).
4. *e.g.* Brahma Samhita 18; Śrīmad Bhāgavatam 3.8.10-14; Caitanya-caritamrta, Adi-lila, 20.287.
5. Śrīmad Bhāgavatam, 3.8.10-15.
6. Monier-Williams.
7. Caitanya-caritamrta, Adi-lila, 5.77. Tr. His Divine Grace A. C. Bhaktivedanta Swami Prabhupāda, ISBN 978-91-7149-661-4, 2012.
8. Caitanya-caritamrta, Madhya-lila, 21.59-21.71.
9. Caitanya-caritamrta, Adi-lila, Tr. His Divine Grace A. C. Bhaktivedanta Swami Prabhupāda, ISBN 978-91-7149-661-4, 2012. Glossary.
10. Brahmānda Purana, Motilal Barnarsidass, Delhi, 2002, p. 3.
11. This arrangement is across the Puranas generally. The reference to it as a planetary system known as the Bhū-mandala is found succinctly in: Srimad-Bhagavatam, 5.16.5.
12. Eric Huntington, *Creating the Universe*, Washington, 2019. p. 38.
13. Siva Purana, *Umā,Samhitā,* Ch. 18, 45-46 (Motilal Banarsidass, Delhi, 2002, Vol. 3, p.1527); Brahmanda Purana, 1.2.19.77.
14. Viśnu Purana: Tr. Manmath Nath Dutt, *Vishnu Purana* (*A Prose English Translation of Vishnupuranam*), Calcutta, 1896, pp. 116.
15. Śrīmad Bhāgavatam, 5.20.
16. Śrīmad Bhāgavatam, 5.20.24.
17. Viśnu Purana: Tr. Manmath Nath Dutt, *Vishnu Purana* (*A Prose English Translation of Vishnupuranam*), Calcutta, 1896, pp. 116;127.
18. Śrīmad Bhāgavatam, 5.20.
19. Śrīmad Bhāgavatam, 5.20.29 & 5.20.34.

20. See Tony Prince, *Universal Enlightenment*, 2020.
21. Caitanya-caritamrta, Adi-lila, 5.51.
22. Caitanya-caritamrta, Adi-lila, 5.52.
23. Madhya-lila, 20.269.
24. Madhya-lila, 15.172; 15.175; 19.152-3; 20.269; 21.50; 21.51-52.
25. Madhya-lila, Tr. Prabhupāda, 15.172; 15.175; **20.269**; 21.51-52.
26. *Ibid.*
27. Madhya-lila, 21.51.
28. Madhya-lila, 15.175; 20.269; 21.50; 21.51-52.
29. *e.g.* Bhagavad Gita, 8.17, 9.8; Iso Upanishad 15; Śrīmad Bhāgavatam, 1 - 8 (numerous) ; Caitanya-caritamrta, Adi-lila 5.50, 51, 54, 57; Madhya-lila, 15.175; 20.269. For word-by-word transliterations see Tr. His Divine Grace A.C. Bhaktivedanta Swami Prabhupāda.
30. Madhya-lila, 15.172; 15.176.
31. *e.g.* Madhya-lila, 20.282.
32. *e.g.* Caitanya-caritamrta, Madhya-lila, 19.152-3, which is from the point of view of the Bhakti tradition, and Krsnaism, but the principle is the same for any approach.
33. This is very clear in many sources. For example, in the Śiva Purana the *Prakrti* or *pradhana* which is "prior" to matter, is already *Maya*.
34. Accounts of the seven *Dwipas* and their surrounding oceans are found in Mahabharata and the Puranas: Viśnu; Agni; Brahma; Brahmanda; Kurma; Linga; Matsya; Markandeya; Vayu; Padma and Śrīmad Bhāgavatam, and others. It also occurs in other sources such as the Harivamsha.
35. *e.g.* Viśnu Purana 2.2, 2.4; Śrīmad Bhāgavatam 5.20. 2, 18,19,24,29,34,35; Caitanya-caritamrta, Madhya-lila, 20.218
36. Śrīmad Bhāgavatam 5.20.35.
37. *Ibid.*
38. Śrīmad Bhāgavatam, 10.89.51.
39. *Ibid.*
40. Śrīmad Bhāgavatam 5.20.34.
41. Caitanya-caritamrta, Adi lila, 5.15.
42. Caitanya-caritamrta, Adi lila, 5.16-7.
43. Śrīmad Bhāgavatam 5.20.35.
44. Caitanya-caritamrta, Adi lila, 2.5; 5.34; 5.38.
45. Caitanya-caritamrta, Madhya-lila, 19.153.
46. Śrīmad Bhāgavatam, 10.89.51.
47. *e.g.* Śrīmad Bhāgavatam, 5.16.2.
48. *e.g.* Śrīmad Bhāgavatam, 5.1.31.
49. Śrīmad Bhāgavatam, 10.89.47.
50. *e.g.* Śrīmad Bhāgavatam, 6.8.23-25.

51. Śrīmad Bhāgavatam, 9.5.5.
52. Śrīmad Bhāgavatam, 9.5.6.
53. Śrīmad Bhāgavatam, 6.10-14, see Tr. His Divine Grace A. C. Bhaktivedanta Swami Prabhupāda, The Bhaktivedanta Book Trust, e-book, 2011.
54. *e.g.* Śrīmad Bhāgavatam, 6.8.23-25.
55. Śrīmad Bhāgavatam, 9.5.5.
56. Śrīmad Bhāgavatam, 10.89.49.
57. Śrīmad Bhāgavatam, 10.89.50.
58. Śrīmad Bhāgavatam, 10.89.52.
59. Śrīmad Bhāgavatam, 10.89.52-3.
60. *e.g.* Śiva Purana, *Umā Samhita*, 24. (Motilal Banarsidass, Delhi, 2002, Vol. IV, p. 1551 *ff.*)
61. Śrīmad Bhāgavatam, 10.89.52.
62. Śiva Purana, IV, *Vāyavīya Samhitā*, Ch. 5, 5 (*Ibid.*, p. 1926)
63. Caitanya-caritamrta, Adi-lila, 1.7-11.
64. The principle of genetic inheritance is a cornerstone of the principle of the evolution of the species. It's one principle of a network of principles. It is the *principles* we should see, rather than their absolute expression in the stuff of material phenomena.

    We currently understand evolution in terms of material phenomena, considered as though it is something separate from what that material phenomena, through the principle of evolution, comes to create, as *us*.

    But there is no separation. Our experience of being is a construct of brain function, and so is the matter that we see involved in the principle of evolution. Our attachment to the idea of separation, is rooted in the personal "who I am" idea, which lurks behind even objective thinking. When we transcend that attachment we can see that what collectively evolves, at the centre of that network of principles, in the network mind we are collectively being, is the intelligence we are being, which eventually manifests our knowledge of the brain.

    The biological brain organ is not who we are, nor does its functioning embody in matter, the reality of our being. It only embodies what we are temporarily being. The import of the Hindu corpus in relation to science, is that the material phenomena science studies is *a construct of being*, expressing itself through the principle of the brain. Whilst the only reality is the Self, or *Brahman*.
65. Caitanya-caritamrta, Adi-lila, 4.56.
66. *c.f.* His Divine Grace A.C. Bhaktivedanta Swami Prabhupāda, *Teachings of Lord Caitanya*, London *et al*, 1985, p. 12.
67. See Purport to Caitanya-caritamrta, Adi-lila, 5.232, §3; His Divine Grace A.C. Bhaktivedanta Swami Prabhupāda, *Teachings of Lord Caitanya*, London *et al*, 1985, p. 12.

68. His Divine Grace A.C. Bhaktivedanta Swami Prabhupāda, *Teachings of Lord Caitanya*, London *et al*, 1985, p. 10; p. 12.
69. His Divine Grace A.C. Bhaktivedanta Swami Prabhupāda, *Teachings of Lord Caitanya*, London *et al*, 1985, p. 10; p. 12.
70. *e.g.* Śrīmad Bhāgavatam, 11.25.12. Tr. His Divine Grace Bhaktivedanta Swami Prabhupāda, 2011, ISBN 978-91-7149-632-4.
71. Śrīmad Bhāgavatam, 11.25.12. *Ibid.*
72. Śiva Purana, 1, *Rudra Samhitā*, Sect. 1, Ch. 9, 58-61.
73. Śiva Purana, 1, *Rudra Samhitā*, Sect. 1, Ch. 16, 37-39.
74. *e.g.* The Śiva Purāna, *Rudra Samhita*, Sect. I, Ch. 13, 47-53. (Tr. J. L. Shastri, Motilal Banarsidass, Delhi, 1970, Vol. I, p. 234)
75. The Śiva Purāna, *Rudra Samhita*, Sect. II, Ch. 3, 34. (Tr. J. L. Shastri, Motilal Banarsidass, Delhi, 1970, Vol. I, p. 284)
76. *e.g.* The Śiva Purāna, *Vāyavīya Samhitā*, Ch. 7, 3. (Ed. Motilal Banarsidass, Delhi, 2002, Vol. 4, p. 1932); Kurma Purana 1.16.94; Brahma Purana 2: 46.67; 83.6; 83.17.
77. Caitanya-caritamrta, Adi-lila, 5.77.
78. *e.g.* Caitanya-caritamrta, Madhya-lila, 21.59-21.71.
79. Brahmanda Purana, I.I.3.38.
80. The initial paper, now well known, was: Don N. Page and William K. Wootters, *Evolution without evolution: Dynamics described by stationary observables*, Phys. Rev. D 27, 2885, 15 June 1983.
81. Brahma Samhita, Verse 1, *translation and explanation of Tīkā*, pp. 9; 17; 33; Verse 5, *Tīkā translation*, p. 62; Verse 33, *Tīkā translation*, p. 181; Verse 40; Verse 40, *Tīkā translation*, pp. 232-234; p. 247; *The eighteen-syllable mantra*, p 140.
82. Caitanya-caritamrta, Adi-lila, 5.59.
83. The Śiva Purāna, *Rudra Samhita*, Sect. I, Ch 6, 21; 24. (Tr. J. L. Shastri, Motilal Banarsidass, Delhi, 1970, Vol. I, p. 196)
84. The essence of this is in Brahmanda Purana 1.2.32.83-87.
85. Linga Purana, Vol. I, Section 1, Ch. 4, *Inauguration of Creation*, 51-53. (Motilal Barnarsidass, Delhi, 1990, p. 15)
86. Kurma Purana, Vol. I, Ch. 4, *Description of Creation by Means of Prakrti*, 10. (Motilal Barnarsidass, Delhi, 1998, p. 40)
87. Śiva Purana, 1, *Vidyeśvara Samhitā*, Ch. 5,10.
88. Monier-Williams.
89. Monier-Williams.
90. Monier-Williams.
91. *Ibid.* 15; 16-18.
92. *Ibid.* 26.

These descriptions sound physical and material. But this of course refers to the *symbolic* way in which *Śiva* is *represented* in the culture associated with the religion. Except that we most commonly find *Śiva* represented with four arms, not ten.

The various features are symbols of various things. For example, *Śiva*'s body is dusted entirely with ash. This takes on a cultural "meaning" of its own, and in Indian culture it is sometimes expressed literally by men who cover their naked selves with ash, because they wish to "appear as" *Śiva*.

We should first appreciate one basic thing about the Puranic stories: It is Mythological symbolism aimed at awakening the reader from precisely the kind of mind that fails to see it is *Mythological symbolism*, and takes it literally.

93. The Śiva Purāna, *Rudra Samhita*, Sect. I, Ch 6, 16-18. (Ed. J.L. Shastri, Motilal Banarsidass, Delhi, 1970, Vol. I, p.196)
94. Alexander Lipski, Ed. Joseph A. Fitzgerald, *The Essential Śri Ānandamayī Mā*, Delhi, 2007, p. 19.
95. Subala Upanishad of Śukla-Yajurveda, Khanda IX, in *Yogic Philosophy and Practices* (*Thirty Minor Upanishads*), Tr. K. Nārāyanasvami Aiyar, 1914, p. 71-75.
96. The Śiva Purāna, *Rudra Samhita*, Sect. I, Ch 6, 16-18. (Ed. J.L. Shastri, Motilal Banarsidass, Delhi, 1970, Vol. I, p.196).
97. The Śiva Purāna, *Rudra Samhita*, Sect. I, Ch 6, 16-18. (Ed. J.L. Shastri, Motilal Banarsidass, Delhi, 1970, Vol. I, p.196).
98. Siva Purana, Pt. 1, Ch. 9, *Rudrasamhitā*, Section 1, (Description of Śivatattva) 27.
99. The Śiva Purāna, *Rudra Samhita*, Sect. I, Ch 6, 19-20. (Ed. J.L. Shastri, Motilal Banarsidass, Delhi, 1970, Vol. I, p.196)
100. The Śiva Purāna, *Vāyavīya Samhitā*, Ch. 16, 8. (Ed. Motilal Banarsidass, Delhi, 2002, Vol. 4, p. 1826)
101. Siva Purana, Pt. 1, *Rudrasamhitā*, Section 1, Ch. 6, 20-21.
102. Siva Purana, Pt. 1, *Rudrasamhitā*, Section 1, Ch. 6, 24.
103. Nirālamba Upanishad, 2. (Tr. K. Nārāyanasvami, Aiyar, *Thirty Minor Upanishads*, Madras, 1914, p. 19)
104. The Śiva Purāna, *Rudra Samhita*, Sect. I, Ch 6, 27-31. (Ed. J.L. Shastri, Motilal Banarsidass, Delhi, 1970, Vol. I, p.197)
105. The Śiva Purāna, *Rudra Samhita*, Sect. I, Ch 6, 27-31. (Ed. J.L. Shastri, Motilal Banarsidass, Delhi, 1970, Vol. I, p.197)
106. *Ibid.*, Ch 6, 33-38.
107. e.g. The Śiva Purāna, *Vidyeśvara Samhita*, Ch 5, 10; *Rudra Samhita*, Sect. II, Ch. 43, 28. (Ed. J.L. Shastri, Motilal Banarsidass, Delhi, 1970, Vol. I, p.50; p. 471)

108. Śrila Rūpa Gosvāmi, *Laghu Bhagavatamrta*, Tr. HH Bhānu swāmī, Com. Śrila Baladeva vidyābhūsana, 1.20.
109. Śrila Rūpa Gosvāmi, *Laghu Bhagavatamrta*, Tr. HH Bhānu swāmī, Com. Śrila Baladeva vidyābhūsana, 1.14.
110. Śrila Rūpa Gosvāmi, *Laghu Bhagavatamrta*, Tr. HH Bhānu swāmī, Com. Śrila Baladeva vidyābhūsana, 1.23, commentary.
111. Śrila Rūpa Gosvāmi, *Laghu Bhagavatamrta*, Tr. HH Bhānu swāmī, Com. Śrila Baladeva vidyābhūsana, 1.12.
112. Śrila Rūpa Gosvāmi, *Laghu Bhagavatamrta*, Tr. HH Bhānu swāmī, Com. Śrila Baladeva vidyābhūsana, 1.21.
113. Śrila Rūpa Gosvāmi, *Laghu Bhagavatamrta*, Tr. HH Bhānu swāmī, Com. Śrila Baladeva vidyābhūsana, 1.14-17.
114. The Śiva Purāna, *Rudra Samhita*, Sect. I, Ch 6, 19-21. (Ed. J.L. Shastri, Motilal Banarsidass, Delhi, 1970, Vol. I, p.196)
115. Śrila Rūpa Gosvāmi, *Laghu Bhagavatamrta*, Tr. HH Bhānu swāmī, Com. Śrila Baladeva vidyābhūsana, 5.146-147.
116. The Śiva Purāna, *Rudra Samhita*, Sect. I, Ch 9, 38-39. (Ed. J.L. Shastri, Motilal Banarsidass, Delhi, 1970, Vol. I, p.212).
117. The Śiva Purāna, *Rudra Samhita*, Sect. I, Ch 9, 30. (Ed. J.L. Shastri, Motilal Banarsidass, Delhi, 1970, Vol. I, p.211).
118. The Śiva Purāna, *Rudra Samhita*, Sect. I, Ch 9, 31. (Ed. J.L. Shastri, Motilal Banarsidass, Delhi, 1970, Vol. I, p.211).
119. The Śiva Purāna, *Rudra Samhita*, Sect. I, Ch 9, 38-39. (Ed. J.L. Shastri, Motilal Banarsidass, Delhi, 1970, Vol. I, p.212).
120. The Śiva Purāna, *Rudra Samhita*, Sect. I, Ch 9, 40. (Ed. J.L. Shastri, Motilal Banarsidass, Delhi, 1970, Vol. I, p.212).
121. The Śiva Purāna, *Rudra Samhita*, Sect. I, Ch 9, 41. (Ed. J.L. Shastri, Motilal Banarsidass, Delhi, 1970, Vol. I, p.212).
122. The Śiva Purāna, *Rudra Samhita*, Sect. I, Ch 9, 58. (Ed. J.L. Shastri, Motilal Banarsidass, Delhi, 1970, Vol. I, p.213).
123. The Śiva Purāna, *Rudra Samhita*, Sect. I, Ch 9, 42-43. (Ed. J.L. Shastri, Motilal Banarsidass, Delhi, 1970, Vol. I, p.212).
124. The Śiva Purāna, *Rudra Samhita*, Sect. I, Ch. 9, 46. (Ed. J.L. Shastri, Motilal Banarsidass, Delhi, 1970, Vol. I, p.212)
125. The Śiva Purāna, *Rudra Samhita*, Sect. I, Ch. 9, 47. (Ed. J.L. Shastri, Motilal Banarsidass, Delhi, 1970, Vol. I, p.212)
126. This depiction is known as the Nataraja, and is the basis for the cover illustration of this book. The concept of *Śiva* as the cosmic dancer has its roots in the Vedas. See C. Sivaramamurti, *Nataraja in Art, Thought and Literature*, National Museum, New Delhi, 1974, Ch. 7, p. 78.

127. Nirālamba Upanishad, 2. (Tr. K. Nārāyanasvami, Aiyar, *Thirty Minor Upanishads*, Madras, 1914, p. 19)
128. Nirālamba Upanishad, 2. (Tr. K. Nārāyanasvami, Aiyar, *Thirty Minor Upanishads*, Madras, 1914, p. 19)
129. *e.g.* Abhinavagupta, *Tantrāloka* 5.7.
130. Monier-Williams.
131. e.g. The Śiva Purāna, *Vidyeśvara Samhita*, Ch 5, 10; *Rudra Samhita*, Sect. II, Ch. 43, 28. (Ed. J.L. Shastri, Motilal Banarsidass, Delhi, 1970, Vol. I, p.50; p. 471)
132. The Śiva Purāna, *Vidyeśvara Samhita*, Ch. 5, 10-11. (Ed. J.L. Shastri, Motilal Banarsidass, Delhi, 1970, Vol. I, p.50)
133. *e.g.* Śiva Purana, *Rudra Samhita*: Kumārakhanda Section IV, Ch. 1. (Ed. Motilal Banarsidass, Delhi, 2002, Vol. 4, p. 711)
134. e.g. The Śiva Purāna, *Vidyeśvara Samhita*, Ch 5, 10; *Rudra Samhita*, Sect. II, Ch. 43, 28. (Ed. J.L. Shastri, Motilal Banarsidass, Delhi, 1970, Vol. I, p.50; p. 471)
135. The Śiva Purāna, *Rudra Samhita*, Sect. I, Ch 6, 32-38. (Ed. J.L. Shastri, Motilal Banarsidass, Delhi, 1970, Vol. I, p.197).
136. The Śiva Purāna, *Rudra Samhita*, Sect. I, Ch 6, 32-38. (Ed. J.L. Shastri, Motilal Banarsidass, Delhi, 1970, Vol. I, p.197).
137. Kurma Purana, I.31.24-25.
138. Kurma Purana, I.31.22.
139. Kurma Purana, I.31.26.
140. Kurma Purana, I.31.30.
141. Kurma Purana, I.31.36.
142. Skanda Purana, IV.ii.53.4.
143. Skanda Purana, IV.ii.53.18-19.
144. Throughout the text but also specifically, Kurma Purana, IV.ii.53.18-19.
145. Skanda Purana, IV.ii.53.4.
146. Skanda Purana, IV.ii.53.18-19.
147. Kurma Purana, I.31.39-40.
148. This is the term used by Barry Long, in *The Origins of Man and the Universe*, Routledge & Kegan Paul, 1998.
149. Skanda Purana, IV.ii.53.84.
150. Skanda Purana, IV.ii.53.42-45.
151. Monier-Williams
152. Brahmānda Purana, 1.1.5.66-68.
153. Brahmānda Purana, 1.2.7.150 *ff.*
154. Brahmānda Purana, 1.2.36.222b-224a
155. Harivamsha, The Prelude, 6.40.

156. Harivamsha, 272.18-37, (Manmatha Nath Dutt, *A Prose English Translation of Harivamsha*, Calcutta, 1897, p.787).
157. Harivamsha, Bhavishya Parva, 26. 11 footnote. *Ibid.*, p.887.
158. Harivamsha, Bhavishya Parva, 26, 26-27. *Ibid.*, p.888.
159. The Śiva Purāna, *Rudra Samhita*, Sect. I, Ch 6, 32-38. (Ed. J.L. Shastri, Motilal Banarsidass, Delhi, 1970, Vol. I, p.197).
160. Skanda Purana, IV.ii.53.89-91.
161. Skanda Purana, IV.ii.53.89-91.
162. Caitanya-caritamrta, Madhya-lila, 20.251; Adi-lila, 5.77.
163. Padma Purana II.39.20-25.
164. Padma Purana II.39.20-25.
165. Padma Purana II.39.20-25.
166. Padma Purana II.39.20-25.
167. Padma Purana II.39.20-25.
168. Padma Purana II.39.20-25.
169. See, for example, Padma Purana V. 82. 65-73a.
170. Kurma Purana I.5.21.
171. The Śiva Purāna, *Vāyavīya Samhitā*, Ch. 13, 16-21. (Ed. Motilal Banarsidass, Delhi, 2002, Vol. 4, p. 1819)
172. Padma Purana V. 69. 70-78.
173. Harivamsha, Bhavishya Parva, Ch. XII, 15-18.
174. Harivamsha, Bhavishya Parva, (*The Creation of a Lotus After Dissolution*) Ch. XI, 2-17.
175. Padma Purana 1.39.153-154.
176. Harivamsha Ch. XII, Bhavishya Parva, 15-18.
177. The Śiva Purāna, *Rudra Samhita*, Sect. I, Ch 7, 7. Ed. J.L. Shastri, Motilal Banarsidass, Delhi, 1970, Vol. I, p.200.
178. The Śiva Purāna, *Rudra Samhita*, Sect. I, Ch 7, 8. Ed. J.L. Shastri, Motilal Banarsidass, Delhi, 1970, Vol. I, p.200.
179. The Śiva Purāna, *Rudra Samhita*, Sect. I, Ch 7, 9-14. Ed. J.L. Shastri, Motilal Banarsidass, Delhi, 1970, Vol. I, p.200.
180. Caitanya-caritamrta, Adi-lila, 5.77.
181. *e.g.* The Śiva Purāna, *Rudra Samhita*, Sect. II, Ch 23, 14. Ed. J.L. Shastri, Motilal Banarsidass, Delhi, 1970, Vol. I, p.380.
182. The Kurma Purana is one exception to the wider description of the *Brahman* as being without *Gunas*. It regards the *Brahman* as consisting of the *Gunas* in equilibrium. However, the *Brahman* is not a "finite entity". The *Gunas* must indeed originate from the *Brahman*, because everything in the world of *Prakrti* originates from the *Brahman*, including the Purusa who agitates the *Prakrti*. But nonetheless, the *Brahman* is widely described as having no qualities or *Gunas*.

183. See note above.
184. The Śiva Purāna, *Rudra Samhita*, Sect. I, Ch 7, 20-21. Ed. J.L. Shastri, Motilal Banarsidass, Delhi, 1970, Vol. I, p.201.
185. Ibid. Ch. 7, 23, p.201.
186. Ibid. Ch. 7, 26, p.201.
187. Ibid. Ch. 7, 28-31, p.201.
188. Kurma Purana, I.9.7.
189. Kurma Purana, I.9.8-9.
190. Rig Veda 10.90; White Yajurveda, Adhyāya 31; Atharvaveda 19.6.
191. Kurma Purana, I.9.8-10.
192. Kurma Purana, I.9.60-61.
193. Kurma Purana, I.9.31.
194. Kurma Purana I.9.38-39.
195. Nārāyana here means 'the one who lies on the water'.
196. Kurma Purana I.9.40.
197. Kurma Purana, I.9.44-45.
198. Kurma Purana, I.9.47-48.
199. Kurma Purana, I.9.50.
200. Kurma Purana, I.9.55.
201. Siva Purana, *Vidyeśvara Samhita*, Ch. 7, 10-11. (Ed. J.L. Shastri, Motilal Banarsidass, Delhi, 1970, Vol. I, p.55).
202. Siva Purana, *Vidyeśvara Samhita*, Ch. 7, 12-14. (Ed. J.L. Shastri, Motilal Banarsidass, Delhi, 1970, Vol. I, p.55).
203. Vāyu Purana, 55.24.
204. Siva Purana, *Vidyeśvara Samhita*, Ch. 7, 16-18. (Ed. J.L. Shastri, Motilal Banarsidass, Delhi, 1970, Vol. I, p.56).
205. Vāyu Purana, 55.26.
206. Siva Purana, *Vidyeśvara Samhita*, Ch. 7, 19. (Ed. J.L. Shastri, Motilal Banarsidass, Delhi, 1970, Vol. I, p.56).
207. Siva Purana, *Vidyeśvara Samhita*, Ch. 7, 20-21. (Ed. J.L. Shastri, Motilal Banarsidass, Delhi, 1970, Vol. I, p.56).
208. Siva Purana, *Vidyeśvara Samhita*, Ch. 7, 22-23. (Ed. J.L. Shastri, Motilal Banarsidass, Delhi, 1970, Vol. I, p.56).
209. Siva Purana, *Vidyeśvara Samhita*, Ch. 7, 24-25. (Ed. J.L. Shastri, Motilal Banarsidass, Delhi, 1970, Vol. I, p.56).
210. Siva Purana, *Vidyeśvara Samhita*, Ch. 8, 4. (Ed. J.L. Shastri, Motilal Banarsidass, Delhi, 1970, Vol. I, p.58).
211. Arthur Avalon, *The Serpent Power*, New York, 1974.
212. Brahmanda Purana 1.2.32.88-90.

213. *c.f.* His Divine Grace A.C. Bhaktivedanta Swami Prabhupāda, *Teachings of Lord Caitanya*, London *et al*, 1985, p.12; His Divine Grace A. C. Bhaktivedanta Swami Prabhupāda, *Srī Caitanya-caritamrta*, Ādi-līlā, 2012, Introduction.
214. Caitanya-caritamrta, Adi-lila, 2.51.
215. Caitanya-caritamrta, Adi-lila, 5.77.
216. Śiva Purana, Part 1, *Rudra Samhitā*, Sect. 1, Ch. 6, 33-38.
217. Padma Purana, Shrila Vyasadeva, Part VI, Patalakhanda, 83, 53-59a.
218. Śrīmad Bhāgavatam, 10.33.24.
219. Śrīmad Bhāgavatam, 10.33.25.
220. Śrīmad Bhāgavatam, 1.3.28 & and extensively throughout Caitanya-caritamrta.
221. Monier-Williams.
222. Śiva Purana, *Rudra-Samhita*, Section II (Narrative of *Sati*), Ch. 21; 22. (*Ibid.*, Vol. 1, pp. 369-379)
223. Siva Purana, *Vidyeśvara Samhita*, Ch. 7, 10-11. (Ed. J.L. Shastri, Motilal Banarsidass, Delhi, 1970, Vol. I, p.55).
224. Linga Purana 17. 33-36. (*The Linga Purana*, Motilal Barnarsidass, Delhi, 1990, pp.60-61).
225. Kurma Purana, I.26.73.
226. Kurma Purana, I.26.100.
227. *e.g.* Siva Purana, *Vidyeśvara Samhita*, Ch. 5, 26-29. (*Ibid.*, Vol. 1, p.51)
228. Siva Purana, *Vidyeśvara Samhita*, Ch. 5, 26-31. (*Ibid.*, Vol. 1, p.51)
229. Siva Purana, *Vidyeśvara Samhita*, Ch. 16, 106-107. (*Ibid.*, Vol. 1, p.105); *Kotirudra Samhita*, Ch. 12, 53. (Motilal Banarsidass, Delhi, 2002, Vol. 3, p.1301)
230. Siva Purana, *Vidyeśvara Samhita*, Ch. 16, 106-107. (Ed. J.L. Shastri, Motilal Banarsidass, Delhi, 1970, Vol. I, p.105)
231. See, for example, Siva Purana, *Vidyeśvara Samhita*, Ch. 5. (Ed. J.L. Shastri, Motilal Banarsidass, Delhi, 1970, Vol. I, p.49).
232. Siva Purana, *Kotirudra Samhita*, Ch. 1, 9. (Motilal Banarsidass, Delhi, 2002, Vol. 3, p. 1260)
233. The Śiva Purāna, *Vāyavīya Samhitā*, Ch. 34, 7-12. (Ed. Motilal Banarsidass, Delhi, 2002, Vol. 4, pp. 2054-2057)
234. The Śiva Purāna, *Vāyavīya Samhitā*, Ch. 34, 14. (Ed. Motilal Banarsidass, Delhi, 2002, Vol. 4, pp. 2054-2057)
235. The Śiva Purāna, *Vāyavīya Samhitā*, Ch. 15-16. (Ed. Motilal Banarsidass, Delhi, 2002, Vol. 4, pp. 2054-2057)
236. The Śiva Purāna, *Vāyavīya Samhitā*, Ch. 15-16. (Ed. Motilal Banarsidass, Delhi, 2002, Vol. 4, pp. 2054-2057)
237. The Śiva Purāna, *Vāyavīya Samhitā*, Ch. 34, 14. (Ed. Motilal Banarsidass, Delhi, 2002, Vol. 4, pp. 2054-2057)

238. Linga Purana 17. 33-36. (*The Linga Purana*, Motilal Barnarsidass, Delhi, 1990, pp.60-61).
239. Radha Tantra: *The Rādhā Tantra*, Tr. Måns Broo, Routledge, 2017, (E-book) Second Patala, opening paragraph *ff*.
240. Radha Tantra: *The Rādhā Tantra*, Tr. Måns Broo, Routledge, 2017, (E-book) Second Patala, opening paragraph *ff*.
241. Radha Tantra: *The Rādhā Tantra*, Tr. Måns Broo, Routledge, 2017, (E-book) Second Patala, opening paragraph *ff*.
242. Siva Purana, *Kotirudra Samhita*, Ch. 12. (Motilal Banarsidass, Delhi, 2002, Vol. 3, p. 1296)
243. Siva Purana, *Kotirudra Samhita*, Ch. 12. (Motilal Banarsidass, Delhi, 2002, Vol. 3, p. 1296)
244. Siva Purana, *Kotirudra Samhita*, Ch. 12, 26-27; 32. (Motilal Banarsidass, Delhi, 2002, Vol. 3, p. 1298-1299)
245. Siva Purana, *Kotirudra Samhita*, Ch. 12, 45. (Motilal Banarsidass, Delhi, 2002, Vol. 3, p. 1300)
246. Siva Purana, *Kotirudra Samhita*, Ch. 12, 46. (Motilal Banarsidass, Delhi, 2002, Vol. 3, p. 1300)
247. Siva Purana, *Kotirudra Samhita*, Ch. 12, 49. (Motilal Banarsidass, Delhi, 2002, Vol. 3, p. 1300)
248. Śiva Purana, *Rudra-Samhita*, Section I, Ch. 12; 51-54. (*Ibid.*, Vol. 1, p.228)
249. Siva Purana, *Kotirudra Samhita*, Ch. 12, 48. (Motilal Banarsidass, Delhi, 2002, Vol. 3, p. 1300)
250. Siva Purana, *Kotirudra Samhita*, Ch. 12, 51. (Motilal Banarsidass, Delhi, 2002, Vol. 3, p. 1300)
251. Siva Purana, *Kotirudra Samhita*, Ch. 12, 52. (Motilal Banarsidass, Delhi, 2002, Vol. 3, p. 1300)
252. Siva Purana, *Kotirudra Samhita*, Ch. 12, 53. (Motilal Banarsidass, Delhi, 2002, Vol. 3, p. 1300)
253. Siva Purana, *Kotirudra Samhita*, Ch. 12, 53-54. (Motilal Banarsidass, Delhi, 2002, Vol. 3, p. 1300)
254. Monier-Williams.
255. Monier-Williams.
256. Padma Purana, V. 69. 6-78.
257. Garga Samhita, 1.2.49. ark:/13960/t42s4634q
258. Brahma Samhita, 2.
259. Garga Samhita, 1.2.17. ark:/13960/t42s4634q
260. Garga Samhita, 1.2.18-19. ark:/13960/t42s4634q
261. Siva Purana, *Vidyeśvara Samhita*, Ch. 13, 42-43. (Ed. J.L. Shastri, Motilal Banarsidass, Delhi, 1970, Vol. I, p.82)

262. Siva Purana, *Uma Samhita*, Ch. 15, 16-17. (*The Śivapurana*, Part III, Motilal Barnarsidass, Delhi, 2002, p.1513); Kurma Purana I.24.72.
263. Siva Purana, *Vāyavīya Samhita*, Ch. 2, 31-24. (Ed. Motilal Banarsidass, Delhi, 2002, Vol. 4, p. 1914); Brahmanda Purana, 1.2.20.2b-4a.
264. Kurma Purana I.10.65b-66a.
265. Kurma Purana I.51.38-39a.
266. Kurma Purana I.51.39b-40a.
267. Kurma Purana I.51.40b-41a.
268. Kurma Purana I.51.40b-41a.
269. Kurma Purana I.51.41b-42a.
270. Kurma Purana I.51.42b-43a.
271. The Śiva Purāna, *Rudra Samhita*, Sect. I, Ch 6, 32-38. (Ed. J.L. Shastri, Motilal Banarsidass, Delhi, 1970, Vol. I, p.197).
272. Kurma Purana I.9.23.
273. Garga Samhita, 1.2.18-19. ark:/13960/t42s4634q
274. Garga Samhita, 1.3.17. ark:/13960/t42s4634q
275. Caitanya-caritamrta, Madhya-lila, 21.59-21.71.
276. Brahma Samhita 5.40.
277. Schopenhauer, Arthur, *The World as Will and Representation*, Tr. EFJ Payne, New York, 1969.
278. Paingala Upanishad, Adhyāya I. (Tr. K. Nārāyanasvami, Aiyar, *Thirty Minor Upanishads*, Madras, 1914, p. 44)
279. Monier-Williams.
280. Monier-Williams.
281. His Divine Grace A.C. Bhaktivedanta Swami Prabhupāda, *Teachings of Lord Caitanya*, London *et al*, 1985, p.1.
282. His Divine Grace A.C. Bhaktivedanta Swami Prabhupāda, *Teachings of Lord Caitanya*, London *et al*, 1985, p.345.
283. Caitanya-caritamrta, Adi-lila, 5.93.
284. Caitanya-caritamrta, Madhya-lila, 20.292.
285. Monier-Williams; V. R. Ramachandra Dikshitar, *The Purana Index*, Vol. III, 1955 (p.771).
286. Monier-Williams.
287. Monier-Williams.
288. Śrīmad Bhāgavatam, 3.20.16
289. Caitanya-caritamrta, Adi-lila, 2.51.
290. Caitanya-caritamrta, Adi-lila, 5.77.
291. Kurma Purana, I.9.22.
292. Kurma Purana, I.9.6.
293. Caitanya-caritamrta, Adi-lila, 2.19.

294. Śrīla Jīva Gosvami (commentary); Śrīla Bhaktivinoda Thākura (explanations), et.al., Śri Brahma-samhitā, Vrndavana, Uttar Pradesh, 2003.
295. Caitanya-caritamrta, Madhya-lila, 21.59-21.71.
296. Maitri Upanishad 5.2, §4. (Hume, *The Thirteen Principal Upanishads*, OUP, 1921, p. 424).
297. Ralph T. H. Griffith, ; Arthur Berriedale Keith; Ed. Jon William Fergus, *The Vedas*, 2017, ISBN: 978-1541294714, *Foreword*, 'Some Remarks on the Veda', 1. General view.
298. Skanda Purana IV.ii.97.139.
299. Brahmanda Purana 1.2.13.127-129.
300. Anjana Chakraborty; (Guide: Das Roy, Snigdha), *A Study of the Evolution of Soma in Vedic Mythology and Ritual*, 2017, Assam University, Department of Sanskrit; Also *e.g. Satapatha Brahmana*, 1.6: 3, 4,5,6,7,15,16.
301. Rig Veda, 10.85.3.
302. Corbett, Lionel *et al.* "Hallucinogenic N-Methylated Indolealkylamines in the Cerebrospinal Fluid of Psychiatric and Control Populations", *British Journal of Psychiatry* 132 (1978): 139 - 144;

Steven A. Barker, "N, N-Dimethyltryptamine (DMT), an Endogenous Hallucinogen: Past, Present, and Future Research to Determine Its Role and Function", *Front. Neurosci.*, 06 August 2018 | https://doi.org/10.3389/fnins.2018.00536.
303. Jiménez-Garrido, D.F., Gómez-Sousa, M., Ona, G. et al. "Effects of ayahuasca on mental health and quality of life in naïve users: A longitudinal and cross-sectional study combination". *Sci Rep* 10, 4075 (2020). https://doi.org/10.1038/s41598-020-61169-x
304. Andrew R. Gallimore, Rick J. Strassman, "A Model for the Application of Target-Controlled Intravenous Infusion for a Prolonged Immersive DMT Psychedelic Experience", *Front Pharmacol.* 2016; 7: 211. Published online 2016 Jul 14. doi: 10.3389/fphar.2016.00211.
305. Andrew R. Gallimore, Rick J. Strassman, "A Model for the Application of Target-Controlled Intravenous Infusion for a Prolonged Immersive DMT Psychedelic Experience", *Front Pharmacol.* 2016; 7: 211. Published online 2016 Jul 14. doi: 10.3389/fphar.2016.00211.
306. Davis AK, Clifton JM, Weaver EG, Hurwitz ES, Johnson MW, Griffiths RR. "Survey of entity encounter experiences occasioned by inhaled N,N-dimethyltryptamine: Phenomenology, interpretation, and enduring effects", *Journal of Psychopharmacology*, 2020;34(9):1008-1020. doi:10.1177/0269881120916143;
307. *e.g.* Adi-lila, 2.4-5; 2.12; 2.14-15; 2.26; 5.31-34 (likens to the Sun); 5.37-8; 5.51; Madhya-lila, 6.268; 19.153-154; 20.159-160; 24.144; 25.33;25.156.
308. Caitanya-caritamrta, Adi-lila, 5.25; 5.36.
309. Caitanya-caritamrta, Adi-lila, 1.5; 4.55-56; 4.9.

310. Michael Pascal, Luke David, Robinson Oliver, "An Encounter With the Other: A Thematic and Content Analysis of DMT Experiences From a Naturalistic Field Study", *Frontiers in Psychology*, Vol. 12, 2021, https://www.frontiersin.org/article/10.3389/fpsyg.2021.720717. DOI=10.3389/fpsyg.2021.720717. ISSN=1664-1078.
311. Griffiths RR, Hurwitz ES, Davis AK, Johnson MW, Jesse R. Survey of subjective "God encounter experiences": Comparisons among naturally occurring experiences and those occasioned by the classic psychedelics psilocybin, LSD, ayahuasca, or DMT. *PLoS One*. 2019;14(4):e0214377. Published 2019 Apr 23. doi:10.1371/journal.pone.0214377
312. Siva Purana, *Umā Samhitā,* Ch. 18, 45-46 (Motilal Banarsidass, Delhi, 2002, Vol. 3, p.1527); Curds & whey: Brahmanda Purana, 1.2.19.77.
313. Viśnu Purana.
314. Śrīmad Bhāgavatam, 5.20.
315. Śrīmad Bhāgavatam, 5.20.24.
316. Śrīmad Bhāgavatam, 5.1.33.
317. Kurma Purana, Part 1, Ch. 45, 4. (Motilal Barnarsidass, Delhi, 1998, p. 296, according to list order.)
318. Viśnu Purana.
319. Śrīmad Bhāgavatam, 5.20.
320. Śrīmad Bhāgavatam, 5.20.29 & 5.20.34.
321. Śrīmad Bhāgavatam, 5.1.33.
322. Explicated, for example, in the Brahma Samhita. *Brahma Samhita*, Śrīla Jīva Gosvami (commentary); Śrīla Bhaktivinoda Thākura (explanations), *et.al.*, Śri Brahma-samhitā, Vrndavana, Uttar Pradesh, 2003. ISBN 81-86737-10-3, p.300.
323. Siva Purana, III, *Umā Samhitā,* Ch. 18, 45-46 (Motilal Banarsidass, Delhi, 2002, Vol. 3, p.1527)
324. Viśnu Purana.
325. Śrīmad Bhāgavatam, 5.20.
326. Śrīmad Bhāgavatam, 5.20.24.
327. Śrīmad Bhāgavatam, 5.1.33.
328. Kurma Purana, Part 1, Ch. 45, 4. (Motilal Barnarsidass, Delhi, 1998, p. 296, according to list order.); Siva Purana, III, *Umā,Samhitā,* Ch. 18, 59-60 (Motilal Banarsidass, Delhi, 2002, Vol. 3, p.1527)
329. Viśnu Purana.
330. Śrīmad Bhāgavatam, 5.20.
331. Śrīmad Bhāgavatam, 5.20.29 & 5.20.34.
332. Śrīmad Bhāgavatam, 5.1.33.
333. *e.g.* Śrīmad Bhāgavatam, 5.1.32, but also across the corpus generally. There are, however, variations. Brahmanda Purana, for example, lists: Bhūrloka,

Bhurvaloka, Svarloka, Mahasloka, Janaloka, Tapasloka and Satyaloka. (Brahmanda Purana, 1.2.19.155-156.)

334. Siva Purana, *Umā Samhitā,* Ch. 18, 64. (Motilal Banarsidass, Delhi, 2002, Vol. 3, p.1528)

335. Siva Purana, *Umā Samhitā,* Ch. 18, 67. (Motilal Banarsidass, Delhi, 2002, Vol. 3, p.1528)

336. Siva Purana, *Umā Samhitā,* Ch. 18, 73-74. (Motilal Banarsidass, Delhi, 2002, Vol. 3, p.1529)

337. Siva Purana, *Umā Samhitā,* Ch. 18, 75. (Motilal Banarsidass, Delhi, 2002, Vol. 3, p.1529)

338. Srimad Devi Bhagavatam, 8.4.1-28.

339. Caitanya-caritamrta, Adi-lila, 5.17.

340. Śrīmad Bhāgavatam, 10.89.47.

341. Śrīmad Bhāgavatam, 10.89.50-53.

342. Caitanya-caritamrta, Adi-lila, 5.110-111.

343. Mahabharata, Shanti Parva, Mokshadhāma Parva, Section CCCXXXVII. (https://www.sacred-texts.com/hin/m12/m12c036.htm, accessed April 17, 2022)

344. My attempt to verify this yielded no conformation.

345. Lagu Bhagavatamrta, 2.43.

346. Laghu Bhagavatamrta, 2. 40-41.

347. Kurma Purana, I.49.40.

348. Padma Purana, VI.229.40-44.

349. Padma Purana, III.8.7-10.

350. Brahma Purana, 1.18. 71-76. (Tr. A Board of Scholars, Motilal Barnarsidass, Delhi, 2001, p. 112)

351. Siva Purana, *Umā,Samhitā,* Ch. 18, 58-60 (Motilal Banarsidass, Delhi, 2002, Vol. 3, pp.1526-1527)

352. Kurma Purana, Part 1, Ch. 45, 4. (Motilal Barnarsidass, Delhi, 1998, p. 296)

353. Kurma Purana, Part 1, Ch. 49, 1. (Motilal Barnarsidass, Delhi, 1998, p. 314)

354. Kurma Purana, Part 1, Ch. 49, 12-13. (Motilal Barnarsidass, Delhi, 1998, p. 316)

355. Kurma Purana, Part 1, Ch. 49, 19b-22. (Motilal Barnarsidass, Delhi, 1998, p. 316)

356. Kurma Purana, Part 1, Ch. 49, 26b-27a. (Motilal Barnarsidass, Delhi, 1998, p. 317)

357. Kurma Purana, Part 1, Ch. 49, 33. (Motilal Barnarsidass, Delhi, 1998, p. 317-318)

358. Kurma Purana, Part 1, Ch. 49, 40. (Motilal Barnarsidass, Delhi, 1998, p. 318)

359. Vetam Mani, *Purānic Encyclopaedia*, Motilal Barnarsidass, Delhi, 1975, *Manvantara(m)* (p. 482).

360. Caitanya-caritamrta, Madhya-lila, 21.59-21.71.
361. Skanda Purana, Part 2, I.ii.40.174.
362. Vetam Mani, *Purānic Encyclopaedia*, Motilal Barnarsidass, Delhi, 1975, *Manvantara(m)* (p. 482).
363. Brahmanda Purana, 1.2.6.7-14. (*The Brahmanda Purana*, Part 1, Motilal Banarsidass, Delhi, 2002, p. 58.)
364. Brahmanda Purana, 1.2.31.77-80. (*The Brahmanda Purana*, Part 1, Motilal Banarsidass, Delhi, 2002, p. 309.)
365. Brahmanda Purana, 1.2.35.181-186a. (*The Brahmanda Purana*, Part 1, Motilal Banarsidass, Delhi, 2002, p. 358.)
366. Brahmanda Purana, 1.2.29.34. (*The Brahmanda Purana*, Part 1, Motilal Banarsidass, Delhi, 2002, p. 290.)
367. Brahmanda Purana, 1.2.29.35-36. (*The Brahmanda Purana*, Part 1, Motilal Banarsidass, Delhi, 2002, p. 291.)
368. Brahmanda Purana, 1.2.31.72-73. (*The Brahmanda Purana*, Part 1, Motilal Banarsidass, Delhi, 2002, p. 308.)
369. *Puranic Encyclopaedia*, Motilal Barnarsidass, Delhi, 1974, *Manvantara*, p. 482.
370. Calculated from Vettam Mani, *Puranic Encyclopaedia*, Motilal Barnarsidass, Delhi, 1974, p. 482.
371. Brahma Purana, Part 1, Ch. 18, 14. (Tr. A Board of Scholars, Motilal Barnarsidass, Delhi, 2001, p. 108)
372. Siva Purana, *Umā,Samhitā,* Ch. 18, 29 (Motilal Banarsidass, Delhi, 2002, Vol. 3, pp.1525)
373. Kurma Purana, I.49.9-10. (*The Kurma Purana*, Part 1, Motilal Barnarsidass, Delhi, 1998, p. 315)
374. *e.g.* Brahmanda Purana, 1.2.24.80-83; footnote 1. (*The Brahmanda Purana*, Part 1, Motilal Banarsidass, Delhi, 2002, p.240)
375. Linga Purana, Sect. 1, 107.51-52; 55-56.
376. Linga Purana, Sect. 1, 107.55-56.
377. Varāha Purana, 87.1 (*The Varāha Purāna*, Tr. A Board of Scholars; S. Venkitasubramoniaiyer, Part 1, Motilal Barnarsidass, Delhi, 2003, p. 202)
378. Varāha Purana, 87.4. (*The Varāha Purāna*, Tr. A Board of Scholars; S. Venkitasubramoniaiyer, Part 1, Motilal Barnarsidass, Delhi, 2003, p. 203)
379. Arthur A. Macdonell, *A Sanskrit-English Dictionary*, New York, 1893, (*Amrita*: "immortal"; "nectar-like"; "consisting of nectar").
380. Varāha Purana, 86.1.
381. Varāha Purana, 85-89.
382. Varāha Purana, 86.1.
383. Caitanya-caritamrta, Adi-lila, 5.77. Tr. His Divine Grace A. C. Bhaktivedanta Swami Prabhupāda, ISBN 978-91-7149-661-4, 2012.

384. Manmatha Nath Dutt, *A Prose English Translation of Harivamsha*, Calcutta, 1897, Bhavishya Parva, Ch. XXIV, p. 887, footnote.
385. Brahmanda Purana, 1.2.15.12-13.
386. Brahma Purana, 2, Ch. 56, 81-82.
387. Brahma Purana, 2, Ch. 56, 84-88.
388. Brahma Purana, 2, Ch. 56, 84-88.
389. Brahma Purana, 2, Ch. 56, 89-91.
390. Brahma Purana, Pt. 2, Ch. 59, 5-10.
391. Linga Purana, Section II, Ch. 12, 30-31.
392. Śrīmad Bhāgavatam, 8.8.5; Monier-Williams, *Indian Wisdom*, London, 1875, pp. 430-431.
393. Brahma Samhita, 29, Tātparya (Śrīla Jīva Gosvami (commentary); Śrīla Bhaktivinoda Thākura (explanations), *et.al.*, *Śri Brahma-samhitā*, Vrndavana, Uttar Pradesh, 2003. ISBN 81-86737-10-3, p.161)
394. Brahma Samhita, 5, Tātparya, footnote. (Śrīla Jīva Gosvami (commentary); Śrīla Bhaktivinoda Thākura (explanations), *et.al.*, *Śri Brahma-samhitā*, Vrndavana, Uttar Pradesh, 2003. ISBN 81-86737-10-3, p.77.)
395. Brahma Samhita, 5, Tātparya. (Śrīla Jīva Gosvami (commentary); Śrīla Bhaktivinoda Thākura (explanations), *et.al.*, *Śri Brahma-samhitā*, Vrndavana, Uttar Pradesh, 2003. ISBN 81-86737-10-3, p.77.)
396. Brahma Samhita, 5, Tīkā. (Śrīla Jīva Gosvami (commentary); Śrīla Bhaktivinoda Thākura (explanations), *et.al.*, *Śri Brahma-samhitā*, Vrndavana, Uttar Pradesh, 2003. ISBN 81-86737-10-3, p.58.)
397. Śrīla Jīva Gosvami (commentary); Śrīla Bhaktivinoda Thākura (explanations), *et.al.*, *Śri Brahma-samhitā*, Vrndavana, Uttar Pradesh, 2003. ISBN 81-86737-10-3, Preface, p.xxiv.)
398. Brahma Samhita, 56; 33, Tātparya. (Śrīla Jīva Gosvami (commentary); Śrīla Bhaktivinoda Thākura (explanations), *et.al.*, *Śri Brahma-samhitā*, Vrndavana, Uttar Pradesh, 2003. ISBN 81-86737-10-3, p.191.)
399. Brahma Samhita, 2, & Tīkā and Tātparya (Śrīla Jīva Gosvami (commentary); Śrīla Bhaktivinoda Thākura (explanations), *et.al.*, *Śri Brahma-samhitā*, Vrndavana, Uttar Pradesh, 2003. ISBN 81-86737-10-3, pp. 35-42.)
400. Brahma Samhita, 2, Tātparya (Śrīla Jīva Gosvami (commentary); Śrīla Bhaktivinoda Thākura (explanations), *et.al.*, *Śri Brahma-samhitā*, Vrndavana, Uttar Pradesh, 2003. ISBN 81-86737-10-3, p. 39.)
401. Brahma Samhita, 56, Tātparya (Śrīla Jīva Gosvami (commentary); Śrīla Bhaktivinoda Thākura (explanations), *et.al.*, *Śri Brahma-samhitā*, Vrndavana, Uttar Pradesh, 2003. ISBN 81-86737-10-3, p. 304.)
402. Garga Samhita, 5.15.34.
403. Garga Samhita, 5.15.36.
404. Padma Purana, 1.39.126.

405. Padma Purana, 1.4.87.
406. Brahma Samhita, 29, Tātparya (Śrīla Jīva Gosvami (commentary); Śrīla Bhaktivinoda Thākura (explanations), *et.al.*, *Śri Brahma-samhitā*, Vrndavana, Uttar Pradesh, 2003. ISBN 81-86737-10-3, p. 161.)
407. Srimad Devi Bhagavatam, 8.4.1-28; Śrīmad Bhāgavatam, 5.1.31.
408. Thomas S Kuhn, *The Structure of Scientific Revolutions*, 3rd Ed., Chicago, 1996, p. 121.
409. Brahmanda Purana, 1.2.24.45-47.
410. Brahmanda Purana, 1.2.24.51-54.
411. Brahmanda Purana, 1.2.24.51-55.
412. *c.f.* Tejaswi Katravulapally, *Journey Through the Vedic Thought*, "Stanza-6: The Holy Sacrifice", 2020, p. 98; Brahmanda Purana, 1.2.28.15-16.
413. Sri Aurobindo, *The Secret of the Veda*, Pondicherry, 1998, p. 64.
414. Sri Aurobindo, *The Secret of the Veda*, Pondicherry, 1998, p. 225.
415. Brahmanda Purana, 1.2.28.15. (Ibid. Vol. 1, p. 279.)
416. Sri Aurobindo, *The Secret of the Veda*, Pondicherry, 1998, p. 442 (footnote 1).
417. Sri Aurobindo, *The Secret of the Veda*, Pondicherry, 1998, p. 547; p. 547, footnote 11.
418. Sri Aurobindo, *The Secret of the Veda*, Pondicherry, 1998, pp. 132; 165; 387.
419. Brahmanda Purana, 1.2.24.51-54.
420. Brahmanda Purana, 1.2.28.15-16.
421. Brahmanda Purana, I.I.1.82-83.
422. Brahmanda Purana, 1.2.7.15-20.
423. Śiva Purana, Part III, Ch. 15, *Umā Samhitā,* 26. (Motilal Banarsidass, Delhi, 2002, p. 1513.)
424. Śiva Purana, Part III, Ch. 15, *Umā Samhitā,* 28. (Motilal Banarsidass, Delhi, 2002, p. 1513.)
425. Śiva Purana, Part III, *Umā Samhitā,* Ch. 16, 1-2. (Motilal Banarsidass, Delhi, 2002, p. 1514.) The names are: Raurava, Sukara, Radha, Tala, Vivasvat, Mahajvala, Taptakumbha, Lavana, Vilohita.
426. Brahmanda Purana, 1.2.21.21-22.
427. Brahmanda Purana, I.I.3.29-31.
428. e.g. Śrīmad Bhāgavatam, 5.16.25;
429. Eric Huntington, *Creating the Universe*, Washington, 2019. p. 38.
430. Brahmanda Purana, 1.2.18. 82-84.
431. Śiva Purana, Part III, *Umā Samhitā,* Ch. 18, 17. (Motilal Banarsidass, Delhi, 2002, p. 1524.)
432. Kurma Purana, I.49.9-10. (*The Kurma Purana*, Part 1, Motilal Barnarsidass, Delhi, 1998, p. 315)
433. Śiva Purana, Part III, *Umā Samhitā,* Ch. 18, 18. (Motilal Banarsidass, Delhi, 2002, p. 1524.)

434. Śiva Purana, Part III, *Umā Samhitā,* Ch. 18, 19. (Motilal Banarsidass, Delhi, 2002, p. 1524.)
435. Manmatha Nath Dutt, *A Prose English Translation of Harivamsha*, Calcutta, 1897, Bhavishya Parva, Ch. XXIV, p. 887, footnote.
436. Brahmanda Purana, 1.2.19.80-84.
437. Brahma Samhita, 1, Tīkā. (Śrīla Jīva Gosvami (commentary); Śrīla Bhaktivinoda Thākura (explanations), *et.al.*, *Śri Brahma-samhitā*, Vrndavana, Uttar Pradesh, 2003. ISBN 81-86737-10-3, p.17.)
438. Brahma Samhita, 62, Tīkā. (Śrīla Jīva Gosvami (commentary); Śrīla Bhaktivinoda Thākura (explanations), *et.al.*, *Śri Brahma-samhitā*, Vrndavana, Uttar Pradesh, 2003. ISBN 81-86737-10-3, p.322.)
439. Brahma Samhita, 5, Tīkā. (Śrīla Jīva Gosvami (commentary); Śrīla Bhaktivinoda Thākura (explanations), *et.al.*, *Śri Brahma-samhitā*, Vrndavana, Uttar Pradesh, 2003. ISBN 81-86737-10-3, p.62.)
440. Brahma Samhita, 40, Tīkā. (Śrīla Jīva Gosvami (commentary); Śrīla Bhaktivinoda Thākura (explanations), *et.al.*, *Śri Brahma-samhitā*, Vrndavana, Uttar Pradesh, 2003. ISBN 81-86737-10-3, p.233.)
441. Uttara-gopāla-tāpanī Upanishad (13), quoted in Brahma Samhita, 3-4, Tīkā. (Śrīla Jīva Gosvami (commentary); Śrīla Bhaktivinoda Thākura (explanations), *et.al.*, *Śri Brahma-samhitā*, Vrndavana, Uttar Pradesh, 2003. ISBN 81-86737-10-3, p.55.)
442. Brahmanda Purana, 1.2.19.160.
443. Monier-Williams.
444. Monier-Williams.
445. Brahmanda Purana, 1.2.19.161-163.
446. Brahmanda Purana, I.I.3.34.
447. Brahmanda Purana, I.I.1.43-44.
448. Brahmanda Purana, I.I.1.43-44.
449. Brahmanda Purana, I.I.3.33; 1.2.19.164.
450. Brahmanda Purana, 1.2.19.165-168.
451. Śiva Purana, Part III, *Umā Samhitā,* Ch. 18, 67. (Motilal Banarsidass, Delhi, 2002, p. 1528.)
452. Brahma Samhita, 56; 33, Tātparya. (Śrīla Jīva Gosvami (commentary); Śrīla Bhaktivinoda Thākura (explanations), *et.al.*, *Śri Brahma-samhitā*, Vrndavana, Uttar Pradesh, 2003. ISBN 81-86737-10-3, p.191.)
453. Śiva Purana, *Rudra Samhitā*, Section 1, Ch. 7, 37-39.
454. Brahmanda Purana, I.I.3.32-33.
455. Brahmanda Purana, I.I.3.34.
456. Brahmanda Purana, I.I.1.43-44.
457. Brahmanda Purana, I.I.3.34.
458. Brahmanda Purana, I.I.1.43-44.

459. Brahmanda Purana, I.I.1.43-44.
460. Brahmanda Purana, I.I.3.33; 1.2.19.164.
461. Brahmanda Purana, I.I.3.33.
462. Brahmanda Purana, I.I.1.43-44; I.I.3.32.
463. Brahmanda Purana, I.I.1.43-44; I.I.3.34.
464. Brahmanda Purana, I.I.1.43-44.
465. Śrīmad Bhāgavatam, 6.16.37.
466. Brahmanda Purana, I.I.3.34.
467. Monier-Williams, *A Sanskrit-English Dictionary*, Oxford, 1899 (1956, 1960), p. 156.
468. Brahmanda Purana, I.I.3.34.
469. Brahmanda Purana, I.I.1.43-44.
470. Brahmanda Purana, I.I.1.43-44.
471. Brahmanda Purana, I.I.3.33; 1.2.19.164.
472. Brahmanda Purana, I.I.3.33.
473. Brahmanda Purana, I.I.1.43-44; I.I.3.32.
474. Brahmanda Purana, I.I.1.43-44; I.I.3.34.
475. Brahmanda Purana, I.I.1.43-44.
476. Brahmanda Purana, I.I.3.38.
477. Brahmanda Purana, 1.2.19.189.
478. Brahmanda Purana, 1.2.20.1-2a.e
479. Brahmanda Purana, 1.2.19.193.
480. Brahmanda Purana, 1.2.19.193.
481. Brahmanda Purana, 1.2.19.192.
482. Brahmanda Purana, 1.2.19.195.
483. Brahmanda Purana, 1.2.19.196.
484. Brahmanda Purana, 1.2.19.196-197.
485. Brahmanda Purana, 1.2.19.195.
486. Brahmanda Purana, 1.2.20.1-2a.
487. Brahmanda Purana, 1.2.20.1-2a.
488. Brahmanda Purana, 1.2.21.21-24.
489. Brahmanda Purana, 1.2.21.21-22.
490. Brahmanda Purana, 1.2.18. 82-84.
491. Brahmanda Purana, 1.2.21.25.
492. Brahmanda Purana, I.I.3.
493. Brahmanda Purana, I.I.3.38.
494. Brahmanda Purana, I.I.3.34.
495. Brahmanda Purana, I.I.1.43-44.
496. Brahmanda Purana, I.I.1.43-44.
497. Brahmanda Purana, I.I.3.33; 1.2.19.164.
498. Brahmanda Purana, I.I.3.33.

499. Brahmanda Purana, I.I.1.43-44; I.I.3.32.
500. Brahmanda Purana, I.I.1.43-44; I.I.3.34.
501. Brahmanda Purana, I.I.1.43-44.
502. Brahmanda Purana, 1.2.32.94-95.
503. Monier-Williams.
504. Avatamsaka Sutra: Thomas Cleary, *The Flower Ornament Scripture*, Boston & London, 1993.
505. Atharva Veda 8.8.
506. Agni: Rig Veda 4.4 (1). Visva: Rig Veda 2.29 (5); 10.87 (15).
507. Monier-Williams.
508. Brahmanda Purana, 1.2.32.96-97.
509. Brahmanda Purana, I.I.5.62.
510. Brahmanda Purana, I.I.5.53-55B.
511. Brahmanda Purana, I.I.5: 35; 28; 51-52.
512. Brahmanda Purana, I.I.5: 46b-47; 51-52; 55B.
513. Brahmanda Purana, I.I.5: 36; 42; 46b-47.
514. Brahmanda Purana, I.I.3.38.
515. Brahmanda Purana, I.I.5, 60-62.
516. Brahmanda Purana, I.I.5, 63-65.
517. Brahmanda Purana, I.I.5, 34 *ff*.
518. Nirālamba Upanishad, 2. (Tr. K. Nārāyanasvami, Aiyar, *Thirty Minor Upanishads*, Madras, 1914, p. 19)
519. Śrīmad Bhāgavatam, 8.6.19-21.
520. Brahma Samhitā, 29, *Tātparya*. Śrīla Jīva Gosvami (commentary); Śrīla Bhaktivinoda Thākura (explanations), *et.al.*, *Śri Brahma-samhitā*, Vrndavana, Uttar Pradesh, 2003. ISBN 81-86737-10-3, p. 161.
521. Manmatha Nath Dutt, *A Prose English Translation of Harivamsha*, Calcutta, 1897, Bhavishya Parva, Ch. XXIV, p. 887, footnote.
522. Plotinus, *Enneads*, 4.8.1. Tr. Stephen MacKenna, 2nd Ed. Revised B. S. Page, Faber & Faber, London, p. 357.
523. Śrīmad Bhāgavatam, 8.6.23.
524. Śrīmad Bhāgavatam, 8.6.24.
525. *c.f.* Śrīmad Bhāgavatam, 8.6.23, Tr. His Divine Grace A.C. Bhaktivedanta Swami Prabhupāda.
526. Śrīmad Bhāgavatam, 8.6.24.
527. Śrīmad Bhāgavatam, 8.6.25.
528. An exception is the Harivamsha Purana, Bhavishya Parva, 26.11-31.
529. Monier-Williams, RTL 108. Also Amarasimha; Halāyudha; Hemacandra.
530. The term is taken from Grof & Grof, *Spiritual Emergency*, New York, 1989; Grof & Grof, *The Stormy Search for the Self*, New York, 1990.
531. Śiva Purana, Part III, *Śatarudra Samhitā*, Ch. 22, 17-18.

532. Śiva Purana, Part III, *Śatarudra Samhitā*, Ch. 22, 16.
533. Śrīmad Bhāgavatam, 8.8.5; Monier-Williams, *Indian Wisdom*, London, 1875, pp. 430-431.
534. Śiva Purana, Part 1, *Rudra Samhitā*, Sect. 1, Ch. 6, 33-38.
535. Śiva Purana, Part 1, *Rudra Samhitā*, Sect. 1, Ch. 6, 8-18.
536. Monier-Williams (*makara*).
537. Skanda Purana, Part 6, II.vi.4.8-9. (Montilal Banarsidass, Delhi, 1951, 1998, p. 287.)
538. Skanda Purana, Part 2, I.ii.5.104b-109. (Montilal Banarsidass, Delhi, 1950, p. 48.)
539. Skanda Purana, Part 2, I.ii.2.43-45. (Montilal Banarsidass, Delhi, 1950, p. 14.)
540. Skanda Purana, Part 8, III.i.29.34-41. (Montilal Banarsidass, Delhi, 1953-2002, p. 185.)
541. Śiva Purana, Part 1, *Vidyeśvara Samhitā*, Part 1, Ch. 2, 41. (*Ibid.*, p. 41.)
542. Brahma Samhita, Verse 1, *translation and explanation of Tīkā*, pp. 9; 17; 33; Verse 5, *Tīkā translation*, p. 62; Verse 33, *Tīkā translation*, p. 181; Verse 40; Verse 40, *Tīkā translation*, pp. 232-234; p. 247; *The eighteen-syllable mantra*, p 140.
543. Śrīmad Bhāgavatam, 8.6.25.
544. *c.f.* Śrīmad Bhāgavatam, 8.6.23, Tr. His Divine Grace A.C. Bhaktivedanta Swami Prabhupāda.
545. Śrīmad Bhāgavatam, 8.6.24.
546. Śrīmad Bhāgavatam, 8.6.25.
547. Śrīmad Bhāgavatam, 8.7.11.
548. Śrīmad Bhāgavatam, 8.7.13.
549. Śiva Purana, Part III, *Śatarudra Samhitā*, Ch.15, 16.
550. Caitanya-caritamrta, *Madhya-lila*, 2.49.
551. Caitanya-caritamrta, *Madhya-lila*, 2.51.
552. Caitanya-caritamrta, *Antya-lila*, 1.148; *Madhya-lila*, 2.52.
553. Śiva Purana, Part III, *Śatarudra Samhitā*, Ch. 22, 20-23.
554. Caitanya-caritamrta, *Adi-lila*, 4.196.
555. Śiva Purana, Part III, *Śatarudra Samhitā*, Ch. 22, 45-48.
556. Śiva Purana, 1, *Rudra Samhitā*, Sect. 1, 6.58-59.
557. Śiva Purana, 1, *Rudra Samhitā*, Sect. II, 23.13.
558. Śiva Purana, 1, *Rudra Samhitā*, Sect. II, 23.13.
559. Padma Purana, V, 69.6-55; 60-78; Brahma Samhita 3-4; 26.
560. Skanda Purana, Part 8, III.i.50.47-53. (Montilal Banarsidass, Delhi, 1953-2002, p. 337)

About the Author

Brian Capleton holds a doctorate in music and is an alumnus of Trinity College of Music (now Trinity Laban Conservatoire of Music and Dance), The Royal College of Music, and Wolfson College Oxford. He formerly lectured at the Royal National College, and his earliest publications were in the field of music, musical instruments, and musicology. He now writes both fiction and non-fiction. His fiction employs Mythic Symbolism, drawing on cross-cultural influences from Hinduism to Renaissance Neoplatonism. His work is now founded on omnist and SBNR themes and in particular presents transpersonal spirituality and its relevance in the context of the contemporary endeavour to scientifically understand the brain.

For more information: briancapleton.com

www.ingramcontent.com/pod-product-compliance
Lightning Source LLC
Chambersburg PA
CBHW020134130526
44590CB00039B/164
9781739258207